HELPING RELATIONSHIPS THROUGH SELF-LOVE

COLETTE PORTELANCE

HELPING RELATIONSHIPS THROUGH SELF-LOVE

**A Creative
Nondirective Approach
to Psychotherapy and Education**

PSYCHOLOGY SERIES

By the same author
Authentic Communication

English translation
Diana Halfpenny

Copyediting
Services d'édition Guy Connolly

Proofreading
Marie Lanctôt-Junger

Design and typography
Guillaume P.-Lavigne

Cover design
Marc Sénécal, Ruse Design

Back cover photograph
Ginette Laforest

Distribution

USA:
Seven Hills Book Distributors
49 Central Avenue
Cincinnati
OH 45202, USA
Tel. (513) 381-3881
Fax (513) 381-0753

*United Kingdom, Northern Ireland
and Irish Republic:*
Lavis Marketing
73 Lime Walk, Headington
Oxford, OX3 7AD UK
Tel. (0865) 67575
    44 865 67575
Fax (0865) 750079
    44 865 750079

Originally published as *Relation d'aide et amour de soi, L'approche non directive créatrice en psychothérapie et en pédagogie,*
© 1990 Les Éditions du CRAM Inc.

All rights reserved. Reproduction in whole or in part by any means without the written consent of the publisher is prohibited and will be considered a violation of copyright.

© 1994 by CRAM Publishers Inc.

1030, Cherrier Street East
Suite 205
Montreal, Québec
H2L 1H9
Tel. (514) 598-8547
Fax (514) 598-7758

Legal deposit, 4nd quarter 1994
Bibliothèque nationale du Québec
National Library of Canada
ISBN 2-9801489-4-6

Printed in Canada

For Nelson and François

**for loving me
and believing in me.**

TABLE OF CONTENTS

INTRODUCTION 7

Chapter 1
THE CREATIVE NONDIRECTIVE APPROACH (CNDA) 11

A. THE NONDIRECTIVITY PHENOMENON IN QUEBEC 11

B. ROGERIAN NONDIRECTIVITY 12

C. THE CREATIVE NONDIRECTIVE APPROACH 15

D. THE DIRECTIVITY/NONDIRECTIVITY DIALECTIC 15
   1. Nondirectivity according to the CNDA 16
      a) The importance of the helping relationships 17
      b) Attitude 18
      c) The nature of a human being 20
      d) Power 20
      e) Conditions for developing a creative nondirective attitude . 22
        • Responsability 22
        • Acceptance 27
        • Love 30
   2. Directivity according to the CNDA 33
      a) The container concept 33
      b) The container according to the CNDA 33
      c) Positive features of container-directivity 36

Chapter 2
RESPECT FOR THE WAY THE BRAIN FUNCTIONS 41

A. LOZANOV AND SUGGESTOLOGY 41

B. THE BRAIN 42
  1. The horizontal structure of the brain 42
    a) The left hemisphere 44
    b) The right hemisphere 45
  2. The vertical structure of the brain 47
    a) The hindbrain 48
    b) The midbrain 51
    c) The forebrain 54

Chapter 3
RESPECT FOR THE WAY THE PSYCHE FUNCTIONS 57

A. THE LIFE OF THE PSYCHE 57
  1. The psyche 60
  2. The conscious 62
    a) The conscious of imbalance 64
      • Overexploiting the rational conscious 64
      • Underexploiting the rational conscious 69
    b) The conscious of balance 71
  3. The unconscious 73
    a) The unconscious and intuition 74
    b) The unconscious and affective life 77
    c) The unconscious and influence 85

B. PSYCHIC FUNCTIONING 96
  1. Psychic needs 97
    a) The need for love 98
    b) The need for security 100
    c) The need to be heard 104
    d) The need for acknowledgment 110
    e) The need to assert oneself 113
      • Power 116

- Authority 122
- Transference and counter-transference 124
  - f) The need for freedom 129
  - g) The need for creativity 133
  - 2. Psychic needs and the emotions:
     An unsatisfactory psychological process 138

C. EMOTIONS 144

D. COMPLEXES 148
1. The abandonment complex 150
2. The sibling rivalry complex 156
3. The insecurity complex 161
4. The castration complex 164
5. The guilt complex... 167
6. The inferiority complex 170

E. DEFENSE MECHANISMS 173
1. Repression 175
2. Introjection 176
3. Escape and avoidance 179
4. Rationalization 184
5. Confluence 186
6. Self-punishment 190
7. Projection 193
8. The adoption of a persona 201

F. PATTERNS 206
1. The bully and the victim 209
2. The deserter and the abandonee 218
3. The invader and the invadee 222
4. The judge and the offender 228
5. The missionary and the disciple 232
6. The savior and the protégé 239
7. The superior and the inferior 244
8. The dominator and the dominee 249
9. The manipulator ans the manipulatee 253

Chapter 4
*RESPECT FOR THE PROCESS
OF LIBERATION AND CHANGE* 259

A. AWARENESS 262

B. ACCEPTANCE 265

C. RESPONSABILITY 269

D. EXPRESSION 273

E. OBSERVATION 278

F. CHOICE OF PROTECTIVE MECHANISMS 281
   1. The explicit request 286
   2. Verification 292
   3. Choice of entourage and environment 298
   4. Territory and limits 302
      a) Invasion 304
      b) Life goals 305
      c) Priorities 307
      d) Organization and discipline 308
   5. New life experiences 311
   6. Transformation of expectations into goals 315

G. THE SHIFT TO CREATIVE ACTION 318

Chapter 5
*RESPECT FOR THE DIFFERENT
TYPES OF INTELLIGENCE* 321

A. DISCOVERY OF DIFFERENT TYPES OF INTELLIGENCE 321
   1. Lack of love 322
   2. Lack of motivation 322

TABLE OF CONTENTS

B. TYPES OF INTELLIGENCE 325

C. RATIONALISTS 327
    1. Intellectual characteristics 327
    2. Affective characteristics 328
    3. Relational characteristics 329
    4. Reference points 330
    5. Skills 331
    6. Difficulties 331
    7. Ways of perceiving and learning 332
    8. Psychotherapeutic case study 333
    9. Educational case study 335

D. PRAGMATISTS 337
    1. Intellectual characteristics 337
    2. Affective characteristics 337
    3. Relational characteristics 338
    4. Reference points 338
    5. Difficulties 339
    6. Ways of perceiving and learning 339
    7. Psychotherapeutic case study 341
    8. Educational case study 343
    9. Personal experience 346

E. ESTHETES 347
    1. Intellectual characteristics 347
    2. Affective characteristics 348
    3. Relational characteristics 349
    4. Reference points 350
    5. Skills 350
    6. Difficulties 351
    7. Ways of perceiving and learning 352
    8. Psychotherapeutic case study 353
    9. Educational case study 355

Chapter 6
THE PARAMOUNT IMPORTANCE OF THE HELPER 361

A. THE TEACHER AS HELPER 363
  1. The teacher, the lifeblood of the education system 363
  2. Teacher-training programs 368
     a) Training centered on the teacher 368
     b) Training centered on inner work 370

B. PSYCHOTHERAPEUTIC INNER WORK AS PART
   OF THE TRAINING FOR ALL HELPERS 374
  1. Preparation for self-knowledge 374
  2. Preparation for the multidimensional approach 376

C. THE HELPER AND PSYCHOTHERAPY 383
  1. Training of creative nondirective psychotherapists 383
     a) Competence 383
     b) Letting go 386
     c) Discipline 388
     d) Pleasure 389
  2. Stages in the training 390
     a) Stage 1 390
     b) Stage 2 391
     c) Stage 3 392
  3. Course methodology 393
  4. Trainers 394

CONCLUSION 399

BIBLIOGRAPHY 403

INTRODUCTION

There is nothing miraculous about the approach outlined in this book; it is, rather, the result of many years of inner work. It could, in a way, be seen as the subjective synthesis of my personal and professional experience on the one hand, and my theoretical training on the other. As the approach evolved, it became imprinted with the suffering that was responsible for bringing me to my true self. This suffering, in which fear, anguish, sorrow and repressed anger all had a part, was what, in the end, made me into a happy person. It was the school in which I learned how to be a mother, wife, teacher, psychotherapist and instructor of the approach I advocate. In my suffering I felt solitude, abandonment and rejection; I suffered from lack of love and recognition, from fear of loss, of not pleasing, of disappointing; I suffered from guilt and shame; I suffered from feelings of invasion, doubt and powerlessness; I suffered from my dependence, my fragility, my vulnerability—in short, I suffered from life. For a long time I wanted to pull the suffering out by its roots: simply extract it, as you would a bad tooth. I wanted to deny it, ignore it, destroy it, but in spite of my efforts it grew stronger. Then, finally, I came to the realization that it had something to say to me, and that I needed to listen to it, as I would listen to a sad child. Over the years of inner work, I learned that I had to welcome it, accept it and listen to what it wanted to teach me. By accepting suffering, I discovered happiness and the joy of living, inner peace and the ability to love myself. Similarly, I discovered that embracing suffering was—and still is—the best way of learning how to help myself and others. It taught me that, if all I used were ready-made theories and techniques, I wouldn't be of much use to anyone. My psychotherapy-directed inner work, and the resulting personal growth, brought me to the realization that I bore the ineluctable responsibility for the success or failure of all my relationships.

This lengthy journey toward self-discovery, during which I spent many days studying, analyzing, researching, and thinking, was responsible for quickening my interest in all things related to people and their relationships, and particularly in counseling, which is often referred to in this book as a "helping relationship." Over the years, as I became better acquainted with the subject, I realized that counseling was not the sole prerogative of psychologists and psychotherapists. In fact, it is accessible to all who are involved in a relationship in which one of the protagonists is helping the other deal with a psychological problem. There are many people who claim—and with good cause—that they are "involved" in this sort of helping relationship: the nurse who takes a personal interest in her patients' problems, the teacher who helps one of his students through an emotionally troubled period, and the father who stands by his son when the latter is having difficulty in school are all giving important psychological assistance. Not to mention all the people who volunteer their time just to listen to those in less fortunate circumstances. In all their various situations, these people are legitimately acting to help others.

The term "counseling" can be applied or defined in many different ways. In the following pages, I have tried to develop the psychotherapeutic aspects of counseling, which I define as an approach that aims to prevent and to cure an individual's mental and functional difficulties. A fairly large section of the book will be devoted to education, because of the primarily "preventive" role I ascribe to the educational sciences.

There are many different schools of thought within the field of psychotherapy, just as there are many different psychological theories. The psychotherapeutic approach defined in this book is one that I developed, and which arose out of my years of experience with psychotherapy, teaching and training. I call this approach the Creative

INTRODUCTION

Nondirective Approach (CNDA). This new approach is based on the Carl Rogers' theories of nondirectivity, and those of Georgy Lozanov on suggestology. One of the primary objectives of this book will be to disseminate this new approach, by defining it and by laying bare the psychological foundation on which it is based. Ways of implementing the CNDA will be dealt with in another book.

I am not trying to claim that I have made a brand new discovery, and even less that I have sole possession of the truth in this particular branch of counseling, where I am far from the first to have done research. Nothing, after all, springs into being fully formed from Jupiter's thigh. Every creation is a continuation of that which preceded it, and its unique properties come from each individual's subjective experience. There are, therefore, as many truths as there are creations. In a spirit of respect for what has already been done in this field, I have set forth the principles of the Creative Nondirective Approach (CNDA), comprising an approach based on the interconnectedness of an individual and his entourage, and the way they grow, evolve and change. What the CNDA definitely is not is an educational or psychotherapeutic "method": it is rather an "attitude" that the helper should try and develop, an "inner state" that can be cultivated through self-examination, through deeper knowledge of his real self, and through love for himself as a person. This approach does not emphasize resolving problems, but rather focuses on the subject himself, as a person, and is designed to give him the opportunity of getting to know himself, of conquering his inner world, of freeing himself from the burden of repressed emotions, of fulfilling his creative potential and thus regain control over his life.

It is impossible to master this approach without first studying human psychology in depth, or acquiring an intimate knowledge of how human beings function, and how the person interacts on an emotional level with his entourage and his environment. Since he will inevitably feel personally implicated, the reader cannot view the approach as a simple intellectual exercise, regarding it as purely cognitive and rational material; to get the most out of this book, he must start out ready to invest something in it, ready to get involved. When reading it, he must be attentive to the echoes of his own subjective responses, and be ready to draw parallels between the subject matter and his own life experience. When approached in this manner, the book becomes an effective medium for self-examination, for inner growth and for spiritual renaissance.

Because the CNDA is based on respect for a person's intrinsic wholeness, for the way his brain and his psyche function, for the way he perceives the world and for his adaptability to change, this approach emphasizes the helper as a person, and the importance of his training. It postulates that the most important ingredient in any successful helping relationship is the helper's own continuing inner work. This book therefore is intended for specialists in physical and mental health care, for teachers and pedagogues, for parents, and for anyone who would like to foster healthier and more effective professional relationships in their work environment. But ultimately, and above all, this book is intended for anyone, regardless of his type of employment, who believes in the importance of inner work and of finding the path to change and freedom within himself, who seeks to find his hidden potential and become the master of his own destiny.

The CNDA invites you into the heart of your Self, where you will discover the key to your own fulfillment, and be equipped for involvement in a helping relationship through self-knowledge, and true love for yourself as a person.

CHAPTER 1

THE CREATIVE NONDIRECTIVE APPROACH

A. THE NONDIRECTIVITY PHENOMENON IN QUEBEC

Everywhere in the Western world, and consequently also in Quebec, the past half-century has seen a shift—particularly in educational circles—from a rather radical form of directivity toward certain reasonably satisfactory attempts at nondirectivity. The pendulum then swung back, bringing the previous strict attitudes back into vogue. In light of this, the extreme shifts that characterize the evolution and growth of humanity need to be counteracted by a search for balance.

The directivity phenomenon that marked Quebec before the Quiet Revolution of the 1960s, had a remarkable effect on the educational theories of that era. It was maintained by the religious, political and ideological powers-that-be, and was characterized by the tendency of certain persons in authority to impose beliefs and ideologies that they presented as absolute, universal truths, to be applied indiscriminately to all individuals regardless of culture, age, education or life history. Thus upheld, directivity dominated those on whom it was imposed by sustaining feelings of inferiority and guilt, and stifled creativity by imposing uniformity and showing a lack of respect for individual differences and personal subjectivity. Although this phenomenon has yet to disappear completely, it is generally acknowledged that the situation has improved greatly.

In the 1960s, in the name of human freedom, the need for creative expression, and respect for the individual, major reforms took place that revolutionized Quebec society, opening the door—notably in the field of education—to less directive approaches. As put forward by Lewin and Rogers, these approaches surreptitiously crossed the border between the United States and Canada and influenced a people ready to cast off the yoke that was beginning to crush them.

Unfortunately, in many cases, this period of profound change in Quebec brought about an overall acceptance of the new and a massive rejection of the old, which cut us off from some of the values essential to our equilibrium. Thus the concepts of discipline and training were more or less disregarded in favor of freedom of expression and freedom of action. Disequilibrium, then, took on another face, and dissatisfaction found other causes. Just as "directivity" had resulted in our being crushed, so "nondirectivity" brought about a feeling of insecurity. What were the reasons for this phenomenon? Why was the Rogerian nondirective philosophy—which represented near-irrefutable human values—unable, when applied to education, to satisfactorily respond to people's real needs?

B. ROGERIAN NONDIRECTIVITY

Although he was preceded by Lewin and followed by, among others, Gordon and Gendlin, Carl Rogers is generally recognized as the foremost proponent of the nondirective current in Western psychology, particularly in the therapeutic and educational circles of the mid-twentieth century. Rogers' theory is founded on the hypothesis that each human being naturally tends toward the kind of fulfillment, actualization, and growth that increase his well-being (Rogers, 1942). This tendency means that the road to self-creation lies within each person, and that only he can tell what is good or bad for him and knows the answers to his problems. Following this conviction, Rogers believes that any approach that intends to help cannot be directive. Therefore the "helper"—be he doctor, psychologist, teacher, therapist or parent—should necessarily be "nondirective" if the "helpee" is going to move toward self-actualization. This is why Rogers, after initially calling his philosophy a "nondirective approach," later spoke of a "person-centered approach." The name change also came in response to the negative connotation of nondirectivity, to which had been attributed, in a great many cases, the idea of "laissez-faire."

What, though, are the characteristics of the Rogerian person-centered nondirective approach?

Rogers conceives of nondirectivity as an attitude. The person-centered therapist is thus recognized as having an empathetic, congruent, accepting attitude: empathetic in the sense of being able to understand and respect the client's frame of reference; congruent because the therapist knows how to be attentive to what is going on inside himself; accepting in that the "other" is unconditionally accepted for what he is (Rogers, 1942). The Rogerian approach, centered above all on real-life experience and particularly on the emotions, sets no clear limits on acceptance, which in my view bears qualification; I will return to this question later.

When applied to psychotherapy, group activities, teaching, education or helping relationships, the nondirective or person-centered approach as conceived by Rogers has not always had the miraculous effects so fervently desired. The majority of those who have tried to put it into practice have run up against serious obstacles that caused them to either become more directive than they were in the first place or to modify the approach to make its application more satisfactory.

In fact, the numerous attempts at applying the Rogerian approach failed for specific reasons.

Besides the fact that it has been misunderstood and misinterpreted, the Rogerian approach has in some cases been improperly applied. First, it seems to me to be difficult to parachute people who have been trained "directively" since birth into an entirely nondirective setting. It is a mistake to believe that one can take charge of one's life overnight when one has always been guided or led by the outside world. Becoming independent is in this case a progressive learning process, one that must be undertaken with respect for the psychological functioning of the human person and his rate of growth. Imposing nondirectivity without taking a human being's psychology and his natural rate of development into account is, paradoxically, being directive. Attempting to change a person or group by throwing them headlong toward a nondirective approach runs counter to the very principles of nondirectivity. Can we, in the name of freedom, destroy values and realities which have existed for centuries without a care for those who believe in them? Can we, in the name of equality, wipe out such deeply rooted realities as father, mother, teacher, leader? Can we, in the name of ideology, forbid the concept of "role"? And can we, with a wave of the hand, dismiss the authority represented by the simple fact of being a "father," a "teacher," a "boss" or a "president"?

Let us say that I am a nondirective contributor in the Rogerian sense, but because of who I am and because of my role as leader, teacher or psychotherapist, I impose my nondirectivity and become in a certain sense directive, even though I may not wish to become so. Therein lies the paradox of Rogerian nondirectivity: those who apply it have not always achieved satisfactory results because of the insecurity caused by the lack of structure that it generates. I am convinced—and I will demonstrate this later—that the need for security is fundamental to human functioning, and that satisfying this need is essential to the process of liberation, growth and change. Simply put, making people insecure inhibits their evolution.

When I first read Rogers in the early 1960s, I admit that the principles of his philosophy, presented in *On Becoming a Person* and *A Way of Being,* and applied to education in *Freedom to Learn* and to psychotherapy in *Counseling and Psychotherapy* more than just impressed me. Yet I quickly realized that I could not be satisfied unless I were to adjust this approach—in my educational practice, in the way I raised my four children, and later in my work as a therapist and at my training center—according to who I am and the people with whom I was working: my children, students or clients. In this way, inspired both by Carl Rogers and by the originator of suggestology, Dr. Georgy Lozanov, and based on my research, and especially my personal experiences as a parent, teacher, leader, psychotherapist and trainer, I succeeded in creating my own approach, which I call the Creative Nondirective Approach, or CNDA.

C. THE CREATIVE NONDIRECTIVE APPROACH

The CNDA is an affective, relationship-based approach that fosters creativity through respect for a person's overall psychological and physiological makeup, for his rate of progress from one stage to another, for the process of change and for his self-creation.

I call this approach "creative nondirective" because it is based on the "directivity/nondirectivity" dialectic, and the development of a person's creativity, through respect for that person and for his evolution.

I believe it is important to a basic understanding of the approach to define the exact nature of the directivity/nondirectivity dialectic as I perceive it, and to show that any dialectic of this nature tends to foster growth of a person's creative potential.

D. THE DIRECTIVITY/NONDIRECTIVITY DIALECTIC

According to the CNDA, nondirectivity in its purest state cannot exist, because of two important limitations: the fact that the helper himself is still pursuing his own inner work, and the setting. The CNDA does, in fact, include a fairly large amount of directivity, and it is paradoxically the dialectical conjunction of the directive part with the nondirective part that makes the approach creative.

To clarify the explanation, I have grafted the ideas of "container/content" to the ideas of directivity/nondirectivity. Thus the CNDA is an approach that is clearly made up of "content-nondirectivity" and "container-directivity."

1. Nondirectivity according to the CNDA

Like the Rogerian approach, the CNDA is a humanistic approach that is centered on the person. Creative nondirective psychotherapists do not hide behind their theories and their techniques; on the contrary, they experience the helping relationship as a human relationship. In spite of their professional competence, they have their limitations, as do all human beings, and their actions are based as much on who they are as on what they know. It is therefore obvious that their work will probably be affected by their life experience, by their psychological blocks, their strengths and weaknesses. It is just not realistic to believe that helpers have to solve all their own problems before they can help others. Even if he has progressed through a great deal of inner work, any person involved in a helping relationship can become vulnerable when going through periods of difficulty, insecurity and real anguish. Even those psychotherapists who claim to be neutral are subject to this phenomenon. In fact, they are precisely the ones who fall victim to it completely unawares, which can be twice as harmful for the client.

Whatever approach he may use, the counselor cannot program himself as he would a robot. He is a human being, and as such will react—at least internally—to what is going on around him. The more he tries to program himself, and cut himself off from his emotions, the less he is able to help, because a ignored emotion could become a defensive issue for him. If he lives, loves, suffers and cries in his personal life, then he is able to listen to the joys and sufferings of others. But just as this ability to live out his desires and emotions constitutes one of the counselor's strengths, the inability to do so, or the negation of emotion, could easily become a source of projections, judgments, interpretations and habits of "taking charge." Also, when the counselor rephrases a situation out of his own experience rather than using the patient's frame of reference, his observations become directive. In training its practitioners, the CNDA greatly emphasizes the importance of inner work. The counselor can only aspire to a creative nondirective approach if he has that self-knowledge and that ability to distinguish between what comes from him and what comes from the client. However, as the counselor is not perfect, and, in spite of his ongoing training, may make errors in judgment in this area, nondirectivity in the content of his approach is, in actuality, a goal he will spend his whole life working toward.

Even if nondirectivity in its purest state does not exist, it is nevertheless true that the counselor who is integrating it into his approach will remain constantly aware of the need to respect others, and to continue his own inner work, because he is aware that this approach is limited by its essentially perfectible nature.

Having said that, creative nondirectivity, as far as its content—that is, its actual substance—is concerned, is not a method and is even less a teaching or therapy technique. First and foremost it is, like Rogerian nondirectivity, an attitude of complete respect for the innermost nature of each human being. Based on Rogers' theory that each individual carries the potential for this own fulfillment within himself, this attitude of respect that sustains the helping relationship relieves the counselor of the power he wields over the lives of others and allows him to regain control over his own life. It is precisely this recovery work that enables him to progressively develop a creative nondirective approach to counseling.

The terms "relationship," "attitude," "nature" and "power" are central to the whole concept of the CNDA and deserve to be discussed individually, as do the conditions for developing a creative nondirective attitude.

a) *The importance of the helping relationship*

Counseling, or the helping relationship, by definition, touches on two areas: "helping" and "relationships." Specialists in the field have tended to stress the former and, unfortunately, neglect the latter. The CNDA philosophy lays great emphasis on the "relationship" aspect, in the belief that it is not possible to help someone unless we, as helpers, have managed to establish a relationship with the helpee that is defined by a respect for the roles of each of the parties.

Two people can be said to have a relationship when feelings of trust and affection, which have a positive effect on the unconscious, are present. We should not be deluded into thinking that it is possible to have a satisfactory relationship if affection, trust and, by extension, mutual influence are not present. What I am saying is this: the psychotherapist cannot truly help his client, a professor his student, or a parent his child, unless he radiates an attitude of love for, and faith in, himself and the other.

The term "relationship," as used here, does not refer to a system of techniques, methods or concrete procedures for establishing contact and solving problems. Rather, it refers to a kind of relationship that is sustained by feelings which, although not always expressed as such, are nevertheless perceived through the parties' attitudes. When the client feels that his psychotherapist likes him and believes in him, and the psychotherapist feels that the client likes him, too, and trusts him completely, then the kind of relationship necessary for the counseling process has been established. This key event usually takes place during the first therapy session, the first day of classes or the first meeting, and it marks the real starting point of a helping relationship. This event is, in fact, difficult to pinpoint since it definitely does not belong to the realm of the conscious mind, but rather to that of the unconscious.

This moment may, of course, be followed by the ups and downs that mark every helping relationship and which, precisely because it is a relationship, take the helpee as well as the helper through different stages of questioning, doubts, and regressive as well as propulsive periods. It is nevertheless true that, in spite of the difficulties along the road, counseling is only relevant if it is sustained by an attitude of trust and love.

b) Attitude

The notion of "attitude," developed by Rogers and largely reiterated by Lozanov (1978) and Lerède (1980) in suggestology, is a notion that is essential to the CNDA, and one without which creative nondirectivity would not exist.

An attitude is a psychological disposition that radiates unconsciously from a person, revealing his emotions, his intentions and his real thoughts. It refers to the helper's inner state, which he communicates unawares, in all his relationships, through non-verbal language: intonation, delivery, how loudly or softly he speaks, his facial expressions, his gestures and, above all, the energy waves given off by his physical body.

The effects of the helper's attitude on the helpee's unconscious cannot be measured as such, but are nevertheless of considerable significance as far as his mental stability, and therefore his behavior, is concerned. Here we have the most subtle and effective form of influence there is, precisely because it cannot be controlled. If, for example, the helper harbors judgments, feelings of aggression and intentions to dominate, his non-verbal language will necessarily reflect his inner reality and have a negative and disturbing effect on the helpee's unconscious. It is not enough to present an impeccable exterior, to say encouraging words and to do commendable things to help others. Above all, the helper must feel—live—what he presents, says and does. If there is any contradiction between his verbal and non-verbal language, between his actions and the underlying attitude, between the "seeming" and the "being," then the helpee will receive a twofold message—the conscious message and the unconscious one—and it will trouble and perhaps even disturb him.

The helping attitude is therefore essentially a genuine one, and essentially nondirective in the sense that there is no underlying need to prove, to manipulate or to dominate, but rather a desire to respect the nature and the development of others.

It is an attitude that has nothing to do with the "seeming" or the "doing" and everything to do with the "being." This means that it is impossible to become "nondirective" overnight, since nondirectivity presupposes a lengthy process of inner work, in which one acquires knowledge, acceptance, respect and love for one's individual essence, for one's own nature.

c) The nature of a human being

The nature of a human being is defined as the set of characteristics that define and distinguish him, and without which he would not exist.

It is generally acknowledged that education often has the effect of distancing man from his innermost nature, that is, from that which makes him unique, rather than bringing him closer to it. This is due to the fact that it overrides individual differences by trivializing real-life experience, or by crushing those who try to distinguish themselves. Such current educational practices stand in the way of self-knowledge, inhibit creative potential and impede the process of growth and actualization.

The CNDA's goal is to reveal the inner self, and it therefore proceeds differently. Although it upholds the notion that there are common aspects that unite people of all races, ages and religions, it also recognizes individual differences, and draws them out rather than banishing them. This recognition is mainly conveyed by the helper's attitude: the more he works at attaining his true nature, at manifesting his own differences, the more he will radiate an attitude of respect for the nature of those he helps, and the less he will attempt to exert power over others.

d) Power

It is impossible to discuss the notion of "power" without touching on a subject that is an issue not only in political, economic, social and cultural circles, but also in everyday human relationships. Wherever there are attempts at imposing uniformity, man grasps at power as a means of distinguishing himself, of expressing himself in order to prove that he exists, of pushing himself forward and taking his place. The "imposition of power" reigns, at the expense of "self-empowerment."

By "imposition of power" I mean the ascendance we take over others: that which incites us to suppress them and try to change them. By "self-empowerment" I mean the individual's ability to use inner power that manifests his difference, in order that he may be empowered to create himself, empowered to free himself from what education has grafted onto him, and empowered to actualize himself as much as possible.

The creative nondirective philosophy holds that the only person in the world over whom we can have power is ourselves, and that the only power we have over others resides in the power of unconscious influence arising from our attitude. In other words, we cannot change others deliberately, only unconsciously; not by what we do but by who we are. Moreover, this influence will only prove positive and effective if it takes place within the context of real self-acceptance, and acceptance of the other. This is the reason the CNDA defines itself as an affective, relationship-based approach.

Let me tell you the story of a client called Jasmine (not her real name). When she first came to see me, Jasmine was 31 years old. Her biggest problem was her relationship with her mother. She told me that they were on extremely bad terms, that she found this very draining, and that it had been going on for as long as she could remember.

Why had Jasmine and her mother been involved for years in an essentially destructive relationship? Because each of the women wanted to change the other. Ever since her teenage years, Jasmine had been trying to change her mother and, at the age of 31, she still had not succeeded. She had tried everything: challenging her, confronting her, blaming her, criticizing her, judging, ridiculing and avoiding her. Nothing had worked. Both of the women were searching for the chink in the other's armor, the Achilles heel where she could be wounded, crushed, perhaps even destroyed. Explanations and justifications succeeded only in exacerbating their confrontations.

After many years of this, Jasmine had such a negative self-image that it had seriously affected her belief in her own potential. What was she to do? She could see no way of improving her relationship with her mother—and she was right. As long as both she and her mother wanted to change the other ("imposition of power") without attempting to change themselves ("self-empowerment") then the difficulties would go on indefinitely. When the CNDA helped Jasmine discover that the answer to her problem was to stop attempting to take power over her mother and above all to regain the power over herself that she had given away, then her anxieties slowly began to disappear. She realized that she had spent her life giving others the power to dominate her, to hurt her and to destroy her, and that she had to regain that power. She was able to do so by adhering to her own pace, as she progressed through the stages of the psychotherapeutic process of liberation and change, which I will discuss further in Chapter 4.

Regaining power over our lives means first getting to know ourselves so that we can develop our potential and bring a positive, loving influence to bear on others through a creative nondirective attitude. However, a creative nondirective attitude, based on inner work, can only be developed under certain conditions.

e) *Conditions for developing a creative nondirective attitude*

I stated previously that one cannot acquire creative nondirectivity overnight. It can only be fully actualized if the helper has integrated into his life the ability to take responsibility for who he is, if he has attained a high level of self-acceptance and acceptance of others and if he maintains, for himself as well as for others, a profound ability to love.

- ***Responsibility***

The mental attitude suggested, encouraged and upheld in all our institutions and, indeed, throughout our whole society is one of refusing to look at oneself, the better to watch, judge, condemn or idolize others. This attitude, which is based on comparison and evaluation, results in a state of dependence and creates permanent competition, thus reflecting only the most infinitesimal part of each human being's intrinsic wholeness.

The CNDA suggests the opposite approach. It transfers attention away from others and directs it inward. It trains one to think first of oneself, to work toward knowing, understanding, accepting and above all, loving oneself. This attitude used to be labeled egotistical and was thus rejected. It is, in fact, the most liberating and "helping" attitude there is. After all, how can anyone know, understand, listen to, respect and love others if he cannot first attain those goals within his own self? How can he accept another person, with all his strengths, weaknesses and contradictions, if he does not first accept his own? It is precisely this ability to concentrate on ourselves that renders us capable of responsibility.

Responsibility refers to an individual's ability to be accountable, to come to terms with himself, and to actualize himself in the fullest possible sense.

Regaining power over our own lives is a lengthy learning process. To attain that goal we must develop the ability to accept the consequences of our choices and our decisions. By making others responsible for our problems, troubles, emotions, expectations, difficulties, failures, frustrations and deceptions, we give them power over us, and lose our freedom. However, when we integrate responsibility and accountability into our lives, we automatically find the road to independence and satisfaction. In many cases we have been taught to make others responsible for all the unpleasant things that happen to us, and so we blame them, judge them, criticize them and above all try to change them to make ourselves happy. Unfortunately, it is not that easy to change others, especially not if we reproach, judge and criticize them. Thus our attempts to change others usually end in failure, and this fosters permanent dissatisfaction. By trying to change ourselves, rather than desperately attempting to change others, we are adopting a responsible attitude.

In order to develop this attitude, we must first become aware of our tendency to blame and to want to change others, and we must have a deep desire to regain power over our own lives by trying to change ourselves. Without this awareness and this deep desire, nothing is possible. We must also accept the fact that learning responsibility takes time because we must first get rid of our futile habits in order to adopt a more effective approach toward others, and this is not always easy. However, if we are prepared to abide by our rate of integration, we will achieve encouraging results. They will be evident in greater self-knowledge, an increasingly strong feeling of freedom, a more vivid expression of our creativity and, above all, by a unique feeling of self-love.

In order to attain that goal, it is crucial that we try and train ourselves to look inward when we feel disagreeable emotions or are disappointed, rather than blaming, judging or accusing, and also that we train ourselves to take responsibility for both our past experiences and our current problems. We are the only ones who can solve those problems in a satisfactory manner.

Responsibility, however, is not a one-way street; there is traffic moving in both directions. There are always two parties in any relationship, and integrating our responsibility means becoming accountable for our own past, but not for that of the other party. The more I learn to be responsible for my emotions, desires, choices, expectations, frustrations, and so on, the more I am able to free myself from taking responsibility for other people's feelings. It is because of this, because I have learned to be responsible and to give back to the other what belongs to him when he makes me responsible for his problems, that I can become increasingly independent, free and creative.

When the concept of responsibility has been fully integrated, one is no longer subject to others, nor is one subject to life's events; one gradually develops an inclination toward action that becomes innate, and thanks to which, one comes to know inner freedom, success and satisfaction.

For example, let me tell you about a client called George (not his real name). When he came to see me for the first time, George had severed all connections with his friends because he felt used by them, and had the overwhelming impression that he was neither appreciated, recognized nor even liked by anyone. He had decided to withdraw from all his relationships because when he was with others he had the feeling that he did not exist. He resented his friends for using him when it suited them, and dropping him when they no longer needed him. Even after he confronted them, the situation did not change. In psychotherapy, George realized that he experienced the same feeling in his family, professional and social life as well. Unfortunately, the idea of withdrawing from the world and seeing nobody did not satisfy him either, and this was, in fact, what had led him to come and see me. Realizing that neither unsatisfying relationships nor total solitude were what he wanted, he was looking for a way to meet people without feeling used. The creative nondirective approach taught him not to satisfy his deep-seated need for love at his own expense, by giving everything to others. George realized that, in doing so, he was giving others the power to use him as they wanted, and then making them responsible for his own troubles. He wanted others to acknowledge him, but never asserted himself, never emphasized his limits, never asserted his needs for fear of losing people's love. Paradoxically, in giving others power over his life, he got exactly the opposite of what he wanted: indifference.

For George, there was only one solution left: changing himself. He devoted a lot of time and energy to this because it required that he look at himself in a way he had never done before. In doing so he realized—with some pain—that he let others take precedence because he did not love himself. How then could he ask others to love him when he did not love himself?

By taking responsibility for his problem, he opened a door that he had always kept closed before: the door of self-knowledge and self-love. Although this door is extremely difficult to pass through, one of its redeeming features is that, sooner or later, it leads to freedom and creativity. This is the reward for those who decide to take responsibility for their lives.

George's case is not unique. There are many people who are at the mercy of the power they have given to other people. Regaining that power is not always easy, because it implies getting rid of patterns that have been entrenched for years. The process of becoming accountable for one's life is a long and arduous one, but it is definitely liberating! Once achieved, true freedom and independence cannot be lost.

But how far exactly does this responsibility go? Are we responsible for things we are forced to submit to? Let me answer that question with another example. During my career as a psychotherapist, I have dealt with a certain number of clients, both men and women, who had been abused; Jean-Paul was one of them. When he was in high school, Jean-Paul lived with his parents in the city, and they decided to send him to work on a farm one summer during the holidays. His time was divided between the farmhouse and the fields; in the morning he helped the farmer's wife with the housework and in the afternoon he worked in the fields with the farmer. Within a week, the woman in question, who was approximately 40 years old and had no children, sexually abused him and forced him to perform acts that he found revolting.

When he came to see me, Jean-Paul was 32 years old. He had never told anyone else about his experience, first because the woman had threatened him in a number of ways, and second because he was ashamed of it. He had been unable to touch a woman since then and, at 32, was left a lonely and extremely depressed person.

Was Jean-Paul responsible for that experience, which for years had ruined his life?

In my opinion, responsibility here does not concern the event so much as the manner in which it is dealt with. Let me explain what I mean. Jean-Paul was an only child, whose mother was possessive and very invasive. At a very young age, he had assimilated a pattern of passively allowing himself to be invaded and dominated by others. In his case, taking responsibility for the manner in which he dealt with the event meant working on how he related to this invasion. Maintaining a "victimized" attitude only means that one will fall deeper and deeper into depression. In all the abuse cases I have seen, I have observed serious problems of invasion and repressed aggression. Victims of abuse are people who have been constantly invaded, not only on a physical level, but also in their psychological, emotional, intellectual and professional space, and who have almost never reacted. Publicly denouncing the abusers is, in itself, not enough to solve the problem. What is needed is an in-depth psychological transformation, the goal of which is to regain power over one's own life by integrating responsibility.

In psychotherapy, the idea of responsibility is closely associated with the idea of nondirectivity. In other words, nondirectivity is not possible without responsibility. In fact, it is because he takes responsibility for his own troubles, fears, defense mechanisms and patterns, that the psychotherapist is able to prevent himself, as far as is possible, from projecting them onto his client through judgments, comparisons, interpretations or patterns of taking charge. According to the CNDA, responsibility is the path *par excellence* to independence and freedom. If the client does not fully integrate his responsibility, then the helping relationship is in danger of becoming a dependent relationship, where each party waits for the other to change, where the therapist becomes a savior, a judge or a spokesman. In teaching the creative nondirective approach, I concentrate first and foremost on integration of responsibility. Without this key element, the helping relationship becomes directive and the helpee is unable to attain the desired independence and freedom.

Of course, learning creative nondirectivity through responsibility is not like discovering a secret passageway into a magic kingdom. The path that leads there is real, and the goal cannot be reached without going through a lengthy process of acceptance.

- *Acceptance*

Rogers considered acceptance to be a key element of nondirectivity. According to him, it referred to a characteristic of the psychotherapist that enabled him to be receptive to the client, with all that he is, unconditionally and without judging him. The CNDA holds that acceptance is the ability of the helper to be receptive to the helpee with total respect for what makes him different.

An accepting counselor is one who is able to "receive" the other, with all his past history, life experience, emotions, needs, desires, thoughts, opinions, tastes, way of life, behavior, outward appearance, choices and decisions . . . all without making a judgment.

I share Rogers' belief that judgment is the biggest obstacle to being receptive, to listening and to change. We are all products of an education largely based on judgment and observation of others and, because of this, we quickly learned to impose, on ourselves as well as on others, judgments that inhibit creative expression. Surely our first step on the road to acceptance should be to accept ourselves as judging creatures, without feeling needlessly guilty. I believe that by accepting and observing the negative consequences of the judgments we bring to bear on ourselves, we facilitate the process of change. Acceptance and observation teach us to what extent the harsh light in which we perceive ourselves limits our ability to develop our latent potential and reduces the possibility of self-actualization. When we cultivate this remarkable manner of perceiving ourselves without judging, we also learn to be receptive to others with complete respect for who they are. As we go through this lengthy process, we come to the realization that it is impossible to help others, in any way whatsoever, unless we are prepared to devote ourselves to ongoing inner work. In training therapists for counseling, I devote the first year of courses to teaching future psychotherapists how to look within. This kind of inner work must, however, be gradual, and can only be accomplished in a spirit of receptiveness and self-love.

The road to "receiving" the other is a lengthy learning process because it starts out with accepting oneself. But, at this point, I part company with Rogers; he speaks of "unconditional" acceptance, which has lent itself to numerous interpretations. Of course, I share Rogers' belief that total acceptance of the other, as a person, remains essential to the process of growth, freedom and creation. However, we must not forget that every helping relationship touches on two areas: helping on the one hand and the relationship on the other.

Moreover, in any helping relationship, the helper's acceptance of the helpee must never, under any circumstances, be detrimental to the helper's respect for himself. This helper/helpee dialectic—acceptance of the other and self-acceptance, respect for the other and self-respect—has, over the years, brought me to the realization that there are certain limits to the idea of acceptance.

As counselors, it is important for us to accept the client just as he is. However, if the latter exhibits an invasive pattern of behavior, and tries to take advantage of us in some way, what then? Should we accept him, reprimand him, reject him? This type of situation creates a problem for so-called "unconditional" acceptance. There are some things that, as counselors, we could not accept without lacking respect and love for ourselves. This is why I believe that acceptance is limited by self-respect, which Rogers addressed with his idea of congruence. In real life, though, how is one to define the boundary between acceptance of the other and self-acceptance?

As helping people and even simply as people it is important, out of respect and love for ourselves, that we not permit our physical, mental and professional space to be invaded. It is also important that we not allow our limits to be disregarded. Finally, it is essential that we not feel pressured into taking responsibility for the emotions, the troubles, the problems, the expectations and the choices of others, whether they be our clients', our students' or our children's. Where does that leave acceptance, then?

Accepting the other with his problem of invasion, accepting and understanding that he finds it difficult to respect the limits of others and has a tendency to make others responsible for his problems—that is one thing. Accepting that he invade us and make us responsible for his problems is another. If we accept the other just as he is, and at the same time respect ourselves for who we are by defining our limits, then our attitude may be influential in helping the other to respect himself and respect the space and limits of others. This is the first major modification I would like to introduce to the idea of acceptance, which is essential to the CNDA.

Secondly, I believe that it is humanly impossible for a helper to be unconditionally accepting of all the people he helps because of his essentially perfectible nature. "Unconditional acceptance" is a goal to be achieved. It is an ideal that all creative nondirective psychotherapists are working toward because, for human beings, growth is faster and more efficacious in an atmosphere of total acceptance. However, we must not forget that, although the helper has come a long way in his inner work, he is nevertheless still developing. In his relationship with the helpee, as I said before, he will encounter stumbling blocks that will bring him face to face with his own limits and his own weaknesses. In certain cases, these will place him in a state of "non-acceptance" that he will have to deal with. In fact, dealing with these states gives him an opportunity for growth, as he learns to become more accepting.

The CNDA posits that acceptance of the helpee is based on the ability of the helper to take responsibility for his own life experience, for his limits, for his space. It is also based on his progress toward accepting himself as he is, on his love for himself and for others.

- *Love*

Help is neither effective nor long-lasting unless it is based on love. The helper—parent, professor, educator, doctor, group leader or psychotherapist, as the case may be—who does not harbor a deep love for himself, for all human beings and for his work is, in my opinion, merely doing a routine, technician's job.

Love is such an important and fundamental concept that man has been trying for centuries to pin it down and define it, perhaps so that he might attain it and live it out. For the CNDA, love is a concept that has no meaning unless it starts with the self; in other words, there can be no love of others unless there is first love of oneself. *This is why I define love as the ability to act in such a way that we constantly foster the satisfaction of basic needs, both physiological as well as psychological, which ensure our well-being, our inner balance and our physical, psychological and spiritual health. Love is a question of self-respect and the ability to choose what is good for the self; without it there can be no love for others.* This premise will be discussed in greater depth because it is central to this book, and because I believe that our love of life is in direct proportion to our love of self.

In fact, love is what gives soul and life to relationships, to work and to our daily activities. We must never forget that the helpee needs love just as he needs air to breathe, no matter what his age, occupation or social standing. In fact, this conviction is the foundation of the CNDA. The person applying the creative nondirective approach is first and foremost someone who is learning, on a daily basis, to love himself, his work and the people he helps. Since the need for love is fundamental to an individual's balanced development, the person who feels loved will move more rapidly toward a solution to his problems, toward self-knowledge and toward independence. The love that the counselor communicates through unconscious influence is of tremendous importance for the client's development—all the more so if it has been noticeably lacking in the client's life. I would even go so far as to say that the helper's love for the helpee is what makes it possible for the latter to grow in loving himself and to become the master of his destiny. One cannot learn to love oneself and love others without first having been loved.

Although I believe that love is a priority in any helping relationship, I do not wish to go to the extreme of advocating obligatory and universal love. Man is made to love and be loved, but this does not necessarily mean he should be obliged to love everyone unconditionally. Lack of love for oneself and for others is a fact of life. The counselor is only human; he helps others with what he has, and this inevitably includes his failings and his weaknesses. By positing love as the driving force in the helping relationship, I am not advocating perfection—far from it. Rather, I am trying to stress how important it is that helpers be constantly striving to develop love for themselves, because it is an indispensable prerequisite for loving others.

Thus, the "content" of the creative nondirective approach is based on the dialectic in the helper/helpee relationship and, more particularly, in the unconscious influence of the helper's attitude. As such, it combines love for oneself with love for others, and respect for oneself with respect for others. A natural consequence of this is that independence develops, freedom is gained and creative potential is liberated.

In short, when I speak of content-nondirectivity, I mean the ability of the helper to respect and accept, as far as possible, the feelings, emotions, impediments and problems experienced by the helpee, as well as his tastes, needs, desires, lifestyle and manner of being, his opinions and his thoughts. Content-nondirectivity is an attitude that is essential for the psychotherapist, as well as the teacher or the parent. Being nondirective, in this sense, means accepting the client, the pupil, the child; it means listening in an active way, being warm and attentive, and thereby allowing him to express freely what he experiences, without hindering this process through advice, judgments, moralizing or comparison, and without compelling him to conform to introjected norms, beliefs or systems, and helping him not to feel constrained by psychological methods of pressure or coercion from his emotions.

This kind of "content-nondirectivity" is what makes it possible for each one of us to find within ourselves the solutions to our problems, our questions, our anxieties and our plans. And this same nondirectivity can bring the helper (and the helpee) to the realization that the only obstacle to self-actualization and freedom is not events, and not others, but our own selves. However, nondirectivity in the "content" has no meaning unless it goes hand in hand with a directive approach in the "container."

2. Directivity according to the CNDA

a) *The container concept*

The verb "to contain" means "to hold together, hold in, keep within limits" (*Webster's New Collegiate Dictionary*). The content needs to be received, held, restrained even, by a container. Otherwise it becomes lost, dispersed, and may well disappear.

The container gives form to the content, lends it body, structure and unity, and imparts coherence and definition. The container's distinctive feature is that it names and defines. The mere act of naming something gives it form and the act of defining gives it meaning and reality. By naming something, we give it birth; by defining it, we give it life.

When we define a thing, we circumscribe it, organize it, structure it and, in a manner of speaking, encompass it so that it acquires a certain capacity. Defining a thing means describing it, giving it meaning, specifying its component parts. Defining a thing also means clarifying it through elimination of foreign elements.

b) *The container according to the CNDA*

Without a container, there is no content. In fact, the two need each other. The CNDA posits that the content—or respect for an individual's feelings, his life experience and his rate of progress—calls for a container which, in this case, is made up of the "what," the "why" and the "how" of the approach. Whereas the content is in a state of flux and varies from one person to the next, the container is clear, precise, structured, solid and rather stable.

In order to illustrate this explanation, let us turn for a moment to the concepts of imagination and fantasy. Imagination, as the "power of forming a mental image" (*Webster's*) is, in a manner of speaking, the container that holds our fantasies, which are the "creation of the imaginative faculty" (*Webster's*). The ability to imagine is common to all individuals, and can thus be likened to a stable container. Fantasies, on the other hand—or the "content" of the imagination—are different for everyone.

So it is for the "content" and the "container" with respect to the CNDA. The content of the CNDA is essentially nondirective, since it respects the feelings, individual differences, life experience, opinions and choices—all elements that vary from one person to another. Container nondirectivity is, however, in my opinion, not only misleading but a total aberration, based on a theory that is completely divorced from reality; misleading because "laissez-faire" attitudes lead to anarchy and chronic insecurity; an aberration because the mere act of calling oneself nondirective and defining nondirectivity becomes, conversely, directive. In any situation, if the helper puts forward a nondirective approach, he is imposing his nondirectivity, which then becomes an unrecognized form of directivity. For this reason, the creative nondirective approach can be described as "content"-nondirective and "container"-directive.

The container refers to the limitations of time and space, to guidelines, structures, methods, rules, requirements, limits, programs, organization, approach and philosophy. Whereas the content, because it is centered on attitude and its contributing factors, is in a state of flux and varies from one person to the next, the container is, on the whole, stable, and is so in every case.

The container owes its stability to its structure and its specific form. However, it does not have the kind of definitive stability that we find in "closed-structure containers." We are dealing here with "open-structure containers," which leave enough room for modifications to the structure as well as to the organization, and space for improvements to its defining elements—and hence to the philosophy itself. Indeed, there is a certain paradox inherent in the idea of "open-structure containers," since it encompasses both stability and flux. Stability here, though, is synonymous with consistency, continuity and balance, not with stagnation and inertia. In that sense, the container's stability refers to evolution and progression; it is, in fact, a kind of "fluctuating stability," which makes it both reassuring and alive.

This fluctuating stability is a distinctive feature of the creative nondirective approach container; it is a kind of container that leaves room for evolution while at the same time recognizing the encompassing presence of structures, definitions, and the particular features of the philosophy.

Rogers' nondirective approach is itself based on a container of specific elements (empathy, congruence, acceptance, rephrasing and so forth). If they are not present, the approach loses its name and its very existence and becomes something else. The content can only be worked out in the context of a definition, a method, a philosophy and its particular features. In my opinion, without this container, it is not possible to establish a therapeutic, parental or learning relationship.

The Centre de relation d'aide de Montréal (Montreal Counselling Centre) is a training ground for "creative nondirective psychotherapists." The vocational training course offered there applies the principles of "content"-nondirectivity and "container"-directivity, which derive from those of the creative nondirective approach. Each person feels respected for who he is, for his differences; each person develops at his own rate, because he is not confronted or provoked, judged, evaluated or criticized. The course, on the other hand, is based on a clearly defined philosophy, structured and organized around the CNDA. It is based on a definite program, the guidelines are clearly presented, the limitations of time and space well defined and the course requirements clearly specified.

I am firmly convinced that healthy nondirectivity can only exist within the context of steadfast directivity, because this provides an environment that is both reassuring and creative.

c) Positive features of container-directivity

Container-directivity refers to a kind of directivity that respects the person and that has nothing to do with gaining power over other people's lives. A helper who is directive in this sense takes a firm stand without being either overbearing or confrontational. Taking a stand presupposes an ability to recognize oneself, to love and to affirm oneself, and hence a great deal of self-confidence and a strong sense of inner security, which the helper can only acquire through lengthy inner work. It is a paradox, but experimentally true, that the "imposition of power" follows from insecurity and lack of confidence in one's strengths and potential. The more self-confident you are, the stronger your belief in your own talents, and the greater your ability to affirm yourself and to take a stand with detachment and humility. In that event, you have nothing to prove to yourself or to others. Because you have become strong yourself, you no longer feel threatened by the strength of others.

Being container-directive means clearly setting one's limits of time and space, and defining one's organizational and administrative requirements; for teachers, psychotherapists and group leaders, it also means choosing the theoretical direction of their practice and the component parts of their approach. This attitude is reassuring, and allows clients to situate themselves and discover whether or not that is the right place for them. The more clearly the counselor defines the "container," the more he encourages the clients' ability to make choices, to define themselves, and to be free in their relationships with others. His content-nondirectivity and his respect for individual differences encourage the creative freedom necessary to his clients' self-actualization, as long as that freedom is accompanied by a reassuring framework. The human need for security is not only psychological, it is also a physiological need, associated with the very structure of the brain, as will be seen in the next chapter. A lack of formal structures is unsettling and can delay the growth process considerably, because energy necessary for creative actualization is dispersed.

I believe that the child-centered approaches that were introduced as pilot programs in the early 1960s failed because the "container" and "content" concepts in educational theories were not properly understood. The lack of structures, of clear recommendations, of a definite framework, created insecurity, dissatisfaction and a dispersal of energies. I further believe that the failure of educational reforms and of certain therapeutic approaches have resulted from the reversal of "content" and "container" as posited by the person-centered approach. They made the container nondirective through a lack of formal structure, and the content directive through evaluation, advice, judgment, interpretation, criticism and reproach, but the end results have been extremely disappointing, and have required an endless succession of reforms.

Container-directivity is essential, as it fulfills the fundamental human need for security. Another positive feature is that it reassures without mothering, protecting, or taking charge. Content-nondirectivity is equally essential in promoting respect for the individual and fostering independence. In the final analysis, the container/content dialectic alone is responsible for ensuring balance, growth and a learning process that leads to freedom and creativity in human beings.

THE FOUNDATION OF THE CNDA

The goal of the CNDA is to reveal the individual to himself by freeing his creative powers; it is based on the global approach to man. This approach presupposes that the helper be thoroughly acquainted with every aspect of his humanity, and that this be channeled through his own self-knowledge, and a great respect for individual differences, which is in turn informed by the respect he feels for his own difference.

It is obvious that the CNDA is not the only philosophy that is concerned with the global approach to man. It is found in many schools of thought, dealing with medicine, psychology and education. However, the CNDA is unique in the way it conceives and applies a holistic approach; this conception is based on respect for the way a human being's brain and mind function, and how all his various aspects interrelate, on respect for different kinds of intelligence and learning abilities, and finally, on respect for his process of liberation and evolution. This approach also assigns the helper a pivotal role in the helping relationship; it is he who, through his attitude of respect for human wholeness, fosters knowledge and love of self as well as the liberation of creative potential.

CHAPTER 2

RESPECT FOR THE WAY THE BRAIN FUNCTIONS

A. LOZANOV AND SUGGESTOLOGY

The study of how the brain functions was the basis for the contemporary Bulgarian physician Dr. Georgy Lozanov's research and discoveries in suggestology. Following on the work of Pierre Janet, Lozanov realized in the course of his medical practice that, if one wishes to help an individual, it is impossible to dissociate his physical side from his psychological side; that one cannot deal with a human being's physiology without affecting that person's psyche, and vice versa. Impressed by the findings of the Russian professor V.M. Banshchikov, which suggested that humans use only about 4% of their brain's potential, Lozanov studied at great length the brain's operation and its repercussions on the individual's psychology and behavior (Lerède, 1980). This study became one of the most important foundations of his entire theory and practice.

It was after my encounter with the Western suggestology specialist Jean Lerède, in 1980, that I discovered Lozanov; his wonderful influence so piqued my interest in the science of suggestion that I made it the subject of my doctoral thesis. Now that I have been involved in education for nearly 20 years, I can see—thanks to my research into suggestology—that in a way I am a born suggestologist. I have been unconsciously applying some of the basic principles of suggestology in my educational approach for years. I believe, incidentally, that if we are interested in a particular theory or approach, it is because it already has some resonance within our past and our life experience. The fact remains, though, that suggestology has taught me a great deal and that my research on the subject has unquestionably influenced—and continues to influence—my approach as a parent, teacher, psychotherapist and trainer of creative nondirective psychotherapists. I can no longer address a group or an individual on a professional level without respecting, among other things, the structure of the brain and the repercussions it has on the mind and on behavior. For these reasons, and as a result of my educational and psychotherapeutic experience, this respect has become a basic component of my personal approach, and later, of the creative nondirective approach.

But what is involved in respecting the way the brain functions? The therapist who wishes to respect brain function must first understand the physiology of the human brain, and especially its impact on the psyche.

B. THE BRAIN

The human brain, writes Dominique Chalvin in *Utiliser tout son cerveau* ("Using Your Whole Brain," 1986, p. 18), is an organ made up of approximately 30 billion neurons, each devoted to a particular faculty. These neurons, in constant interaction with one another, constitute a twin structure: the horizontal or hemispheric structure, and the vertical or evolutive structure.

1. The horizontal structure of the brain

The most revealing and determining research into the horizontal or hemispheric structure of the human brain has been conducted by the American surgeon Roger Sperry, winner of the 1981 Nobel Prize for Medicine. N. Geshurnd writes, in *Scientific American* (197X), that according to Dr. Sperry the two cerebral hemispheres, while seemingly identical, are in fact asymmetrical and have different functions. Surgical operations have revealed that, depending on which hemisphere is "lobectomized," different brain functions in humans are affected; for overall action of the "two brains" to be possible, however, joint action by both hemispheres is required.

Until now, in the political, social, educational and medical realms, a dominant role has been ascribed, in the name of objectivity and science, to the left hemisphere; it has been considered the dictator of brain function. This practice has been partly responsible for overburdening it on the one hand, and on the other, inhibiting the development of the right hemisphere. Gabriel Racle, writing in *La pédagogie interactive* (1983, p. 124), believes this physiological discrimination in favor of the rational hemisphere has had serious consequences in educational and social realms, in that it puts at a disadvantage those who apprehend reality more easily via the right side of the brain. Recent studies, continues Racle, seem to demonstrate that this is the case in emotionally and socially disadvantaged children.

Furthermore, since most approaches to human beings, in society, at work, at school, in the home and even in healing settings, address themselves mainly to one side of the brain, there is a resulting disequilibrium, and this explains the numerous cases of fairly serious physiological or psychological illnesses. Hence the proliferation of patients in the offices of doctors, psychotherapists and psychologists. It is important, then, that all those involved in health, including educators, develop a more global approach to the brain that respects the interaction between the two hemispheres. This approach should not only be curative but also—and especially—preventive, such that equilibrium of brain function is re-established and maintained, and thus any type of disorder, whether physical or mental, is prevented.

"An ounce of prevention is worth a pound of cure": so goes the saying. Yet just look at how much time, energy and money are invested in healing, to the detriment of prevention. Prevention means training all those involved in health to respect human beings' normal, balanced functioning. And to do this, one must be aware of the nature of the human organism; one must know among other things how the brain functions normally, and learn to respect that function in practice, thus contributing to the development of healthy, balanced persons.

But what exactly are the fundamental differences between the functions governing each brain hemisphere?

An old Zen adage quoted by Racle (1983, p. 43) states: "The hemisphere that speaks does not know; the hemisphere that knows does not speak." The "hemisphere that speaks" is the left hemisphere.

a) The left hemisphere

It is important to note first of all that the characteristics of the left hemisphere in most right-handed people apply to the right hemisphere in left-handers. As stated previously, we are dealing here with the hemisphere that speaks, hence the one which governs language, rational thought and the capacity for abstraction and analysis. It is the hemisphere of linear thought, logic and objectivity, as well as grammatical, syntactic, semantic and mathematical ability. According to Racle, most educational systems are based on how it operates. Those same systems rank students based on intelligence tests that are too often designed solely as a function of the rational/verbal side of the brain. Its functioning is required almost everywhere in society, because of the excessive value placed on qualities of objectivity, intellectual ability and the logical, coherent language of reason, to the detriment of the language of the heart.

This example of educational practice suitably supports this affirmation: not only are students ranked solely on the basis of the left hemisphere; they are also evaluated solely according to their intellectual, rational and logical performance and according to their abilities in grammar, spelling and mathematics. As a rule, the importance given at school to the right hemisphere does not go much beyond the bounds of the ideologies inscribed in the curricula. On the practical level, the evaluation system forces teachers to put the accent on cognitive learning. In classrooms, at all levels, little importance is given to the corporeal, affective, imaginative and creative dimensions. In this sense school, instead of being the preventive setting it should be is rather, because of its unbalanced approach, the breeding ground *par excellence* for physical and mental ailments. It is school that, along with the family, provides the greatest number of patients for physical and mental health professionals. Neglecting the right hemisphere is a grave error that bears correcting because, in our day, no one escapes the rigors of schooling.

b) The right hemisphere

For most right-handers, the right hemisphere, according to Racle (1983, p. 43), is the physiological center of irrational, non-verbal thought; that is, everything having to do with insight, fantasies and emotional life. It apprehends shapes, sounds, faces and things in a global fashion. It is the hemisphere where opposites, metaphors and analogies are wholly perceived. Termed the artistic hemisphere by Racle, it specializes in sensory expression, creativity, synthesis, affectivity and subjectivity. Its input, in all fields, is not only desirable, it is essential. Scientific discoveries are not the sole prerogative of the left side of the brain. On this subject, Jean Chevalier (1984), in an article entitled "La pensée rationnelle n'a pas réussi à tuer la pensée symbolique" ("Rational thought has been unable to kill off symbolic thought"), recounts that it was while playing a Bach sonata on the piano that Einstein experienced the insight that led to his relativity theories. In fact, any theory is born first and foremost of its author's life experience. It is quite possible that all the world's great discoveries that have benefited mankind resulted from the joint efforts of both hemispheres. These discoveries are "positive," in the sense that they are the product of equilibrium, complementarity and interrelation.

Furthermore, it seems apparent that the left hemisphere's attributes are masculine or *yang*-type qualities, while those of the right hemisphere are more feminine, *yin*-type qualities, and it is this conjunction of male and female in each of us, or what Jung termed the anima and the animus, that ensures our equilibrium. The fact that society favors development of the left hemisphere explains the popularity of encounter groups, therapeutic approaches and spiritual associations that tend to center their approach on the right hemisphere. People naturally seek to restore a balance that has been lost. The danger is that, with such practices, they may well fall into a disequilibrium as great as the initial one, by placing too great an emphasis on the irrational hemisphere; that is, going from the "cult of rationality" to the "cult of intuition."

A balanced approach must always respect the overall operation of the two hemispheres. When exclusive attention is paid to the rational side of the brain it makes a person dry, cold, skeptical and critical; it upholds systems of evaluation, comparison and power; it disembodies and dehumanizes, by creating people who, believing themselves superior, become almost monstrous. On the other hand, favoring the right hemisphere fosters dependence; it leads to a loss of structure and of qualities of actualization; it means denying oneself a solid shape that surrounds and reassures, an essential container for self-actualization. "Man is neither angel nor beast," wrote Pascal in the 17th century, "and ill fortune decrees that he who wishes to play the angel must play the beast."

As I have said before, if we exploit the feminine or *yin* qualities of the self excessively, we move toward a disequilibrium as profound as that which currently results from the over-exploitation of masculine qualities. In this sense, the contributions of the women's liberation movements in Quebec and elsewhere in the world have had considerable impact; they have enabled women to develop their *yang* potential. And it is women's development of their masculine sides—that is, the "container" aspect of being—that has made it possible for them to define themselves, to take a stand, to increasingly take their place in society and to free themselves from male domination. However, if a woman who exploits the left side of her brain simultaneously loses the resources of the right side, she is no further ahead. Society has no need for left-brain–hypertrophic women, but rather women who, while affirming themselves and taking their rightful places on an intellectual and hierarchical level, at the same time bring to the world all the wealth of their sensitivity, their intuition and their creativity; women who, by virtue of their presence, ensure the dialectical balance of the pairs "intuition/reason," "objectivity/subjectivity," "analysis/synthesis" and "affectivity/intellection."

It is this dialectical balance that the CNDA seeks to respect. When I train future creative nondirective psychotherapists, my approach always addresses both sides of the brain, encouraging the expression of the emotions, fantasies, intuition and creativity without destroying the contribution from the rational faculties. Experience has convinced me that a therapeutic or educational approach that addresses only the left hemisphere impedes creativity, because it lacks subjective content, and therefore lacks difference. Similarly, an approach that addresses only the right hemisphere maintains dependence because it lacks a framework, or an objective container to support it, define it, and make it manifest.

The joint action of both sides of the brain is crucial to man's overall development as well as to the synergistic action of the three levels of the brain's vertical, or evolutive, structure.

2. The vertical structure of the brain

The second cerebral structure is called vertical or evolutive because it has developed over thousands of years by the superimposition of three different brains that are characterized by specific functions. According to the evolutive model proposed by Paul D. MacLean and outlined by Gabriel Racle (1983, p. 43), the present human brain is made up of three superimposed layers that developed during the Secondary, Tertiary and Quaternary geological eras, and which retained the characteristics of this formative process, reflecting "our ancestral relationships to the reptiles, ancient mammals and newer mammals." Paul D. MacLean's graphical presentation (see Figure 2.1), reproduced from Dominique Chalvin's *Utiliser tout son cerveau* (1986, p. 24), enables us to visualize each of these three brains: the hindbrain, midbrain and forebrain.

Figure 2.1

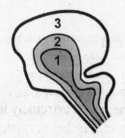

1. **Hindbrain**
2. **Midbrain**
3. **Forebrain**

a) The hindbrain

The hindbrain, also known as the primitive, archaic or reptilian brain, is an extremely small brain that developed during the Secondary Era. As Chalvin explains, it corresponds in humans to the brain stem's nervous systems (p. 25). It is the center of behavior associated with survival and preservation: behavior manifested in automatic gestures, pre-planned itineraries and repeated actions. It is associated with the routine and imitation so characteristic of humans. That is to say that a minimum amount of rituals, stereotypes, set rules and precise frameworks is necessary to human beings because they ensure a certain degree of security.

In fact, man requires some framework, structure or organization in order to feel secure. It is this psychobiological need that inspired the CNDA. The creative nondirective therapist responds to this need for security by being directive in the container of his or her approach, proposing definite frameworks and clearly setting the "rules of the game"— for to respect the hindbrain is to respect our need to feel secure within a framework, surrounded by familiar elements.

To the question "How does the therapist make someone feel secure by setting up a framework?" I would reply using the following example. One day, a woman called me to explain that her eight-year-old daughter had a problem, and that she would like to bring her to me for therapy. I never meet a child of that age without also meeting the people most involved in his life: the parents. The mother complained that her child was completely crazy: insolent, hysterical, and totally undisciplined. She believed her daughter to be seriously disturbed and psychologically ill; she herself felt discouraged and powerless to the point of crying. I learned during my first meeting with this woman that she had adopted a completely nondirective attitude with her daughter, on the pretext that under no circumstances did she want to bully her child—all because she had suffered the crushing weight of her own parents' strictness. So the child never went to bed at the same time, ate at extremely irregular hours and pretty much did whatever she wanted. Furthermore, the mother was completely exhausted from attending to her daughter's every whim, but never taking time for her own needs. The systemic relationship that had been built up between mother and daughter had resulted in a strong sense of insecurity for both of them, because it had been built on the principle of "laissez-faire." The child felt a great sense of insecurity because of a lack of routine, ritual, rules and stability; the results of the way she had raised her child made the mother just as insecure as her daughter.

The same problem arises in school: students require the security of rules set by their teachers. If they are faced with an instructor who displays no consistency in setting requirements, they will become very insecure and adopt undisciplined, even insolent behavior. Learning about freedom cannot take place in a laissez-faire, anarchical context; rather it must take place within a structure, an organization that provides a sense of security and makes room for individual differences. "Container-directivity" is not only desirable but essential, on the express condition that it be accompanied by nondirectivity where the content is concerned.

When I was teaching high-school students, I never really experienced any of the difficulties commonly known as "discipline problems." Mine was, it must be said, an extremely structured and disciplined approach. My classes were always meticulously prepared, my limits clearly presented and my requirements precisely expressed. In my classroom, though, the teenagers were always free to express their life experiences and their feelings; there was quality time given over to nonjudgmental listening, and to pleasure, humor, *joie de vivre* and creativity. In such an atmosphere, even the most recalcitrant students found their niche, and their interest for the class increased. They felt that I loved them very much. The greatest joy I had in teaching adolescents lay in the relationships that I built with them during class. They brought me a great deal and I thank them for it today. They taught me, in their candor and their genuineness, that human beings are capable of anything as long as they feel secure and especially when they feel accepted and loved for who they are. For me, teenagers were great instructors, and I would like to express my sincerest gratitude to the men and woman they have become.

The need for security linked to hindbrain functions, then, is expressed in terms of a framework, as I have just demonstrated, and also in terms of familiar elements.

How does one convey security via familiar elements? Readers will note my fondness for using examples as answers; in this case, that of little Julian springs to mind. One day, when Julian was about two years old, his mother, who had never left him since his birth, decided to entrust him to her neighborhood daycare center because she had to go back to work. When she left Julian with the caregiver in the morning, he went into a crying fit the likes of which she had never seen before, and with good reason: the child had been, in a sense, parachuted into an environment unknown to him, with a caregiver he had never met. Cut off from familiar elements, he experienced a great deal of insecurity, and as a result his mother had, for some time after that, considerable difficulty finding a daycare center that would take him.

In any new situation or new learning process, people need to feel the sense of security that familiar elements bring. For example, if Julian had known his caregiver, he would probably have adapted quite easily to his new surroundings, to the new games and new framework of the daycare center. The same applies in school: when learning a new concept, the student needs a foundation of familiar elements to feel secure. This is the requirement imposed by the makeup of the child's hindbrain. To fail to respect this natural functioning is to run the risk of impeding the learning process, of slowing evolution—even of traumatizing the child. It is thus important to the human educational approach that this need for security be respected. This is the only way of allowing people to experience the effectual and lasting changes required by the midbrain.

b) The midbrain

The midbrain is also known as the limbic system, the ancient brain or the paleocortex. Corresponding to the brain of the ancient mammals, it is located at the base of the brain, near the cortex, and lies on top of the hindbrain. According to Chalvin (1986, p. 26) it includes those parts of the brain that are not part of the forebrain: the hippocampus, amygdala, septum, cingulate gyrus and hippocampal gyrus. It is the part of the brain that governs emotion and imagination, adaptation, motivation, change, long-term memory and evaluative experience. I cannot overemphasize the midbrain's importance to the make-up of the human brain: because it is the center of emotion, it is at the heart of the brain's and of man's functioning.

Dominique Chalvin (1986) stresses that the limbic system operates independently of the upper cortex (p. 27). Between the two upper levels of the brain, communication is one-way; that is, the midbrain influences the cortex, but the reverse is not true. In other words, emotion acts upon the functioning of reason, which is unable, in all its logic, objectivity and abstraction, to influence emotion.

In a way, the limbic system is to the brain what a conductor is to an orchestra. It receives information of an experiential or cognitive nature and decides whether or not to convey that information to the forebrain. It impedes passage of any information that provokes negative emotions in the cortex; conversely, it accepts information that generates pleasurable emotions and transmits them directly to the forebrain. It has a determining influence on the cortex that is not reciprocal.

Since it is the heart of emotion, the midbrain is also the center of motivation. When an individual has an experience that produces pleasurable emotions, he is motivated to continue that experience. However, if the experience provokes unpleasant emotions, he will refuse to continue, or even remember it. Finally, an experience that generates no emotion in a person remains a useless one, because it is non-motivating. This is the case with certain learning experiences.

In education, for a student to properly integrate what he has learned, he must be emotionally involved with the experience—it must be a pleasurable one. Otherwise he will lack motivation and learn little. The same is true of psychotherapy and counseling. For both child and client, the educational or psychotherapeutic relationship must be a pleasurable experience, otherwise there will be neither learning nor change. This is proof that what keeps a patient in psychotherapy is definitely not the psychotherapeutic technique but rather the loving and accepting attitude on the part of the psychotherapist. Similarly, what determines whether a student likes a course is determined not by the material but by the teacher's attitude. Finally, what determines whether or not a child will be happy within the family is the parents' affective attitude. Love is the key to motivation. Children, patients and students all require teaching and assistance from people who love them and who love their work—people who, through their attitude, uphold motivation, foster change and facilitate learning.

To ensure that knowledge of any kind is properly integrated, persons applying the CNDA must respect the functioning of the midbrain. Their approach and attitude must, above all, touch the person being counseled on an emotional level and in a pleasurable way. They must respect the fact that before anything can be learned and integrated it must first be conveyed by experience. It is pointless for the psychotherapist or teacher to transplant theoretical knowledge that does not echo in the life experience of the client or the student. This type of knowledge never becomes integrated and can only be regurgitated at exam time and forgotten immediately afterward, or perhaps brought up as after-dinner conversation meant to impress. If the knowledge we acquire is to foster change, then it must be integrated; that is, it must be informed by the helpee's emotional and life experience. And to hasten the process of change, teachers and therapists must not forget that the production of images is also a function of the midbrain. Thus, the use of imagery in educational or therapeutic approaches speeds up the process of change. Images are one of the most powerful factors for growth and change that we know. This is why the CNDA allows imagination to play a prominent role in the psychotherapeutic process and the process of integration.

When I was teaching high-school students, I had a particular interest in poetry and storytelling. When I worked with these literary genres, I noted that the students made remarkable progress, not only in their acquisition of intellectual knowledge but also in their self-awareness and creativity. I saw a notable improvement in interpersonal relations in the classroom, displayed in a greater respect for individual differences and which evolved from the discovery of each student's creative potential. In the majority of cases, students who had been evaluated as "weak" by the system displayed an ease of expression when using images that surprised their classmates. Consequently, their self-esteem grew, and there was harmony between their feelings and their learning process.

I recall the case of one particular student, whom I will never forget. He had obvious and serious difficulties with written French. In Grade 9, when I met him, he was still writing phonetically and did not respect any of the rules of grammar, spelling, sentence structure or punctuation. This was extremely discouraging for both him and his teachers. This student had succeeded in reaching Grade 9 because he was quite proficient in mathematics, science and the other subjects. He was, it goes without saying, a very intelligent student, but one who had evidently experienced impediments in learning written language. Yet once we tackled poetry, I was the first to be surprised by his creative talent. He manipulated images with an irrational logic I found astonishing; he was truly a budding poet. At a literary soirée that I organized, during which each of my students had to read a poem to the invited guests, his words touched the entire audience and he turned out to be the star of the evening. This student was unquestionably possessed of superb creative talent; he handled metaphor naturally, like a professional. I was deeply moved by his creations. Later, he continued to write and brought me all of his stories and poems, week after week. At the end of the year, there was some slight improvement in his written language, but it would have been some time before any discernible improvement could have been made, and unfortunately he never reached that point. In Grade 10, he changed schools, and his French teacher couldn't see past the form and appreciate the content. He failed his French course, and left school for the job market.

A uniquely theoretical approach will not reach the "heart" of the brain and may well, in difficult cases, lead to failure. The student mentioned above had been touched by imagery and it had awakened forces within him that he was unable to develop later. Imagery is the ideal path for students or clients experiencing learning or psychological difficulties.

Following that path means respecting the normal functioning of the brain; it also means reaching those whose learning or growth has too often been impeded because of experiences that were too negative and caused too much suffering. This is why the CNDA lays great emphasis on imagery. I have always achieved remarkable results with images in my experience as an educator, psychotherapist, group leader and instructor, and so I created two psychotherapeutic methods centered around imagery, which I call Cram-Art and Projecto-Cram. These methods are remarkably effective in counseling, on the one hand because they respect brain function, and on the other because they act gradually, at the conscious and unconscious levels simultaneously. When used by a creative nondirective psychotherapist, these methods (which will be described more fully in a future book) produce astounding results simply because their application is accompanied by a constant concern for respecting hindbrain function, via the security brought about by structure, and for respecting midbrain function via the predominant role given to emotion and imagination. Indeed, it is the respect inherent in these two methods for the first two levels of the brain that enables them to reach the third: the forebrain.

c) The forebrain

The forebrain, or neocortex, is far more voluminous than the midbrain and hindbrain and dominates them to a large degree. As Chalvin (1986,

p. 30) states, it is the mark of humanity's superiority over the animal world, in the sense that it governs language, abstraction, organization, thought and the association of ideas. He adds that it also controls rational thought and consciousness; the latter, using the data it receives, analyzes and accumulates, develops thought processes, structures images produced by the midbrain, and organizes action. In governing rational thought, the forebrain acts like a computer; that is, without sensitivity or heart. Were an educational or psychotherapeutic approach to address only this level of the brain, without involving the hindbrain and midbrain, it would be a superficial approach indeed. The neocortex is nothing more than storage space for knowledge that, without the intervention of the hindbrain and midbrain, is not properly integrated and is fast forgotten.

However, an approach whereby the forebrain is neglected would also be a fairly sterile one; first of all because human beings need to learn, understand and express themselves through language just as much as they need to be loved and feel secure, and secondly because the brain is a whole, and it can only function normally as a whole. It is this synergistic conjunction of rational and irrational thought, of verbal and non-verbal language, of emotion and reason that ensures human evolution. Without this synergy, people act in a piecemeal fashion, without ever reaching the balance they seek.

Unfortunately, the training generally provided to health and education professionals does not prepare them to treat people with consideration for the way their brains function. Yet one of the priorities of the CNDA is to raise creative nondirective psychotherapists' awareness, preparing them to respect the overall functioning of the human brain so that they are able to contribute to the creation of healthy, balanced individuals.

CHAPTER 3

RESPECT FOR THE WAY THE PSYCHE FUNCTIONS

A. THE LIFE OF THE PSYCHE

The somatic aspect in man cannot be dissociated from his psychological aspect. Similarly, the way a person's brain functions is inseparably linked to the operation of his mind. Some specialties to see man from a uniquely physiological point of view, others from a uniquely psychological one. Although it is true that, in touching upon one aspect of an individual's personality, one can reach them all, it is also true that a twofold approach is necessary to reach people in a more global manner. Reducing an individual to one or the other of these component parts is, in my opinion, similar to the way some therapeutic approaches concentrate on activating only the irrational hemisphere, or the way some teaching methods focus solely on the actualization of the rational hemisphere—and can be just as harmful. That said, it is reasonable to ask ourselves what the psychological aspect tells us about human beings that we have not already gathered from our knowledge concerning the brain. In general terms, would it not be sufficient to link the physiology of the right hemisphere and of the midbrain to unconscious mental activity, and the physiology of the left hemisphere and of the forebrain to conscious mental activity?

However interesting these parallels might be, they do not do justice to the subtle nuances that characterize our psychic realm. In fact, the word "psyche" comes from the Greek meaning "soul." Whereas the brain, and in a general sense the soma, are palpable, visible and concrete, the soul is immaterial, imperceptible and abstract. When dealing with the mind, one enters into another dimension: an invisible, spiritual—etymologically speaking—and incorporeal dimension which, despite having been the object of extensive studies from the 18th century onward, remains very mysterious. In fact, everything that has been written about the psyche is based not on certainties but rather on hypotheses, which all too often have been presented as absolute truths. Freud, Jung, Assagioli, Lozanov, Lerède and many others, founded their theories on hypotheses born, in large measure, of their intuitions and life experience.

These attempts at giving our psyche some sort of structure, however hypothetical it may be, at least serve to confirm the existence of immaterial life. This proves once again that man not only needs to feel, he needs also to name something in order to give it life. In other words, he needs the container just as much as the content. In his process of growth and learning, he depends on the contribution of the left hemisphere just as much as that of the right. The very fact of having intuited, structured and defined psychic existence is what lent it being. The fact that humans are endowed with an invisible, incorporeal dimension has even been acknowledged by modern physics, especially since the discovery of certain subatomic particles. Indeed, in his latest book *L'esprit et la relativité complexe* ("The Soul and Complex Relativity"), published in 1983, Jean Charron provides scientific proof for the existence of "psychic" particles attached to electrons, whose properties are supposedly similar to those of the human soul. The French physicist's demonstration confirms what Jungian deep psychology had already guessed, and what religious beliefs have been based on for thousands of years.

The soul, the spirit and, more recently, psychic existence have always raised questions for man and have never ceased to bring him face to face with the unfathomable. To enter into a man's psyche is to penetrate a world of uncertain boundaries, of boundless properties, of an indefinable nature; it means entering a multidimensional, polysemic world full of hypotheses and infinite potential—in short, the true center of our emotional, imaginative and intuitive existence and of our unconscious influence.

In modern western society, geared as it is toward the rational and the material, there are many people who have trouble believing that we may have immaterial and irrational aspects. It is, in fact, very much in the nature of science to want to explain and define everything, to understand and organize it—in short, to know all things. Science apparently cannot accept that any aspect of humanity might escape its investigations. And yet, after centuries of research, there are still some human dimensions that refuse to be reduced to scientific formulas. In the beginning was the dialectic of light and shadow, which is still the underlying element of all life. Science sheds light on the universe, yet the realms of darkness are growing. Whatever cycles nature might impose, the rhythm of day and night will never change, for there is no light without shadow. In that sense, humanity is like the line of the horizon: the closer you get to it, the more it recedes into the distance.

According to the method centered on the person, the helper must accept that there will always be something he will not understand about the helpee. It is precisely this "something" that stimulates evolution and leads us to attain higher goals. Without this call from the unknown, without this opening up of the conscious mind toward the infinite, there can be no real growth. It is not so much what we know that helps us move on, as that which we do not know. Man has such a strong need to learn that he is attracted by everything there is to know, including the unknowable. However, if he wants to grow and change, he must accept the fact that he still has everything to learn, and accept the limits of human reason.

It is precisely this conviction that is the CNDA's guiding light. Thus, the creative nondirective helper is able to accept that each helpee is partly in sunshine, partly in shadow. Awareness and acknowledgment of these two realities will mean that his approach respects the nature and inner truth of each human being. A psychotherapeutic approach that claims to know all, to organize and direct everything is one that might easily overlook the psychic realm, since this aspect does not lend itself to easy organization or direction; the individual in question alone has the keys that will enable him to explore it. For this reason, the CNDA supports the Rogerian theory that the road to actualization lies within, and each person carries within himself the solutions to his problems. Helping someone therefore becomes a question of fostering his ability to go within and to get in touch with the innermost source of his freedom. Helping someone in a propulsive way also means acknowledging not only what that person seems to be, but also what he might be—in all his grandeur, beauty and singularity—although it is not apparent. The greatness of man cannot be measured merely by what is seen, but also by the impenetrable and indefinable elements that radiate from his psychic realm. The CNDA respects the immateriality of this world and for this reason is a creative nondirective approach.

However, recognizing that man is imbued with the invisible, and that mystery permeates his psychic existence, is not enough. This immateriality must be given a container, a meaning, a definition, a structure, which is precisely what the best-known specialists in this field have done, notably Freud and Jung, who have inspired most of those currently attempting to define the human mental apparatus.

The CNDA's notion of psychic existence is a purely hypothetical one—as are all the others—which has meaning for me only because it reflects part of my life experience, and because I experience its advantages on a daily basis.

1. The psyche

Freud divided the psychic apparatus into three parts: the conscious, the preconscious and the unconscious. Drawing upon his professional experience, he gave each of them a well-defined meaning based on his own hypotheses. This is not the place to enlarge upon the

Freudian notions of psychic existence, but in order to elucidate the CNDA's hypotheses, I will adopt the notions of conscious and unconscious.

The CNDA holds that the mind is made up of two indivisible parts: the conscious and the unconscious. Just as Jung did in *Psychology of the Unconscious* (1963), I identify the conscious with reason and the powers of rational thinking, and the unconscious primarily with the more irrational aspects of the mind. Viewed in this light, the irrational comprises everything that cannot be ordered, structured or organized according to reason, or that is not immediately perceived by it. Sensations, emotions and intuitions, which are part of the irrational, are first discerned by the unconscious before being perceived by the conscious. In many cases, unconscious perceptions never make it to the conscious level of the mind, but they are nevertheless present in the unconscious and may affect a person's relationships even though he does not perceive them. The more all-powerful the rational conscious becomes, the more the irrational language of the unconscious is obscured.

Suppose we dislike being around a certain person. In his presence our unconscious will perceive a certain level of uneasiness. It will take steps to defend itself against these unpleasant emotions, before the conscious becomes aware of the irrational language spoken by the body and the feelings. Unconscious perception is immediate and all-encompassing, whereas conscious perception is often delayed and fragmented. The conscious observes, reflects, analyzes, compares, classifies, structures, and arranges and brings organization to ideas, thoughts, realizations, material. The unconscious grasps sensations and emotions in their entirety before making them available to the conscious, which may or may not admit them. For the conscious to admit the irrational language of the unconscious, it must be attentive to the latter's sensory and affective side, but this attentiveness is often distorted by defense mechanisms, which work in the mind on an unconscious level. Any attempt at liberating the psyche must, as shall be discussed further on, be channeled through an awareness of these defense mechanisms, which inhibit the irrational language of sensations and emotions and which frequently cause reason to have a disruptive effect on the psychic realm.

In his relationships with his entourage and his environment, an individual always apprehends the sensations and emotions that influence his reason on an unconscious level. Even the most apparently reasonable speech originates in the emotive and sensitive life of the speaker. Political speeches, economic decisions, teaching methods are all based on a whole variety of emotions, most of which are unconscious. This fact has led me to form the following hypothesis: the unconscious functions like the midbrain in the sense that it influences the conscious, but the reverse is not true. This means that in terms of the psyche, the irrational mind, which includes the sensory, affective, intuitive, spiritual and creative faculties, initially perceived unconsciously by the mind, influences the activity of the rational conscious. In other words, all rational or logical activity has a sensory, emotive or intuitive basis, of a primarily unconscious nature.

This hypothesis can more easily be understood by defining these psychic processes, as conceived by the CNDA, and by demonstrating their reciprocal functions as well as the way they interact in relation to psychic existence.

2. The Conscious

By using the term "conscious" I am referring to that part of the psyche which is the center of rational thought, of the kind of thinking that guides the mind's intellectual, volitional, cognitive and verbal functions. This is the faculty that allows man to apprehend, accumulate, classify, structure and organize knowledge and to develop verbal language. The conscious also makes it possible for human beings to know themselves, and to attain a significant level of awareness regarding themselves, their entourage and their environment. Isolated from the rest of the psyche, it is a faculty devoid of sensitivity, which perceives reality objectively. In fact, it can be programmed like a computer. One could advance a hypothesis stating that the physiological center of the conscious is most probably the forebrain or the "evolved" brain, so called because of its relatively recent formation in terms of phylogenetic development.

Fortunately, the "conscious" is not isolated from the rest of the psyche, any more than the neocortex is independent of the midbrain, where the emotions are located—for everything in the human body is interconnected. This is why conscious perceptions or realizations are never entirely devoid of sensibility, since they are influenced, to a greater or lesser extent, by the irrational unconscious and by the midbrain. However, the degree to which the unconscious influences the conscious, and emotion influences reason, varies from one person or from one situation to the next. It varies from person to person because it depends on what I call the "psychic state of the individual," that is, everything that he has accumulated in his psyche in terms of sensations, emotions, feelings and knowledge since conception. The degree to which emotion can influence reason also depends on how a person is affected by his present entourage and environment. Finally, it depends on how defensive that person is. If, for example, the helper's attitude is geared toward the psyche in its entirety, without giving precedence to either the conscious or the unconscious side, then the joint action of both faculties will likely be more balanced. The more an emotion is denied, as much by the individual himself as by his entourage, the more the perceptions of his "conscious" mind will be divorced from his needs, interests and preferences and, consequently, the more they will be sterile, distorted and a source of imbalance. On the other hand, if the irrational intervenes, conscious perceptions become better adapted to the individual's real needs; they become more closely connected with his feelings and his intuition and hence more subjective.

The psyche is not, however, always fully exploited. Approaches that deal exclusively with the conscious, and those that completely inhibit its contributions, lead to an imbalance, and this is manifested on both a physical and a psychic level.

a) The conscious of imbalance

• Overexploiting the rational conscious

Jean Lerède played a significant role in raising and developing the question of hypertrophy of the conscious in his wonderful book *Les troupeaux de l'aurore* (1980). He states that no matter how evolved man may be, he is never capable of perceiving everything on a conscious level, of apprehending, understanding and resolving everything by reason alone. And yet this is exactly what man tries to do, with more or less pathetic results. Lerède goes on to say that the powers of reason and the achievements of science have not been sufficient to improve man's lot; neither have they found an effective means of averting the planet's impending ecological destruction, and even less the tendency to physical and psychological deterioration in every individual. There are places in the world where thousands of men and women are dying of hunger, where children are condemned to unrelenting physical labor to earn a meager living, where those who claim their right to be different are imprisoned for it, and where innocent people are tortured in order to maintain the reign of terror that keeps the leaders in power. In the so-called "civilized, wealthy" countries, reason has come up with increasingly subtle forms of power, blackmail and intimidation to feed the public with disinformation, to enslave men, and to make them dependent by imposing uniformity on their thoughts and behavior. Almost everywhere in the world, the omnipresent power of rational thinking has led to the death of freedom and man has become completely imbalanced.

What good is there in the evolution of science alone, in concentrating exclusively on the conscious in order to improve man's lot and find a solution to his permanent insecurity and deep dissatisfaction? Of what use is the monopoly of reason in the effort to wipe out the threat of ecological, physical and moral destruction that hangs over humanity's head like a sword of Damocles?

It would seem to be the hypertrophy of rational thinking that has led man to build a world founded on comparison, evaluation, competition and performance, that compels him to use force to achieve power. He is the author of his own imbalance because he has concentrated solely on external criteria for his edification. His ever-increasing need for intellectual performance, for visible success and spectacular results has led him to neglect a very important part of himself and stifle his affective, intuitive, spiritual and creative faculties.

I am reminded here of a case involving a 15-year-old girl, Helena, whose parents, in desperation, had finally brought her to see me. Their daughter, who had always been their pride and joy, had, over the past several months, completely changed. She had always been head of her class but suddenly, in Grade 11, she was barely able to achieve a passing grade. In the two weeks before she came to me for consultation, she had categorically refused to go to school, saying that it left her feeling judged, criticized, ridiculed and rejected. At our very first meeting, she told me a lot about herself. She was an only child of parents who were well-off and respected in their professions. From an early age she had worked at developing her abilities not only at school but also through private lessons in English, Spanish and Latin. Her father was extremely proud of his daughter, and never failed to show off her linguistic talents when company came, by having her speak in all the languages she knew. Consequently, Helena grew up believing that her self-worth was based on the attention she received from others. All her life, she had existed only as a product of other people's admiration for her intellectual and linguistic accomplishments, without ever stopping to think about herself, or about how this never-ending performance was affecting her.

Fortunately for her, adolescents do not spare anyone. Her classmates had, in fact, rejected and ridiculed her until her whole value system broke down. Praised for years by her parents and teachers for her intellectual accomplishments, she was now the object of her fellow students' scorn because of those same accomplishments. As she had only ever existed in terms of the esteem of others, she was unable to survive in an environment where her worth was not acknowledged, and was close to collapse. During her CNDA-directed therapy, Helena discovered that she did not, in fact, know herself at all because she had created a persona that conformed to the ideal her parents had imposed upon her. It took some time before she was able to get in touch with the real Helena, all the more so because she was still living at home with her parents. They were ready to do anything to save their daughter, but even so they found it hard to re-evaluate their beliefs and especially their own need to keep up appearances. The process involved the whole family, and I believe that Helena came through it because her parents truly loved her. The step their daughter was taking was difficult for them, but they really tried to adapt to the situation. Helena changed schools the following year, repeated her last year of high school, and decided to become a Kindergarten teacher. Dealing with this decision required a great deal of renunciation and humility on the part of her father, who had hoped his daughter would follow in his footsteps and become a lawyer. Helena, who had learned to go beyond the performance and "learning for the sake of learning" mindset in order to get in touch with herself, was hoping to learn self-respect, not only regarding her career choice, but also in her ability to be independent in all areas of her life.

In fact, the child that is raised exclusively according to the "learning for the sake of learning" ideal that stresses intellectual accomplishments above all else will sooner or later run into difficulties; overexploiting rational thinking and the conscious leads to a kind of imbalance, based on the principle of accumulation.

Thanks to a mechanical, repetitive impulse generally acquired at school, the conscious is able to accumulate the facts it is presented with, retain them and regurgitate them in verbal or written form at a given time. By accumulating facts in this way, man is able to increase his knowledge. Society today, and especially the educational milieu, is in the habit of overexploiting this principle: "learning for the sake of learning," with no participation, no integration. Parents want their children to accumulate knowledge but do not care what their feelings are. An evaluation system that measures the accumulation of facts, to the exclusion of almost all else, obliges teachers to gear their teaching methods toward verbatim ingestion of material. The child is taught everywhere—at home, at school, and elsewhere—to amass and display his knowledge in the same way one might amass and display material wealth at social gatherings, in the street and at fashionable parties. Those who have knowledge are richly rewarded: in society with constant praise, and at school with high marks—these being the only motivation for "learners," their reward for consistent regurgitation at exam time. What this means is that many young people hate school because they feel bad in most learning situations; emotions that are desagreeable influence negatively their process of learning. So they acquire diplomas that attest merely to forgotten or non-integrated facts, as in the case of Helena.

In fact, "knowing" and "having" belong to the same realm. The more people know, and the more they have, the more they believe they are important and advanced, because social standing definitely does not depend on the kind of person we are, but rather on our material and cognitive acquisitions. In order to maintain a praiseworthy social image, an individual can require his conscious to accumulate facts and store them, without confronting them with who he is, what he feels and what his intuitions are. By bringing knowing and being into constant contact with each other, the CNDA hopes to avoid this error. The training for creative nondirective psychotherapists stresses that the theories taught in the courses should be integrated with the students' feelings, using an approach that respects the overall functioning of both the brain and the psyche.

However, in order to integrate theory with emotions, the student must first learn to be attentive to his feelings. There are many people who are not aware of what they feel, nor of what happens within them, because they have been told that a subjective approach to one's experiences is a sign of weakness, and of little worth. Formal education is replete with expressions that support the sole exploitation of the conscious: "be reasonable," "take an objective approach," "smarten up," "be sensible," "think about it," "let's look at this scientifically," "grow up," and so on. Constant repetition of these programming formulas has cut many people off from their feelings, and consequently from themselves. Moreover, being cut off from one's feelings does not mean that they are not there, but simply that they are obscured. This was, in fact, what had happened to Jacqueline, an extremely sensitive, emotional woman who had spent her life subduing her emotions in order to appear reasonable and conform to her mother's ideal. When she came to see me, she was 43 years old, an age at which, generally speaking, the "person" wants to break free from the "persona."

Jacqueline had expended so much effort on denying her emotions that she no longer felt them. She didn't react, no matter what happened, and no matter whether the occurrence was a sad or happy one. She was lifeless, soulless—in a word, almost dead. What led her to seek counseling was a profound desire to die; she had no significant other to provide her with friendship or love, and felt like an automaton, like a robot activitated by a routine built on survival. Life, for her, had neither meaning nor value. For a long time she had been satisfied with her intellectual accomplishments and professional achievements, but, when she came to see me, these had lost all power to gratify her. Being well informed about psychology, she was able to make some very interesting explorations into her past, her life history and their inevitable impact on her present situation. However, these theoretical and intellectual realizations had not helped her with her problem. Jacqueline wanted to rediscover the zest for life she had lost at a young age, when she decided she wanted to become the model of a "reasonable" woman.

I couldn't help her with rational explanations and theoretical knowledge because she was already well-versed in these areas. Neither do I believe in provoking emotional discharges in order to free an individual from his inhibitions. Crises of this sort often make the person even more vulnerable, or instead strengthen his defenses. I will elaborate on this later. For Jacqueline, the path to freedom lay in gradually exploring the unpredictable realm of the imagination. She was, as I have said, a very sensitive woman, but she had blocked herself off from her emotions because she was afraid she couldn't control them. Projecto-Cram's projective technique and the CNDA allowed her to progress at her own pace and, with their help, she got in touch with her affective nature without losing control. She gradually lost her fear of emotions, and this freed her to experience them and live them out. The concrete results of this were that Jacqueline left her job as vice-president of a large company to learn new skills working with exceptionally gifted children. Since her new life was more enlivening than her previous one, and since she had been successful in demystifying her emotions, she became more genuine in her approach to others because she no longer felt the need to be always reasonable and efficient. This woman who had neither laughed nor even smiled during the first few months of consultation eventually discovered within herself an extraordinary zest for life, and was able to treat herself to "unreasonable" pleasures and fantasies that made her feel alive. Through therapy, she learned not to know facts but to know herself. She had spent her life denying her own and others' subjectivity in order to be the model of a woman who is knowledgeable and who displays what she knows. Now she wanted to maintain a balance between her emotional and rational dimensions, without favoring one to the detriment of the other.

Both this example and the preceding one illustrate how dangerous an overexploited rational conscious can be, whereby imbalance in the individual can lead to imbalance in the world. Nevertheless, overexploitation of logical thought is not the only cause of man's imbalance. To my mind, the consequences of under-exploiting the conscious faculties are just as serious.

• *Underexploiting the rational conscious*

An acquaintance of mine called me one day to tell me that, for the past two months, she had been experiencing terrible depression. She had become so vulnerable and impressionable that she had lost all control over her emotions, frequently having fits of crying and of anger. She had no idea why since, to the best of her knowledge, nothing unpleasant had happened in her life over the past several months. On the contrary, she was loved and supported by her husband and children. As she was talking a curious coincidence emerged: her hyperemotive behavior had started at roughly the same time as her new therapy sessions. In order to expand her self-knowledge and travel further along the path of self-examination she had, on the recommendation of a friend, gone into a type of psychotherapy that used emotional discharges in order to free people from the burdens of the past that have accumulated in the body. Because of her vulnerability, and after she had come to the above realization, she decided to stop attending the sessions for a while. One week later, she was her old self again.

Therapeutic approaches that incite such expressions of emotion are, in my opinion, dangerous and often harmful. By eliminating the contribution of the conscious faculties, they make the client very impressionable and dependent on the psychotherapist. Since they only deal with the irrational, they often result in a loss of structure, and deprive the individual of self-mastery. During and after the sessions, he is at the mercy of his entourage and his environment. The absence of structure and power over his life leave him prey to an ever-increasing sense of vulnerability and fragility which he cannot shake off. For this reason, expressions of emotion should never be provoked or directed from outside but, when they occur naturally, should be attended to and respected in their intensity, without being exaggerated, trivialized, belittled or inhibited by therapists. A person who experiences emotional suffering needs someone who will be receptive to him in a structured way and who will listen to him. In such a context, he can progress toward autonomy at his own pace because he alone controls the process. He is not directed by the psychotherapist but guided from within. In this manner, he never oversteps the natural limits that ensure appropriate action by the rational and irrational faculties, thus maintaining balance within the psyche.

b) The conscious of balance

The center of rational, logical and verbal thought is the conscious. It does not merely perceive external facts and reality, it is also able to recognize what comes from inside the person: his needs, his emotions, his desires, his resistance. In other words, thanks to the activity of the conscious, man is not only able to acquire knowledge but also self-knowledge. In this sense, the CNDA's goal is not so much to increase man's field of knowledge as to raise his level of awareness concerning what is happening around him and especially within him.

Raising our level of awareness does not only mean increasing our intellectual knowledge. If we want to use and integrate the knowledge we acquire, and if it is to benefit man's overall evolution, we must transcend the "learning for the sake of learning" mindset and develop a heightened, more all-encompassing awareness, one that addresses every facet of our human nature: our feelings, our desires, our fears, our defense mechanisms, our intuitive, imaginative and creative potential, our strengths, our limits and our weaknesses. Once the rational conscious is no longer merely trying to store and consume facts, theories and techniques, then it becomes a more human conscious.

A conscious based on human values is one that is turned inward, ready to welcome the intuition, emotion and feeling without which integration would not be possible; it is also one that draws its knowledge from being. Having understood how the brain functions, we can now grasp that the need to know and learn does not originate in the rational conscious. In fact, as I know from personal experience, we feel a desire to know more about something if, in a given situation, someone or something has awakened a pleasant sensation in us.

The first time I saw an exhibition of Salvador Dali's paintings, I was deeply moved by both the painter and his works. Because of this, I was on the lookout for any comment, allusion, article or interview about the surrealist painter, whom I found quite simply exceptional. During the course of my travels in Europe and America, I was able to see a large number of his paintings and, in addition, acquire many reproductions of his works, in the form of postcards, slides and posters. Because his paintings had affected me emotionally, I wanted to know more, not just about Dali, but also about surrealism and the surrealist painters.

One thing intrigued me, however. Why is it that I was—and still am—particularly affected by this type of painting? How does Dali move me? What reason can I give for my receptiveness to this particular kind of art? For me, it was love at first sight, and this inspired me to learn about Dali, his paintings, life and thought as well as the characteristics of surrealism. Through this I also learned more about myself; I realized that my response to Dali and his painting was an echo of my particular penchant for risk, my intense love of life and my desire to be different, my immeasurable thirst for freedom, and my deep-seated need to forge ahead and to continuously create and recreate my life.

Because Dali's works had moved me, I not only enlarged my field of knowledge, but raised my level of awareness. I went beyond storing cognitive data to discover myself through my discovery of surrealist painting.

This is, in my opinion, the way to achieve balance in the conscious. An external suggestion touches us within, and starts a "conscious" process that fosters our development, our personal evolution, our self-knowledge and our understanding of the world. Any therapeutic or educational approach oriented toward results must adhere to this principle. The CNDA-trained psychotherapist, teacher or group leader is constantly aware of the need to respect the way a person functions. The helpee, whether he be a client, student, or group member, will progress much more rapidly in terms of his physical and psychological health if he works with a helper whose attitude and approach are directed at his psyche in its entirety, not merely at its intellectual or rational aspects. The overall approach to the conscious is propulsive, in the sense that it fosters an atmosphere of verbal and non-verbal exchanges that results in surprising progress as long as the helper understands the importance of using the helpee's feelings in order to trigger increasingly higher levels of awareness. Otherwise, he is not abiding by the natural operational pattern of his psyche, which dictates that emotion influences reason. If the helpee is not deeply touched by what affects him, then the evolutionary or healing process may well be greatly retarded or quite simply blocked. For this reason, the CNDA always deals with the sensory conscious, such that any attempt at therapy or education unites both the "doing" and the "knowing" with the "being," encouraging, not the accumulation of facts, but the integration that is first and foremost informed by self-knowledge. This is precisely what science needs to make its discoveries useful in solving humanity's present problems: a sensory conscious faculty, one that recognizes the influence of the irrational on the way it functions; an overall approach that respects man for his physiological and psychological nature; and, finally, a way of intervening that addresses what Jean Lerède referred to as the two kinds of thought with which human beings tackle the world: rational, conscious thought and irrational, unconscious thought.

3. The unconscious

The unconscious is the irrational part of the psyche that constitutes the realm of intuition, of spiritual and creative life, of the psyche's sensory and especially its affective perceptions, of direct, automatic, spontaneous reactions of non-verbal language and attitude. According to my hypothesis, unconscious activity always precedes conscious activity; the rational is born of the irrational in the same way that the faculties of the forebrain are influenced by those of the midbrain. As I have already observed, the unconscious influences the conscious but the reverse is not true. As conceived by the CNDA, the sensory and affective faculties influence the rational faculties; thus, any approach that deals solely with the conscious, bypassing the unconscious, will probably prove unfruitful. This hypothesis calls into question the whole process of therapeutic and educational approaches, and it is therefore imperative to clarify the role intuition and emotion play in mental processes, as conceived by the CNDA. This clarification will help us to recognize that a person's entourage and his environment are crucial to the composition of the human psyche's irrational unconscious.

a) *The unconscious and intuition*

Intuition is an irrational faculty of the unconscious which gives this part of the psyche the properties of immediate sensory knowledge belonging to real needs, pertinent choices, and appropriate decisions leading to complete actualization of the self and of one's mission in life.

For several years now, as certain types of psychological and spiritual approaches have proliferated, intuition has been given a power and meaning that make it almost independent of the rest of the psyche, a sort of infallible force used here, there and everywhere by some to control the lives of others. In reality, intuition is just as fallible as reason is, and the way it functions is directly related to the complexity of our psyche.

If we believe intuition to be infallible, then we grant absolute and irrevocable power to those who use it in order to control the lives of others, and we give similar power to those who pretend to speak in its name. Indeed, mere mention of the word "intuition" can give an individual incredible influence over others, and convey a sense of importance that fosters dependence. I do not believe in an all-powerful intuition. Neither do I believe that some people have intuitive powers that give them the right to guide or direct my life. I would never grant anyone that kind of power over me because I am firmly convinced that intuition, as a psychic phenomenon, is fallible.

If rational objectivity is usually subjectively influenced by a person's emotions, then intuitive activity is often disturbed by the defenses thrown up by the forces of reason. Indeed, my hypothesis posits that intuition is an irrational psychic phenomenon whose functions are therefore necessarily linked to the unconscious mind's sensory and affective perceptions. When confronted with a particular emotion, a person will often adopt a hyperdefensive attitude of rational control toward it, because it makes him afraid. This fear prompts him to use his rational faculties defensively, thus disturbing the normal functioning of the intuitive faculty, and sending messages that are not, in fact, intuitive but defensive. In other words, the quality of intuitive activity is in direct proportion to the ability of the sensory faculty to listen to emotions and sensations, and it can only be attained once the rational faculties are let go of.

People who are truly intuitive have nurtured an exceptional ability to listen to their feelings, their emotions and their sensations. They have learned to recognize the limits of reason and to open themselves up to the language of the unconscious. For most of us, this learning process is a lengthy and at times difficult one. Lengthy because current educational methods usually do not prepare us for listening to and expressing our sensory, affective and emotional life, and difficult because self-awareness implies the ability to confront all our fears, including the fear of death and the fear of madness. Truly intuitive people have demystified emotion; they have stopped running away from it and are able to confront it. They have worked at freeing themselves from many of the repressed burdens that accumulate in the body and in the psyche, and have got rid of their hyperdefensive attitude, the archenemy of intuition. Anyone who protects himself from emotion or who runs away from it will not have access to immediate awareness, because he must first address his emotions, then his physical sensations, before delving into the depths of the unconscious.

Sensations and emotions lead to intuition because, if we are attentive to them, they can help us tune out our rational faculties and open the doors to a world where reason no longer operates. When a person goes through a painful period of mourning, separation or rejection, reason is powerless to alleviate his physical suffering. At such times, exercising the faculties of reason will only cut that person off from his feelings and from himself. The long-term, negative effects this type of process has on the body are well known. Suffering belongs to the realm of emotions and sensations and it is through them, and only through them, that suffering can be dislodged. If we attempt to use reason to relieve our suffering, then we block the vital energy needed to free it, because alleviating mental pain, which is by nature irrational, is not within the power of the rational faculties. Suffering, then, cannot be healed by reasoning. Reasoning can not make suffering disappear; it can at best anesthetize it, but it can be healed by the ability to listen to it and experience it. Once the suffering has been acknowledged, it will leave room for more subtle messages from the intuitive faculty, thereby allowing the individual to experience his spiritual dimension. Paradoxically though, this most profound of experiences can only be attained after listening to and giving expression to the body and the emotions. Without this process one cannot really speak of spirituality, but only of emotional escapism and defense mechanisms. To my mind, the spiritual experience can only be defined as the end result of work on the body and on one's affective aspect. To truly live out this experience is to know a healing and nourishing inner peace; it means attaining that deepest level of the unconscious which takes us beyond our differences and unites us with the rest of the universe.

However, anyone who wants to tame his sensory, affective faculties, develop his intuitive and creative faculties and his spiritual life needs at least as much preparation and training as the person who wishes to develop his rational faculties. And since, in general, the education system focuses solely on the conscious aspect of the mind, intuitive potential remains by and large unexplored, and the vast numbers of people who use it to impact the lives of others tend to do so in an uncontrolled manner. In the name of intuition, these people often act without restraint, showing no regard for present freedom or feelings in the here and now. True intuition holds the freedom of others as a sacred trust. It is discreet, connected to the inner life and is not concerned with proselytizing. The truly intuitive person uses this extraordinary faculty to help him direct his own life, but never the lives of others. Let me repeat that developing intuitive qualities means listening to our feelings, our emotions, demystifying our affective states. It means learning to tune out our conscious faculties, because intuition, as a faculty of the unconscious and a means of understanding and perceiving our psychic dimension, is inextricably linked to our affective life.

b) *The unconscious and affective life*

The unconscious, seat of the irrational, does not perceive, nor does it transmit, data of a cognitive, intellectual or verbal nature. It does perceive and transmit information of an intuitive, sensory and mainly affective nature, and it retains all the data it receives in its memory. In contrast to the conscious, which sometimes forgets a certain percentage of the ideas, events and facts it has recorded, the unconscious retains all the sensations it has perceived providing they are associated with an event of an affective nature. This content, held in reserve by the unconscious, emerges each time a new situation incites the unconscious memory to recall past experiences. On this point I differ with Freud, who believed that the past conditioned and determined the present. Lozanov's notion of suggestology, which influenced the CNDA, posits that the present summons up the past and gives it meaning. The next story provides an interesting illustration of this point.

One day a young girl of 17 whom I will call Esther came to consult me. She was from a dysfunctional family, and her past was marked by insecurity. Esther worried that her parents might separate, and was very frightened of her father because he had a loud voice and would sometimes get terribly angry at her mother. She lived in constant fear of being hit or beaten by him, yet this fear was completely unfounded, since her father adored her and had never touched her except in an affectionate, loving way. Esther's relationship with this man was marked by a certain ambivalence. Rationally, logically, she could see no reason for her negative attitude toward him since he had always been a good father to her. Emotionally, though, she could not like him, and felt all the more guilty and ungrateful for it. As she got older, her rejection of her father and consequent feelings of guilt became stronger. Her only thought was to leave home in order to get away from it.

Since I knew that Esther was very fond of music, I often used it as a tool to initiate the CNDA-directed psychotherapeutic work we were doing together, and on one particular day I put on one of Elvis Presley's songs, "Love Me Tender." As soon as she heard it, she began to cry and tremble like a little child. What could be the matter? How could merely listening to a certain kind of music trigger such an emotional upheaval? I accompanied Esther in her pain, being careful to neither magnify, belittle or block it. She cried for a long time before she realized why she was so upset about her ambivalence toward her father. In her emotional state, Esther was able to relive an event she had experienced when she was about eight years old and that she had completely blocked out. She was watching television when she became aware that her parents were arguing. Since this was a regular occurrence, she didn't pay much attention until her mother started screaming. She turned around in time to see her father beating her mother and shouting obscenities. When I asked her what she had been watching on television when the incident occurred she asked, surprised: "Does it matter?" Then she paused for a few seconds and answered "Yes, of course! I was watching an Elvis Presley movie."

It took some time before we were able to unravel the whole story, but it serves as a good illustration of how the unconscious acts in a given situation. When the incident occurred, Esther, who had been watching Elvis on television, experienced an intense feeling of fear. Her unconscious, center of her affective life, recorded the fear and associated it with the corresponding auditive stimulus: the music of Elvis Presley. Whenever Esther heard his songs, she would feel very sad and ill at ease, but had never understood why. Her conscious had forgotten the event, probably because it was too difficult for her to deal with, but her unconscious had retained the corresponding emotions and sensations. Each time the sensation in question manifested itself she felt afraid, but the situation which had initially caused the fear remained obscured. Esther understood, then, why she hated her father although she had been able to find no logical reason for it.

I would like to make clear that it is not in the least necessary to relive past events in order to be freed from the pain they can cause. The important thing is to be liberated from the emotional burden associated with the event, which is retained by the psyche.

In my personal as well as my professional life, I have observed that the unconscious records and retains everything having to do with emotions or feelings, and that suppressed emotions disrupt balanced functioning and get in the way of freedom. This observation has led me to put forward the following hypothesis: *affective life is at the heart of the psyche and the unconscious, and human beings' balance depends above all on their emotional life, past and present*. If, during the course of his life, an individual has experienced events which brought him mostly negative and unpleasant sensations, his psyche will be disturbed and, in a manner of speaking, unwell. If, on the other hand, life has filled him with pleasant feelings, his psyche will be that much more healthy. In other words, what is important here is not the nature of events in themselves but rather the affective circumstances associated with them, as Michel Lobrot so succinctly stated in *Les forces profondes du Moi* ("The Deep Currents of the Self," 1983). An event that is very disturbing for one person may be only slightly troubling for someone else.

On this topic, I recall the case of two teenagers whom I met a few years ago, Paul and Trevor. On their way home from a party where they had consumed a considerable quantity of alcohol, the motorcycle they were riding crashed and they ended up in hospital, for quite a long time. Paul, who came from a close-knit family, had a visitor every day; often, the whole family came to see him, and he realized how very fortunate he was to be esteemed and loved by those close to him. All in all, he perceived the accident as a minor, somewhat unpleasant incident and, thanks to the postive emotional atmosphere provided by his family, he emerged mentally strengthened from his experience.

Things were quite different for Trevor, who had lived in a foster home after his parents had abandoned him; he had no one to support him through this difficult time. He relived the sense of rejection that he had experienced before, feeling abandoned and forgotten by everyone, even to the point of considering suicide. It was a hellish experience that left him wounded and profoundly devastated.

For Paul, the serious consequences of the accident were offset by pleasant and reassuring emotional circumstances. For Trevor, though, the pain he experienced as a result of the accident was augmented by internal suffering caused by his deep sense of rejection. Because there was no one to love him, his affective life was basically a write-off, and this caused him profound psychic disturbance, for the emotional life is at the heart of man's psyche.

The case of Paul and Trevor reminds us that even though an event may be perceived as objective reality by the rational conscious, it resonates in the subjective realm of those who have experienced it. The intensity of this echo depends on each individual's emotional experience. *What a human being feels in the here and now is, to my mind, worthy of profound respect. No one anywhere can discuss, explain, analyze or judge others' feelings. It is the truest and most personal part of every individual.* To ridicule, reject or deny a person's emotive and affective life is to destroy him, and annihilate his source of self-expression, of creativity, of life itself. What one feels is absolutely incontestable, undeniable, irrefutable; one's emotions are the cornerstone of one's being, the heart of his inner self. To reject an individual's emotion is to deprive him of his right to be: his right to demonstrate not only his individuality but his essential nature. Too many people have been robbed of their vital energy because their past experience has never been heard and acknowledged.

To live means having one's heart, one's whole body imbued with feelings of joy, pleasure, satisfaction, pride, happiness, and also sadness, grief, aggression, anger, jealousy and pain. To live means allowing ourselves to acknowledge and express, in a responsible manner, the emotions and feelings that reside within us.

A person's feelings here and now constitutes his reality. To listen to them is to respect and liberate them. An educational approach that denies them denies, by extension, the person himself. Furthermore, an emotion that is neither recognized nor liberated does not disappear, but remains lodged somewhere in the body and in the psyche, and will return sooner or later in the guise of illness.

Trevor's problem lay not just in having had painful emotional experiences, but also and above all in not having been able to share his pain with anyone. The need to be heard explains the current popularity of counseling; for many people, the psychotherapist is the only person in the world who listens to them and accepts them. This is why non-judgmental listening and total respect for feelings are cornerstones of CNDA-based counseling. In fact, the CNDA holds that life experience constitutes what I call the "content of the approach," and can only be addressed in a nondirective manner. As we shall see further on, listening is an art that few possess. Changes come about—man is reborn—when we are listened to in a respectful and essentially nondirective atmosphere. For this reason, the training for creative nondirective psychotherapists puts a great deal of emphasis on listening; not just to others, but first and foremost to oneself. An essential prerequisite for the latter is the process of attaining personal freedom and ultimate self-creation—a process that, in fact, very few helpers have initiated or pursued.

The only way to help Trevor, and those in similar situations, is by listening in a nondirective manner, and by maintaining an attitude that conveys respectful acceptance, love and faith on the part of the helper. I am firmly convinced that this combination forms the basis for an effective educational and therapeutic approach. All the counseling techniques, and all the teaching methods in the world will be of little use if they are not put into practice by counselors and teachers who maintain a loving and accepting listening attitude.

A person's emotional world is so vulnerable that it can only be addressed nondirectively, and in a comprehensive fashion. Our emotional life is of such complexity that when problems arise, rational thinking alone is unable to resolve them. Reason cannot operate effectively in this confusion of pleasant and unpleasant emotions, of positive and negative feelings that constitutes an individual's "psychic state."

However, in order to satisfy logical thinking's legitimate need to understand, it is important to properly distinguish emotion from feeling, and in so doing comprehend how a person's "psychic state" is formed and what effect it has on his relationships with others.

Emotion is a physiological phenomenon expressed by an intense, comprehensive and isolated reaction to a given situation or person, and which is manifested through such well-known physical symptoms as palpitations, trembling, flushes, increased heart rate, and so on (Sillamy, 1983).

Feelings are a psychic phenomenon that build up and become embedded in the psyche. In contrast to emotion, which disappears as soon as the real or imagined trigger is gone, feelings are maintained by the imagination and hence persist long after the actual emotional event, inhabiting an individual for months, or even years.

For example, if a person is frightened of air travel, he will feel the fear in his body whenever he takes an airplane, but will be relieved of it as soon as the plane lands. His fear will then be no more than an unpleasant memory, a certain sensation of physical discomfort which will eventually disappear. When he gets off the plane, the emotion will diminish in intensity, but the physiological symptoms may recur intermittently, whenever the fear recurs in his imagination.

Feelings, however, do not appear quite so suddenly. They are formed slowly, and take root within a person's psyche over a period of time, usually without his knowledge. Thus, the feeling of true love is built up little by little, and persists even when the loved one is absent. It would be impossible, for example, to uproot the love of a mother for her child, because it is anchored deep within her and in most cases will never disappear. Human feelings and emotions experienced during the course of a lifetime constitute a complex whole: the psychic state. But how exactly is this psychic state formed?

Because an infant's rational faculties are not developed at all *in utero*, and only very little during its first few months of life, it perceives the world in an unconscious manner. Its first few years are therefore particularly important because all its contact with the outside world is of a sensory and affective nature. For the newborn to react positively to the touch, voice and smell of its primary caregiver, these stimuli must be accompanied by positive emotions, because of the close link between sensation and affection. When a mother holds her baby, the sensations and energy she radiates communicate her own feelings and emotions to him. If those emotions are generally positive, the infant will pick up on this and will consequently be more likely to feel happy and develop well. If, on the other hand, feelings of indifference and rejection emanate from the mother, they will permeate the baby's psyche, and his evolutionary progress will be disturbed or retarded.

It goes without saying that human beings are usually born with the physical and psychic potential necessary for healthy development. Already at birth, the baby displays certain physical and psychological tendencies inherited from its parents. However, in spite of his innate assets, it cannot be denied that the newborn is completely dependent on his entourage and environment for healthy, problem-free development. From a merely physiological point of view, the baby needs food and warmth for biological survival.

Children, however, and human beings in general, do not only have physical needs, they also have psychological ones. A warm, well-fed child will not develop "normally" without affection, both given and received. The mother's and father's love has such a powerful, direct influence on the child's psyche that, without that love, his psychological evolution will be seriously disrupted or retarded.

This means that it is not enough to provide a child with physical necessities; if we do not also provide love, we are quite simply gambling with his inner balance. The need for love is just as fundamental as the need for food; it is a question of psychic survival.

Because it has not yet acquired language-related verbal structures, the only input the infant is able to perceive is the affective language related to sensations. Since this language is non-verbal, it acts spontaneously and directly on the infant's psyche, with immediate results. At a sensory and unconscious level, the newborn is able to perceive his mother's emotions whether or not she wants it to, and whether or not she tries to hide them. This is why it is essential for the loving mother to hold her baby often—at least every time she gives him milk. In fact, it is vital for the infant to be touched in order for him to absorb the love he needs. The lack of contact is just as disturbing as the lack of love. I cannot emphasize enough the importance of touch in human relationships. Physical contact that conveys love is worth a thousand words, because it communicates true feeling.

Unfortunately, a puritanical education system has banned physical contact from human relations, burdening it with almost exclusively sexual connotations. By denying people's need to touch, it has suppressed the truest language of love and life, the irrational and non-verbal language of the unconscious.

I wish to reemphasize at this point that the irrational language of the unconscious reflects an individual's psychic state, which is not made up of any single feeling or emotion. On the contrary, it is made up of the accumulated affective residue left by past experience and of the present influence exerted by his entourage and his environment.

c) *The unconscious and influence*

The influence of environment and entourage is crucial to the formation of the unconscious mind's affective contents. The younger a child is, the more important external influences become, since he has not yet erected his rational structures and his protective barriers. He perceives everything around him in an emotional and sensory manner, with almost no intervening defenses. Little by little, year after year, his psychic state is developed; how balanced it is depends on the influence of his entourage. But the contents of his psychic state, formed as a result of the emotional impact of past experience, will always be with him. The CNDA does not, in fact, consider the unconscious to be a reservoir for past contents which influence the present and inevitably determine its outcome. My approach resembles Lozanov's theory of suggestology on this point, in that the present situation summons the past, since information which accumulates in a person's unconscious over the course of his life is always present and available in his psyche, and his current situation calls it forth. In reality, a current situation can summon forth blocked emotions—as we saw in the case of Esther—just as it can activate creative potential. Let me state, however, that not all the information that accumulates in the unconscious throughout a person's life is linked to unpleasant emotional burdens. The unconscious, as the center of irrational and intuitive faculties and creative potential, also has the ability to record everything associated with pleasant emotions. For this reason, it contains all kinds of positive reserves. Just as a current situation can assist in unblocking repressed emotions, so it can also, as Lozanov specifies, activate the creative powers. Seen in this light, the advantage of this hypothetical conception of the unconscious is that it directs man toward the future instead of always bringing him back to a past that no longer exists. Here we see the present summoning up the past in order to dismantle blockages and free creativity.

Thus we see that man's interaction with his environment and the people around him in the here and now of everyday situations can either foster or inhibit his freedom and evolution. Here again we see a similarity between suggestology and the CNDA: our human unconscious is indivisibly linked with our situation, relationships and communication. As the child builds relationships with those who take care of him, he also builds his psyche. But, since man is always building relationships, this basic structure is neither immutable nor inflexible; through his contact with the outside world he can constantly reconstruct his psychic state, by becoming aware of troubled feelings and taking the responsibility for finding a more healthy environment and an entourage that will help him attain evolution and actualization. In other words, if he has had emotional experiences that have negatively affected his psyche, he is able to transform his psychic state and achieve a degree of balance by immersing himself in pleasant affective influences. This is the most likely explanation for so-called miracles of transformation, which are in fact due merely to a change in external circumstances. This is why the helper's influence is a determining factor in the growth of the helpee. It also explains why it is sometimes so beneficial to leave one's surroundings and live somewhere else. This does not mean that we can "run away" from ourselves, but it does mean that our constant interaction with those around us and with our environment exerts a great deal of influence on us. If we remain locked into the same surroundings, always evolving with the same people, then we will be subject to the same kind of influence. Consequently, we will be maintaining the same patterns and the same kinds of dissatisfaction. Changing our environment means bringing new influences to bear on ourselves, thus transforming previous ones and developing in ourselves the ability to question them.

I would like to illustrate my theory with my own example of changed environment. I was born in a small Québec town close to the Ontario border. I stayed there until I left to get my diploma from the Teachers' College, where I was a boarder for four years. After completing my studies in educational science, I returned to my home town to teach at the high school there, where I stayed for 18 years, continuing my university studies on a part-time basis. After so many years in the same place, I felt an urgent need for renewal and change. I felt that I was no longer able to achieve self-actualization where I was. Since I had just completed a master's at the Université de Montréal, I decided to do my doctoral work in Paris. This decision was not easy to carry out, however, as it affected not just myself but my partner and our four children, aged 13, 10, 7 and 3 at the time. It took almost two years before we were able to carry out our project, which involved a certain degree of separation for all of us. By selling all we had, we were able to raise enough money and, on June 25, 1982, we landed in Paris where all six of us lived like students for three years. This is not the place to dwell on all the preparations beforehand, and all the adventures after our move. Suffice to say that this extraordinary experience was a turning point for all of us, on many levels. We all made a great deal of progress in freeing ourselves from labels and patterns of dependence in which we had been trapped. We discovered new interests, new possibilities, and these led each of us further along our respective paths to self-actualization. Our new surroundings influenced us in remarkably enriching ways. By immersing oneself in new influences that impact one's unconscious, one necessarily creates an avenue of transformation.

I am returning here to the notion of responsibility that I touched on in the first chapter. Since human beings are imbued with the influences that have affected their lives from birth onwards, they may exhibit a tendency to passivity, putting themselves at the mercy of external influences and maintaining an attitude of victimization whereby they blame others for their afflictions. This is an irresponsible attitude that maintains dependence and inner suffering, because it forces us to submit to the power that we have given to others. Making those in charge of our upbringing—whether parents or teachers—responsible for our problems is harmful on two counts: we deprive ourselves of any possibility of freedom, and we expend energy that provides no satisfactory return. In behaving this way, we enter into a sort of endless genealogical "blame chain": we blame our parents, they blame theirs, and so on *ad infinitum*. Once we realize that the present also influences psychic functioning, in addition to the past, it is much more effective for us to take the responsibility for choosing a new entourage and environment that exert a liberating, regenerative influence on our unconscious. We can take control of our lives by bringing about changes that are propitious to our greater well-being. Of course change frightens us and makes us insecure, but it also has the power to heal and propel us forward. Nor is it necessary to proceed with radical changes; sometimes even the smallest modifications to our everyday life can free us from the stranglehold of routine, with a surprisingly liberating effect. By consciously placing ourselves in new situations, even the simplest ones, we are providing our unconscious with unfamiliar data elements, thereby not only enriching it but also assisting with a progressive softening of the core within, hardened by misoneism, repetition and routine.

The advantage of this view of unconscious influence, adopted by the CNDA, is that it casts psychic existence in a positive light. I do not believe now, nor have I ever believed that the structures of the unconscious are inflexible. I do not believe now, and I have always refused to believe that our childhood experiences inevitably affect our entire lives and that, in the case of negative experiences, there is no room for hope. To believe that is to deny the impact of current life, the possibility of change and the action of external influences on the psyche. I am firmly convinced—and my experience backs me up—that it is always possible to achieve a greater state of well-being, to transform one's innermost self through the sustained impact of new and positive influences in the present, and through working to free oneself from emotional burdens accumulated in the past. Of course it is not possible to alter the past events that caused psychic disruption in the first place, but there is no doubt that one can, at any age, transform the psychic state that resulted from these events by instigating propitious changes and pleasant emotional experiences through the conscious choice of a healthy entourage and environment, and also through inner work.

I cannot emphasize too strongly the importance of the environment which, like Lozanov, I consider to be a fundamental element in the process of change. The whole history of our planet and of man's evolution is directly linked to environmental mutations. To cite only one example, we now know that certain species of prehistoric mammals became extinct because climactic conditions—and consequently vegetation—could no longer permit their survival. Similarly, man appeared on the planet when the optimum natural conditions for his survival began to appear.

Michel Lobrot, in *Les effets de l'éducation* ("The Impact of Education," 1974) demonstrates the overwhelming importance of environmental influence on man's overall development. If twins are separated at birth and placed in completely different surroundings, their development is based on the relative richness or poverty of their environment. The same phenomenon can be observed in children, or even adults, who are obliged during the course of their life to change their living situation; they exhibit definite personality changes, ranging from the most disappointing regression to the most surprising progress.

Environment's determining influence on man is not limited to early childhood. In fact, it influences him throughout his life. Thus, a rich environment ensures progressive development of brain functions and psychic reserves for any person, no matter what his age. But what exactly constitutes a "rich" environment?

Externally speaking, a rich environment includes both natural and cultural elements. The equilibrium inherent in nature imbues man's unconscious with feelings of calm, relaxation and balance. Nobody disputes any longer the beneficial effects of nature on the human psychic state. One of the best cures for depression is to go outside for some form of physical exercise. I believe that man needs to re-energize in the great outdoors because it provides an effective means of looking within, in a society almost exclusively concentrated on the external.

Let us now turn to the beneficial influence of culture. When I lived with my family in Paris and was traveling in many European countries, I came to understand the importance of surrounding oneself with cultural influences of all kinds. The artistic wealth of architecture, sculpture, painting and music contributes considerably to the stimulation of our unconscious powers. Moreover, the CNDA's approach uses the symbolic value of artistic works as a language that works gradually but effectively on the unconscious to liberate emotional blocks or free creative powers.

Providing a human being with a rich external environment means fostering the development of what Lozanov referred to as "latent potential." This is why, at the Montreal Counselling Center, part of the training psychotherapists receive in the CNDA takes place in natural surroundings of exceptional beauty, where each person can use his free time to wander at will along the forest paths, follow the meanderings of the river, take up a physical activity of his choice or quite simply let himself be soothed by the calm, beauty and purity of this secluded spot, still unsullied by the ravages of pollution.

The influence of the environment is also evident in our interior surroundings, at work and at home. The size of a room and the way it is decorated, its lighting, the arrangement of the furniture and especially the choice and harmonization of colors are all elements that act upon an individual's unconscious to induce well-being or lack of same. Fixing up one's surroundings at home or at work means granting oneself the pleasure of feeling happy there. I hang pleasingly evocative works of art or artistic reproductions in my classrooms, and decorate them in soft, warm colors, to make people welcome and put them at ease.

Generally speaking, the physical layout of a place reflects the inner space of those who live there. For this reason, no environment is ever neutral, but always emits vibrations that are either agreeably or disagreeably perceived by the unconscious of those who inhabit it. These sensory contributions, communicated to the irrational part of one's being by the environment, are all the more positive if they are accompanied by affective stimuli from the people around us.

The entourage is of considerable importance in determining unconscious influence on the psyche. A person's unconscious perceives first and foremost the emotions and feelings expressed through the attitude of the people around him. These influences have a determining effect on the development of his psychic state, since the unconscious retains all the affective vibrations it receives. This proves the vital importance of all relationships, whether with family, friends, lovers or colleagues, as far as an individual's psychic health is concerned. If he lives in an environment that emits negative affective vibrations, then he may be harboring an inner disturbance that can only serve to upset his balance and diminish his zest for life. On the other hand, if he feels accepted, recognized, respected and loved by those around him, not only will he progressively transform his psychic state, he will also develop his creative faculties. It is therefore essential to build an entourage in which one feels at ease—just as essential as training people (psychotherapists, group leaders, teachers) who, thanks to their inner work, emit propulsive vibrations based on their genuine and respectful attitude with regard to individual differences. The results of psychotherapeutic and educational approaches depend overwhelmingly on the attitude of the helper. For this reason, the CNDA places the helper himself at center stage. He is the most important determining factor in the helping relationship.

Of course, all these influential phenomena that act upon the unconscious only attain reality in people's life experience. It is not easy for the rational conscious, which believes itself all-powerful and accepts limitations with difficulty, to gain access to the irrational dimension; it is, in fact, a place in which the structures and analytical investigations of logical thought cannot be implemented. To enter it, one must be in touch with those realms that can bring about imbalance if they are controlled or denied. I repeat that, since the unconscious is the center of the irrational dimension, the only hypotheses we can conclude from it are those based on our own life experience. The main hypothesis that emerges from my assertions on this subject is that the unconscious is the principal center of true influence.

Influence is a primarily affective phenomenon. In other words, external influence is either received or blocked by feelings and emotions. One cannot influence another person solely with rational explanations, logical arguments and even less so with justifications and analytical expositions. In order to let himself be influenced by others, a human being needs to be affected in a manner he perceives as pleasant. Nobody will stay for long under the influence of a person who is not genuine and whose presence makes him ill at ease.

As Rogers states, man has a natural tendency to grow in the direction of his own greater well-being and he will automatically refuse to transform under pressure from an influence that makes him feel uncomfortable.

What are the hallmarks of true influence? It is manifested through deep, internal changes as opposed to superficial external ones. Of course, threats and exhortations can cause a person to change some external aspect of his behavior in order to avoid undesirable consequences, but positive and favorable internal change only occurs as a result of unconscious influence based on a genuine and congruent attitude that reaches out to a person, affecting him deeply. Thus, our influence over others depends overwhelmingly on who we are, and not on what we say or do. In order for our words and actions to be effective in transforming others, they must be upheld by positive intentions, emotions and feelings that serve to confirm them. If this congruence of the verbal and the non-verbal, as supported by Lozanov, is absent, then our words will not get through. Thus, man influences his entourage through his attitude, and since attitude is the reflection of who he is and what he experiences, and since he is never fully conscious of the complexity of his emanations, he influences others without being aware of it—often when he least expects it. In fact, it is not possible to consciously choose to influence or not to influence another person. Whether we like it or not, we influence others by our emanations. And this influence cannot be effective unless the "other" is reached in his affective dimension.

RESPECT FOR THE WAY THE PSYCHE FUNCTIONS

For this reason, creative nondirective training emphasizes attentiveness to the self, with particular emphasis on the feelings in the here and now. Thus helpers are better able to stay in touch with those they help, to listen to their emotions and to approach them in a genuine manner, so that the words they speak correspond to their own feelings as much as possible. In fact, CNDA-trained counselors work constantly at reconciling their reason and emotion in order to radiate a reassuring and congruent unconscious attitude; one that reaches out to the helpee and touches him by its authenticity and simplicity. Only a real attitude, devoid of artifice, can truly reach us.

This idea explains the influence of "gangs" on young people. Although adults often perceive this as a negative phenomenon, it continues to thrive because adolescents feel, often for the first time in their lives, that the leader and the rest of the gang listen to them, value them and accept them as they are. Appearances to the contrary, young people often exert a mutually beneficial influence, because they give each other the attention and respect so seldom shown by their parents and teachers. Sensitive to the congruence of the messages they receive, adolescents reject the language of adults when it is not genuine, or when it conveys morals or principles divorced from feelings. As I stated before, all influence is channeled through emotions and feelings. Any therapeutic or educational approach that is disconnected from real life is a sterile approach that blocks evolution because affective life is at the heart of the psyche. However, tapping into feelings and emotions does not mean that the rational faculties should have no say. For an influence to be positive, the conscious and the unconscious must be in harmony, and it must address the rational through the irrational. To exclude the rational from communication by exclusively emphasizing feelings is to deprive the individual of self-mastery. Triggering emotions and playing on someone's feelings is manipulation, pure and simple. And manipulation is the most prevalent form of negative influence, maintaining dependence and blocking evolution. People who manipulate are very good at thoughtlessly trying to satisfy the lack of love in others' lives; they stimulate the affective realm through special attention and exaggerated praise, while actually satisfying their own desire to dominate and control. This is how they achieve their own ends, and they can become threatening when they lose control of their "subjects."

One always feels troubled in the presence of manipulators, or those whose non-verbal messages contradict their spoken language. If we have not learned to listen to these troubled feelings, we will never be able to benefit from the accuracy of our intuitions, and we will remain in damaging relationships and situations, never using our inner power to guide us toward greater well-being.

We can see here how the entourage and environment have a significant evocative effect on the unconscious and how, as a result, all of us have a great deal of influence on the world around us. It also becomes clear that man and his environment are interrelated, and that external influences do not affect everybody in the same way. It all depends on the individual's psychic state, which, as we have already discussed, is shaped by emotional and sensory experiences throughout his life.

However, ontogeny is not the only context within which the psychic state is shaped. It has a much larger source, since the unconscious is not merely a reservoir for the affective states formed during the course of our human life. There is an intangible link between us and the histories of our family, our country and our world. We all have a personal unconscious, as discussed above, but there is also another unconscious, which I refer to as the genealogical, cultural and collective unconscious. This psychic component is not merely the reservoir of our own life experiences; it also retains experiences passed on from our parents, grandparents, great-grandparents, and so on. Genetic influences that appear over the course of several generations also have their psychic counterparts. It is obvious that our ancestors did more than pass on their genes; they also brought psychic influences to bear on us through their experiences, their past and their affective states. Thus, we are born with a certain amount of psychic baggage that makes us, from birth onward, inwardly different from one another. Our unconscious is also imprinted with psychic characteristics which have come down to us from the real-life history of the people we belong to; they have been transmitted over generations through the influences of entourage and environment, and they forge a common bond between us and others who have received the same historical and cultural heritage as we have. Finally, there is something within the human unconscious that unites man with the rest of the world, beyond beliefs, values, race, culture and language. This is what Jung referred to as the "collective" unconscious, which contains humanity's common experiences and which unites all men beyond space and time.

All this phylogenetic and ontogenetic baggage is present in the unconscious and assists in shaping an individual's psychic state. This state is, in fact, the end result of interaction between his affective states, which have been influencing him during the course of his life. And this psychic state, which is born of his emotional life and which can be perceived in all this individual's relationships with his entourage and his environment, can only be reached when he is attuned to his feelings and is able to express them. Our emotional and sensory feelings are our guides as we explore our unconscious world. Only they can unite and unify the complexity of the psyche and its affective experiences. They constitute the heart of the unconscious and the psyche, the core of the psychic state and source of all influence. The memory of past events and experiences is not what matters; the important thing is whatever remains of them on the affective, emotional and sensory level. The conscious memory of events is of no help in moving man toward greater well-being; what he needs to do is free himself from the emotional burdens accumulated during those events. It is, in fact, this emotional burden retained within the body and the psyche which is responsible for blocking the vital and creative energies, and which brings on physiological and psychological illnesses of a more or less serious nature. As a psychotherapist or teacher, one can help another person only by carefully recognizing his feelings in the here and now and his affective state and feelings, and by respecting the need of the rational conscious to understand and to know.

Because they are aware of the importance of psychic equilibrium, helpers trained in the CNDA are prepared to implement a comprehensive approach that effectively combines the rational and the irrational components of the psyche; an approach that calls up both the emotional life, cornerstone of the unconscious, and reason, cornerstone of the conscious, in such a way that the helpee retains power over his life, and will under no circumstances give anyone else power over him. The CNDA is an approach that fosters the development of creativity and the learning of true freedom, through its respect for the normal and comprehensive functioning of the psyche.

B. PSYCHIC FUNCTIONING

Psychic functioning, as conceived by the CNDA, is based on stated hypotheses according to which affective and emotional life are at the heart of the psyche and in which the unconscious is the principal center of influence, due to its ability to receive and emit the kind of non-verbal language that conveys an individual's true emotions, feelings and intentions. This concept of the psyche is based on the axiom which states that human beings are essentially "relational" beings, in the sense that they are constantly—whether they like it or not—in relationship with an entourage and an environment, with which they interact and by which they are influenced.

It is not in man's nature to isolate himself from the rest of the world. The stories of isolation that one reads about do not really resonate positively in people's emotional experience. Examples of individuals isolated by external forces or who withdraw voluntarily from the world do not tend to be very encouraging. Man is made to live in the company of others, and when he flees because reality has become unbearable for him, he often finds even greater suffering. Human beings need other human beings, and to deny this reality amounts, in my opinion, to denying the many interdependent links that exist within the natural world. Nothing can live detached from the rest of the universe. The earth is not sufficient unto herself; in relation with the rest of the solar system, she needs the sun, the moon, the stars and the planets. Her needs, like man's, are linked to her relationships with her surroundings. Any attempt to separate man from the rest of the world is a purely mental operation that only has meaning for the rational conscious, divorced from the rest of the psyche. It has no reality outside of the mind; indeed, I put forward the hypothesis that it is the result of defensive attitudes adopted as a protection against others, in order to escape from pain. This suffering, however, can never disappear when it is avoided, but only when it is attended to.

I cannot conceive of a human being completely devoid of relationships. As far as I know, such a creature cannot exist, and if he did exist, he would not be human. Living alone means continuing to live with others, if only in the mind, in the realms of the imagination and in association with the environment. Man is born out of relationships: that of his father and mother, and of himself with his mother during gestation. And it is precisely because he is essentially a connected being that he has psychic needs which must be satisfied if he is to attain well-being and inner balance.

1. Psychic needs

To ensure his physical equilibrium, man needs to breathe clean air, eat good food, sleep well, keep his body fit through physical exercise and experience his sensuality and sexuality in a satisfying manner. Equally important, he has psychic needs which are born of his relationship with the world around him and which, if they remain unsatisfied, will threaten his psychological balance.

The CNDA's preoccupation with the wholeness of each human being leads it to consider man's psychological aspect just as much as his physiological one. Because of the constant interaction between body and mind, neglecting one of these dimensions is tantamount to harming the other. And since the CNDA respects the functioning of man's physiology, it also respects the fundamental psychological needs whose satisfaction forms the basis for his inner harmony and happiness.

The theory of needs was extensively developed by the Gestalt school of therapy. It was also part of the inspiration for the CNDA, except that here it is viewed in a different light: that of creative nondirectivity. But what exactly are man's fundamental psychic needs; how does the CNDA define them?

A psychic need is an immaterial form of nourishment that originates in relationships and that is essential to an individual's normal, healthy functioning. Thus, in order to find the harmony and satisfaction he desires, man needs love, security, attentiveness, recognition, affirmation, liberty and creativity.

a) *The need for love*

Inextricably linked to the way the psyche and the brain function, the need for love is, as I have said before, one of man's most vital needs, no matter what his age. A child who is not loved will suffer serious psychological damage and his psychic state will be distorted. An adult who is not loved is often prey to fears that keep him from fulfilling his potential, to frustrations that make him hate other people, to depressions that prevent him from enjoying life or to psychosomatic illnesses that rob him of his vital energies.

I do not subscribe to theories that consider the need for love to be a dependent kind of need. Love is man's most essential psychic nourishment. To try to rationally convince oneself that one can live without love is to use that rationalization to reinforce one's defense system, thus concealing the suffering caused by a lack of love. Dependence does not arise from the need to love and be loved, which are natural to human beings, but from the irresponsible attitude that makes the other accountable for our lack of love. Dependence comes from attributing the cause of our problems to others, from giving them power over our lives. And when we find the means of satisfying our fundamental, vital needs, we have, by that very fact, broken free from our dependence. The person whose natural need for love is satisfied is much more free and independent than someone who is trying to fulfill that need. The person who eats his fill is not obsessed by food; because his physiological need is satisfied, he can break free from it and turn to other pursuits. A child who lacks love is very dependent, clinging and monopolizing all his caregivers' time and attention. When his need for love is fulfilled, he is able to separate from them for a while and pursue other activities, without feeling abandoned. Love is the key to motivation, it gives zest for living, creating, developing and helping others develop.

Evelyn, who had been coming to see me for about a year, turned to me one day and said, using more or less these exact words: "You don't know how much I suffer from being so lonely. I find it unbearable not to have anyone in the world waiting for me, or thinking of me, and not to have anyone to be with and to love. I feel that there is nothing worth living for. Nothings interests me. There are days when I just want to die, because life seems so pointless and futile." Jacinthe, a friend from France, wrote to me recently, saying: "I'm so lonely it hurts. I don't like the way I look any more because I have no one to love." How far are we prepared to go to satisfy our need for love?

Steven was 28 years old. He had come to see me because his eighth relationship in a row had ended in heartbreak for him. All the women that he had ever been involved with had dumped him, though he did everything he could to keep them. He was so afraid of losing them that he never refused them anything. Our human need for love is so great that sometimes we are ready to deny ourselves, destroy ourselves, become a puppet in the hands of others so as not to lose their love.

It is just as harmful to become dependent so as not to lose the love of others as it is injurious to use rationalization to deny one's need for love. Lack of love cannot be satisfied either by turning overwhelmingly toward rational thought or by giving way completely to the "other." In both cases, there is negation of self, and a lack of love for the self, and, as I have said before, the ability to love and be loved is in direct relation to the ability to love oneself.

This concept brings us back to the importance of relationships. How can a person learn to love himself if he has not been loved? The man who does not love himself is a man who has never felt love, a man who has been rejected, judged and denied in his past. The task of leading these "poorly loved" ones to a true love experience falls on the shoulders of teachers and psychotherapists. We recall that when the psyche is surrounded by pleasant influences, it becomes transformed; in fact, the love of his entourage awakens in man the love of self, and allows him to love with a deep and unshakable respect for who he is. The three indivisible components of man's fundamental need for love are: love oneself, love others and be loved by them. Satisfying this need is the key to his inner balance and evolution. CNDA-trained psychotherapists are aware of this need; since they are constantly striving to cultivate love of self and take responsibility for their own affective deficiencies, they know how to encourage love of self in their clients. They are careful to radiate, as much as possible, a loving and respectful attitude, without taking responsibility for their clients', their students' or their patients' affective deficiencies. They are aware that the best way of helping others remedy their failings, develop their love of self and take responsibility for their own affective deficiencies is, first and foremost, for the helper to concentrate on his own inner work. True helpers are neither theorists nor technicians, but psychotherapists to the core whose primary means of helping others lies in the unconscious influence emanating from their inner selves.

Thus, knowing about man's fundamental needs is not enough unless we, as helpers, are constantly striving to satisfy our own need for love, security, attentiveness, recognition, affirmation, liberty and creativity.

b) *The need for security*

Our knowledge concerning the overall functioning of the human brain has made it possible for us to understand the importance of the need for love, connected to the functioning of the midbrain, and the importance of the need for security, connected with the functioning of the hindbrain, and how both factors affect man's balance.

How can we satisfy our need for security? It is important to know that we cannot make someone secure by protecting them, sparing them or taking charge of them, but rather by developing a well-defined "container," by acquiring self-discipline and by showing love. There is a close connection between "container" directivity, as defined earlier, and fulfillment of the need for security.

As a parent, teacher, psychotherapist and trainer I have had ample opportunity to observe the importance of structure and discipline to achievement and to a sense of security.

I cannot begin to count the number of teenagers and adults who have experienced failure, repeatedly and on many levels, because their upbringing and schooling, based as they were on "laissez-faire" or impulse, had deprived them of a reassuring structure and the kind of self-discipline that promotes action. Nothing makes a child more insecure than a parent who changes the rules according to his mood at the time, a teacher who says "yes" and "no" in the same breath, or a psychotherapist who sets no limits. The helpee needs a helper who knows what he wants, who takes a definite stand, who is capable of giving appropriate choices and making decisions. However, it is impossible for the helper to be explicit, organized and sustained in his approach if he is not self-disciplined, and if his professional life is not clear-cut, structured and consistent.

I have seen so many people who were not happy with themselves, who were dissatisfied because they never managed to finish what they started. We all know that we will not get something merely by wanting it; we must also submit to a certain process and a certain amount of work. But how can we accomplish this without structure, organization and self-discipline? And how can we attain our goals when we have been taught by people who always took charge and did our work for us?

To take over from someone else is to suggest that he is incapable and, consequently, to initiate feelings of profound insecurity in him that will prevent him from attaining self-actualization and creativity. When a parent raises a child in an over-protective atmosphere, or according to the principle of laissez-faire, he is turning him into an insecure, diminished and passive creature, who will give others power over his life. Such a creature can never take a stand, distinguish or actualize himself. He will live in constant fear, permanently dissatisfied and perpetually unhappy.

Since the need for security is so fundamental to our well-being, it is important that helpers give those they help a sense of security by giving them the responsibility for their feelings and power over their lives, and also by laying out well-defined limits that will not fluctuate according to the helper's mood.

The thorny issue of rules and limits cannot be settled so quickly. Rules are everywhere: in society, at home, at school, at work, and so forth. The advantage of these rules is that they uphold a certain degree of order and also that they create a feeling of security. Each environment has its own set of rules; one need only go to a friend's house or to a different school, change jobs or travel to another country to notice the way demands vary according to one's surroundings. Thus we can state that rules are not universal absolutes. The preoccupation with standardizing structures so that no one might distinguish himself from the next person has prevented the individual from learning his personal limits. Some people are so caught up in conforming to the crowd mentality that they are completely cut off from themselves. Who can obey a rule that is implemented for the set purpose of imposing conformity? This sort of rule is very difficult to implement successfully because it is born of the insecurity and lack of self-confidence of the person who introduced it.

A structure is meant to give security, but only under certain conditions; the rule must be a clear reflection of the helper's personal limits, and not the consequence of an introjected principle or belief. It must also be implemented with love. If the helper implements a rule derived from an external principle that he has adopted without checking whether or not it is in accordance with who he is, then the rule will only give rise to insecurity, and cause insolence, disobedience and lack of discipline. I firmly believe that the rules and limits of every parent, teacher and psychotherapist must be established with complete self-respect.

I have tested the relevance of the above statement in my relationship with my four children. I always set my limits according to who I am, without letting myself be influenced by relatives, neighbors or books. Of course, all of my children at one time or another have asked me a question that went something like this: "Mom, why can't I watch TV when I get home from school, like all my friends do?" or "Mom, why can't I ride my bike to school? My friend Meagan does." These challenges never caused me to question the way I had decided to raise my children.

Children, students and clients find it much easier to accept the limits imposed by their parents, teachers and psychotherapists when they are imposed in accordance with the latter's self-respect, and not with norms, principles or values borrowed from others. The impetus for questioning a limit should come from within the self, never from a source outside the self. I will change the limit I have set not because it is different from other people's, but because it no longer meets my needs or no longer corresponds to who I am.

One day when I was a teenager, about 14 or 15 years old, my father imposed a restriction on my activities and, because I didn't like it, I said: "When I have kids, I'm going to let them go out every night." My father, whom I have always loved, answered: "Well, my girl, you can certainly try to do a better job than I have, if you can." I have never forgotten those words and even today I recall them with profound emotion. My father was so real and so honest that his demands could not but communicate his innermost essence, his values, principles and beliefs. He defined his limits with such conviction, clarity and love that what I got out of them was inevitably beneficial for me. I was lucky to have a father who loved and acknowledged me, listened to me and made me feel secure. He gave me the basics and, in that sense, he really couldn't have done better. And it was precisely because he gave me security and a great deal of love that, later on, I was able to reject those principles which didn't suit me and replace them with ones that conformed to who I was. And when I did this, I lost neither his love nor his respect.

A teacher who does not know how to take a stand and still respect others cannot teach us how to take a stand while respecting ourselves. Structures give security when they are clearly laid out with total respect for our emotions and our individual differences, and when they are informed first and foremost by love. Loving someone and providing him with a secure environment are inseparable acts. François Lavigne, writing in *Psycho-Mag* (1987) recounts the disturbing effects on children of "affective deficiencies" and "authoritative deficiencies." A child who is insecure is just as troubled as a child who is not loved. This is why the helper must consider both these needs, which form the basis for the CNDA's philosophy of "content" and "container." For if the need for security is associated more with "container" directivity, the need to be listened to is undeniably linked to "content" nondirectivity.

c) *The need to be heard*

To be a truly attentive listener is such a rare gift that many different kinds of specialists get paid just to listen to people. Very few people know how to listen, and those who really take the time to listen to others are few and far between. Too often, when we listen to others, we busy ourselves with other tasks, or let events, other people or objects distract us. Too often also, as we listen, we try to bring the conversation around to ourselves, waiting for the slightest opportunity to step in and occupy center stage.

So what exactly does it mean to really listen to someone? Listening means taking the time to be warm and attentive, welcoming the other and exhibiting total acceptance of who he is by putting aside one's own preoccupations.

Many human beings suffer because no one takes the time to listen. Parents are often too busy or preoccupied to "find the time" to stop and listen to their children. Teachers have so much to show and tell that they have little time left over to listen to their students' emotions. Specialists in the fields of physical and mental health, for their part, are frequently so enslaved by their theoretical and practical knowledge that they attempt to use their clients to reinforce their own theories and professional techniques rather than listening to their clients' needs.

True listening requires time, attention, warmth and acceptance; it means really being there. If the helper does not ensure an attentive and welcoming presence as well as a great deal of acceptance, then he is not really listening.

The person who is being listened to should feel that, when he is speaking, only his problems, his experience and his difficulties have any claim on the helper's attention. He should feel that what he is saying is, in the here and now of the relationship, of the utmost importance to the listener. This importance should be conveyed not merely by the listener's external attitude, but also by a real and sustained interest in everything about the speaker. Finally, the person being listened to should feel, without a shadow of doubt, that the interest he perceives on the part of the other stems from the fact that he is loved and accepted for who he is.

The kind of listening that judges, advises or interprets is neither "accepting" nor "helpful." Learning to listen means first and foremost learning to accept oneself in a context where judgment, advice and interpretation give way, as far as possible, to that warm, welcoming, attentive kind of listening that every individual needs in order to blossom and open up to others. However, the road to total self-acceptance is a circuitous one, with many obstacles. Man tends toward perfection, and in order to achieve it he must also realize how difficult it is to accept certain parts of himself. Accepting oneself and others requires time and tolerance, and when a therapist or a teacher has trouble accepting a client or a student, all he can do is admit his limitations and use that difficulty to progress one step further along his own road to self-acceptance. Paradoxically, accepting our inability to accept sometimes places us on the path of acceptance and change, which leads toward a greater ability to listen to ourselves and others.

In counseling, this kind of listening presupposes that the helper has acquired the qualities of congruence and empathy so esteemed by Rogers.

I believe that congruence is of fundamental importance to educational and psychotherapeutic relationships. Congruence refers to the ability to listen to what we are feeling and express those feelings as they arise. It also refers to the ability to accept and present ourselves as we are. In other words, a congruent attitude comprises two specific elements: the ability to listen, know and accept ourselves on the one hand, and on the other, the ability to express, in a verbal and nonverbal manner, both who we are and what we are experiencing.

Creative nondirective psychotherapists are trained to listen to themselves, to feel what is happening within them, to be aware of emotions when they appear, to deal with them without evasion and to accept themselves in a non-judgmental manner. This is the first step toward developing a congruent attitude, but it is not the last. Being congruent also means expressing who one truly is and what one is truly experiencing in the here and now. This second step requires working out one's fears and needs. People often say the opposite of what they feel, out of a need to be loved and acknowledged, and out of fear of being judged, ridiculed or rejected, or hurting or disappointing someone.

Not wanting to make Estelle unhappy, and not wanting to appear egotistical or unsympathetic in the eyes of his family, Ernest had agreed to let his mother-in-law live with him and his wife. After all, he owned a big house, and was sufficiently well off to provide for her needs until she died. However, he found it extremely difficult to deal with his new living arrangements. He suffered from the loss of intimacy between himself and his wife, and felt invaded as soon as he walked through the door to his home. Acutely aware of his growing uneasiness, he became even more attentive to this woman, whom he privately considered an intruder in his home. His home life deteriorated to the point where, one day, without warning, he announced to Estelle that the company he worked for had transferred him to a town several hundred miles away, and that he had decided to find a little pied-à-terre there where he would stay during the week. This announcement precipitated a crisis within their marriage, and only then did Ernest reveal the real reason for his exodus. Although he had been aware of his reaction to the new situation, he had not communicated it. In other words, he had displayed a lack of congruence in his behavior, causing a crisis, which is exactly what he had wanted to avoid.

A great deal of inner work is necessary before one can acquire congruence, including a commitment to oneself that the helper cannot uphold if his defense mechanisms block off his emotions and his anxieties. This inner work implies that the candidate-in-training be ready to confront his fear of emotion and his fear of losing control.

Congruence cannot be learned from books. It can only be learned from inner work and from the experience provided by relationships. On this topic, Rogers describes the result of his personal experiences, in *On Becoming a Person:*

> *In my relationships with persons I have found that it does not help, in the long run, to act as though I were something that I am not. It does not help to act calm and pleasant when actually I am angry and critical. It does not help to act as though I know the answers when I do not. It does not help to act as though I were a loving person if actually, at the moment, I am hostile. It does not help for me to act as though I were full of assurance, if actually I am frightened and unsure. Even on a very simple level I have found that this statement*

seems to hold. It does not help for me to act as though I were well when I feel ill.

What I am saying here, put in another way, is that I have not found it to be helpful or effective in my relationships with other people to try to maintain a façade; to act in one way on the surface when I am experiencing something quite different underneath. It does not, I believe, make me helpful in my attempts to build up constructive relationships with other individuals. I would want to make it clear that while I feel I have learned this to be true, I have by no means adequately profited from it. In fact, it seems to me that most of the mistakes I make in personal relationships, most of the times in which I fail to be of help to other individuals, can be accounted for in terms of the fact that I have, for some defensive reason, behaved in one way at a surface level, while in reality my feelings run in a contrary direction (pp. 16–17).

Throughout these passages, Rogers stresses the importance of expressing his emotions, of showing his real self. This is a key element of congruence, without which it could not exist. But, in order to express the truth that lives within us and by which we are made, we must also be ready to listen to ourselves, to know ourselves and to accept ourselves for who we are. Rogers builds here on what he said previously:

[. . .] I find I am more effective when I can listen acceptantly to myself, and can be myself. I feel that over the years I have learned to become more adequate in listening to myself; so that I know, somewhat more adequately than I used to, what I am feeeling at any given moment—to be able to realize I am angry, or that I do feel rejecting toward this person; or that I feel very full of warmth and affection for this individual; or that I am bored and uninterested in what is going on; or that I am eager to understand this individual or that I am anxious and fearful in my relationship to this person. All of these diverse attitudes are feelings which I think I can listen to in myself. One way of putting this is that I feel I have become more adequate in letting myself

be what I am. It becomes easier for me to accept myself as a decidedly imperfect person, who by no means functions at all times in the way in which I would like to function (p. 17).

Congruence is really born of a learning process. Learning to become congruent means learning to be ourselves, accepting ourselves as we are, and learning to listen to what we feel. Through this learning process the psychotherapist learns to observe himself and accept his own imperfections, to acknowledge, without judgment or condemnation, the times when he was lacking in congruence and to accept the consequences of that. Relying on my own psychotherapeutic experience, I cannot believe that it is possible to truly help others to be themselves, to find the solutions to their problems and the right path for them unless, in my role as therapist, I am congruent, or at least aware of the times when I lack congruence, for I am convinced that creative nondirectivity is not possible without it. Once again we see how the CNDA trainee cannot avoid undertaking inner work, learning how his psyche functions, freeing up emotional blocks, listening to his feelings and developing his creative potential. This learning process really is a prerequisite for empathy.

Congruence, which is, in a manner of speaking, the ability to listen to oneself, is also a prerequisite for true empathy, which is the capacity to listen to another: to his emotions, his needs, his frames of reference and the way his psyche functions.

Being empathetic requires that we be sufficiently able to know and listen to ourselves so as to avoid projecting what belongs to us onto another. As he listens to "the other," the empathetic psychotherapist is able to perceive who he is, what he experiences and what he does, and accept him with all his differences. This ability to recognize the other for who he truly is encourages the real person to be born.

Rogers, who introduced the notion of empathy to nondirective psychology, had this to say on the subject: "[. . .] I find that when I can accept another person, which means specifically accepting the feelings and attitudes and beliefs that he has as a real and vital part of him, then I am assisting him to become a person" (p. 21). In other words, the helper must not only be able to accept and "be conscious" of himself, but also take responsibility for what he feels and for who he is in such a way that the helpee regains power over himself by assuming responsibility for his own feelings. Thus, the psychotherapist who has learned to distinguish his own emotional structures and his own needs from those of his client is capable of listening to him, of entering into his world without getting caught up in it, and can reflect, through his way of listening, the client's *modus operandi*, his emotions, needs, beliefs, values, and frames of reference; all this, while respecting and accepting him for who he is. This kind of interaction cannot take place unless we develop self-love and acknowledge who we are.

d) *The need for acknowledgment*

We have all heard stories of people having sunk into alcoholism, drug dependency, depression or even madness because they were never acknowledged. Man has a fundamental need to be acknowledged in a positive way. In my opinion, the concept that an individual does not need to be acknowledged by others as long as he acknowledges himself is only partially true. Self-acknowledgment is built in the same way as love and acceptance of the self. Anyone who has been put down all his life will have trouble finding within himself any reserves of self-worth. Being acknowledged by others is a prerequisite for self-acknowledgment.

Despite this fact, educational institutions frequently fail in the task of building up their pupils, which results in a lack of self-confidence, inferiority complexes, the need to prove oneself and even lying. In an attempt to be acknowledged, some people become boastful, and attribute to themselves qualities, abilities and achievements which they do not possess.

One day Lisa, a woman of about 35, came to my office. The only daughter among five children, she had never been acknowledged by her father, who had always treated her as a sort of servant. While her four brothers went to university, Lisa's father persuaded her to work toward a secretarial career so she could be the "girl Friday" for his four companies. Constantly put down and made to feel inferior, Lisa had left her job after a long period of depression, as a result of which she had started to see a therapist and begun to re-examine her whole life. For many years, she had wanted to prove to her father that she was as intelligent as her brothers. She had given her job all she had, working overtime in order to tackle, in addition to her regular secretarial duties, the company's accounting, day-to-day business, organizational structure and even upcoming projects. Her father never acknowledged his daughter's exceptional abilities, instead taking all the credit himself. Convinced that she was worthless, Lisa always felt compelled to work extra hours in order to prove her competence.

Her inferiority complex was also apparent in a tendency to boast. Far from earning her the recognition she desired, though, it only brought her rejection. When she first came to see me she projected such a positive image of herself that I had trouble believing her story. It took some time for Lisa to realize that the superiority she exhibited was, in fact, the expression of a profound sense of inferiority, and that she brought rejection on herself because she portrayed the opposite of who she was. Lisa could not acknowledge herself either as a secretary or a woman because her father had never acknowledged her as such. And since the need to be acknowledged was vital for her, she unconsciously acted in such a way as to perpetuate—even increase—her suffering in an attempt to satisfy that need. While in therapy, Lisa decided not to go back to work for her father. She changed jobs and was so successful in her new work situation that she was promoted to the position of secretary to the executive director in less than a year. It was then she realized that, in spite of her suffering, those years spent working for her father had been an exceptional training ground, that secretarial work was really the right field for her, and not at all demeaning. She also realized that changing jobs had been beneficial in other ways: her new entourage had been quick to acknowledge her qualities and, since that fundamental need was satisfied, she no longer felt the need to boast or to prove her worth.

When a fundamental need remains unsatisfied, we often tend to adopt extreme behavior patterns which repel the satisfaction we seek. A person who needs love will tend to cling to others, but will be rejected because of this; again, a person who desires acknowledgment will often be boastful, trying to prove his worth, but his behavior will most likely be met with criticism, which will merely serve to reinforce his inferiority complex.

So far we have seen that when the need for acknowledgment is not satisfied it can lead to suffering, and even imbalance. We have also seen how, in order to achieve self-acknowledgment, people need to be acknowledged by others. In fact, acknowledgment is propulsive, and in counseling—as in education—the foundation of acknowledgment is faith. When the therapist firmly believes in the client's abilities, he is acknowledging him and helping him move forward. Rosenthal and Jacobson, in their book *Pygmalion in the Classroom,* provide overwhelming proof of this. Based on extensive experimental studies, the book relates real-life experiences which should cause us to question many educational approaches. From among many examples, I mention here the case of a teacher who was given a class of students with learning disabilities, but was told that it was a class of "enriched" students. His conviction and faith enabled him to achieve remarkable results with them.

If, as a teacher or therapist, one is convinced that the person with whom one is working—whether he be a student or a client—is incapable of succeeding or pulling through, then one will radiate an attitude that may well endanger the positive outcome of the helping relationship. A teacher who does not believe in his students' abilities condemns them to mediocrity and maintains their feelings of inferiority. A psychotherapist who does not truly believe that his client will resolve his difficulties will only succeed in confirming the latter's self-doubt and in inhibiting profound, effective change. The helper's faith is essential to the helpee's steady forward progression. Suggestology states, moreover, that faith is one of the key elements in the attitude of the suggestologist, because faith is the key to acknowledgment.

But what exactly is faith? To have faith means to believe in something so strongly that one's belief has the power to create it. As for our own actualization, we are the product of those who have believed in us, of those who have trusted us. They are the ones who lit the spark which we are now able to tend.

I believe it is the job of therapists and teachers to light and tend that spark of faith in each of the people they help. In training creative nondirective psychotherapists, we are constantly trying to discern the strengths of our students, and to help them discover, through our deep and unshakable faith, their potential for greatness, and lead them toward their greatest possible self-actualization. Faith is creative in the sense that the individual who is acknowledged learns to acknowledge himself and to open wide the doors of self-assertiveness.

e) *The need to assert oneself*

Satisfying one's need for love, security, attentiveness and acknowledgment is intimately linked to the need to assert oneself. Human beings need to take the kind of stand that, through words and actions, confirms who they are and openly announces their presence and their differences. A case in point would be Lisa, and her need to be acknowledged by her father as a woman and as an excellent secretary. What immured this woman in her suffering was that she never dared tell her father of the injustice she felt, nor dared set requirements and limits for herself: she was always afraid to reveal her pain. Because of her lack of self-confidence, she adopted instead a defensive, boastful, superior attitude that was completely untrue to her inner self, and which kept her firmly in her "girl Friday" role. Her lack of love, acceptance, attentiveness and acknowledgment toward herself prevented her from defining her needs, limits, demands and desires. Lisa submitted to the domination of her father and brothers, repressing her inner revolt and thus depriving herself of all that she desired. Unless we assert ourselves, we have nothing, and we cannot become anything. He who does not assert himself knows the pain of going unnoticed.

Of course, being assertive can be frightening. Taking a stand means running the risk of displeasing others, and perhaps losing them. Unfortunately, many people prefer to play down their respect and love of themselves rather than lose the love of others. However, since one cannot be loved unless one loves oneself, such people end up gaining very little. In fact, it is futile for us to subdue or deny ourselves in order to maintain the approval of our entourage: we end up losing others anyway, in addition to losing ourselves. Nobody really likes half-hearted people. I am reminded here of the story of Julie, who when she was still very young decided to become quiet and self-effacing like her father, whom she adored. By his example, he had taught his daughter how to avoid disturbing and displeasing others. Julie had come to the conclusion that, in order to be loved, she must always say "yes," always say what others wanted to hear, and always do what others wanted to see. She was the most subdued person I have ever met. Hyperrational, always on the defensive, she showed no reaction to anything. I sometimes had the feeling I was talking to a robot, to a being with neither soul, depth nor personality. Here was a woman who had been "molded," in such a way that she did not know who she was, what she wanted or what she was feeling.

I met Julie at a lecture I gave at her place of work; she came to see me as a result of a particular event that shook her otherwise firmly entrenched defense mechanisms. Her father, whom she had left two years previously and whom she had steadfastly refused to see since that time, had been diagnosed with general cancer and had expressed an urgent desire to see her before he died. This situation forced Julie to re-examine her position: she was unable to refuse her father's request, but she was also unable to agree to it. Thus she found herself in a double bind that caused her a great deal of anguish. Cut off from herself and from her emotions, Julie found herself, for the first time in many years, in a situation that succeeded in threatening her inner world. All the emotions she had repressed over the course of her life were now being released in the form of intense anxiety. As she learned to listen to her inner self, she found out that, for many years she had been stifling an intense hatred for her father. She could not stand his coldness, his indifference, his half-heartedness. She despised him for being so weak and for having passed his futility on to her. Through the CNDA-directed process, Julie discovered that she had stopped seeing her father for two reasons: first, because she saw in him a reflection of all that she didn't want to see in herself, and secondly because she was afraid of venting all her suppressed rage on him.

Emotions that are repressed through lack of assertiveness do not disappear. They become lodged within us, in our bodies and in our psyches, and their obstruction affects our behavior and personality, both of which become progressively more subdued. Indeed, the vital energy that we need for actualization and self-assertiveness is diminished, as part of it is used to repress the emotions and keep them on hold. The idea of having to shake off this emotional burden can be frightening. The attitude of the creative nondirective psychotherapist and the characteristic techniques of the approach gradually facilitate a gentle liberation of emotions, thus allowing the client to experience the pleasures of self-acceptance and of being listened to, and also to discover that he can assert his ideas and his differences without being afraid of the feelings that come with them.

Drawing on my professional experience, I have come to the conclusion that the greatest obstacle to self-assertiveness is fear of our emotions. Because of this, our statements of principles, ideas and opinions tend to lack warmth, and the consequent rejection makes us afraid to assert ourselves again. For an idea to be accepted, it must resonate in a person's feelings and life experience. There can therefore be no self-assertiveness unless there is contact with the emotion that gives rise to it, sustains it, confirms it and, above all, makes it personal to a particular individual.

In counseling, it is not possible to deal with the client's need for self-assertiveness without touching on the concepts of power, authority, transference and counter-transference.

• *Power*

The concept of power is often raised in educational and psychotherapeutic circles. Moreover, it is present in the political, economic, religious and social milieux as well as in interpersonal relationships. We come across it at work, in love relationships, and between friends. If one were to do a study on the psychological aspects of power—which would doubtless be extremely interesting—one would almost certainly conclude that the need to dominate is at the root of all our inferiority, superiority and insecurity complexes. In other words, the helper with a propensity for playing power games, whether on a conscious or unconscious level, has to work on bringing his own complexes to light. First, he must identify them; then, in therapy, he should try to recognize and accept his dominating tendencies. Also, he should try to acquire control over his life by becoming responsible for his own liberation, according to the steps laid out in the developmental process. Asserting oneself by exercising power over the helpee means maintaining the latter's dependence and destroying the confidence necessary for the kind of bonding process that is favorable to personal growth. That said, however, let us explore how the psychotherapist manifests power over his clients, and the teacher, power over his students.

It is usually the helper's defense mechanisms that are responsible for placing him in a position of power. When he is emotionally affected or involved, or when he experiences fear, anxiety or doubt about himself and is not in touch with these feelings, he may unconsciously adopt a defensive attitude of power vis-à-vis the helpee. This attitude of control and domination is embodied by interpretation, advice, confrontation, evaluation and also by a certain kind of fanaticism and "technicism."

Interpretation, one of the most subtle and dangerous forms of power in the helping relationship, is the primary method by which the therapist expresses his ascendance over the client. The psychotherapist who uses interpretation does so not by using the client's own experiences, and by being ready to listen, but rather by using ready-made theories or his own personal experiences. Theory-based interpretation puts all clients in the same pigeonhole, regardless of their differences. In cases such as these, the power of absolute knowledge prevails over individual subjectivity, and this type of interpretation cannot help but be harmful and annihilating because it gives the theory precedence over the person. We find this kind of behavior among helpers who use theories to help them feel secure. The other type of interpretation, which is much more common, takes place when the helper constantly refers to himself. He would be better off going into therapy himself, and really dealing with his concerns, rather than interpreting the client's experiences based on his own. In these kinds of situations, the psychotherapist exercises a subtle form of control over the client: the power of using his own life experience to control the client's life. This attitude inevitably leads to confusion. After all, since the client looks up to his psychotherapist as an authority in his field, he has a tendency to "buy" everything about this person, whom he consults because he acknowledges his competence in the art of helping people. He is therefore completely open to all the therapist's words and actions, to which he attaches more importance than he does to his own feelings and values. Interpretation, then, is a way of gaining power over the client, and the psychotherapist would do well to work on his own attitude toward it, by developing greater self-awareness.

In psychotherapy as well as in education, power is expressed in terms of the projects that certain therapists and teachers have for their clients and pupils. The psychotherapist who directs his client toward this decision or that choice, or who tries to impress upon him this belief or that value is, essentially, adopting a directive, power-based attitude which is harmful, not helpful. This kind of "helper" should remember that his own growth process, while well and good for himself, is not necessarily so for others. For example, because he has just gone through the painful ordeal of an imposed separation himself does not mean he should recommend total conjugal harmony for his client. Just because for him, having children brought much joy, freedom and happiness does not mean he should encourage others to start families too, whatever the cost. The helpee's path, however circuitous it may be, is nevertheless his own path, with all its uniqueness and difference. It is possible for some to find fulfillment in divorce, whereas others may find it in religion, or in their social life. In the end, there is no ideal way. There is only the way uniquely suited to each one of us. The helper must never forget that his way is right for him, but is not necessarily so for others, and that each helpee's way will lead him along a completely different path. Never mind where he is going; the important thing is that he is *en route*—at his own pace, using whatever means and taking whatever detours he deems necessary—to the place where he will find happiness and well-being.

Apart from the tendency to interpret and direct the client, there are other means by which the therapist can exercise power over the client. He may do so through confrontation or provocation, often stemming from a judgmental attitude. In general, these two methods serve to mobilize the client's defense mechanisms, disregarding his rate of personal growth. Using confrontation and provocation in one's work yields apparently remarkable results in surprisingly little time. One can indeed succeed in changing an individual's behavior by these methods, but this does not mean that his psychic state has been altered. On the contrary, this approach merely succeeds in reinforcing his defense mechanisms and his behavior patterns. The psychic state will only be transformed when the therapist's attitude of acceptance, faith and love leads the client to a positive experience of relationships and authority. In psychotherapy, it is the way the helpee feels and experiences his relationship with the helper—and not the external pressures that shut him off from himself and force him to maintain his persona—that effects his transformation.

Confrontation does not demystify the psychic dimension, nor does it help the individual to comprehend or confront what is happening inside him; it merely serves to modify his behavior, or his observable reactions. When someone is coerced in this fashion, he will alter his reactions to the external world without being overly concerned about his inner world, that is, about the way he is dealing with the change, and of its relevance to himself and his own self-development. True change comes from within, and an approach that does not deal in confrontation encourages in-depth transformation simply by respecting the individual's need for security and his personal rate of development. Simply dealing respectfully with the client and working with who he is and what he says, both verbally and non-verbally; simply adhering to his pace, without protecting him and without taking charge of him or judging him, is enough to open him up to himself and to elicit far-reaching transformations—because they are in accordance with who he is. Congruence, not confrontation, on the part of the therapist should be the order of the day. The mere fact that he is genuine in expressing his feelings and limits has a remarkable effect on the process of change and evolution.

The confrontational therapist would do well to examine and accept whatever it is within him that is prompting him to behave this way. Is it a personal problem? Might it be a need to elicit a reaction, to get concrete results? Could it be a deep-seated insecurity, a need to save the other at any cost? A defense mechanism, perhaps? Or could it be something else entirely? The urge to confront is a revealing one, that emanates from the psychotherapist himself. Be that as it may, there are, within each human being, certain forces in constant opposition to one another. The CNDA maintains that the psychotherapist's role consists not in forcing the client to progress through confrontation, but rather in leading him toward realization and acceptance of the contradictory forces within him and of helping him bring order to them through observation, reformulation and elucidation.

The helping relationship, whether in education or psychotherapy, requires that the helper use both the right and the left hemispheres of his brain. He needs to use his rational faculties in order to observe, establish connections, and to draw up syntheses and elucidations based on what the helpee has said; he also needs to know when to silence those faculties and call upon the irrational ones, by which he can feel, perceive and intuit. If reason, however, in addition to occupying its rightful place, also interferes with the irrational, then it creates an imbalance in the counseling relationship, maintaining the client in a state of confusion without implementing any real changes. A good creative nondirective psychotherapist or teacher is someone who is capable of observing, analyzing, synthesizing, elucidating and deducing, but who is also able to be moved, who feels and can be affected; in short, someone who lives life to its fullest. If this is not the case, then the helping relationship is not so much a "relationship" as a cold, disembodied kind of "help," with no effective long-term impact, which merely displaces the client's suffering, neither facing up to it nor freeing him from it. As long as the helper's counsel does not emanate from his head, his heart and his body, his approach cannot be deemed comprehensive, nor will it produce results that are anything more than fragmentary, divorced from any sensationalistic external appearances. This is where we touch on the problem of therapeutic techniques that aim for observable results. When the therapist gears his practice toward obtaining concrete results and proving the effectiveness of his approach, then he is using counseling as a means of ego massage, not as a means of helping others and helping himself. Therapists feel the need to be acknowledged and the need to assert themselves the same way all human beings do; however, when these needs are not allowed into the conscious mind, when they are not accepted, they have a negative effect on the therapeutic or educational relationship, through sensationalism, fanaticism and "technicism."

Indeed, in order to be acknowledged, and to satisfy his need to assert himself, the helper might use a certain theory or technique and present it as absolute truth, as if nothing else were valid. He may use this method to establish authority over his clients or pupils, thus rejecting everything that exists apart from himself and his practice. This attitude reveals a certain degree of fanaticism, the kind that grounds psychotherapy in a particular doctrine or technique that completely ignores the human qualities of the psychotherapist and the client, and gives the theory or technique precedence over the personal development of the individuals involved. The therapeutic process should not be experienced solely as a product of a rigid theoretical or practical framework. To me it is of the utmost importance to link the success of any counseling or educational relationship to the human qualities of the helper, as a person.

At the opposite end of the spectrum from fanaticism and "technicism" is utter confusion. The helper who has neither opinions, positions nor directions will necessarily evoke within the helpee a great deal of insecurity preventing the latter from defining and acknowledging himself. As psychotherapists and educators, it is vital that we assert ourselves by knowing as much as possible—through our own inner work—about who we really are, what we really believe in and what our actual values, beliefs and ideologies are, so that we can take a stand, firmly and without ambiguity. It is extremely important that the people we deal with know exactly what our theoretical, therapeutic and practical positions are. It is just as essential, however, that these positions, though presented in a clear and precise manner, not be put forward as absolutes or universal truths, but rather as one truth among many: our truth, which can give way to others. This manner of asserting oneself firmly, with respect for what exists outside oneself, allows the client or the pupil to make a fully informed choice, based on his needs.

The creative nondirective therapist is thus trained to know, acknowledge and love himself sufficiently well to be able to assert himself, to clearly define himself and to sincerely believe in the qualities of his approach, so that he can present it without imposing it, respecting his inner truth as well as external reality. He does not define himself by opposing his approach to others, but rather by possessing deep inner conviction, born of self awareness and life experience. Indeed, a psychotherapist's choice of approach is based solely on who he is: the approach merely serves to confirm his nature. He cannot use it honestly and effectively unless it reflects his attitude. I do not believe that either the technique, the approach or the theory used by a psychotherapist can, in and of themselves, bring about a transformation. Rather, it is the way certain elements are used that encourages change, the elements being, on the one hand, the psychotherapist's attitude and personality and, on the other, the client's needs, inner processes, emotions, defense mechanisms, behavior patterns and life experience. The psychotherapeutic process takes place in the context of a two-person relationship; and it is precisely these two people who can move it forward, as long as they realize the importance of their commitment to the process and to their respective roles.

And in his role as therapist, whether he wants to or not, the psychotherapist or educator represents an authority figure in the eyes of his clients or students.

• *Authority*

Lozanov (1978) has this to say on the subject of authority: "It is a nondirective influence that inspires confidence and the spontaneous desire to follow an example." In other words—and this is what the CNDA emphasizes—the notion of authority is associated with the concepts of influence and receptivity. The creative nondirective therapist must come to terms with his role as an authority figure. What is important for him is not so much "having" authority as "being" an authority. Seen in this way, authority is less a question of power than a question of influence.

What significance does this notion of authority have for the creative nondirective approach? Quite simply this: if the helpee is to foster the inner receptiveness necessary for his own liberation, then he needs to have confidence in the helper. He needs to acknowledge the latter as a competent person, able to support him through the educational or psychotherapeutic process, and it is the helper's attitude that is responsible for creating this atmosphere of trust. The authority I am speaking about here is the kind that consists not of threats or punishments, but of self-confidence and self-love. It is based on the therapist's innermost qualities, on his professional awareness, his integrity, his responsibility, his respect for himself and others, on his self-awareness and on his concern for keeping abreast with important, ongoing research in his field. It is also connected to his ability to assert himself, to be container-directive as regards his approach, and nondirective as regards the contents of that approach. His authority is not based on psychic constraints; rather, it makes one feel secure, inspires confidence and facilitates the act of letting go.

The helper who can acknowledge himself as an authority figure for the people he helps does not become their friend, but is able to fully come to terms with the role he must play until the conclusion of the helping relationship. There may be some students or clients who will attempt to transform the helping relationship into friendship, to avoid working on their attitude to authority, but this will only inhibit their acknowledgment of self and prevent them from going through certain necessary stages on the road to independence. This type of client will often pry into the psychotherapist's life, or even try to reverse the roles by asking questions or by manipulating the situation in every possible way. Others will remain after the session is over in an attempt to solve the enigma that frightens them so. As long as the therapist avoids falling into these traps, he is in a position to help his clients confront their fears and acquire a concept of authority that is simple, natural and non-threatening. In addition to being a warm, complete, sensitive, vulnerable person, he must take a stand and clearly define his limits, for this is precisely what it means to be an authority figure.

Helpees, whether they are children, teenagers or adults, all need good role models with whom they can identify, to learn more about themselves and to eventually become free and independent. These role models have to take a stand and come to terms with their respective roles, whether they be fathers, mothers, teachers, psychotherapists or instructors.

This is where the creative nondirective therapist in training needs to work on his self-assertiveness and self-acknowledgment. He can accomplish this through learning about who he is, through a progressive enrichment of all his inner dimensions, through more in-depth theoretical knowledge and through sound practical training. All this is necessary because, since he is in a position of authority, he will inevitably be confronted with his clients' transference problems, and with his own counter-transferences.

- *Transference and counter-transference*

Introducing the notion of transference to the CNDA appears to me to be a fundamental step. My experience as an educator, group leader and especially as a psychotherapist and trainer of creative nondirective psychotherapists puts me in transferential situations practically every day. Because of this, I feel compelled to include this element of Freudian psychoanalysis in the therapist training curriculum by adapting it to the CNDA and by emphasizing its significance. Sooner or later, all psychotherapists will become determining transferential surfaces for their clients, just as all teachers will become so for their students.

But what exactly do we mean when we speak of transference? Transference is the term given to the client's transferring, onto the psychotherapist, the emotions and feelings he has experienced during his infancy with respect to authority figures.

The notion of authority is closely associated with that of transference. And, generally speaking, the people who represented authority for the child are the father, the mother or other primary care-givers. In a transferential situation, the client will experience feelings and emotions for his psychotherapist—as an authority figure—similar to those he experienced for one of his parents, or a significant other from his childhood.

What happens in a situation like this? When the helpee transfers onto the helper in this way, the latter is not perceived as he really is. If, for example, the client transfers his father figure onto the psychotherapist, he will feel the same emotions for him as he used to feel for his father, and this will prevent him from getting in touch with the psychotherapist's true nature. The transference can be positive or negative—the client will either love him or hate him—but in either case it can only be a factor for growth if the psychotherapist or teacher is prepared to deal with it. In general, during the course of the therapeutic process, the client will go through both kinds of transference, but many clients complete only the positive transference stage, never touching on the negative one. Thus they move from one therapeutic stage to the next without ever delving deeply into themselves. What explanation can we give for this phenomenon?

When the psychotherapist is not familiar with transference, and has not dealt with it in his own inner work, he may unconsciously block his clients' expressions of negative transference. This situation often occurs with "life-saver" therapists for, indeed, if the psychotherapist has a tendency to protect the client in order to avoid causing him pain—and especially to shield himself from his own suffering—then the client will unconsciously register this attitude and be inclined to conceal his negative feelings so as to spare his psychotherapist. In that case, the therapeutic process will go around in circles for several sessions, finally reaching a dead end. It is therefore vital that the therapist be aware of this phenomenon and work on accepting his pain, subduing it and facing up to it. He will thus be in a position to attend to the suffering of others without wanting to save or protect them, and consequently he will be able to manage his own counter-transference situations.

How is it, though, that transference can be a progressive element within the process of liberation and change, and how can it contribute to the transformation of the psychic state? I wish to put forward here a highly personal appreciation of the beneficial effects of transference, based primarily on my professional experience.

When the client transfers positive feelings of admiration and idealized love onto the teacher or psychotherapist, his psychic state is transformed due to the identification phenomenon, by which his personality is shaped. Throughout his life, the child's personality is shaped as he imitates his parents' behavior, and this process continues into adolescence, as he identifies with role models ranging from his parents and teachers to "gang" leaders. Each human being must pass through these stages in order to stand out from the crowd—to find himself and assert his right to be different. He must first discover his identity, in order to use his adolescence as a means to, ultimately, "constitute himself as an independent being and creator of his own model, and hence his own values" (Sillamy, 1983).

Unfortunately, these periods in which we more readily identify with role models do not always progress toward a blossoming of our own creative personality: the two-year-old boy who copies his father may well, at the age of ten, no longer wish to be like him. Not all fathers are positive role models for their children. Often admired, even idolized, they can nevertheless disappoint us. Some, because of divorce, may leave a very young child, and no longer have any contact with him. The child is deprived of a male role model, and something is broken in the formation of his character. The child may turn to other role models, but these, too, can lead to repeated disappointments and, since it has not been accomplished in a satisfactory manner, the identification process continues through transference. In relation to his psychotherapist, the client will therefore tend to recreate the feelings of admiration and idealized love that, as a small child, he felt for his father, his mother or other primary care-givers. The helper thus becomes, in the eyes of the helpee, an ideal to be attained. Through positive transference onto this model, the helpee will pass unscathed through the identification stages necessary for his self-discovery. As long as the helper does not change the therapeutic relationship into one of love or friendship, the helpee's successful completion of these stages will gradually direct him toward the need to assert and distinguish himself. If the helper does transform the relationship, then the whole therapeutic process will end up being harmful and possibly even disastrous for the helpee. It is imperative that the therapist be ready to come to terms with his professional role, and remain an authority figure for the client.

The client, assisted by his psychotherapist, must also go through negative transference if he is to shape and define his unique personality. This stage is a crucial one because it allows him to sort out his repressed emotional blocks with the psychotherapist. Going through the negative transference stage means finding a way of expressing past negative feelings toward a parental figure who served as a transferential surface, and, most importantly, it means working on the attitude that alienates him from authority. Facing up to repressed fears, to stifled feelings of hatred and rage means first recognizing, then accepting, and then liberating them. When the client has been able to work on negative transference with his psychotherapist, everything that has represented authority for him becomes demystified. What he has previously perceived as threatening becomes harmless because he has found the courage to confront that concept of authority which was so frightening. He discovers that there is no longer a need to rebel, and that instead of defining himself through opposition he can define himself according to who he really is.

Once the client has gone through the stages of transference and discovered who he really is, he also discovers who the psychotherapist really is. This is where another type of relationship, free from interference, begins, in which the two people involved each have different roles: the psychotherapist is always a psychotherapist, and the client always a client. We are not speaking here of friendship—much less intimacy—but rather of a psychotherapeutic relationship in its conclusive stages. The psychotherapist remains an authority figure, and this is, in fact, what allows the client to really feel his inner transformation with regard to authority. He realizes that he knows how to deal with it and not feel threatened, because he stays in contact with who he is and who the therapist is.

However, this whole process cannot adequately come to fruition unless the psychotherapist, and especially his counter-transference, are recognized as important factors in it.

The concept of counter-transference was proposed by Freud, countered by Lacan and taken up by the English psychoanalysts Paula Heimann, Margaret Little, Lucia Tower and Annie Reich. According to Heimann, Little, Tower and Reich, the concept has to do with the psychotherapist's reaction to the client's transference. Even though the helper may rationally apprehend that he is not the specific target of any feelings the client transfers onto him, but is acting merely as a transferential surface, he can nevertheless be affected, even deeply distressed by the situation. When it arises, if he has not worked at self-awareness and at becoming attuned to his feelings, he may very well project his own experience and his own discomfort onto the helpee, thus compromising the positive development of the helping relationship. The way he reacts to the helpee's transference shows him which areas of his own personal exploration he needs to work on in order to avoid interpretations and projections, which lead to confusion and chaos. For this reason I believe that "regulating" psychotherapists is a vital issue. At our training center, we provide the psychotherapist-trainees with experienced "regulators" who assist them in resolving their counter-transference experiences and continuing their own inner work, without which their approach would be nothing more than a disembodied technique, or the application of a cold and soulless theory.

In fact, creative nondirective psychotherapists can be "regulated" such that, in a psychotherapeutic situation, they are never out of touch with themselves, and will not fail to distinguish their experiences from those of their client. This regulation makes it possible for them to uncover and accept their strengths and weaknesses and also to assert themselves with complete authenticity.

Because it is so closely associated with the expression of our experience, our differences and our innate authenticity, the need for self-assertion is indeed a fundamental need which, if left unsatisfied, leaves us imprisoned and bereft of freedom.

f) *The need for freedom*

Human beings have such a fundamental need for freedom that imprisonment is used as "punishment" for those who have misused it. Prisoners, however, are not only found behind bars. There are many human beings who are imprisoned by norms, conventions, beliefs and principles—and many more who are trapped in relationships. True freedom depends much more on our inner circumstances than on our external ones, and the man who does not feel free will be perpetually unhappy and unable to escape his personal hell.

Learning to be free is not an easy thing when one lives in a world ruled by manipulation, dependence and irresponsibility. I believe that, of all our needs, the need for freedom is one of the hardest to satisfy because of its close association with the needs for love, acknowledgment and assertion. In order not to lose the love and acknowledgment of others, man often throws away his own freedom. But he may not recognize that love needs space. By sacrificing his freedom, he is throwing away his chance to experience the profound joy that true affection and acknowledgment of the self can bring.

If we want to be free, we have to learn to love, acknowledge and assert ourselves. But what exactly does freedom mean? *Freedom is the ability to make decisions, follow through on choices and accept the consequences*. As I write this, a number of stories spring to mind about people who never make choices because they are afraid to accept the consequences of their decisions.

But what happens when we are incapable of any kind of choice or decision? Often, circumstances—other people and events—end up deciding for us, and we become puppets in their hands. We become passive, fearful, frustrated beings because we let others, fate or so-called *force majeure* run our lives. Some forms of belief are destructive: we should remember that having faith in "higher powers" does not mean totally abandoning ourselves to external circumstances. "Heaven helps those who help themselves," goes the proverb. In other words, there is no freedom without responsibility. As long as I do not avail myself of the power to make my own decisions and follow through on my own choices, I am at the mercy of—and dependent on—the external world, whether material, human or spiritual, which threatens to engulf me. Fear of the consequences makes man deny and enslave himself, annihilating his need for freedom and giving him a feeling of worthlessness.

I recall the story of Edmond, who came to see me after his third and most serious suicide attempt. He was 23 years old at the time and still living at home with his parents. Smothered, almost destroyed by an all-powerful, overbearing mother, he was unable to leave home because he was afraid he wouldn't be able to make it on his own. He had been over-protected by his mother to the point where he was convinced that he could do nothing without her. Because of this, he was deeply afraid of change. Trapped in this relationship that controlled his life, he was torn between feelings of powerlessness and a need for freedom. Since his mother had always made all his decisions for him, and since she was opposed to his leaving, he was completely unable to make the decision to move out. He was afraid of losing his parents' love, afraid of being cut off and afraid of the consequences if he were to leave.

In therapy, Edmond realized that the real reason he had come to see me was because, deep within, he hoped to escape. He even admitted hoping, as he was unable to make that decision, that I would do it for him. I did not, of course, for two reasons: first, because, through his transference, I would have been maintaining the pattern established between him and his mother; and, second, because advice always sustains dependence and takes away freedom. Edmond had to accept responsibility for his problem and decide for himself what course to take. My job was to make sure he knew that I had profound faith in his abilities, acknowledged his strengths, accepted his weakness and indecision and felt sincere affection for him.

Edmond came to the realization that he had always felt indebted to his mother so that, whenever he thought about leaving, he would be overcome by guilt and immediately accuse himself of being an ungrateful son. His guilt and fear made him feel alienated, depriving him of the vital need to be free in his relationships with others. In addition, he was constantly dogged by the feeling that he owed something to everyone around him.

Edmond's case is not unique. There are many people who are utterly trapped by their relationships, and Rose was one of these. She was 54 years old when we first met; I remember her story well because it touched me deeply. She had been married for 30 years and, since her wedding day, her friends and sisters had envied the way her husband, Augustus, treated her. He was a truly charming, gentle man, who for all those years had anticipated his wife's every wish. Materially speaking, she lacked nothing; nor did she ever feel deprived of affection or tenderness. Everything seemed to indicate that the man she had married was almost perfect, and certainly ideal for her. And yet Rose was not happy, and this caused her constant guilt. She had such a good husband—why should she feel unhappy or dissatisfied? But she was and, rationally, she was unable to overcome her distress. What was the reason for her unhappiness?

Thanks to the therapeutic process, Rose came to the realization that her husband's generosity made her feel obliged to repay him by always being at his beck and call. Because of this sense of obligation she felt suffocated by her relationship, and alienated from herself and her husband.

For Rose, separating from her husband was out of the question—the solution to her problem simply did not lie in that direction. Instead, she worked on learning to listen to her inner self and on breaking out of the "I am unworthy and must repay you" mindset she had fallen into, more or less unawares. Because she took responsibility for her unhappiness, Rose was able to come to terms with it without compromising her husband's love and attentiveness. As she regained her freedom to be and to act, she recovered her inner balance and *joie de vivre*.

Many relationships are based on just this kind of mutual alienation, because most people tend to believe that they have to pay others back for what they receive. In June 1982, when I arrived with my family in Paris, the six of us still hadn't found a place to live. While we were looking for an apartment, we took two rooms at the Foyer international d'accueil de Paris. Because this temporary arrangement was expensive for us, a friend offered to lend us her mother's apartment, near the Parc Montsouris. We stayed there for two weeks before moving into "our" place, on rue d'Arsonval in the 15th *arrondissement*. After we had moved in, I asked my friend how much I owed her for her generous hospitality. She answered: "Nothing at all. Perhaps one day you'll be able to help someone else in the same way." The instant she said that, I understood what freedom was. Up until that time, I had spent my whole life feeling obligated to the world. These days, I can accept gifts without feeling indebted, and I give freely, without expecting anything in return. Thus, I have broken free from a number of alienating relationships based on the "I am unworthy and must repay you" mindset.

Freedom is priceless, and I believe we must sometimes accept loss rather than compromise on this key need, for without it we cannot experience true love. And our freedom is compromised when the only reason we give is to pay back what we have already received, or to make someone feel obligated.

If I choose to be free, I have to accept the consequences. Sometimes our friends don't want us to break free from the alienation of our relationships; they don't want to lose their power to trap us by making us feel obligated for what they have given us. Accepting the consequences of our decisions is often hard, but apparent defeat can translate into victory in terms of autonomy, inner freedom and self-love.

Learning to be free does not mean that we should stop caring about others' feelings, or stop listening to and loving them. It does, however, mean that we should break free from restricting behavior patterns, and we can do so by taking responsibility for our experience as well as for our choices and decisions, accepting the resulting consequences, and giving back to the other the responsibility that is rightfully his. Going through with this liberating experience is the only way for us to live in harmony with others, respecting both who they are and who we are. This step is essential in developing our individual differences and creative potential. It is also absolutely necessary for the satisfaction of other basic needs because, generally speaking, when one psychic need goes unfulfilled, all the others are affected. An unfulfilled need causes suffering, a lack of inner harmony and a certain imbalance which will not disappear until the need is satisfied. This is also true for other needs, such as the need for creativity.

g) *The need for creativity*

Creativity is a natural human function. Encouraging creative expression increases our intellectual, imaginative and practical abilities, helps us learn to be free and actualizes our latent potential.

Since creativity is a natural human function—a psychobiological one, according to Jean Lerède—and a fundamental need, even an urge, as defined by Michel Lobrot (1974), we could say that the more a person creates, the more complete his life is. Truly creative individuals, those whose creativity plays a role in their inner development, are alive, motivated, committed people who are involved with their lives— people who are actors in life, not bit players or spectators.

Because creativity comes naturally to all human beings, it follows that everybody can create, regardless of age or social status. Unfortunately, although this function is innate to man as a species, it is not necessarily developed in individual members of that species. In educational settings, sadly enough, the necessary conditions for encouraging creativity are not always present. In the absence of a favorable affective environment, or an atmosphere of respect for individual differences, creative abilities are stifled and consequently the child's or teenager's natural growth patterns are impeded. In order to create, children—and adults as well—need to discover their true nature and give their spontaneity free rein. Similarly, in order for their potential to be liberated, they also need people around them who love them and have faith in them.

Discovering one's true nature means freeing oneself from introjections that block actualization of the creative process. Some people have been so conditioned by what the education system has grafted onto them that they have trouble realizing who they are and what they want to become. Too often they are what others want them to be: nothing about them is really theirs. Indeed, as they grow older they learn to fit themselves into pigeonholes and to make their behavior conform to others' expectations. They are alienated, imprisoned by the way others perceive them. Seen in this light, certain education systems tend to favor the "persona" at the expense of the "person."

However, there comes a time when the effort of maintaining the "persona" makes us feel distressed. The person inside wants to be let out. The stage is set for a confrontation between the person and the persona, and unless the person emerges victorious, that is, occupies the space that rightfully belongs to it, serious neuroses or even psychoses will result. When the person does win, the individual will feel the need to create because, by giving birth to his inner person, he is actually creating himself.

This is always a difficult stage to go through. It is the moment of truth, the point at which, if he wants to be healed, the individual must allow the person inside him to live by focussing on it, listening to it, accepting it as it is and above all by loving it. This stage of giving birth to the person, of establishing contact with one's true nature is called "renaissance". In constrast to the initial birth experience, here the subject is the conscious author of his continuing renaissance. This birth of the person, and the concomitant death of the persona, can only come about in a tolerant, loving atmosphere. Together, they necessarily give rise to spontaneous expression, the liberation of creative potential and self-love. As the individual gets in touch with his inner person, this automatically leads him to discover whatever makes him different from others—in other words, with the source of his creativity.

Since our creativity is a way of expressing our differences, or that which is unique in each individual, it varies in accordance with our emotions, with the personal history of each of us: why we are alive and why we are here on this earth.

Because of his differences, man has something to give to others. This is what I call his "mission in life." But he cannot contribute his unique gift unless he demonstrates his creativity. If this difference, this singularity that is his alone because it is shaped by his feelings, is not acknowledged by his teachers, or if he chooses to conform to a lifestyle or a set of social norms that does not acknowledge who he is, and if he supports those norms, then he is stifling his creativity. And when a person's creativity is stifled, life, more often than not, has no interest for him: he lacks self-motivation and does not know the joy of being alive. He is like a puppet that lets itself be controlled by others, or by external circumstances. Stifling our creativity means hindering our renaissance, our self-manifestation, and consequently the fulfillment of our mission in life—that is, the reason why we were born.

As our life unfolds, and as we learn how to be free, our creativity develops. I demonstrate that I am alive and I affirm my differences through the expression of my creative powers.

It is written in the Bible that God created the world. Whatever our actual beliefs may be, this statement reveals a great deal about the phenomenon of creation as a symbol. Indeed, by creating the world, God—or the god-symbol, which carries different names within different belief systems—made himself manifest to man. To a significant extent, then, God exists through his creation. In fact, he is his creation. From this, I can hypothesize that God is the symbol of the creative impulse by which man, also, can manifest himself. If my hypothesis is correct, then human beings need to create in order to actualize themselves. The created work is a springboard; it is the external realization of our inner creative powers. Without that realization, man cannot become actualized; he cannot even exist. Thus my human qualities and my inner creative powers are confirmed through my acts of creation. By taking God out of man, by making him an entity external to man, certain religions distorted the divine symbol, diminishing man's stature and taking away his power and his strength. Thus man lost the power over his own life and came to be at the mercy of God's representatives here on earth. He had to wait for God to answer his prayers, because he had forgotten God was also within him, and was the expression of his own creative energy. And when man loses control over his life, he simultaneously loses any hope of exploiting his creativity, or of attaining freedom. The possibility of creation, self-creation and renaissance is therefore excluded.

Creativity is an innate potential that asks only to be set free. I believe that this innate creative potential provides an explanation for Rogers' view that man tends naturally toward self-actualization. But this hypothesis can be taken even further. If creativity is in fact at the root of man's natural tendency toward self-actualization, then the act of creating is an essentially therapeutic one because it sets man free, enabling him to assert his right to be different. It is also both preventive and curative, in part because the creative act takes place within the context of a relationship.

Creativity is associated with a relationship in the sense that it constitutes a connection between the creator and his works and also between the creator and others. Creation leads to self-creation—a constant process of renaissance—through exploitation of the self, revelation of the self to others and to oneself, as well as going beyond oneself. Creation not only validates the creator, as we have just emphasized, it also makes him manifest. In fact, by liberating his latent potential, his hidden strengths, his buried talents, his inner powers, the creative act ends up creating the creator; as Paul Valéry suggests, to create is to bring forth a creative work that brings forth the creator. Creating means ceaselessly striving for self-mastery; it means discovering, transforming, actualizing ourselves; it means learning to love ourselves.

There is an obvious correlation, or "interrelation," between the creator and his work. As Yves Landry (1983) has written, one projects oneself onto an external object which acts upon the subject of the self. Interrelation, or interinfluence of the subject and the object are inherent to the creative process: the creator, or subject, transforms the matter, or object, which in turn transforms him, going round and round in an endless, spiralling cycle. Each act of creation by the creator represents a step further along his path to self-creation.

This subject-object dialectic can also be found in the relationship between the creator and others. Every relationship has the potential to be both creative and self-creative. As I stated previously, when two people enter into a relationship, they exert an influence over each other, which can transform them for better or for worse. The psychotherapeutic relationship is the context *par excellence* in which both the psychotherapist and the client can be transformed, and in which the process of creation and self-creation can become actualized. However, this relationship cannot be creative in this sense unless the helper has adopted a nondirective attitude based on respect for individual differences, on responsibility and on love, thus encouraging self-creation and empowering the helpee to be the creator of his own life.

The attitude of the therapist or teacher is a crucial element in the psychotherapeutic or educational process. To be effective, any person who takes on a "helping" role should strive unceasingly for inner transformation in order to attain increased self-knowledge, and a greater manifestation of his latent potential. To achieve this, in his relationship with the helpee, the helper should be constantly creating himself, using his strengths and especially his mistakes to question and transform who he is. In this way, his unconscious influence will become increasingly beneficial and propulsive for the helpee. This is why the CNDA emphasizes that the helper's mistakes should be seen as symptoms of a troubled feelings that needs to be worked on. Errors of judgment, interpretation, comparison, confluence, taking charge, protection or content-directivity could all be related to the helper's defense mechanisms, which he has set up to protect himself against undefined or unaccepted emotions, blocks or fears. The helper can, however, seize upon them as an opportunity to know, understand and exploit himself more fully.

In other words, our approach is not based solely on the acquisition of knowledge and techniques. It is my belief that a therapist's actual competence is in direct proportion to his capacity for self-creation. Even though he may work on increasing his knowledge and his ability, a good helper is someone who is concerned first and foremost with knowing how to *be*. When he makes mistakes in his practice, he uses them as a springboard toward self-creation. He is not a technician who mechanically applies the steps of a method learned by rote, but a creative being who is aware that a technique is only a meaningless instrument unless it is channeled through our human qualities. Thus, the creative nondirective helper is a person who uses his mistakes not to put himself down but to move himself forward. This is why the nondirective approach is creative. It lets both helper and helpee partake in an ongoing process of self-creation, as they seek to satisfy all their basic needs.

2. Psychic needs and the emotions: An unsatisfactory mental process

The satisfaction or lack of satisfaction of our basic psychic needs is always accompanied by corresponding pleasant or unpleasant emotions. If his needs are satisfied, a person will feel peace, joy and happiness. If one of his needs is not fulfilled, he will be disturbed, defeated or unhappy, because the balanced functioning of the human psyche depends on the satisfaction of man's fundamental needs. This link between needs and emotion is central to the psyche. When a need goes unsatisfied, this disturbs our inner balance, initiating an entire mental process which, once triggered, will frequently repeat itself. The subject in question, meanwhile, has no understanding whatever of the mechanisms that are at work within him—of the source of the mental process. This repetition of the unsatisfactory mental process may continue for months or even years, overwhelming the subject by its constant recurrence. He is at the mercy of an internal mechanism that has invaded him completely, and that causes him to fall, repeatedly and incessantly, into traps which, try as he might, he is helpless to avoid. Understanding how that mechanism works is the only way out of the vicious circle he is in.

The CNDA's concept of the unsatisfactory mental process can be seen in diagram and flow-chart format in Figures 3.1 and 3.2.

The cycle of the unsatisfactory mental process is shaped over the course of a person's life, and becomes imprinted in his psyche as a result of repeated, distressing emotional experiences. Basically, these painful experiences have left a fundamental need unsatisfied; they have affected his psyche to such an extent that he has unconsciously created a protective "system," which he implements each time a new event makes him unconsciously relive painful feelings. This event becomes the trigger for the whole internal process.

Figure 3.1

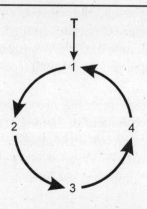

Figure 3.2

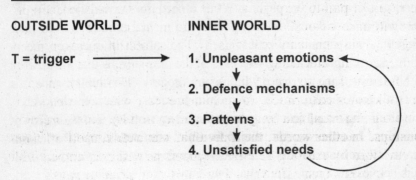

For example, if this person feels that his father and mother rejected him or didn't listen to him—to a degree that made him suffer and left a deep void within him—he will build up an entire internal protective process, which will automatically be triggered each time when, in his daily activities, he feels rejected or not listened to by someone whose opinion he values. We can see, then, how lack of attentiveness and acceptance can trigger the mental process, but how does this process unfold?

Let us start with the actual trigger itself. Man is not isolated from the outside world; in fact, he interacts with it constantly. In this sense, there is a certain amount of mutual influence between the person and his entourage and environment. The way the external world influences the person, however, depends on his emotional state. For this reason, the same event or trigger will have different effects on different people. Indeed, the trigger (T), initiated consciously or unconsciously by one's entourage, can release either pleasant or unpleasant emotions (1) within the psyche.

If the emotions thus released are pleasurable, they energize us, freeing our creative potential; if they are not, they may block the vital energy necessary for self-actualization. Unpleasant emotions are more deep-seated and more vivid if they are caused by a complex, or—as Mucchielli (1980) puts it—by an "area of excessive sensitivity." This area, which is at the heart of the psyche, is the result of painful experiences. In an attempt to escape his pain, man will unconsciously resort to defense mechanisms (2) to protect himself. These mechanisms form a sort of shell that prevents him from becoming attuned to his feelings and his emotions. In search of substitute satisfaction, he will adopt and continually repeat a certain kind of pattern (3), or mental process, which feeds his unconscious, habitual and long-term inability to have satisfying relationships. In other words, the individual who cuts himself off from his emotions by erecting defense mechanisms will only end up with his basic needs unsatisfied (4). I call this "the price to pay."

René was 28 years old when he first met Aline. With her intelligence, self-confidence and extreme good looks she literally bowled him over. Two years later, their relationship was still going strong. He felt that they communicated well, and he enjoyed their intense discussions on such topics of shared interest as psychology and the arts. René was convinced that Aline was the ideal woman for him.

One issue, however, began to overshadow their apparently strong relationship. As wonderful as she was, Aline seemed icily indifferent to René's need for affection, rejecting his sexual advances. During the first year they went out, he waited patiently, thinking she needed to get to know him better. But since they were so close on an intellectual and social level, he started to have doubts about the supposed reserve of the woman he adored. They talked about everything under the sun, but the topic of love and sexuality was never even raised.

René finally came to see me because in this, as in all his relationships, he felt that he could not assert himself as a man. There was more to this than frustrated sexual desire: René was becoming increasingly dissatisfied with the way women refused to acknowledge his masculinity.

René was the youngest of four brothers, and his mother had never tried to hide her disappointment at having had another boy. Because she had really wanted a girl, René felt that his mother had never recognized his male qualities and, because he loved and admired her, this caused him a great deal of suffering. His need to be acknowledged was so strong that he did everything to gain his mother's acceptance, hiding his anger and pain from her, denying and repressing his feelings out of fear of rejection or humiliation. As he grew older, he spent a lot of time with her, listening to her and so on—to the point of forgetting his own needs.

In therapy, René discovered that whenever he became involved with a woman, he would repeat the same pattern he had adopted toward his mother: he would put her on a pedestal, devoting himself to her needs and desires. Moreover, he always attracted eminently superior women who, inevitably, made him feel inferior: fear of rejection and humiliation ruled out any possibility that he might become an equal in the relationship. He realized that the conversations he had thought so stimulating were really just monologues, with himself in the role of the enrapt listener. The feeling that he didn't measure up prevented him from making a move, expressing an opinion or desire, or sharing his needs or emotions. This made him an excellent friend, but not the lover he really wanted to be. Thus, his fear of rejection (emotion) caused him to repress his desires (defense mechanism) in an attempt to be acknowledged (need). What he ended up with, of course, was the opposite of what he wanted: his need for love and acknowledgment went unsatisfied.

The first thing René had to do was learn how to listen to himself, how to recognize the strengths, desires, needs, feelings and emotions that he had always denied and repressed in order to please women. Thanks to the psychotherapeutic process of self-development, directed by the CNDA, he made amazing discoveries about the way his psyche functioned, and this led to rapid and satisfactory progress.

This case provides an illustration of how the unsatisfactory mental process unfolds. It has been summarized in Figure 3.3.

Because he felt that he was not acknowledged as a man (Trigger), René experienced a number of unpleasant emotions (1), but did not share them with anyone. Because he denied and repressed them (2), these emotions triggered an involuntary response (3) that was activated every time he got involved with a woman and that always left him with the same feeling of dissatisfaction (4).

Most of us have experienced or will experience something along the lines of René's story. Only our realization that we are prisoners of

Figure 3.3

OUTSIDE WORLD

Trigger ⟶
- *non-acknowledgment of masculinity*

INNER WORLD

1. Emotions
  - *grief*
  - *sadness*
  - *jealousy*
  - *fear of abandonment*
  - *fear of others*

↓

2. Complexes
  - *abandonment*
  - *sibling rivalry*

↓

3. Defense mechanisms
  - *rationalization*
  - *justification*
  - *explanation*
  - *accusation*
  - *judgment*
  - *escape*

↓

4. Unsatisfied needs
  - *need to be loved*
  - *need to be listened to*

an unsatisfactory mental process, and our efforts to understand it, will open the doors to change. Demystifying this inner process entails becoming familiar with each of its component elements. I will therefore follow the same procedure I used in explaining fundamental needs, expanding on each stage of the unsatisfactory mental process in turn: emotions, complexes, defense mechanisms and patterns.

C. EMOTIONS

Emotions constitute the very essence of the way the psyche functions and, as such, are at the heart of the unsatisfactory mental process. If his needs are satisfied, an individual will experience joy and inner peace. However, if one or more of his fundamental needs remains unsatisfied, he will experience such unpleasant emotions as grief, anger, jealousy or fear. Unfortunately, a number of religious or philosophical beliefs hold that our unpleasant emotions are monsters we should run away from, that they are to be denied or repressed whenever and wherever they arise.

Emotions, however, are natural psychological phenomena that one cannot summon or banish at will. They affect us spontaneously, or at regular intervals, through our relationship with the environment and with people in our entourage. When we take a walk outside, for instance, or when we watch a sunset or look at a beautiful work of art, or when we are with someone we love, we can experience a whole range of pleasurable emotions. But concentrating solely on this kind of experience can be dangerous, for just as human energy is bipolar, so also are our emotions. Dr. Stone, the "father" of human polarity, posited that there are two poles of energy in man that complement and attract each other. Denying energy's negative polarity is tantamount to destroying the positive. Similarly, suppressing unpleasant emotions automatically decreases the potential intensity of the pleasurable ones. Instead of using his vital energy to create himself and to express his creative urge, man wastes a significant amount of his potential energy in more or less indiscriminately repressing his emotional experiences. His psyche becomes amputated, leaving him with so little energy that he is almost not alive at all.

In denouncing the repression of emotion I am by no means saying that we should let ourselves be overwhelmed by it. It is just as unhealthy to let emotion rule our life as it is to let it be dominated by reason.

I would like to distinguish here between unleashing previously repressed emotions and expressing, in a responsible manner, emotions experienced in the here and now of a relationship. The ideal context for liberating previously suppressed emotions is with a psychotherapist or, in certain cases, in close personal relationships. Above all, it must happen in an atmosphere of love, trust and acceptance, in the company of someone who conveys a sense of security. As for the other instance, that of emotions experienced in the present, I believe that it is always worthwhile to voice them, particularly in relationships involving significant others: friends, lovers, parents, and the like. This, however, implies that one is capable of listening to one's experiences rather than stifling them through defensive attitudes.

But why do we stifle certain emotions? Believing that unpleasant emotions are monsters that need to be caged and hidden leads us to develop feelings of fear, guilt and shame. In addition to the psychic or physical suffering caused by our painful emotions, we also feel ashamed of them, and this prevents us from being assertive. As we learn to curb these so-called "shameful" emotions, we are actually allowing ourselves to be controlled by the principles and beliefs of the external world.

Nevertheless, hatred, jealousy, anger and fear are only dangerous when they are repressed or denied. Emotion is like a child: when we can't be bothered with it, it bothers us. A suppressed emotion will never disappear; it will become lodged within us, in our bodies and in our psyches, to reappear one day in the form of physical or mental illness, or violent and dangerous emotional release.

However, when we take the time to listen to our emotions, to accept them and express them, they do not wreak havoc in our lives. This is why the CNDA, instead of teaching people to deny their emotions, encourages attentiveness, acceptance, acknowledgment and, above all, responsible expression of personal emotional experience in the here and now of a relationship. Of course, it is easy to articulate emotions that were experienced in the past. Learning to listen to emotions as they arise and voicing them without shame is much more difficult. In itself the feeling is not threatening, but it becomes so when it is repressed, and voiced in an irresponsible and defensive manner. When one person feels emotionally affected, he attacks; the other reacts defensively, inviting aggression. Instead of expressing our emotion and maintaining communication with the other, we are constantly either on the offensive or the defensive. This kind of behavior severs, at least temporarily, certain ties within the relationship, and in the long term tears down what should actually have been built up.

Emotion, then, is not a monster, and even less a shameful disease to be hidden at all costs. It is a natural phenomenon which can do no harm unless it is ignored or treated with disrespect. To deny or provoke it is to deviate from its natural process, which is never violent or threatening when it is attended to and acknowledged in the here and now of the relationship and the present situation.

How is it possible for a helper to accompany others through their natural process of emotional evolution if he reacts with shame and fear to his own emotional experiences? In my opinion, it is not possible for the helper to assist others in using their vital energy creatively unless he has learned to acknowledge and express his own emotions. In this sense, the creative nondirective attitude works at gradually dismantling feelings of shame and guilt, allowing us to listen to what is happening within us. An atmosphere of love and acceptance provides the only forum in which we can embrace our feelings of anger, jealousy and fear, in addition to our outpourings of pleasure, generosity and joy. Sadness, anger, envy are emotions we all experience at one point or another in our lives, but hiding and denying them does not make them disappear from our relationships. When they are not expressed verbally, they will emerge in our non-verbal attitude, whether we want them to or not, and this is perceived at an unconscious level by others. This unconscious perception can become so strong as to seriously trouble the relationship, and possibly destroy it. Indeed, many relationships fail because of what is left unsaid by the partners. They are not able to express their emotion because they are not aware of them, because they never learned to listen to them or because they are ashamed of them. Instead of confiding their innermost feelings to their partner, they overwhelm them with judgments and criticism, all of which will, in the long term, poison the relationship, destroy trust and lead to separation. I believe that being attuned to one's emotional experiences and expressing them in a responsible manner are crucial to making any relationship work. Hiding what we are truly experiencing with respect to our partner is equivalent to hiding ourselves, and presenting a persona in our stead. Inevitably, this persona will end up being unmasked, because of the other's unconscious perception.

I do not believe that any long-lasting relationship is possible unless both partners listen to their feelings and express them in a responsible fashion. It is equally impossible without an honest and respectful appreciation of the other, which neither blames nor spares them. When we spare others, what we are really doing is sparing ourselves, and protecting ourselves from the fear of hurting, disappointing or suffering loss. Paradoxically, however, the more we spare ourselves, the harder it is to get close to others. When we learn to say what we feel in a genuine and responsible manner and understand how to be congruent, then we will have discovered how to have satisfying relationships based on mutual feelings of trust and security.

Since our emotions are at the heart of the psyche and, by extension, of the unsatisfactory mental process, we need to accept and listen to them before we can move on to satisfying our fundamental needs.

As outlined above, when the emotions are denied and not allowed into the conscious dimension, a whole unconscious process is set in motion, imprisoning man in a network of unfulfilling relationships.

I believe that our upbringing has contributed to instilling in us that most devastating of fears—the fear that vitiates every one of the processes leading toward freedom, creation and change: the fear of emotion. And fear, in itself, is the major culprit in the lack of satisfaction of our basic needs. It can take on many guises in its attempts to prevent man from finding the love, security, acknowledgment, affirmation and freedom he needs. Fear of rejection, loneliness, disapproval or criticism, fear of ridicule, judgment, intrusion or commitment, fear also of mistakes and failure and, again, fear of disappointing, displeasing, annoying, hurting or suffering loss and, as well, fear of being mean, or quite simply fear of change, or even madness or death—all these fears cause man to deprive himself of ingredients essential for his inner balance. Unacknowledged fears end up as emotions that block our vital energy, inhibit satisfaction of our needs and poison our affective life—and hence our relationships.

Like all unpleasant emotions, fear needs to be acknowledged in a non-judgmental way. When it is experienced so intensely as to be traumatic, with no possibility of liberating it through expression, then it can cause deep-seated complexes that cannot be uprooted without a great deal of inner work.

D. COMPLEXES

Mucchielli (1980) defined the complex as, among other things, an "area of excessive sensitivity." Brought about by the conjunction of an individual's psychic state and his emotional experiences, the complex leads him to repeat unsatisfactory and painful behavior patterns.

The way complexes are formed in a given individual is directly related to his emotional past. Painful and traumatizing emotional experiences create an "area of excessive sensitivity" in his psyche, which leads him to react strongly to even the most trivial external trigger that makes him unconsciously relive unbearably painful emotions. Indeed, the casual observer is at a loss to understand the extent of the person's reactions to seemingly insignificant events: because of his complex, his emotions arise spontaneously, and are so strong that they cannot be controlled by his rational dimension, and they frequently earn him rejection from his entourage. For this reason, it is not possible to work with and help people without having a thorough understanding of how complexes operate, in order not to condemn the strong reactions of helpees whose emotions bring them undue suffering and disrupt all their relationships.

A complex is not a shameful evil, any more than the intense emotions that give rise to and perpetuate it are. Helping another person to discover his complexes, to understand his so-called "exaggerated" reactions and to regain his inner balance necessarily implies that, as a helper, one has worked on bringing one's own complexes to light.

Becoming conscious of our own complexes is not an easy thing. As Mucchielli reminds us, an individual can very well be aware of his reactions and his pain, without necessarily understanding the mechanisms that cause him to react so violently to certain events. Although the dawning consciousness of one's problem is one of the first steps—indeed an essential one—on the road to freedom, it is not in itself enough to demystify the complex. This book, however, could not do otherwise than encourage people to become conscious of the complexes they harbor, emphasizing that only in psychotherapy can they go through all the stages of the evolutive process. It is precisely this process that makes it possible for each one of us to continue along our personal path toward freedom and acceptance, in our search for balance and independence.

The root of the complex lies within each individual's personal history, buried deep in the emotional baggage linked to his past experiences. For it is not the experience itself that traumatized him, but rather the subject's emotional reaction to that experience. The same event that traumatizes one person can leave another one with nothing more than a bad memory; it all depends on the individual's psychic state, and on how the event resonates in his emotional memory. An incident that others would deem commonplace can cause a huge rift to develop in the psyche because of the strong emotional impact it had for the subject in question. On the other hand, an apparently catastrophic event may have only a negligible affect on the person who experienced it because it was not disturbing for him emotionally.

We can gain a better understanding of how complexes function within a given individual by examining each of the major complexes in turn and explaining, through real-life examples, how they arise and in what manner they manifest themselves.

In his book *Les complexes personnels* (1980) Mucchielli describes six of the most commonly occurring complexes: abandonment, sibling rivalry, insecurity, castration, guilt and inferiority.

1. The abandonment complex

This complex, which is the cause of many psychic dysfunctions, is described by Mucchielli in the following terms: "I would include under this one title a variety of complexes that are often seen as separate, such as the affective frustration complex, the exclusion complex and the rejection complex."

Included among the feelings that most clearly express this kind of complex are the following: the certainty of not being taken into account, of being rejected, not understood, or not loved at all. A whole inner drama is unleashed every time the person feels put aside, excluded or rejected, causing him to question not only his Self, but his very existence. The feeling that he has been abandoned, that nobody takes any interest in him, that he will never be the center of attention, loved or recognized can easily lead to depression, existential emptiness, and finally, the loss of the will to live.

> *Because the "abandonee" is extremely sensitive to the affective attitude of everyone around him, he tends to become obsessed with the quality of others' affection for him, doubting its sincerity and questioning whether his friends are genuine. Having this kind of focus means he is ever-watchful for signs that would belie the love and friendship others profess for him. In order to test the actual limits of other's love or patience, he can be demanding, annoying, even spiteful, and his behavior necessarily becomes inappropriately aggressive, which leads to rejection. When those he thought loved him reject him, he believes he is condemned to permanent emotional solitude. In voluntarily withdrawing, he excludes himself from all human contact, thus reinforcing the complex. If anyone should show an interest in him, what he expects for and insists on, is absolute proof that he is loved unconditionally. His unquenchable thirst for ultimate love can only end in disappointment (p. 57, free translation).*

During the years I spent in clinical practice, I met a significant number of people who were suffering from an abandonment complex. Some stories, which I will use here as examples, made a particularly strong impact on me.

When Emily came to see me, I was impressed by her warm handshake, her self-confidence and her great beauty. She was 27 years old at the time, and had been married to Jorge for four years. She was intending to separate from her husband, whom she was convinced no longer loved her, and had turned to psychotherapy for support. In fact, it was her deep-seated fear of abandonment that caused her to feel rejected and neglected all the time. The only words and actions of her husband that registered with her were those that confirmed her emotional preconception. Indeed, as Mucchielli reminds us, it is characteristic of people with complexes to project their own internal experience onto external reality, and to apprehend only what they dread. Thus Emily, blind to her husband's demonstrations of affection, was only aware of the times when she felt he was excluding or rejecting her. When he sat down to watch television without her she felt excluded;

when he had to stay late at the office, she felt she was insignificant to him; when he forgot to kiss her good-bye in the morning, she felt unloved; when he didn't phone her at lunch from the office, she thought she no longer interested him—in short, any time he did not give her his entire attention, she felt abandoned. For her, his actions, his words, the times when he was silent were all indications of his waning love. By making her feel this sense of deficiency, his very presence caused her intense suffering.

To get his attention, and test his love, she had got into the habit of questioning, harassing and lecturing him relentlessly, which earned her the rejection she feared, and confirmed her doubts about Jorge's feelings for her. This is a defensive reaction typical of "abandonees": they provoke and nag, get rejected and run away. Emily had spent four years confronting and tormenting her husband but she still wasn't satisfied, and so she had decided to call it quits and leave him.

However, as early as the first session, I realized that she loved Jorge deeply and that, even if she did leave, she would have the same problem in her next relationship, because she was unable to modify her behavior patterns. She could run away from Jorge, but she could not run away from herself.

Why did Emily have such an "exaggerated" reaction to such seemingly minor triggers? What traumatizing experience had caused her to develop this "area of excessive sensitivity," leading her to turn the most trivial word or gesture into a painful rejection?

Let me emphasize that it is not necessary to become conscious of the events that led to the formation of the complex in order to be freed from it. Because the complex is an internal mechanism, of an irrational and affective nature, it is not within the scope of the rational conscious to attempt to resolve it. The important thing is to liberate the emotional burden which caused the complex in the first place. I believe that the most effective, and also the gentlest, method of accomplishing this is to work in the realm of the imagination.

Thanks to our work in this realm, Emily was able to free a number of repressed emotions. Moreover, her older sister was able to relate certain events that could have been responsible for her abandonment complex. When Emily was five months old, her mother caught pneumonia and, because it was extremely infectious, she had to stay away from Emily for several weeks. This enforced separation almost certainly had a significant psychological impact. Later, when she was five years old, just as she was starting school, her mother got a job as a waitress, so she was gone every weekend and at least three nights a week. In her absence, Emily's 15-year-old sister took care of her. Emily's mother, who had always been there for her during the first five years of her life, was suddenly almost never at home. Emily was able to recall throwing tantrums in the morning to avoid going to school, and at night, to avoid going to bed. This lasted for almost three years. Then, for the third time in her life, Emily experienced an unbearable sense of abandonment. She had become very attached to her older sister but, at the age of 18, this "second mother" left home to work full-time. Emily could not bring herself to accept the sitters that were supposed to replace her sister. Realizing that her pain was not acknowledged, but rather interpreted as a temperamental outburst, she shut herself off from the outside world, concentrating on her school work and rejecting any form of emotional attachment. But a feeling of emptiness persisted. In spite of her individualistic, defensive attitude, she could not control her inner turmoil when she first met Jorge. She needed love so badly that she couldn't resist getting involved with him, and eventually marrying him. Her love for him was so strong that she was constantly afraid of losing him. This caused her to react disproportionately to the most insignificant event, whether real or imagined, that served to confirm her fears.

When a person with this kind of complex feels abandoned by his partner, he relives the initial sense of abandonment brought on by his relationship with his mother or father. An apparently insignificant situation can trigger a whole range of confused, unbearable emotions that make him unconsciously relive a time of suffering or abandonment, a crisis or a death. The partner that triggers the pain represents the lack of love from the past. He becomes threatening because he is the source of intolerable emotions. The person who manifests this kind of complex is so afraid of being rejected and unloved that he will choose to leave, to abandon the other rather than be abandoned yet again. Moreover, when he feels pushed away, he himself starts to push away, which inevitably leads to the very rejection from which he wanted to protect himself. Running away and rejection are the characteristic defense mechanisms of those harboring an abandonment complex. They run away because the mere presence of the loved one confronts them with their initial lack of love, and they reject in order to punish the other for having hurt them. Their fear of being abandoned is sometimes so overpowering that they choose to live alone rather than endure the suffering. This is the catch-22 that the "abandonee" is caught up in: to escape the suffering of feeling unloved, he runs away or rejects the person he is involved with, but when he is alone, he feels an overwhelming need for love that can only be satisfied by the very relationship he is running from.

Only a partner who truly loves the abandonee, who is well acquainted with the problem and who is therefore able to understand and accept the reactions caused by the complex without assuming responsibility for it, feeling guilty or trying to take charge can help him satisfy his fundamental need.

Although it is not sufficient in itself, the support of such a partner in being gentle, taking time and providing love can help the abandonee in his psychotherapeutic progress toward freedom. When they feel deprived of love, those who manifest this kind of complex may become disillusioned with life itself. In fact, it was for this very reason that Carl, at the urging of his partner, Edward, started coming to see me for treatment.

Carl was the second of three children. When he was only 18 months old his older brother died after being hit by a car. Two months later his sister, Lucy, was born. Absolutely devastated by the death of her son, Carl's mother transferred all her affection onto the only one who could relieve her suffering: little baby Lucy. Feeling neglected,

Carl's behavior toward his mother and sister became aggressive, and so they rejected him. Over the years, he developed a profound hatred for these two women, which he projected onto all members of the female sex. What little love and attention he did get came from his father, who had tried to forget his pain in his work and so was almost never home. Because of his aggressive behavior, Carl never got along well with women. His first experiences of love and sex were with men, but these relationships never lasted long because his lovers never fulfilled his expectations or his emotional void. Fear of being abandoned turned into aggression each time he felt rejected or excluded. The slightest gesture, the briefest silence was interpreted as a sign of rejection and drove him into a terrible rage. Thus, his attitude earned him exactly the opposite of what he wanted, that is, rejection instead of love. Each time a relationship came to an end, he swore he would never get involved with anyone again. But his need for love was so strong that, soon afterwards, caught up in the cycle of non-satisfaction, he would fall into the same trap all over again.

Fortunately for Carl, his relationship with Edward started out on a different note entirely. Up until then, he had never revealed anything about himself to his partners, but he met Edward at a clinic for recovering alcoholics. At one point in the group therapy sessions, Carl told his life story, so Edward was familiar with his past. Because of this, after they had been living together for a few months, Edward (who was having a hard time dealing with Carl's aggressive, nagging behavior) suggested that Carl begin seeing a psychotherapist. I really believe that the protracted healing process we began then could never have come about without Edward's help and support.

When I started working with Carl, I really had no idea where the process would lead him in the content. Because the CNDA lets the client direct the helping relationship, the psychotherapist's job is to be ready to deal with the results, which vary from one person to the next. After uncovering his abandonment complex, Carl went through an initial period of acceptance. This dismantled a number of his defense mechanisms, and reduced his level of aggressivity. We continued in this direction, letting him go through the evolutionary stages as he felt able to experience them. Indeed, whatever pace we may set for ourselves, it is important to realize that one does not shake off an abandonment complex as one would a cold. In a therapeutic context, it takes time, a great deal of acceptance on the part of the helper, and a secure emotional atmosphere if the improvement is not to deteriorate into stagnation. The most important factor is learning to live with the complex. Since the complex is sustained by extremely intense feelings and emotions, the psychotherapist's creative nondirective attitude and his warm and attentive presence form the essential ingredients for the process of liberation and change. This sort of attitude is vital, not only when working with those suffering from an abandonment complex, but also with those harboring other complexes, such as the sibling rivalry complex, for example.

2. The sibling rivalry complex

Sibling rivalry complexes take root in early childhood. In most cases, children are happy to have a little brother or sister, but sometimes the older sibling takes unkindly to being displaced from the center of his mother's and father's attention. This phase in his young life can be relatively brief and painless, as long as the parents include the firstborn in their time spent with the new arrival, and as long as they don't require the older child to sacrifice everything for the younger one. Unfortunately, however, many mothers find the baby's demands all-absorbing, and they end up either punishing or rejecting the older child whenever he asks for attention, makes demands or manifests feelings of jealousy. In other cases, the baby is seen as intruding on the parents' relationship with the older child, and is consequently met with rejection. The parents' attitude in these situations is all-important, for it determines whether or not the child will emerge from this stage in his life with a sibling rivalry complex.

How is this complex manifested in the lives of those who suffer from it? Mucchielli writes that such people experience all their relationships, whether with family members, lovers, friends or colleagues, as a battleground. Their competitive spirit is hard to bear, not only because they always want to be in first place, but also because they react with jealous aggression whenever anyone tries to usurp their position. Since the initial struggle took place within the family unit, every subsequent relationship he has recreates that initial triangle, involving the mother, the brother or sister and himself, causing him to project his envious feelings onto others. The person suffering from a sibling rivalry complex is absolutely convinced that everyone he meets is jealous of him and wants to take his place, and that he has to be constantly competing against a host of rivals to keep what is rightfully his.

Let us return to Carl who, you will recall, lost his claim on his mother's attention when his little sister Lucy, was born. As a result, he began to hate his mother and sister, and his behavior toward them became aggressive. This aggressivity led him to unconsciously seek out relationships in which he had a rival, thus recreating the initial triangle. I return to Carl's story here because it is also relevant in this context: the sibling rivalry complex is often linked to the abandonment complex because the child who feels abandoned has suffered rejection at the hands of his mother or father and has witnessed the younger—or older—brother or sister usurping his rightful place. Before Carl met Edward, he almost always fell in love with a man who already had a partner and he would inevitably get hurt by the resulting triangle; in his fight for first place, he was always the loser, because of his jealousy, hostility, lack of trust and aggression. This fits the pattern for people harboring complexes, whose behavior and attitude often earn them the opposite of what they seek. Because they lost in the initial struggle, they unconsciously place themselves in relationships that repeat the same scenario. They react spontaneously and exaggeratedly to an external trigger that makes them unconsciously relive those past events that brought them such suffering. Moreover, they have no control over the recurrent nature of this trigger, because they are unaware of the internal mechanism that repeatedly activates the process.

Catherine's story will give us a better understanding of how this mechanism works. When Catherine was five years old, her father left the family, and she never saw him again. She was deeply attached to him, and couldn't get over being separated from him. After he left, she frequently had severe night-time asthma attacks, which were so serious that her mother feared for her life. Catherine was 23 when she came to see me. Tall, slender, strikingly pretty and obviously very intelligent, she was undeniably attractive to men but was unable to maintain a relationship for more than a few weeks. As soon as she became attached to someone, she would fear being eventually abandoned, and walk out on him. Her unconscious fear of the pain she had felt when her father left made her reluctant to make any kind of emotional investment.

However, the real reason she had come into psychotherapy was her troubled relationship with her mother and her brother, James, who was a year older than her. Catherine had always identified with her father and, after he left, she became the outsider in a triangle involving her mother and her brother. In her eyes, the two shared a bond from which she was excluded. She did everything to get her mother's attention: tantrums, bribery and, twice, attempted suicide, but nothing worked. Her mother preferred James. Catherine felt such hatred and jealousy for her brother that, at the age of 18, she left home to live by herself. Her brother also left, eight months later, to live with his girlfriend. Thinking that the coast was now clear for her to claim her mother's attention, she began inviting herself over for dinner. But each time she called her mother, she would find that her brother, who just so happened to be visiting, had got there before her. And so the triangle continued: Catherine was convinced that her brother got all the attention, leaving her out in the cold. She was jealous of James; jealous of the bond between him and their mother, jealous of his girlfriend and of his many friends. In fact, her brother was as sociable as Catherine was unsociable.

Catherine's friendships only ever lasted a short period of time because she was always trying to occupy center stage. As a result, she had chosen to withdraw, but found solitude no more satisfactory than painful relationships. Her sibling rivalry complex, coupled with her abandonment complex, made any affective relationship almost torture for her, with each involvement driving her deeper into despair. Instead of being open to her problems, she tried to protect herself from them with a wall of rationalization that completely cut her off from herself and from others. Catherine was ashamed of her pain, anger and jealousy and, because she didn't freely express her feelings, they emerged in the form of explanations, justifications, criticism and disapproval. When others retreated in the face of these, she felt confirmed in her sense of rejection.

Freeing people from these kinds of complexes requires a thorough knowledge of the mental processes involved. Figure 3.4 illustrates the unsatisfactory mental process that Catherine was going through.

Figure 3.4

OUTSIDE WORLD

Trigger ⟶
- *non-acknowledgment of masculinity*

INNER WORLD

1. Difficult-to-deal-with emotions
   - *grief*
   - *sadness*
   - *anger*
   - *fear of rejection*
   - *fear of humiliation by mother and by women (amplified by inferiority complex)*
   ↓
2. Defence mechanisms
   - *denial*
   - *repression*
   ↓
3. Patterns
   ↓
4. Unsatisfied needs

As long as Catherine was unable to discern how the perceived lack of attention from her mother, her brother or her friends acted as a trigger for her, then she was doomed to repeat the same unsatisfactory behavior patterns. Before she could break out of this automatic internal system, she had to uncover and accept her deep-seated need to be loved and listened to. Also, she had to take the necessary steps to satisfy her fundamental needs, for the inner imbalance brought on by their non-satisfaction caused her a great deal of suffering. The creative nondirective approach sheds just this kind of light: the psychotherapist trained in this approach is aware of the mental process and is thus able to elucidate his client's internal mechanisms when he feels sufficiently conversant with the latter's personal history. This is not something he does arbitrarily, but only when the helpee has provided him with specific facts, such that his elucidation does not interrupt the latter's progress, nor impel him in a particular direction.

There are many other examples I could mention to illustrate the sibling rivalry complex, but Alexander's case is probably the most salient. He and his brother worked for the same company, but Alexander was incredibly jealous of Eli, and this had made him very manipulative. He had "bought" his way into everyone's good books with presents, compliments and small favors, and had then proceeded to demolish his brother's reputation, making him out to be a monster. Eli reacted violently to the ensuing rejection that came from almost all sides, which merely served to confirm Alexander's assertions.

One day, the company manager decided to transfer Eli to a branch in another city, where he immediately made a strong positive impression. He soon won everyone over with his honesty, openness, sense of organization and hard work. He was soon made a manager and, over the next two years, went from one promotion to the next. Alexander was beside himself with jealousy and despair. It was almost a year later that he finally sought my professional help. By this time his younger sister, who was having severe financial problems, had gone back to live with their parents. Although he was financially self-sufficient,

Alexander was still living at home, and the arrival of this rival left him feeling alone and abandoned. Recreating the original triangle that had developed between his mother, his brother and himself, he tried to gain the upper hand through manipulation, but this time it didn't work. He tried to pass his sister off as a parasite and a slut but she, in turn, retaliated, giving him the same kind of reputation at home as he had given Eli at work. It was when he realized that his number-one weapon was no longer effective that Alexander broke down.

Alexander felt the need to face up to his inner suffering when his manipulative behavior no longer worked in his favor. The process by which he became aware of his sibling rivalry complex took him to the depths of his repressed anger, pain and jealousy. Above all, it was the ability to accept the feelings that he had repressed as shameful that allowed his inner work to move forward; this allowed him to free himself from the suffering in his past and to lead a simpler life, in which he could be himself and acknowledge his strengths as well as his weaknesses.

Alexander's story provides yet another illustration of the fact that a sibling rivalry complex, left unresolved and unaccepted, can cause us to fall into uncontrollable behavior patterns that prevent us from being at peace with ourselves and with others because we don't know how to protect ourselves from it. This kind of complex, which in itself can generate psychic imbalance, often goes hand in hand with another, equally disturbing kind—the insecurity complex.

3. The insecurity complex

The insecurity complex, as its name implies, arises from an unsatisfied need for security. It is brought about first and foremost by a lack of security and love in an individual's life but—no less significantly—by the insecurity unconsciously instilled in him by those involved in his upbringing. And, finally, it is brought about by the universal, obligatory imposition of principles and beliefs, without respect for individual differences. All these factors contribute to the formation of the insecurity complex, which is manifested through various forms of anxiety and obsession. Haunted by the fear of illness, loss, death, change and the unexpected, the insecure person tends to establish an inner defense structure that, in the end, does not provide sufficient protection to calm his fears—as was the case with Jackie. When I first met her, she was 45 years old and had come to see me for help in freeing herself from an obsessive fear that prevented her from sleeping, leaving home or leading a normal life. A palmist had told her three weeks earlier that he had read death in her hands. I sensed right away that this might be the manifestation of an insecurity complex, and so I accompanied Jackie along the path she chose, with attentiveness, acceptance and love.

Insecure people will often consult all manner of "seers" to relieve their anxieties. They also tend to equip their houses or apartments with locks, safes and the latest alarm systems, and to accumulate money, food, insurance and other things that make them feel secure, just as Jackie did. She never gave anything away, and made others pay for all the favors she did for them. Over the years, she had managed to save thousands of dollars, which she hoarded in case something unforeseen should happen to her. In fact, she was ingenious in thinking up new ways to prepare herself for the accidents, illnesses and catastrophes supposedly awaiting her. Driven by these obsessive fears, she would get up two or three times each night after she had gone to bed, to check that the door was firmly locked, that the windows were tightly shut, that the stove was turned off, and so on and so forth. Each time the phone rang, she began to imagine all the bad news she might hear, so she never answered it. Because of her complex, she mistrusted everyone, and lived in constant fear.

After a number of sessions, Jackie came to understand her internal structures and learned to take a different approach to her complex. When she left psychotherapy, she felt less anxious, but had not been completely freed from her suffering and insecurity. A structure built up over decades can not be torn down in a matter of weeks. The process evolves in stages, at a progressive pace dictated by the client's own experiences.

I talked to Jackie six months later, and learned that she had completely given up her habit of consulting specialists in order to reassure herself. She said that she had just come back from a trip organized by the church she attended. Occasionally, she experienced the same fear and anxiety that had driven her to become a recluse in her apartment, but now she was able to distract herself from them by going out, and this helped her to realize, more and more with each passing day, that her fears had no basis in reality. Her decision to shut herself off from others in an attempt to protect herself had merely aggravated her problem; now, she had adopted a new lifestyle that was more open, giving her the human contact she so desperately needed. Her insecurity complex had not disappeared, but because she was aware of how it operated, she had learned a *modus vivendi* that caused her less suffering. I was astonished at Jackie's progress, since I knew only too well how difficult her life had been.

Jackie's mother had died when she was barely two years old. Her father had remarried a few months later. His new wife was a cabaret singer who felt that Jackie's presence restricted her freedom, so she told her husband he had to decide between her and the child. Shortly thereafter, Jackie was placed in an orphanage. She spent three years there, and was later adopted by a childless couple, with whom she lived more or less happily for many years. In her final year of elementary school, her adoptive father had a serious accident that left him a paraplegic. He lost his job, and his wife—who had very little formal schooling—had to find a way of supporting the family. Since she didn't want to be separated from Jackie, she decided to take in foster children. Suddenly, after having been an only child for seven years, Jackie found herself with an older sister and two younger brothers. Her life was completely turned upside down. During our conversations, she recalled that this period marked the beginning of her unbearable fear and anxiety. She would shut herself in her room, crying quietly, not wanting to add to her adoptive parents' distress.

Jackie's story reveals that the root of her complex was a sense of abandonment and insecurity, caused mainly by the loss of her mother, by the suffering and anxiety unconsciously communicated by her adoptive parents after the accident, and by frequent changes in her surroundings. When she left home to work full time in a garment factory, she was literally terrified. It was at this time that she began to erect inner defense structures. These were meant to alleviate her fears, but the only times she felt even partially at ease were when she was at work or when she visited her parents. Locked as she was into a rigid framework that she had constructed to make herself feel secure—but which was totally unsatisfactory in every respect—it took more than a few sessions of psychotherapy to enable her to break down her defense mechanisms and escape from her anguish. Psychotherapy is not a universal cure-all that can do its miraculous work in a matter of hours. Life always presents us with new obstacles to overcome, new problems to deal with. The main goal of the creative nondirective approach— and the Rogerian approach, as well—is not to help the client solve all his problems, but rather to help him confront them with more inner strength and more confidence in his ability to resolve them. This is the philosophy underlying the CNDA's method of dealing with the complexes of abandonment, sibling rivalry and insecurity, which we have already looked at, and also the castration complex, which is discussed below.

4. The castration complex

Mucchielli defines the castration complex as "a difficulty, for both men and women, in asserting themselves in an independent, responsible fashion and in leading their own lives, due to the castrating influence of their entourage" (p. 62, free translation). He goes on to say that this complex is manifested by a marked lack of spontaneity and initiative, an exaggerated tendency to be shy, submissive, obedient and dependent, and by a complete negation of all sexual desires. In order to mask their weakness, people harboring this complex may become rigid and domineering. In all cases, the subject is completely incapable of leaving the "castrating" parent, no matter how difficult the relationship may be.

There are many possible reasons, continues Mucchielli (pp. 62–63, free translation), why a person might harbor a castration complex. One factor could be the castrating mother, whose attempts to "achieve an ideal of purity" and mold her children's character lead her to humiliate her son or daughter, shame them and stifle their initiatives. Another factor is the mother or father's character assassination of the other parent. A young boy who hears his mother call his father mean and egotistical will refuse to identify with this supposedly monstrous being, thus depriving himself of an indispensable element in his search for inner balance. Through his sole identification with an "ideal mother," such a child's feminine qualities would develop at the expense of his masculinity, as was the case with Eric. At the age of 38, he was still living at home, and never missed an opportunity to criticize or attack his father, whose cruelty had ruined his mother's life—or so he imagined. Eric was very effeminate, and had never had any kind of physical contact with women; even his relationships with other men were, on the whole, platonic. Eric was essentially incapable of expressing his sexuality, and divided his time between his mother, his work and his books. He was extremely perceptive, knew how to manipulate others in order to get what he wanted, and did not hesitate to criticize or dominate those who opposed him in a most "castrating" fashion when things did not go his way. He was, in fact, an extremely sensitive person who could only assert himself when he felt powerful. He managed to get into everyone's good graces through his generosity and helpfulness, and the fear he spread around him, and these traits made those in his entourage dependent on him. Just as his mother had done with him, he manipulated and used others in an extremely subtle way. Indeed, how could anyone feel exploited by such a generous, helpful, attentive person? Like those in his entourage, Eric was unaware of his real motivations and, appearances to the contrary, he experienced a great deal of inner suffering, over which he had no control. As much as he knew how to dominate others, he was powerless when it came to controlling his inner world. Although he projected an image of strength and infallibility, deep down he was overwhelmed by his own vulnerability and weakness.

It is not easy to work with someone who is so afraid of revealing himself. The first time Eric came to see me was after the death of his mother. He was extremely distressed at finding himself alone with his father, whom he had always detested, but he was unable to leave home; even this difficult relationship was better than being alone. During our first few sessions, he told me his life story, with his father, mother and brother at center stage, and himself only in a minor supporting role. I felt that he trusted me but that he was still afraid to show his true self. I was honestly not surprised when, after the fifth session, he announced that he was feeling much better and would not be coming back. I respected his decision, knowing that any attempt to persuade him to continue with the psychotherapeutic process would be tantamount to destroying his trust in me and reinforcing his defense mechanisms. However, I did invite him to come back whenever he wished.

Eight months went by before Eric asked for another appointment, and by that time, he was ready to go further. He had, in fact, been evolving at his own pace all along, slowly increasing in self-awareness and especially self-acceptance. The last time I saw him, he had just left home to move in with another man for whom he had harbored a secret and platonic love for more than five years. As he became less "castrating" himself, he was able to build progressively more real and satisfying relationships with others, and was less afraid of being known for who he was. He was more conscious now of his need to dominate and manipulate in order to hide his weakness. However, he was sufficiently accepting of the process itself to accept the rate at which he was evolving.

Mucchielli emphasizes that many other factors are involved in the formation of castration complexes, such as overprotection, overindulgence, or parents' overwhelming fear of their children's sexuality and independence.

Fear of being humiliated, psychologically castrated or made to feel guilty either blocks an individual's ability to assert himself, or else makes him authoritarian and uncompromisingly self-assertive. In either case, the reaction arises from the suffering brought on by shame and repression, and the individual is unable to rid himself of his sense of inferiority and guilt.

5. The guilt complex

The guilt complex is among those most commonly encountered by psychotherapists. On an emotional level, according to Mucchielli, the person with a guilt complex lives in constant fear of failure or mistakes, and ends up compensating for possible flaws with an overdeveloped sense of duty. Such a person becomes a perfectionist who permits himself neither rest, relaxation nor pleasure, but spends his time scheming in an attempt to avoid the sense of failure he feels when things go wrong. In relating his activities, he has a tendency to minimize his successes and dramatize his failures, but the opinion of others is extremely important to him. He feels a strong need to ask for permission from others and to be acknowledged by them. Since he believes that he is always in the wrong, he either punishes himself, or searches out a form of external punishment in order to relieve his guilt.

In their defensive form, guilt complexes are generally manifested by a judgmental attitude. The person with a guilt complex becomes a dispenser of justice, the one who punishes others for their faults and mistakes. Unaware of his own guilt, he makes certain that others are aware of theirs.

Brought on by an upbringing marked by humiliation, shame, emotional blackmail and negative reinforcement, this type of complex makes the person who harbors it feel guilty of all pleasure, sexual or otherwise, guilty of his flaws, mistakes and thoughts, guilty each time he fails to adhere to the moral and religious principles instilled in him, guilty also of the unhappiness and suffering of others.

When I first met Evan, he was about 40 years old. A few months before he came to see me, he had left Helen, his wife of five years, because he felt that their relationship was slowly suffocating him. His need to be free prevented him from going back to her, but he nevertheless felt a great deal of guilt over the breakup of their marriage—which he believed was entirely his fault—and Helen, who was aware of these feelings, used them to control him. Evan thought that Helen was a wonderful woman, and that it was his fault that she had to endure the strain of a failed marriage. To relieve his guilt, he forced himself to see her regularly, and took upon himself most of the responsibility for raising their two-year-old daughter. In fact, he had arranged things in such a way that he paid dearly for his freedom.

There is a distinct tendency among men and women with guilt complexes to assume full responsibility for others' problems; when their attempts to resolve them fail, they become weighed down with guilt. The other tendency is to pass off all responsibility for their own past and for their difficulties onto others, which is what Helen did. In either case, the relationship suffers. By making Evan responsible for the failure of their marriage, Helen remained unaware of her own involvement, and hence remained unchanged. Instead, she tried to change her husband through accusations and manipulation. As I emphasized in an earlier chapter, when we want to change someone, and wait for that change to happen, the results are necessarily unsatisfactory.

As for Evan, he was bearing all the responsibility for his own behavior in the marriage, and also for Helen's, which completely distorted the relationship. To punish himself, and thus lessen his guilt, he denied his own needs. Because of this, he was constantly conveying contradictory messages to his wife, making real communication almost impossible. Their behavior created a mutual dependence that suffocated them both. Although they no longer lived together, and in fact disliked each other's company, each was incapable of completely cutting off all contact. Before he could make that final break, Evan had to learn to regain power over his own life by refusing to assume responsibility for Helen's behavior. After he became aware of how his mind operated in this situation, he was able to let himself hate Helen, a feeling that he had previously repressed. He realized that in many situations it was Helen, and not himself who was to blame. This attitude was neither unconscious nor compensatory, but an honest reaction to what he had experienced with her. Evan hated Helen for the guilt he had felt on her account, and for how it had made him dependent on her. Later, he was able to understand that he had recreated with her the same structure that had governed his relationship with his mother. With her, as with Helen, he had spent his whole life behaving as though he were guilty of everything, and this attitude had earned him nothing but criticism and disapproval.

His mother was distant, unfeeling and very strong-minded. Evan had always had difficulty relating to her because she simply could not accept her son's delicate, sensitive nature. He was punished severely and made to feel terribly guilty for the most trivial incidents: spilling his milk, losing a scarf or getting a bad mark in school. His fear of her, however, was tempered by a certain admiration—which was perhaps what led him to marry Helen. His wife was just like his mother: tall, slender, distant, and authoritarian. Since Helen was a very determined woman, she had high expectations of Evan; he, in turn, did all he could to win her approval.

Evan, though, was in a no-win situation. When he was with Helen he was made to feel constantly guilty, and when he left her, the guilt followed him. After the marriage broke up, he realized that the only way to avoid being suffocated by his feelings of guilt was to become aware of his complex, through inner work. He was determined not to leave psychotherapy until he had acquired some degree of independence, and this determination sustained him. As stated previously, complexes originate in intensely painful emotional experiences which are relived each time an external occurrence triggers the unconscious recollection of the initial trauma. This is the case for all the complexes we have looked at so far, and it also holds true for the inferiority complex.

6. The inferiority complex

There are many painfully shy people in the world who are deathly afraid of appearing ridiculous. These people are too inhibited to allow themselves any form of personal expression and are so intimidated by others that they will do anything to avoid drawing attention to themselves. They are hypersensitive, profoundly convinced of their own lack of ability and self-sufficiency. Consequently, as Mucchielli notes, they have no faith in themselves and are always putting themselves down. From every standpoint—looks, clothes, abilities, achievements, and so forth—they compare themselves to others and find themselves wanting.

The other way an inferiority complex might manifest itself is through an attitude of superiority, adopted as a form of defense against ridicule. Such people are often boastful, and irritating in their unceasing attempts to prove that they are right, that they know everything and that they are better than everyone else—better looking, more intelligent, more cultured, more capable. They are fond of criticizing others in order to build themselves up, of displaying their knowledge or exhibiting their bodies to satisfy their craving for attention and admiration. Like teenagers, they feel they have to rebel to show their rejection of the status quo.

Mucchielli cites many possible causes for the kind of inferiority complex common among adolescents: a belittling and negative attitude among those responsible for their upbringing, repeated failures at school and, occasionally, physical handicaps.

Jason, who was 49 years old when he began psychotherapy, had been struggling with this kind of complex since early childhood. At school, he had had trouble keeping up with the others, and his consistently poor performance had made him the butt of many cruel jokes at school and also at home, for his older brothers excelled academically. After he had failed a number of grades, he left school at a very young age to begin working. He always felt inferior to his three brothers, who followed in their father's footsteps and went on to university to study medicine, surgery and psychiatry.

When he was 22 years old, Jason married a woman who had children from a previous relationship. In spite of his possessive, jealous behavior, he was ashamed of his wife and rarely took her to visit his family. In fact, he often put her down in the presence of others, to make himself look better. Although he was a regular at the local bars and taverns, he worked tirelessly and made sure his wife and children never lacked for anything. Heavy drinking helped him forget his deep-seated fear of ridicule. When he came home drunk he would behave very arrogantly toward his wife and insult her, but deep down he was terrified that she would one day grow tired of him and leave.

Jason and his wife had four children but his favorite had always been his youngest daughter, Nancy: an intelligent, talented girl. He wanted her to become the professional that he had never been, and was very proud of her good marks at school, sparing no expense to pay for her education. Nancy was a lot like her father, having inherited his sensitivity, generosity and diligence. She and her father were very close; in fact, she was the only one in the family who could really talk to him, or who could get through to him without making him feel threatened. It was Nancy who suggested that he seek treatment for his drinking problem and who, several months later, encouraged him to go into psychotherapy. As he passed through the stages of self-examination, Jason became aware of many factors that contributed to his growing self-esteem. First, he realized that his low marks at school were due not to a lack of intelligence but to a significant emotional void that had inhibited his learning process. In group therapy with other recovering alcoholics, he discovered that his honesty, sensitivity and ability to listen were great assets to the group, and that he was highly regarded among its members, many of whom had gone through ordeals similar to his own.

The time Jason spent in psychotherapy brought him to a far better understanding of his mental processes. He realized why all those contemptuous smiles and mocking glances from his former schoolmates had crushed him, undermining his self-confidence and ruining all his subsequent relationships.

Figure 3.5 illustrates the unsatisfactory mental process that applies to Jason's case.

Figure 3.5

OUTSIDE WORLD   **INNER WORLD**

Trigger ⟶ **1. Emotions**
- *smiles, glances*
                          - *fear of ridicule*
                          - *fear of failure*
                          - *anger amplified by inferiority complex*

                          ↓

2. Defense mechanisms
                          - *criticism*
                          - *superiority*
                          - *escape into alcoholism*

                          ↓

3. Inferior pattern
                          ↓

4. Unsatisfied need to be acknowledged

These chapters out of the lives of Jason, Alexander, Carl, and Jackie—to mention just a few—may resonate in other people's experience, too, for complexes are far from uncommon. They all originate in profound suffering; becoming aware of them, recognizing them for what they are and accepting the fact that they are an integral part of us are all vital stages in alleviating the pain they can cause. We need to treat this "area of excessive sensitivity," rooted deep within the psyche, with great respect; we need to listen to it if we are to protect ourselves from it and, ultimately, become free.

A complex plays a significant role in the psychic makeup of many individuals, making them extremely vulnerable to certain external triggers. Before we can become aware of our mental processes, we need to gradually sort out their component elements and trace them back to the emotions by which they are triggered. Since these emotions are usually painful, we try to escape that pain through the defense mechanisms that we unconsciously deploy, leaving our fundamental needs unsatisfied. These mechanisms are examined in the following section.

E. DEFENSE MECHANISMS

As conceived by the CNDA, "defense mechanism" refers to the means by which the psyche unconsciously protects itself from the unpleasant feelings that emerge from our relationships—either as they are, or as the way we imagine them to be.

When defense mechanisms are first erected, they are nothing less than a means of survival. A child may retreat behind one to escape from unbearable suffering. If he is feeling rejected, for example, he may attempt to avoid a recurrence of that feeling by unconsciously withdrawing, tuning out or running away. This kind of unconscious behavior, however, does have negative physical and mental consequences, since the walls a person puts up to protect himself will eventually suffocate him. Because the energy needed to maintain those walls comes from the same source as his vital creative force, he ends up using only a fraction of his latent potential. His relationships with others also suffer, because his defense mechanisms prevent him from showing his true self, even though he is not aware of this. Finally, he is so busy trying to protect himself that he cannot get in touch with his emotions: he can neither become aware of his mental processes nor satisfy his fundamental needs.

The CNDA, however, does not advocate eliminating defense mechanisms since, in many cases, they are necessary to ensure that the psyche continues to function. Rather than attempting to tear them down, its goal is to help the individual become aware of them so that he can see how they disrupt his relationships and how he is personally affected by them.

Becoming aware of and accepting one's defense mechanisms, and the emotions that activate them, are the two key steps toward mastering one's fears through the use of "protective mechanisms." This means that, instead of deploying them unconsciously, he will be conscious of the process he is involved in. However, before I discuss these protective mechanisms in greater detail, I would like to return to the defense mechanism and examine what methods the psyche unconsciously uses to defend itself against suffering.

The theory of defense mechanisms was first developed by Freud (psychoanalysis) and, later, by Perls (Gestalt therapy). The CNDA draws on these two schools in formulating its own creative nondirective concept of defense mechanisms. Psychoanalysis sees the defense mechanism as a means by which the individual unconsciously protects himself from inner conflict occasioned by the influence of his own drives, desires and instincts on the external world. In contrast to this, the CNDA defines it as a means by which the psyche unconsciously protects itself from the unpleasant feelings that emerge from the real or imagined relationship. These unconscious means can take on different forms: for example, a person might defend himself by stifling all emotional expression, or by attributing his own emotions to others.

In either case, the emotion ends up being denied or repressed because it elicits fear and because it is seen as unacceptable. Instead of expressing our grief, aggression, jealousy, fear or mistrust, we tend to stifle these "shameful" emotions, unconsciously struggling to protect ourselves from them via such inner structures as repression, introjection, escape, rationalization, confluence, self-punishment, projection and the adoption of a persona.

1. Repression

Repression is a defense mechanism that manifests itself at a very early age. To avoid being judged, a child will suppress—that is, avoid expressing—any emotions deemed incorrect or abnormal by those in charge of his upbringing. By repressing his emotions in this manner, he may end up no longer feeling them, thus preventing him from realizing who he is and what he wants.

Repressed emotions can have dire consequences, as the following story illustrates. Lisette came to see me after Jim left her. During their relationship, she had almost never told Jim of her dissatisfaction for fear of hurting, displeasing or losing him, but this had not prevented him from leaving. Losing her partner was hard for Lisette to accept and to deal with. She was angry at him for having hurt her, and consumed by the desire to punish him in some way. On the other hand, she felt guilty for wanting to hurt the man she loved—a man, moreover, whom she had always sheltered when they were still together. Her feelings of guilt became more and more pronounced until she started to believe she was a monster. Because of this negative self-image, she rarely spoke about herself, and completely repressed her feelings, emotions and desires. She was thus unconsciously but inexorably drawn into a behavior cycle that caused her a great deal of distress. The diagram in Figure 3.6 represents this cycle.

Figure 3.6

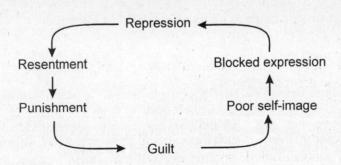

I have observed that this cycle is common to all repressed individuals because they do not allow themselves to express what they experience, and also because they are withdrawn (repression). They get angry at others for not satisfying their needs and for making them suffer (resentment). As a result, they try to get even in underhand ways, attacking the other through insinuation and indirect criticism (punishment), but this leaves them feeling guilty and mean (negative self-image). They unconsciously seek to hide this unpleasant image (inhibition of expression), to repress it (repression), and present instead a façade of kindness, generosity, and forgiveness which draws them back into the same painful, unsatisfactory cycle.

Repression is harmful and destructive for the individual and for his relationships. We have already seen that repressed emotions do not simply disappear, but are registered by the body or picked up by the psyche, thus acting against the subject and eventually crushing him. For this reason I believe it is vital for all helpers to teach their helpees to listen to their emotions, to accept them and to express them in a responsible manner. However, no one can teach what he does not know. The inner work that leads the helper to learn this lesson himself is, in my opinion, an essential foundation for all professionals in the fields of physical and mental health care. It is precisely the helper's nondirective attitude that encourages an awareness of emotions and the gradual dismantling of defense mechanisms, and also fosters acceptance of the emotions denied by those mechanisms. Suppressed emotions do not free us; on the contrary, they imprison us. Repression is a defense mechanism that suffocates even as it protects—as is another mechanism that helps to maintain repression: introjection.

2. Introjection

Marie Petit (1984) defines introjection as "a way of feeling, judging and evaluating that we have borrowed from someone else, usually our parents, and that we have integrated into our behavior patterns without ever assimilating it" (p. 36, free translation).

The introjected attitude or idea is grafted onto a person, preventing him from discovering and displaying his true personality. Because he is imbued with judgments, principles, values and beliefs that are not his, and which he adopted to avoid losing his parents' love, he is unable to define himself or to develop his creativity. Thus, introjection debases man to the level of a mere copyist, depriving him of his status as a creator. It forces him to maintain a persona, draining away vast quantities of vital and creative energy.

The story of Jeanette comes to mind as a possible representation of this particular kind of defense mechanism. Her parents had raised her very strictly and, by the time she was 35, the principles she had been taught were so deeply ingrained that they prevented her from satisfying her need for love and kept her, in spite of herself, both single and celibate. She refused to respond to a co-worker's obvious interest (while still subtly encouraging it) because he was seven years younger than her, divorced, and not a Christian. The introjected attitude she had learned from her parents held that a respectable woman should always marry a man older than herself and that any man who was divorced must be unreliable and dishonest, especially if he was not a practising Catholic.

There is nothing harmful about such beliefs as long as they are well integrated and are part of the individual's true personality. However, when they make a person tormented and unhappy, as in Jeanette's case, something is wrong. There is no absolute truth, no ideal set of principles or beliefs; there is only that which best suits and defines each one of us. What is ideal for one may not necessarily be so for another. When a principle is adopted because it reflects an individual's true self and builds on his own experience, it will necessarily help him toward self-actualization. But when a belief has been grafted onto him, it will only succeed in separating him from his true self, making it impossible for him to satisfy his fundamental needs. The child who patterns his behavior after the principles of his parents and teachers does so precisely because he wants to be loved. Paradoxically, however, those same introjected attitudes will later rob him of the love he needs so much, for introjection leads to the creation of a persona, rather than to the development of a real person.

For example, if we have been taught that feeling jealous is shameful and unacceptable, then we will refuse to acknowledge such feelings when they arise: we will deny them, repress them and hide them from others—but not without consequences. Repressed emotions have an affect on our relationships with others. By inhibiting real communication, they set up barriers between partners, preventing them from satisfying their need for love. Defensive attitudes rob us of the very thing we seek, namely, the satisfaction of our fundamental needs.

No matter what the belief, if it is introjected, it prevents us from attaining complete self-actualization. All those preconceptions about old age that are passed on from one generation to the next can make that period an unfruitful one for some people, as any kind of significant achievement is simply blocked off. It can be devastating to believe that, as we get older, we lose our looks and our memory, become useless and impotent, are no longer able to work or make love; that we become, in fact, somewhat infantile. Armed with these exaggeratedly pessimistic beliefs, conveyed by our educational institutions and reinforced by society in general, people today prepare to face an unhappy old age. Lozanov (1978), the father of suggestology, labeled these beliefs "negative suggestions." It was his opinion that they inhibited the expression of our vital and creative potential.

Being extremely impressionable, children often adopt introjected beliefs that can mark them for life. A story I heard at a conference given by Jacques Salomé in Montreal in September 1987 made a great impression on me, and I will use it here as an example; certain details may escape me, but the essentials remain unchanged. The story goes like this: One day, when Julia was still a little girl, her aunt was giving her a bath. As she washed her, they chatted about this and that and, when Julia pointed to her clitoris and asked her aunt what it was, the latter replied simply: "That, my dear, is a good-luck charm."

When she got out of the bath, the little one ran into the kitchen and said: "Mommy, look! I've got a good-luck charm." Her mother replied: "Good-luck charm? I don't think so! It's more like a bad-luck charm."

An experience like that, coupled with an upbringing of a similar nature, might well lead the child to adopt her mother's negative attitude, allowing this introjection to influence her own attitude toward sex once she matured.

Introjection is a defense mechanism that not only prevents a person from discovering his own personality, but also deprives him of the precious asset that is freedom.

It is impossible to free oneself from introjected attitudes without first becoming aware of them. However, that in itself is not enough. Discovering and respecting our own personality goes hand in hand with dismantling the other personality, the one grafted onto us by our upbringing. Both these steps require that we get in touch with ourselves, that we feel a real need to face up to our inner turmoil and accept ourselves without attempting to escape from ourselves.

3. Escape and avoidance

Escape is a means of fleeing fear. The need to create an unconscious refuge from certain painful experiences is common to all mankind, and each individual adopts his own personal method of retreating from events or people that cause him too much suffering. It is not, in fact, so much external reality he is fleeing from, as the fears it makes him experience. One person may escape into an imaginary world, or become absorbed in his work; another may use sleep, television, sports or music. In fact, many of us avoid reality in one way or another: travel, constant change, sex, drugs, alcohol, cigarettes and food on the one hand; meditation, spirituality, prayer and charitable works on the other.

There is nothing inherently wrong with most of these means of escape. They become harmful when they are used excessively and unconsciously, over a long period, in order to run away from an emotion that cannot be expressed. When a means of escape has been unconsciously adopted as a defense mechanism, it prevents an individual from satisfying his fundamental needs. However, it may legitimately be used in a conscious manner, when an individual chooses to stand back from certain people or situations in order to sort out his emotions, and recognize why he is acting defensively.

The case of Sean might help clarify some of these distinctions. Although he loved his parents, he didn't get along well with them. Each time they had an argument, he would leave the house in a rage, slamming the door, and stay away for several weeks. Once he did go back, it wouldn't be long before they were quarreling again, and he would be storming out with the same inner torment. When he went into psychotherapy, he admitted being very upset by this situation, but felt powerless to change it. Why? Because at home he was not conscious of his feelings. When he was there, he felt an unbearable emotional turmoil from which, unconsciously, he tried to protect himself, using criticism, disapproval and accusations.

While in CNDA-directed therapy, Sean discovered that the reason he went home again after each fight was that he needed to be loved and acknowledged; and each time he was disappointed, because he felt his parents didn't care for him. In order to get their attention, he would lose his temper, make them angry at him and then leave, just like he had done when he was a young child.

Since the family provides the setting in which most of our complexes, defense mechanisms and behavior patterns are formed, it is obvious that by staying in that environment we are perpetuating our unsatisfactory mental processes. We are confronted with the very triggers that were responsible for creating our complexes in the first place. Frequent contact with the family that caused us so much pain and frustration, no matter what our age, may make us relive past suffering—unless we have become aware of our mental processes, and taken steps to consciously protect ourselves. If so, we can avoid falling into the same unsatisfactory behavior patterns that, in the past, prevented us from achieving independence.

This is, in fact, what Sean did. He made a conscious decision to stay away from his family, instead of continuing his involuntary pattern of escape. When we are immersed in an environment that maintains our complexes and behavior patterns by influencing our unconscious, it is difficult—and, in many cases, impossible—to break away and gain a measure of self-awareness. Standing back helps us do just that, and also strengthens the psyche which, like the body, becomes weak and vulnerable in situations of prolonged suffering.

When we realize how we have been running away and why, we can use our means of escape consciously and constructively, instead of falling into the same unconscious patterns and being left with the same unhappiness.

When Sean finally went back to visit his family he was more aware of his mental processes and he knew what triggers to be wary of. He thus had much more power over himself. He was determined not to fall into the same automatic behavior he had exhibited before and, if he did, he knew he could more easily regain control of the situation. In the end, he didn't run away, but consciously chose to withdraw in order to gain a better vantage point.

Escape, as a defense mechanism, is not only manifested by a desire to withdraw into oneself, leave or cut people out of one's life; it is also manifested by avoidance. When Charlotte was with other people, such as friends, family and co-workers, she never disagreed, never expressed her needs or ideas because she was afraid she might offend someone, and be criticized or rejected. The only way she dared voice an opinion was by using such generalizations as "In today's society, very few people would contest that . . . " and "Almost everyone I know seems to think that . . . ." Her unconsciously adopted defensive attitude made her frustrated each time she was in a group situation, for when no one reacted to her vague, impersonal statements, she supposed that the others simply overlooked her.

This defense mechanism could perhaps be traced to Charlotte's adolescence, when she and her mother had gone through a rough period in their relationship. Her mother reacted violently whenever Charlotte expressed an idea that ran counter to her beliefs. Charlotte came to fear these explosions of temper, and learned to either keep quiet, or else speak in generalizations. Although this solved the problem in the short term, it prevented her from satisfying a deep-seated need to be acknowledged. In fact, it was precisely because of an incident of non-acknowledgement in the workplace that she had come into psychotherapy. She was angry that a promotion, which she felt should have been hers, had gone to a colleague who was less qualified and had less seniority than she. Her faultless work and professionalism had been passed over in favor of her colleague's self-assertiveness and ability to express herself. Because she represented all that Charlotte longed to be, her co-worker came to represent a threat, but Charlotte's fear of disapproval prevented her from dealing with the situation by confronting either her colleague or her employer.

Charlotte's habits of repression, avoidance and escape deprived her of a fundamental need. Unless she learned to deal with these involuntary structures which cut her off from herself and her needs, she would be unable to initiate any change. Defence mechanisms, as I mentioned earlier, force us to act unconsciously in order to protect us from unbearable emotions, especially fear. Thus Charlotte had chosen escape and avoidance as means of protection against her fear of criticism and rejection, giving others the power to direct her actions by belittling and negating herself in their name. She never voiced her own opinions and went along with everyone else's ideas in the hope of being liked and acknowledged, but because she was not expressing her true self, no one acknowledged her anyway.

Figure 3.7 illustrates the unsatisfactory mental process that applies to Charlotte's case.

Figure 3.7

OUTSIDE WORLD

Trigger ⟶
- *lack of acknowledgment from employer*

INNER WORLD

1. Emotions
- *envy*
- *fear of displeasing*
- *fear of shocking*
- *fear of judgment*
- *fear of rejection*

↓

2. Defense mechanisms
- *avoidance*
- *escape*
- *repression*

↓

3. Unsatisfied need to be acknowledged

As we have seen before, because defense mechanisms interfere with communication, they supply exactly the opposite of what a person needs. The defensive person involuntarily cuts himself off from his emotions and, since he is not in touch with himself, he is also cut off from others. Therefore, when a person is repressed, takes on introjected attitudes, or resorts to escape or avoidance, he ends up disappointed and frustrated, since this behavior creates more, instead of less, distance between himself and others, and once again, his fundamental needs go unsatisfied. This same phenomenon can also be observed in situations where rationalization is used.

4. Rationalization

Rationalization is a defense mechanism that drives people to use reason as an unconscious means of resolving emotional difficulties. In other words, we tend to rationalize because we are afraid of the feelings that arise within us and that we do not allow ourselves to experience. It is among the most common of all the defense mechanisms, and also the most detrimental to interpersonal relations. Indeed, it obstructs the relationship precisely because it cuts the individual off from his experiences and from himself.

What are the signs that a person is deploying this particular defense mechanism? When he unconsciously suppresses his emotions in order to make justifications, generalizations and explanations, and to intellectualize or moralize. In some manifestations of this defense mechanism we may find a tendency to wield power over others—since he who generalizes and interprets often believes his viewpoint to be the only valid one. But rationalization can also reveal a certain lack of self-confidence. Because our emotions are at the center of the psyche, the very act of expressing them exposes our differences, our innermost being. This requires enough self-love for a person to be able to listen to and acknowledge himself, so that he can show himself as he is, with his innate subjectivity.

There is no doubt that our reasoning faculties are excellent tools for organizing and planning—without them our life would turn to absolute chaos. But we cannot allow our feelings to be ruled by those faculties. In that sense, their role is limited to helping us understand our mental structures, outside of emotional situations. When reason intervenes as the emotion is being experienced, it usually does so in a defensive manner, distorting reality, distracting attention from the real problem and—temporarily at least—severing the links of the relationship.

Another risk of using rationalization is that it can lead us to become dependent on belief systems. Sometimes, we use justifications and explanations to build up a rational case that we end up believing and getting others to believe, and that we hold as absolute truth. In their desire to escape painful emotions, some people may end up convincing themselves that they have no feelings, that they don't need love and that nothing frightens them. In the process, they end up becoming nothing more than rigid, false, impersonal beings.

Thus there are many different kinds of rationalization people use to avoid pain. When they are introduced unconsciously—in other words, as a defense mechanism—their beneficial effects are fleeting: they trap rather than liberate the user. This is so for all techniques that attempt to control the emotions because, just as some types of medication do, they control the pain temporarily, but leave the actual illness untouched.

Although these techniques may constitute a form of protection in certain circumstances, they do not enable us to get to the root of the problem. We must never lose sight of the fact that mental suffering is caused by emotions, and that the only way it can be relieved is by setting those emotions free. There are techniques that claim to control one's emotional experiences and tap the powers of positive thinking, and they can be helpful. However, if they are used as a means of rationalization, they cut the individual off from himself, impede his progress toward self-knowledge, and prevent him from discovering the liberating and creative power of his emotions.

Perhaps Maria's story will elucidate my point. Following a violent quarrel with her ex-husband, she was filled with excruciating feelings of hatred for several months, and even plotted to seek revenge. She was horrified that she could have such feelings and, in an attempt to escape them, she began to practise all sorts of techniques, and to recite lengthy prayers on the subject of love and forgiveness several times a day. After several weeks of these mental and spiritual "gymnastics," she was no further ahead—her hatred had not disappeared but had simply been deadened—so she decided to see a psychotherapist. While in therapy, she got in touch with the feelings that she had repressed and denied because she was afraid of the pain and guilt they could cause her. She realized first that, by accepting her hatred, she could get rid of it and that, subsequently, by shedding light on her mental processes, she could regain power over her life.

For many weeks, she had tried to rationalize her emotions, but it was not until she treated her feelings with respect and followed her instincts that she was able to regain her inner peace and find forgiveness.

Each time we generalize, moralize, interpret another's experience, justify ourselves or feel the need to explain our actions, we lose touch with what we really feel and, consequently, lose touch with others. We all rationalize at one time or another, but if we could heighten our awareness of this defense mechanism, we would have more genuine, more intense, longer and healthier relationships.

In fact, difficulties in relationships often originate in defensive attitudes that sever communication. Rationalization, as we have seen, can be a source of confusion and possible conflict, as can confluence.

5. Confluence

The theory of behavioral confluence was developed primarily by the school of Gestalt therapy. Marie Petit (1984) says that a person who displays confluent tendencies is "unable to distinguish between his own limits and those imposed by his environment" (p. 40, free translation). As conceived by the CNDA, *confluence is a defensive procedure that consists of denying the self in order to become absorbed by the other*. It results from a lack of self-knowledge, self-confidence, self-love and independence.

An individual may begin to display such tendencies when, as he falls out of touch with his own needs and limits, and stops listening to his emotions, he can no longer distinguish between himself and others. Fear of being rejected or criticized, fear of displeasing or disappointing others have led him to adopt other people's thoughts, preferences, beliefs—even their needs and emotions—regardless of whether they correspond to his own. He lives in a state of permanent confusion that prevents him from asserting himself, or fulfilling his potential. He appears to have no personality of his own and is, in fact, extremely dissatisfied because he can never enter into a real relationship with anyone; he loses contact with himself.

Since the "confluent" individual defines himself according to the various people he associates with, he has no opinion on anything, and his ideas change depending on who he is with. The relationships he formed with each of his parent figures were responsible for causing him to introject, at a very young age, the idea that to be loved and acknowledged he had to appropriate everything that others thought, believed and loved. This was how he chose to satisfy his fundamental need for love and self-worth. As he grew older, he repeated this strategy in every new relationship, until his dissatisfaction became acute. His fears—of disappointing, of being criticized, judged or rejected—led him to be so subservient to the other that he himself ceased to exist.

The only way of dismantling this widespread defense structure is for the subject to take responsibility for the consequences of expressing his true thoughts and feelings. This requires that he work on awareness and acknowledgment of the self, both of which require time and commitment.

Confluence is a stumbling block that psychotherapists, parents and teachers alike need to watch out for. If the helper becomes confluent with the helpee, help becomes impossible. Here again we see how crucial it is for the helper, whether he be a group leader, teacher, doctor or psychotherapist, to pursue his own inner work. Self-knowledge, the ability to come to terms with one's differences and to distinguish oneself from the other—these are all indispensable to an effective helping relationship. Let us suppose, for example, that the helpee relates a story from his past that is similar to something the helper has gone through. As a result, the latter may well display some confluent tendencies, projecting onto the helpee his own views, feelings and solutions, and thus driving him deeper into confusion and dependence.

At any given moment, literally thousands of relationships are being formed and destroyed because of confluence. The story of Gloria is a case in point.

When I first met Gloria, she was going through a bitter, vengeful separation from her husband—a process that was making her completely wretched. During the 12 years they had been married, Gloria had always felt she had to subordinate herself to her husband Jean-Paul, whom she admired tremendously. She hardly ever voiced her wishes, needs or opinions and when she did, it was in such a confused fashion that it was hard to understand what she meant. Unconscious of her confluence with Jean-Paul, Gloria never asserted herself because she had been afraid of losing him, but also because she knew only too well how he could turn against people who opposed him, and thus was frightened of what he might do. Jean-Paul was a man who made friends easily thanks to his generosity, sensitivity and willingness to help others. Unfortunately, he often misused their affection to manipulate them.

After she had been in therapy with me for several weeks, Gloria decided one day—following yet another situation in which she chose not to assert herself to avoid a confrontation—to show her true colors. Jean-Paul's reaction to her decision to stand up for herself, which she reached after much suffering and anxiety, cost her her marriage and her reputation. Jean-Paul, who could not accept the fact that his wife might assert herself and define her limits, decided to put her in her place. This sort of behavior is characteristic of manipulative people: when they fail to control the other through manipulation, they attempt to maintain their hold over them through punishment and revenge. Thus, Jean-Paul, whose kindness was widely acknowledged, revealed to Gloria's family and co-workers a number of secrets which she had told him over the years, and even showed around some excerpts from her letters which, taken out of context, could have appeared damning. She was well known in the small town where she lived, especially since she had been a teacher there for over 15 years, but Jean-Paul managed to convince all of their acquaintances that he was a "helpless victim," and just as they felt compassion for him, so they judged and rejected her. After that, she decided to break up with Jean-Paul, move out, and ask her employer to transfer her.

It was not until a few months later that she realized to what extent she had been responsible for her own downfall; her lack of self-confidence had been at the root of her suffering. Her relationship with Jean-Paul had cured her of trying to hold onto others by denying herself. Gloria understood that by resolving this particular pattern in her relationship with her ex-husband, she had freed herself from a habit that had burdened all her relationships. Although the experience had been painful, it had taught her how to define her limits and assert her right to be different. All her life, a confluent attitude had made Gloria content to let others shape her, and in the end she had even decided to run away rather than stand up for herself.

Gloria would never forget the lessons she learned from that devastating experience. First, she realized that she had lost many of her own friends and acquaintances because their attitudes had become confluent with those of Jean-Paul, even though they were not directly involved in the situation. Second, she recognized that by being confluent with certain people, as opposed to asserting her own preferences and opinions, she had alienated some of her friends. On several occasions she had unconsciously reflected her husband's attitude of mistrust and indifference toward some of her close friends and acquaintances, but this was a reflection of his personality, not hers.

The learning process was long and arduous, but when I saw Gloria two years later, she told me that not even for a moment had she ever regretted paying such a high price for her freedom. She knew that the few friends she had left in the community where she had lived and worked for 15 years were true friends. She also appreciated having become a freer, more responsible and more independent person. Even though she had chosen to stop seeing Jean-Paul, she had never felt the slightest desire to criticize him or seek revenge; it was her own choice, and that is why it opened the doors of independence.

Freeing oneself from confluent attitudes allows one to step out along the path to true freedom, and form genuine, satisfying, propulsive relationships. In fact, it is surprising how integrating responsibility into our lives can free us from involuntary habits we have been caught up in. We have seen that this is so for confluence; we will now look at self-punishment in a similar light.

6. Self-punishment

The theory of self-punishment as a defense mechanism was first developed by psychoanalysis and subsequently taken up by Gestalt therapy under the name of "retroflection." The CNDA defines it as a form of defensive behavior by which a person refuses to satisfy his fundamental needs. This denial is achieved through self-imposed suffering based on guilt, and on the fear of how others will react to his true feelings.

Although he is unconscious of this tendency, the person who punishes himself also wants to punish others or make them feel guilty. Let us consider Janet's case: I first heard of her when she was 14 years old. About four years previously, her father had died after a long illness. Since then she had lived alone with her mother. Mixed in with the intense grief she still felt over her father's death was a sense of resentment toward her mother, a desire to punish her for having let her father die. The violence of her feelings frightened her. For this reason, and because she didn't want to be rejected by her mother—as Janet herself had rejected her—she chose to withdraw inward, shutting herself off from the very person from whom she most needed love and attention.

Initially, it was Janet's mother who came to see me. She also was devastated by the death of her husband and had great difficulty dealing with her daughter's refusal to communicate. When Janet finally agreed to come and see me, after repeated requests from her mother, it was obvious that relations between the two were extremely cold and superficial. After she began expressing the anger she felt toward her mother, Janet discovered that she had been feeling responsible for her father's death, and had projected her own sense of guilt onto her mother to avoid the intense suffering this caused her. Also, she was afraid that she would somehow bring about her mother's death as well, and so she punished herself by completely cutting herself off from her mother, denying herself the love she so desperately needed.

Self-punishment is an extremely complex mechanism from which one cannot be freed unless it is brought to light. Unfortunately, some people go so far as to commit suicide in order to escape their excruciating guilt and pain.

People punish themselves in many different ways. Dr. André Moreau (1983) quotes the following examples of punishment on a physical level:

Having an asthma attack because we think we are being abandoned; getting a knot in our stomach because we have to be decisive [. . .]; feeling words stick in our throat because we are angry; having an upset stomach on Monday morning when we have to go back to school or work [. . .]; getting a headache because the children [. . .] won't stop screaming; biting our nails or scratching incessantly; suffering from insomnia because we can't find an outlet for our irritation; becoming impotent because we feel unloved (p. 124, free translation).

And let us not forget such problems as anorexia, bulimia, incontinence, encopresis, and so on. People also punish themselves by taking on extra work, denying their fundamental needs, or cutting themselves off from those they love. They punish themselves by hating themselves, belittling themselves and comparing themselves to others. All this, because they are afraid of the emotions that dwell within them and have the goal, usually unconscious, of manipulating, punishing and making others feel guilty in order to obtain the attention and acknowledgment they desire.

Unfortunately, when a person punishes himself, he is taking the worst route possible to winning the love and acknowledgment of others. In fact, he becomes his own worst enemy because by punishing himself, he is reinforcing his status as a victim, thrusting himself ever deeper into dissatisfaction, dependence and, paradoxically, solitude.

The cycle of self-punishment fits into the pattern of unsatisfactory mental processes, as described above. Janet's particular case is represented by Figure 3.8.

Figure 3.8

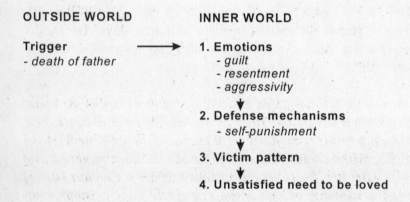

Unless he becomes aware of his self-punishment mechanism, and above all starts dealing with his underlying guilt and his concept of himself as a victim, the subject will neither stop punishing himself, nor come to satisfy any of his fundamental needs. The CNDA-trained psychotherapist helps his client look within himself and accept what he finds there, leading him through successive stages toward inner freedom.

I believe that our educational institutions could address the issue of self-punishment by using consequences instead of punishments, thus becoming part of an increasingly preventive approach toward physical and mental health care. What we are dealing with here is the whole notion of responsibility. By punishing the child, the educator reinforces his own position of power and maintains the other's dependence. The concept of consequences, on the other hand, teaches the child to take charge of his own learning process. Before he can develop this sense of responsibility in the child, however, the educator must clearly set forth his own limits as well as the pleasant and unpleasant consequences of respecting and overstepping those limits. Instead of being punished or made to feel guilty, the child learns to choose, and to accept the consequences of his choice. Rather than learning to protect himself through defense mechanisms such as self-punishment, he will learn to know, acknowledge and assert himself, as well as make choices that address his own real needs. In other words, he will learn how to take responsibility for his own life. In this sense, bringing our projections to light can be a revealing experience.

7. Projection

Projection refers to a mechanism of the psyche that occurs in every relationship a person forms with the people and things around him. In its natural, positive form it is one of the best methods of acquiring self-knowledge. In its defensive form, however, it has the same effect as the other defense mechanisms we have looked at: it disrupts the process by which man builds relationships. This second instance is defined by the CNDA as an unconscious means of transferring whatever we refuse to accept in ourselves, onto others.

A person who uses projection in this manner will attribute to those in his entourage his own needs, habits and emotions, which he cannot allow himself to experience because, unconsciously, he believes them to be bad, abnormal or intolerable.

On this subject, the story of a student from one of my French classes comes to mind. I remember Norman as a boy who just couldn't seem to make friends with anyone in his group. Whenever I asked the students to do a project in pairs or in larger groups, he would simply go off and work by himself. One time, I had asked the students to share in a responsible manner how they felt about school. Norman said that he didn't like school, that he hated all his teachers and that he despised all his classmates because everyone rejected him. A number of his fellow students reacted with surprise, reminding him of the times he had rejected their attempts to befriend him. What had happened, of course, was that Norman had projected his own tendency to reject onto others.

The reason for Norman's difficulty was simple enough. His parents were well-off and had planned to send their son to private school, thinking that the education he would receive there would better prepare him to take his rightful place in society. Norman had desperately wanted to go, but unfortunately he had failed the entrance exams and had no choice but to start attending the local public school. Before he even set foot in it, he was convinced that the teachers were all incompetent and the students uniformly stupid. He convinced himself he wouldn't be there for long anyway, and proceeded to reject the entire school outright.

Thus we see that the introjected attitudes he had picked up from his family caused Norman to project his dislike and rejection of the school onto his fellow students. Because he couldn't accept the idea that he might dislike and reject others, he protected himself from those feelings by externalizing them. The case of another student, Stephen, was very similar to Norman's: the reason he tended to criticize others for being aggressive was that he himself was struggling with repressed aggressivity.

Raymond is another case in point. A born charmer, he was fortunate enough one year to be in a class where the girls far outnumbered the boys. One day he came to see me after class because of a problem he had: he told me that he felt the girls were always after him, bothering him and interfering with his school work. From my vantage point at the front of the class, I had observed exactly the opposite. Since the beginning of the year I had seen him turn on the charm for every pretty girl in the group, with a smile to this one, a wink to that one, a rubbed shoulder here, a compliment there. Without even realizing it, he was using every possible means to make the girls notice him and like him—and he did it very well, too.

But why did Raymond project his seductive nature onto others? Because the idea that charming the opposite sex was a negative trait had been instilled in him by his mother. In fact, Raymond was a lot like his father, who was a charming man with women, although he had never been unfaithful in his life. However, because Raymond's mother had always criticized his father's behavior, Raymond wanted to avoid being like his father for fear of his mother's scorn.

I told him what I had observed, without judgment or criticism. He realized that the introjected rejection of his father's behavior was his mother's, not his. By accepting the seductive side of his personality, he regained the power he felt the girls had been using against him. He also became more aware of his actions and of their consequences. Without changing his essentially charming nature, he was able to see clearly both who he was and what the situation was.

As we have seen, projection—used as a defense mechanism—can be found in many different kinds of relationships, and parents, teachers and psychotherapists are not immune to it. If, by their actions, they project their own fear, anger or introjections onto the helpee, then they hinder the healing process, creating confusion instead of bringing clarity. As always, we return to the CNDA's two fundamental goals: liberating the helpee's creative potential, and encouraging the helper to continually create himself through his ongoing inner work, as he strives toward greater self-knowledge and self-acceptance. The better he can distinguish between what belongs to him and what belongs to the other, the less likely he is to project any of his emotions or be "content"-

directive in his approach. This ongoing inner work is at the heart of the helping relationship, imbuing it with the essentially human qualities that make it more than a mere problem-solving exercise.

Projection, however, is not always a defense mechanism in the sense I have just defined; I believe, in fact, that it is an inherent part of our human make-up. After all, it is perfectly normal for a person to perceive the world in a certain way because of who and what he is. For proof one need only think of how, when the same event is recounted by different people, different aspects of the story will be emphasized. The only objective elements in their stories are those that are immediately visible, whereas their perception of the event itself is colored by the emotions they projected onto it.

As we have seen, if we want to avoid confusion in our relationships, it is vital that we learn to distinguish what we see from what we feel. Through observation we can pick up objective information that is translated into subjective experience. I am being objective, for example, when I observe that Suzanne never looks me in the eye when she is speaking, but I am being subjective if this observation bothers me, and makes me feel uncomfortable. If I go on to assume that Suzanne is a deceitful, hypocritical, untrustworthy woman, I am entering into the realm of projective interpretation, which has nothing to do with the other, and concerns only me.

I can still maintain contact in this sort of situation if I restrict myself to objective observation of the other and if I express my feelings. For example, if I say to Suzanne: "I have noticed that you don't look at me and it makes me feel uncomfortable. I'm worried that you're not interested in what I'm saying, or that you might be disappointed," then I am sustaining the relationship by not making the other responsible for my emotions. On the contrary: I acknowledge, accept and assume them.

What happens in most cases is that, in order to shake off a vague, undefined uneasiness, we project it onto another person. This happens automatically, precisely because we are unaware of our emotions, triggers or inner mechanisms. The CNDA-trained psychotherapist learns to apply this approach to his own life, so that he can differentiate between what he observes (trigger) and what he feels (emotions). By doing so he avoids the pitfalls of projection and its various manifestations, such as criticism, judgment and interpretation. If he does unconsciously project his difficulties onto the other, he may temporarily disrupt the bonding process. Before he can restore it, he must see what his judgment, criticism, interpretation and projection can teach him about himself. If he has projected hypocrisy and deceit onto the other, it is perfectly possible that he himself is hypocritical and deceitful. This may, however, be difficult for him to accept because, based on his introjections, he believes that these traits are reprehensible. It is much easier, after all, for him to attribute these qualities to the other. Often, what bothers us most in other people is the very thing we don't want to acknowledge in ourselves. In that sense, it is certainly more convenient for us to judge them than to judge ourselves. But is it possible for someone to project onto another person something that doesn't initially come from himself?

I believe there is always a connection between what I project and who I am. Sometimes there is a direct connection, as I have just explained, and sometimes it is more indirect. In the case of Suzanne, the projecting person may discover from that phenomenon that he has trouble trusting people who won't look him in the eye because he remembers that his father (transference) never looked at him when they talked, and that he never kept his promises, either.

Be that as it may, whether projection is expressed through judgment, advice, interpretation or criticism, it has nothing to do with the other, and only concerns the person from whom it comes. When we believe the opposite to be true, projection can wreak havoc in a relationship.

Projection really does distort relationships, especially when it is used defensively: as the subject tries to cast off his unpleasant feelings, the object ends up being wrongfully characterized. In doing so, the subject is exerting a certain kind of power over the object: the power to label and criticize him. Instead of telling the other about his feelings, he makes him responsible for them. He doesn't tell the other that he is afraid of losing or disappointing him, afraid of being criticized or rejected; he won't even share his grief, pain, jealousy or aggression with him. Instead, he blames, accuses, judges and criticizes him, disturbing the harmony of the relationship and destroying the other's trust.

Tackling projection can be an extremely difficult stage of one's inner work because it calls into question habits built up over a lifetime, and upsets the power balances in relationships. Some people allow themselves to use their "feelings," "perception" and "insight" to dominate others. They seem to think it is their right to use expressions such as "I can tell ... ", "It seems to me ... ", "I feel that you..." "I sense that you...". They pretend to know others better than they know themselves; they see themselves as dispensers of justice, superior beings who necessarily dominate those around them. Instead of using their insight and feelings to deal with their own life experiences, they use them to try and control the lives of others, through judgment, interpretation and criticism and even through clairvoyance.

However, an intuitive and perceptive person is not automatically granted *carte blanche* to meddle in other people's lives. How many parents have dominated their children's lives through the fear, insecurity and weakness which they unwittingly, and unwillingly, pass on to them? How many people allow themselves to be controlled by "seers," or all the others who claim they can solve the mystery of our lives? This does not mean that seers have no place in today's society. However, they need to be aware of their own strengths, weaknesses and limitations, just as doctors, educators, psychologists, psychotherapists and all those who work in the field of physical and mental health care do. And we who consult them, for our part, need to be aware that they are fallible, just like us. In spite of their ability and training, they may still have a preconception of the client as a mere pawn in their hands, who should implicitly accept whatever they suggest, without questioning whether or not it actually conforms to who or what he is. Clients who allow themselves to be dealt with in this manner will most likely be dependent and dissatisfied. The CNDA holds that the helpee is the true master of his own destiny; he alone may choose, as long as he is able to, what is best for him.

In that sense, working out one's projections has the advantage of furnishing an effective and ongoing means of self-awareness and self-empowerment. It is, in fact, our single most reliable mental barometer. The way man perceives the world is dictated by who he is. When he is feeling good, he sees good things around him. Similarly, when he is feeling ill at ease, when he is feeling sad or anxious or aggressive, he projects his feelings onto what he sees around him, too.

The CNDA-trained psychotherapist learns to clearly differentiate between what he observes and what he feels. The advantages of doing so are twofold: it decreases the frequency of his projections, and—since no one is immune from this defensive phenomenon—it helps him learn from them when they occur. The helper who falls into the trap of judging, interpreting, criticizing or giving advice will learn to use such pitfalls as a springboard to inner work, and discover what his projections have to say about himself.

If, for example, he observes that the helpee is constantly moving his hands, he may realize that he finds this habit irritating. If he is not aware of the distinction between what he sees and how that makes him feel, he risks projecting his irritation onto the other, saying something like: "I can tell you are irritated now," or "It seems to me you feel nervous." Because it speaks of the helper's feelings, this kind of projective rephrasing usually makes the helpee confused.

Defensive projections occur in other types of relationships, causing problems there, too. They color whatever communication there is, so that it merely conveys the partners' defensive reactions rather than their feelings here and now. For this reason, defense mechanisms—and especially projection—prohibit harmonious interaction. They tend to eliminate the atmosphere of trust and affection, replacing it with one of mistrust and rejection. If we want to work out our projections, we must observe and be attentive to our feelings, for we tend to project when we are unaware of our emotions, our suffering and especially our fears. Simply put, we feel uneasy and attempt to rid ourselves of this feeling by attributing it to the other, blaming him for what we are doing ourselves. In doing so, we pretend to know the other whereas in fact we don't even know ourselves, and are not aware of what we are feeling. We set ourselves up as the other's judge, advisor, critic or spokesperson even though we may be completely unaware of his feelings, thoughts or intentions. This kind of interaction is at best superficial and false, and usually ends in failure.

Dealing with one's projective defense mechanisms means regaining power over one's life; it means being sufficiently attuned to oneself to realize the importance of satisfying one's fundamental needs. Working out one's projective structures also means being sufficiently self-aware to stop the other from labeling, controlling, and transferring onto oneself the responsibility for his anxiety, problems, frustrations and failures.

Often, when we lack self-knowledge or self-confidence, we let ourselves be dominated by people who claim to know all about us: our character and temperament, our emotions here and now, our future. However, objective observations aside, no one can do more than put forward hypotheses on these topics while remaining conscious that such hypotheses may not prove true.

One day, as I was leading a study group, I realized that one of the participants sat with her eyes closed while I was talking (objective observation). This made me feel uncomfortable and, as I became aware of my uneasiness, I began to wonder what reason she might have for doing this. Many possible hypotheses came to mind, but essentially they were all an expression of my fears. Perhaps she was tired. Perhaps my ideas didn't interest her. Perhaps she was cutting herself off from me or the group because we made her uncomfortable. I spoke to her after the class, and discovered that she had a serious vision problem. She had in fact closed her eyes to hear me better, to avoid being distracted from what I was saying by her weak eyesight.

Because of their underlying emotions, projection and interpretation can lead us down the wrong path, causing us to falsely pigeonhole others.

Unconscious, unacknowledged projection is by itself an extremely troublesome defense mechanism, but it can also lead to others, among them the adoption of a persona.

8. The adoption of a persona

Children learn at an early age to show the world a façade. This has the advantage of earning them the love and approval of those who are responsible for their upbringing, but it instills in them the notion that revealing their true selves is inadmissible and that, in order to be loved, they must be what their parents and teachers want them to be. This is how a significant part of the child comes to be denied, and replaced with a "better" persona. To maintain this idealized image of himself, he will plumb the most annihilating depths of conformism, and unknowingly tell the most appalling lies. Maintaining this image becomes almost an issue of survival because, in his mind, it is unconsciously associated with love.

Trying to have a real relationship with a persona is not easy. All too often, though, the world becomes a stage, with all the men and women on it merely players. They pretend that they are strong, successful, cool, indifferent, or anything else they believe necessary to profess in order to survive. Unfortunately, they are unaware that this defense mechanism robs them of their freedom. Their persona becomes a prison guard, barring them from genuine relationships, relationships that only real "people" can enjoy. "Personae," however, cannot. Their relationships are overshadowed by lies, by the need to pretend and to prove themselves, and by complete denial of their true feelings and motivations, all of which leads to distrust and dissatisfaction. Unless we are genuine, communication is impossible since our lack of honesty destroys the other's confidence.

It is foolish, however, to believe that we can all be perfectly authentic in every situation. There is a persona in each one of us, and it appears from time to time in order to mask our real feelings when they are deemed unacceptable. On occasion, we have all smiled when we were hurt, appeared indifferent when we were deeply affected, have insisted that all was well when our lives were falling apart. And we all know someone who says he likes something when it actually bothers him, who congratulates us over something he doesn't appreciate, who pretends to love us when he actually despises us, or who projects an image of success, culture or material wealth which completely belies his real situation and his true nature.

Whenever we are afraid of being rejected, judged or ridiculed, whenever we are afraid of hurting or disappointing someone, in short, whenever we experience fears or emotions that we cannot acknowledge because we feel they are unacceptable—this is when we unconsciously adopt this kind of defensive attitude.

As the individual becomes aware of the instances in which he defensively deploys his persona, he can discover the emotion or the complex that is at the root of its automatic appearance. This is, in fact, how Anne was able to improve her relationships with others and shake off a feeling of profound loneliness. She taught at a high school and was universally disliked by her pupils, whom she managed to control with some difficulty. Her relationships with her co-workers were distant and superficial. These two factors combined to make her chosen profession boring and pointless. Her husband was a rich industrialist, and they had one 14-year-old son, who had always been Anne's pride and joy and who over the last few years had become her only reason for living. It was precisely because of this particular relationship that she decided to come into therapy. Her son had always been a model child but, recently, he had become so rude and disobedient that Anne had lost all control over him. He threw all her values back in her face, refusing to cut his hair or do his homework, to spend the evening at home or wear anything but dirty, worn-out jeans. Anne felt completely overwhelmed by the situation and had no one to help her, since her husband was almost never at home.

She came to the first session broken, lost and devastated. She had come to talk to me about her son, hoping that she could learn some way of getting him to listen to reason. I wonder if she suspected, even then, that such changes could only come about through her. Since her son refused point blank to come along with her, she decided, for lack of anything better, to keep the weekly appointment herself; as she told me, I was the only person she could talk to about her sufferings. She was too ashamed of the way her child-rearing skills had turned out to ask for advice within her family or at work. Except in my office, she continued to present an image of success and self-satisfaction that cut her off from her own feelings and from other people.

It was only after several weeks of therapy that Anne was able to look reality in the face. Since her husband was a well-known businessman and the mayor of the town where they lived, her method of child-rearing was based on appearances. Her son had learned to be unfailingly kind, polite, generous and helpful, just like his mother, without taking into account how he was feeling, or what he was getting out of this masquerade. For Anne, her son was visible proof of his parents' success. However, his manners and attitudes did not go over well with his fellow students and, throughout elementary school, he had been relentlessly teased and ridiculed. Since he had been brought up to repress his fears and aggressive tendencies, he simply denied that part of himself that wanted to cry and scream, in order to keep his parents' love. After he started high school, however, it wasn't long before he realized that he would have to change his ways if he wanted to make any friends. At this stage, young people generally prefer to reject their parents rather than lose their friends, and so Anne's son started to rebel against the principles of his upbringing, letting himself be influenced more and more by his peers. Faced with this change, Anne was completely at a loss.

The psychotherapeutic process made Anne aware of how she had deprived herself of satisfactory relationships by maintaining an image that was completely divorced from her reality. She realized that she had spent her life playing a role in order to please her parents, and later, her husband. She also realized that she had raised her son according to the very pattern that had left her alone and unhappy. The unconscious statement behind her son's behavior was that he no longer wanted any part of a persona that deprived him of acceptance and friendship. As she came to understand this, Anne began to see things in a completely different light. Whereas at first she had thought it was her son who needed help, she came to realize that his rebellion had helped her break free from her own persona, and come to understand the origins of her rejection problem.

Often, an event that seems shattering at first can actually pave the way for a liberating renaissance by weakening the persona's hold over the person. The realization that he is harboring a persona may help an individual to free himself from introjected principles and beliefs that deprive him of happiness and prevent him from having healthy, balanced relationships.

As with all the other defense mechanisms, the persona intervenes in people's lives when they either feel, think or plan something that they deem unacceptable. These overly defensive people are in fact very sensitive and very emotional. They are so afraid of their feelings that they "wall themselves in" to hide from them, and they attempt to control others in order to mask their emotional nature, which they consider a weakness. Behavior based on domination, superiority and power, then, is actually defensive behavior that conceals unbearable fears. This act of concealment requires that one deny emotion and fight against oneself instead of against an external "enemy," and this uses up a significant amount of vital energy. The defensive person's worst enemy is, of course, himself: he defends himself fiercely from his own feelings, which he refuses to see and understand because he is afraid of them. But whether his defensive attitude is turned against himself or the other, it leaves him feeling tired, frustrated, unhappy and, in a way he can't quite define, defeated.

When he is on the defensive, it is impossible for a human being to progress because he unconsciously adopts a passive attitude, caused by lack of awareness and unwillingness to see. Since he is incapable of viewing his external triggers objectively and listening to his emotions, he throws himself headfirst into a defensive behavior pattern. This occasionally gives him power over others, but consistently renders him powerless to change himself. He acts involuntarily and despite appearances is—psychically speaking—at the mercy of others.

The counseling profession should stress the importance of understanding this phenomenon. The helper must be aware of his needs, fears, complexes and defense mechanisms because, if he is not, there will come a time when he will involuntarily react in a defensive manner to a certain stimulus. This reaction would probably mobilize the helpee's defense mechanisms and, in the long run, all effective counseling then becomes impossible. This defensive reaction of the second person is an automatic response to the defensive attitude of the first. The relationship, if it still exists at all, then deteriorates to the point where both parties are either defending themselves or attacking each other, but certainly not listening to one other.

On the other side of the coin is the individual who acknowledges his feelings, accepts them and expresses them; he has no need to either defend himself or attack in order to gain the upper hand. Instead, he chooses to face up to his emotions in order to be freed from them. This individual is choosing the path of self-love. Winning or losing for him is not the issue; the issue is to become fully himself. Rather than expend his vital energy in fruitless and unsatisfactory cycles of defense and attack, he chooses to accept what he feels and to let himself experience his emotions; in this way, he uses his energy for creation and self-creation, progressively replacing his unconscious defense mechanisms with conscious means of protecting himself—what the CNDA refers to as "protective mechanisms." If he does not become aware of the way his psyche functions, and if he does not learn to protect himself in a conscious manner so as to satisfy his fundamental needs, he will fall into recurrent mental processes, or patterns. He will be unable to understand these patterns, or why he always has problems with his relationships and why he can never resolve them.

F. PATTERNS

I use the term "pattern" in the sense of an unconscious, recurrent mental process that leads human beings to adopt a repetitive mode of behavior in their dealings with others. More specifically, in their search for love and affection, it directs them toward people with the same psychological functionning, who display the same type of psychological phenomena and with whom they inevitably end up experiencing the same dissatisfaction.

Our patterns originate in the cycle of our unconscious mental processes. As we have seen, this cycle is based on our desire to satisfy our need for love, acknowledgment, acceptance, affirmation, freedom and creation. Certain events or people act as triggers, arousing fear, anxiety, anger, grief or jealousy. Unrecognized and unaccepted because of their supposed shameful nature, these emotions lead us to assume a defensive attitude. When we are on the defensive, although we are not aware of it, we unconsciously seek a substitute instead of satisfying our fundamental needs. For example, if we are afraid that our feelings will be criticized or rejected, then we will conceal them. First, in order to protect ourselves from disapproval and second, because we want to satisfy, if only partially, our need for love and acknowledgment. However, as we well know, instead of fostering relationships, defense mechanisms generally tend to hinder them.

We can speak in terms of a "pattern" when this dissatisfaction occurs consistently, and compulsively, in all our affective relationships. Figure 3.9 reviews the cyclical nature of this unsatisfactory mental process.

Figure 3.9

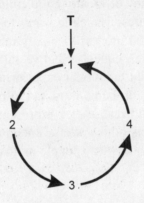

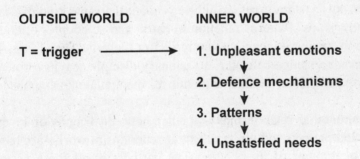

Certain triggers, activated by the people or things around us, can cause us to experience unpleasant feelings (1). When an "area of excessive sensitivity," or "complex," has been created in the psyche, these emotions begin to be felt repeatedly and intensely. To protect ourselves, we unconsciously deploy our defense mechanisms (2), preventing us from satisfying our fundamental needs. Thus, we become trapped in an involuntary process that forces us to adopt the same unsatisfactory behavior (4) in all our relationships.

Constant repetition of the same process creates a pattern: an unconscious, recurrent mental process that directs the individual, in his search for love and affection, toward people who display the same type of psychological phenomena. Patterns are born of relationships and upheld by them; they originate in the child's relationship with his parents or their substitutes. The child wants to be loved and he unconsciously creates a mental process to satisfy that need. He repeats this mental process in all subsequent affective relationships because they remind him of his initial emotional experiences with his mother and father. He always ends up being attracted to people who are psychologically similar to him because they represent his sole experience of love. In turn, he attracts others whose unconscious mental processes complement his own; in this way people mutually sustain each other's patterns.

Each pattern, in fact, attracts a complementary one, creating a "system." Because it is built on unconscious and recurrent interactive behavior, this system necessarily brings about the same kind of dead-end relationships. Patterns function in pairs, and so couples often reflect the following oppositions: bully/victim, deserter/abandonee, invader/invadee, judge/offender, missionary/disciple, savior/protégé, superior/subordinate, dominator/dominee, manipulator/manipulatee.

Innumerable relationships—whether between friends or lovers, doctors and patients, within families, at school or at work—are based on one or another of these pairs. The partners in all these various relationships involuntarily create complementary systems that foster dependence and dissatisfaction. Before they can "clear the air" and establish freer and more authentic relations, it is crucial that they find out what unconscious patterns are hidden beneath the surface of the relationship that prevent them from satisfactorily experiencing their emotions. This, in fact, is the role the creative nondirective psychotherapist plays when he sees people who are having problems in their relationships: he helps them to detect their unconscious, recurrent behavior and the psychic patterns on which it is based.

In order to bring to light and clarify the elements that are characteristic of these various patterns, and how they constitute a system, the helper must be aware of their differences and of how they complement one another.

1. The bully and the victim

Whenever he encounters the least hint of rejection from a person he is emotionally involved with, the bully retaliates angrily, using either verbal or physical violence or any other means of coercion, domination or repression. Early on in his life, he was deprived of the love and security he needed, and this left him overly sensitive to every indication of indifference or rejection. Basically, the reason why the bully frightens others is because he is afraid of them and because he is desperately unhappy. However, as we have seen so many times before, his attitude brings him exactly the opposite of what he seeks: instead of seeking out the love he needs so much, he frightens away those he loves by the repressive way he expresses his suffering. He repeats this pattern in all his affective relationships, every time a feeling of rejection is triggered.

Hidden behind the anger and the will to dominate are deep-seated pain and fear. The fear, in turn, often conceals a different kind of anger, one that the bully has repressed. His irascible, repressive nature does mask a high degree of sensitivity, though. He directs his pain against the other, by being violent and domineering, in an attempt to escape his intolerable suffering. This constitutes an unconscious refusal to feel the pain and the unbearable void within him, in which his pattern originated.

Nobody is born a bully. This behavior pattern is acquired through relationships with others, particularly those in the family. Usually, a series of unbearably painful situations leads to the formation of a counterproductive mental process within the psyche.

Often, a child becomes a bully because his sensitive nature, his feelings or his right to be different have been rejected, perhaps even violently. Since his pain and suffering are neither tolerated nor recognized, he represses his emotions. They burst forth violently and uncontrollably, however, whenever he perceives he is being rejected. He will unfailingly manage to get the other's attention by some method or another, one that is disturbing, liberating and frightening, all at once. His affective experience instills in him an unconscious fear of being rejected for his sensitivity, and that fear incites him to violence, domination and repression. Having been repressed himself for his high degree sensitivity, he represses others. Having been frightened himself by the thought of being unloved, he frightens others. Although he is not aware of it, all his actions and attitudes combine to maintain others in a state of fear and dependence.

Guilt is another effective medium for turning out bullies. When a child is made to feel guilty for his parents' mistakes, their feelings, their suffering, their problems, their failures, mistakes and choices, the child will attempt to escape from that guilt, which is usually unconscious, by throwing frightening temper tantrums. The child may lash out at the adults in question, both verbally and physically, thus maintaining them in a state of subjection.

Paradoxically, although the bully's repressive behavior patterns are counterproductive, he cannot get rid of them because he needs them. His initial need is to pass his suffering onto the other, but his underlying and more vital need is to make sure that others notice him. He has an intense fear of not being loved, and by making others afraid he manages to get their attention and exert a certain degree of control over them. He is, unconsciously, making do with a substitute for his real need to be loved, and he continues to settle for it because he knows of no better way. In fact, he has acquired a deep-seated fear of his sensitive nature, because it has brought him so much suffering.

Experience has taught him that when he shows his sensitivity, he is either rejected or made to feel guilty. In order to protect himself, he unconsciously chooses to deny it, and to live with the consequences of his anger and his repressive behavior.

As we have seen, the bully's sensitive nature was rejected at an early age. To satisfy his need to be loved, he unconsciously chose to deny his feelings of grief and fear and, when the suffering became too great, to pass his pain onto others. But this process necessarily requires a victim, and the bully always manages to find someone with whom to play out his pattern. In some ways, however, he is himself a victim, for he is the one who is rejected and viewed with disapproval by others. He is the one others call "mean" and who is blamed when a relationship fails. He is the one left feeling misunderstood and alone. I would argue that the bully is, in fact, the victim's scapegoat. The only way he can break out of these counterproductive behavior patterns is by becoming aware of his mental processes (see Figure 3.10).

Figure 3.10

OUTSIDE WORLD	INNER WORLD
Trigger ⟶	**1. Emotions**
- rejection	*- fear of losing*
	- grief
	- anger
	(amplified by abandonment complex)
	↓
	2. Defense mechanisms
	- projection
	- repressive judgment
	- domination
	↓
	3. Bully pattern
	↓
	4. Unsatisfied needs
	- need to be loved
	- need to be acknowledged
	- need to be listened to

Thus we see that the bully is actually extremely emotional, and that his anger is no more than a manifestation of his defense mechanism, used unconsciously to protect himself from his acute anguish.

The victim, whose pattern complements that of the bully, also wants to escape from his suffering. He does so by handing the responsibility for his feelings, his powerlessness, his disappointments, his mistakes, his choices, his decisions and his frustrations, over to others. His methods may include complaining and not standing up for himself, only to turn around and accuse, blame and criticize the other. The victim's power is more subtle than the bully's but is no less effective: he can always find supporters to back him up, and join with him in rejecting the one who is desperately seeking love.

The attitude of each partner in the pair is geared toward dominating the other. The bully represses and intimidates; the victim, in turn, makes him feel guilty and rejects him. Observers tend to pity the victim, who unconsciously uses their sympathy to increase the burden of guilt laid on the bully, whether person or institution. One has only to look at the newspapers today, filled with stories about so-called poor victims of society, for evidence of this phenomenon.

But what exactly is a victim, and how does his behavior develop? He is a person who rejects the limits imposed by those with whom he is emotionally involved, and makes them responsible for everything he feels and for all the unpleasant and painful things that happen to him. His behavior, like that of the bully, is caused by lack of love.

A child who feels unloved or who does not get enough attention will take it upon himself to remedy these deficiencies. He may do so by making those in charge of him feel guilty, by becoming restless, whiny, mean, critical, or insufferable. In other words, he will automatically do whatever is necessary to make his mother or father notice him. He soon learns that, when he plays the part of bully or victim, he can make his parents react. Thus, in all his relationships, whenever he is frustrated, rejected or attacked, he will respond by complaining, criticizing and judging, believing that there is no other way of getting love and attention. He learns that there is a certain satisfaction to be gained from making the other responsible for what he feels, since he can make the other react and thus get attention. His pattern therefore requires a bully he can complain about, so as to obtain the sympathetic reaction he desires and the feeling that he exists.

The victim pattern is generally established in the same way as that of the bully: the child reacts to being attacked, repressed or beaten either with violent, angry outbursts or with self-repression. Often, he will lapse into whining and criticism as a form of self-defense. In fact, the repressive attitude of those in charge of raising him may result in a bully/victim pattern in the same child.

We risk establishing a victim pattern in a child if, as mothers or fathers (or their substitutes), we become overprotective toward him, taking responsibility for all the unpleasant things that happen to him. Generally, this type of parent demands perfection from his children; he shields them from mental and physical suffering with one hand and punishes them for the slightest error or imperfection with the other. Such demands and overprotection, however, are in themselves a source of suffering for the child, for they teach him two lessons. First, he learns that if someone loves him then that person will take care of him, relieving him of all responsibility for his feelings, mistakes and choices. He also learns that if he isn't perfect, no one will love him. These lessons foster a lack of self-confidence and establish a permanent fear of rejection. After all, the victim who receives total attention and support, but who also knows the fear of imperfection, will not appreciate being opposed or restricted, for he has unconsciously integrated the idea that being loved equals unconditional approval and permanent satisfaction. When someone puts down limits, expresses a malaise, or refuses to take the responsability for the victim's feelings and problems, he is unable to take it. Indeed, as far as the victim is concerned, these occurrences are a sign of rejection or lack of love. He will most likely try to defend himself by complaining and blaming the other, thus reinforcing his victim pattern. This behavior also increases his dependence on the bully, for when we criticize somebody, we are showing a certain form of attachment. The victim's attitude demonstrates an obvious subservience to his complementary half in the pair, the bully.

The victim is also dependent on his entourage, from whom he seeks support, encouragement, approval and sometimes help. This lack of responsibility, however, deprives him of all independence, as is often the case, for example, with employees who only communicate with their employer via their union. In fact, the bully/victim pattern is a common one in employer/employee relations: all exchanges are based on a "win or lose" formula. This necessarily excludes communication since this formula is based on defense mechanisms, manifested through the defensive and aggressive attitudes of the parties involved. The employer's strength is based on power; that of the employee on coalition. However, it is neither power nor coalition, but feelings, that bring people together. When this sort of formula is put into practice, people and their feelings disappear and only the disembodied issue appears relevant. When we concentrate on facts and problems instead of people, even the winners are losers.

As long as the individual conforms to a standard of behavior that cuts him off from his feelings and emotions, he will continue to be involved in win/lose relationships. When we repress the other as the bully does, or transfer responsibility for everything, as the victim does, we remain trapped in painful, unsatisfactory relationships.

The concept of responsibility is an important one here. If the bully reacts violently, it is because he feels rejected and because he assumes responsibility for the victim's feelings. If the victim complains, it is because he also feels rejected and because he refuses to take responsibility for his own feelings. For, if the latter feels unhappy or any other negative emotion, he is certain that the other is responsible for his suffering, and reproaches him accordingly. The victim has a hard time accepting the limits and weaknesses of others, especially when these interfere with the satisfaction of his own needs. He will inevitably end up in relationships with a bully, thus justifying his complaints and satisfying his need for emotional security. Because he is afraid of losing the other, he constantly searches out this type of subservience, from which he escapes only to fall into another one that is identical in every respect. Thus he will seek out a sensitive type who becomes easily guilt-stricken and who needs love and emotional security just as he does. At first, the victim's new partner will do everything in his power to please him, but after a while he will become exasperated with the other's constant dissatisfaction, interpreting it as a sign of rejection, of lack of love and acknowledgment. Thus begins the cycle of anger and reproach that locks both partners into mutual dependence and dissatisfaction, fed by their unconscious and complementary behavior patterns.

Although both have a vital need for love, both are ready to sacrifice their need for freedom, attentiveness, affirmation and creation in order to attain a certain degree of security; this exchange paradoxically leads to their own ruin. In order to avoid suffering, the victim and the bully both adopt automatic mental processes which bring them the opposite of what they sought. Mary Ann's story provides an excellent illustration of this point.

The woman who consulted me was in her forties, but grief and disappointment made her look years older. She had three sons, aged 18, 21 and 22, who were her pride and joy. However, at the age of 45, she was feeling frustrated and deeply unhappy with her life, so much so that she felt ready to end it. When she was young, her parents had owned a store and had been fairly wealthy, so she had never lacked for any material possession. Unfortunately, her upbringing had suffered from her parents' absence; they were always busy minding the store and had little time to spare for their daughter. They tried to make up for their absence with little treats, but these failed to satisfy her. What she really wanted was her parents' attention, and she learned early on that if she burst into tears, one or the other would come running, even if the store was crowded with customers. Throughout her childhood and adolescence, her behavior reinforced the victim pattern, which she maintained until she met her future husband, Albert.

Albert was 12 years older than Mary Ann, solidly built, handsome and rich. Mary Ann saw in him someone she could always count on, who would deny her nothing. In fact, for the first few months of married life, their relationship was idyllic. In addition to the material comforts she was used to, Mary Ann had the love and constant attention of the man she loved. However, the birth of their first son changed all that. Because her parents' preoccupation had hurt Mary Ann a great deal, she was determined to devote all her time to her children. Feeling rejected, Albert started to show signs of an explosive temperament. Mary Ann saw no way of protecting herself from his temper except by becoming even more devoted to her children, who became her sole *raison d'être*. As they grew up, the children inevitably sided with their mother in the face of Albert's rages, which were becoming increasingly frequent. Through the plaintive, victimized attitude she portrayed for her sons, as well as through the constant criticism she directed toward Albert, she had succeeded in cutting them off from their father, with whom they could not identify. When Mary Ann turned 45 she realized her family was composed of three sons who rejected their manhood, and a violent, irascible husband. Disappointed in her relationship with her husband, and in the results of her overprotective child-rearing methods, she experienced an unbearable feeling of failure and futility which left her almost suicidal. She couldn't accept the fact that her oldest son was a homosexual, and so she blamed it on her husband. However, although she was afraid of Albert, she still felt attached to him, because of the material security and sense of stability he provided. Mary Ann admitted that, in between his violent periods, Albert was more attentive and generous than ever. They were united and made dependent by their common need for love and a mutual fear of losing each other. Mary Ann needed Albert, whom she despised and rejected. Albert needed his wife, whom he attacked with his uncontrollable outbursts of anger. They were both locked into this pattern, and neither could find the key to escape.

I will not dwell on the lengthy inner work they both had to accomplish before they could find inner peace, although I will say it comprised attaining a degree of self-acceptance and coming to terms with the results of their marriage. Getting rid of guilt, no longer taking responsibility for other people's lives, especially those of our children, is one of the most difficult stages to go through in psychotherapy. However, there is simply no other way to achieve peace and independence and, through our unconscious influence, to make others free. Passing through this stage requires that the victim and the bully both understand their mental processes, as represented in Figure 3.11.

Figure 3.11

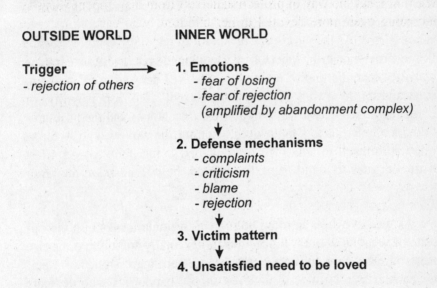

The story of Mary Ann and Albert clearly demonstrates that the bully and the victim have a lot in common: a need to be loved and a fear of losing the other. Their defense mechanisms differ, but the abandonment complex they both harbor is the same, and these common features spell out mutual attraction. Also, they each carry within them the pattern that is the opposite of their own: the bully is also a victim and vice versa. Breaking out of this involuntary behavior pattern starts with self-awareness. However, the work cannot continue satisfactorily unless participants adhere to the steps toward freedom outlined by the

CNDA. The same liberating process also applies to the complementary patterns of deserter/abandonee.

2. The deserter and the abandonee

Driven by a constant and obsessive fear of losing the love of others, of being rejected and being abandoned, the abandonee interprets the smallest lapse of memory, the slightest distraction, the least delay as a sign that he is being pushed away. This is a person who is suffering from an abandonment complex in every sense of the word, and in every one of his relationships.

In order not to be rejected or abandoned, his desire to earn the approval of others knows no bounds. He will deny himself, defer to others and let them walk all over him. He will take responsibility for the feelings, the deceptions, the failures, the choices and the problems of others. Generous to a fault, overly helpful, he will even go so far as to debase himself to avoid the unthinkable: being unloved. As a last resort, in order to avoid being abandoned, he will abandon the other first.

As we have seen so often before, his attitude brings him the opposite of what he desires. Since he is either totally submissive, or else asserts himself through outbursts of repressed aggression, he is neither respected nor truly liked. Even those abandonees who dedicate their whole lives to serving others never succeed in truly inspiring respect. They do not dare stand by their limits or venture an opinion for fear of displeasing others, and because of this they are often either exploited or manipulated. Since they are always taking responsibility for what happens to others, they don't really know who they are or what they want, and this lack of self-love and self-knowledge prevents them from attaining any degree of self-respect or self-confidence.

At an early age, the abandonee was either abandoned, rejected, or else loved not for himself but for what he could give to others. The abandonee could be a child who was literally abandoned by his birth parents, who was placed in a foster home, who suffered the loss of one parent or the other through death or divorce, who overheard his parents' constant bickering, or whose parents were constantly ill, absent, narcissistic or extremely fearful. These children grow up haunted by the fear of loss, of being rejected or deserted. They are convinced that they do not deserve to be loved. Believing that others reject them because they are not lovable, they are by turns helpful, attentive, charming, manipulative and mendacious. Often, they lapse into confluent or persona-based attitudes, simply because they feel that their own person is unacceptable and displeasing. The goal of all this unconscious activity is to please, or at the very least, not to displease. Consequently, they are crushed when they are emotionally rejected or abandoned.

When this happens, the abandonee suffers tremendously. He attempts to escape from his suffering, either by severing relations with the loved one or by running away. In some ways, then, the abandonee doubles as a deserter. He will not try to approach the person who rejected him, though. First, because the rejecter hurt him too much, and second because the abandonee lacks sufficient love for himself and confidence in his own worth. Since he is used to existing by virtue of the other's love, he feels deflated when that love is gone. The only option he can see is to run away, but his suffering inevitably pursues him. So he sets out to prove to the other (his father, his mother, a friend, a lover, and so on) that he is worthy of his or her love. This behavior pattern, however, strengthens the cycle of inner conflict, reinforcing the abandonee's fears, from which he cannot escape.

As we have just seen, the abandonee can easily become a victim, sucked into this kind of pattern because he has a distorted view of his own responsibilities in a relationship. Either he believes himself unworthy of the other's love but tries desperately to please, thus becoming completely dependent, or else he succeeds in convincing himself, by means of projection, that the other is unworthy of his love and that he doesn't need the other, in which case he will become defiantly independent in order to avoid rejection. In either case, though, he is deluding himself. The reality is that others reject him because he has rejected himself, because he lacks self-acknowledgement, self-love and self-confidence. His rejection of self is evidence of his need for greater self-love, for it is precisely this lack that drives him into the arms of a deserter. Breaking out of the cycle means acquiring enough self-love to enable him, in his relationships with others, to put himself first, even at the risk of being rejected, instead of denying himself and putting others first. In short, the abandonee has to accept the loss of his friend's, partner's or parent's love in order to gain his own love. This is his route to freedom; only when he learns to put himself first automatically and in every situation will he stop attracting deserters, that is, those who are afraid of commitment because, in the past, they had been smothered with, or, conversely, deprived of any manifestation of love.

Some deserters, as they were growing up, may have been suffocated by love, to the point of developing a fear of being loved, which is linked to an intense fear of losing their freedom. As soon as the loved one becomes too possessive, the deserter rejects him. Paradoxically, however, the very love he rejects is also what attracts him because it fulfills an urgent need. Thus he is torn between his need for love and his fear of rejection.

What the deserter is doing, in fact, is playing out the pattern that had become a feature of his relationship with his parents. He couldn't do without his mother or father because he needed their love. However, since theirs was a jealous love, he surrounded himself with barriers to give himself some space and protect his freedom. In his emotional dealings, therefore, he tends to commit himself only partially. He rarely lets himself go, and when he does, he becomes withdrawn afterward, fearing he will be consumed by the other's love, just as he was by that of his parents.

Deserters can also display the characteristics of an abandonee. Having been abandoned and rejected, they protect themselves from the painful consequences of love by running away. Their fear of rejection makes it difficult for them to get involved in any kind of relationship.

They often regret indulging themselves or letting down their guard because they are sure the other will be disappointed and/or displeased. For this reason, out of self-defense, they tend to back away from commitment. Instead of being torn between his needs for love and freedom, this kind of deserter may feel the pull of such contrary forces as his need for love and his fear of rejection.

The abandonee and the deserter are inhabited by the same need for love, the same fear of losing the other, the same abandonment complex and the same instinct to run away when rejection looms. Their separate but similar patterns complement and support one another, and this forms the basis for their mutual attraction. Of course, neither one will be able to break out of this cycle unless he first attains a high degree of self-awareness and learns to trust the other implicitly and to be completely honest. All this, so that he can distinguish what belongs to him from what does not.

This is the route Rick and Yolanda chose to take. At our first session, although they told me of their love for one another, they had serious doubts about their future together because they both felt extremely insecure. Rick's job obliged him to be away from home for extended periods of time. All the time that he was away, he worried about losing Yolanda, who was not very demonstrative in her affections.

In psychotherapy, Yolanda discovered that her apparent indifference was actually a means of protecting herself against her fear of losing Rick, which she felt whenever his job took him away. As for Rick, he realized that he had actually chosen that job to avoid dealing with the fear of rejection brought on by his wife's presence. He realized, however, that by running away from Yolanda's reserved disposition, he could not succeed in escaping his own abandonment complex, which followed him wherever he went. We see, then, how an inability to express feelings can cause a rift to develop between people who love each other. Often, fear of disappointing or displeasing the other will prevent one partner from expressing his emotions, but his silence brings about the very disappointment and rejection he hoped to avoid. Once he gains insight into how the patterns are established, he will be freed from constraints in his dealings with others because his fundamental need for love is satisfied. The helper must realize that lack of love is the single most significant factor in the formation of patterns. And lack of love, combined with lack of acknowledgment, is also the source of the invader/invadee pattern.

3. The invader and the invadee

The invader is someone who lacks respect for other people's differences, who violates their limits and their mental, physical and professional space.

A glance at any newspaper will convince you that the world is full of invaders. The wars, revolutions and uprisings that occur with regrettable frequency are all born of invasion in one form or another. Feeling that their beliefs, their right to be different and their freedom have been violated, entire peoples rise up to redress the wrongs done to them, although in many cases they are unable to stop the invaders, who infiltrate others' territory and occupy a place that is not rightfully theirs.

The invader is filled with a need to possess and control others. Brute strength and manipulation are the means he uses. He refuses to allow others to impose limits on his behavior, overstepping boundaries with impunity. Indeed, he will do anything to show he can exceed the limits of others. If he were to accept them, it would restrict the range of his influence and make him extremely insecure. In fact, people imbued with this pattern have a very great need to be acknowledged and made to feel secure because they have often grown up in families where they had no "territory" they could call their own and where the parents' strict discipline was based on introjected principles or beliefs. This was how it was with Max, the oldest of 12 children. His early recollections of family life were relatively happy. He especially remembered how everyone shared with and helped one another. All the boys wore the same clothes interchangeably, shared the same toys and slept in the same room. When one of them was given a toy as a present, he was obliged to share it. Since nobody had any personal territory, nobody set any limits, and this attitude was repeated at the psychological level; there simply was no privacy. The only means of self-protection was withdrawal. Although Max could laugh and have fun with his brothers and sisters, he was unable to share what went on inside him with them. His parents, and especially his father, were strict disciplinarians, severely punishing even minor transgressions.

Having grown up in an atmosphere that was simultaneously easygoing and strict, Max had trouble adapting to school. He resented rules and was constantly trying to break them, despite the rejection or punishment he earned as a result. He had been brought up to share and take indiscriminately, and so had trouble confining himself to what was considered his. Another side effect of his upbringing was that, since the notion of territory and limits is closely associated with the notion of identity, Max didn't really know who he was or what he wanted. In fact, it seemed he could only feel at ease when he occupied another's space. Denying him access to that space was tantamount, in his eyes, to declaring that he was worthless, to not recognizing him. Ultimately, this refusal made him feel like he didn't belong.

Since the invader's definition of self depends on other people, he needs to infiltrate their world in order to feel loved, in order to feel alive. If he is excluded, his need for security and acknowledgment is not satisfied. Because he lacked personal space when he was young, he was forced to find his sense of security by invading the space of others. Coming, as Max did, from a family where everyone was expected to be the same, the invader cannot understand why the world would shut him out, nor can he understand why its values and beliefs differ from his own. So he invades it, placing himself in a paradoxical situation of dominance and dependence. He invades in order to find acknowledgment and obtains, of course, the opposite: rejection.

This is, in fact, what led Max into therapy. He and his partner Linda had been living together for five years. Their first few years together had been happy ones because they shared everything. Little by little, however, Linda had started to define her limits and demarcate her territory, initiating a power struggle. Since Max saw limits as a form of rejection, he simply overstepped them in an attempt to protect himself from the suffering they caused him. Completely ignoring Linda's wishes, he shamelessly pried into her affairs, thus earning systematic rejection. Feeling shut out and worthless, Max tried even harder to worm his way into Linda's well-guarded territory, not realizing that this was the root of his problem.

In fact, Max had the same problem at work. He was helpful and hardworking to the point where he had progressively taken over, not only from his colleagues, but even from his superiors.

These are the unconscious behavior patterns the invader falls into. When others take advantage of his helpfulness, he believes he has the right to infringe on their privacy. However, this manipulative tactic only works until the invadee realizes that he is paying for the invader's generosity with his mental, physical and professional space, and thus his freedom.

The game was up for Max, too. His companion and his immediate superior reacted forcefully to his intrusiveness, leaving him feeling completely lost and rejected, and dangerously close to losing both his job and his relationship. Since he was no longer able to control the others' territory, he felt helpless, even desperate.

It took some time before Max was able to see his actions for what they were. Because he had never differentiated between himself and others, he had to find out who he really was. If he could define his own limits he would know how to respect the limits of others, and how to enforce respect for his, since the invader is also, in some ways, an invadee. Through inner work, he came to accept other people's differences even as he discovered his own.

He was able to acknowledge the fact that Linda's needs, desires and goals were different from his.

Max also discovered how his invader pattern had caused him to disrupt relationships, and he learned to take responsibility for his actions. This allowed him to regain the power he had given to others and use it to direct his own life. However, he also discovered that he was not responsible for Linda's feelings, or for that of his superiors. These people were invadees who had come into his life unconsciously seeking a behavior pattern that would complement their own.

The invadee is someone who, for fear of not being loved, cannot set limits, does not define his mental, physical or professional space, makes neither choices nor decisions and cannot show that he is different.

In order to satisfy his need for love and recognition, the invadee, who is often an abandonee as well, leaves himself wide open to anyone who shows him the least affection. He feels so indebted to this person that he is willing to prostitute himself, metaphorically speaking, in order to be loved. Like the abandonee, the invadee lacks self-respect and will practically hand over his life and all his belongings to anyone who shows the slightest interest in him. He neglects to set up any barriers or means of protection because he is afraid of losing the other. However, defenselessness and lack of freedom are a high price to pay for love and acknowledgment, especially when the love is basically unsatisfactory, since it is based on "indebtedness."

Breaking out of an invadee pattern is extremely difficult. He who succeeds usually has to sacrifice the friendship of those whose affection he tried so hard to earn.

I am reminded here of the story of Victoria. At the age of 39, Victoria came to see me because she was suffering from acute anxiety. This was beginning to impair her ability to function normally, both with her children and with the patients she attended to in her capacity as a nurse. After a while, she finally discovered that the source of her unhappiness lay in the fact that her life did not belong to her. At home, she gave herself completely to her husband, her children, her family and her friends, and at work she let herself be invaded by her patients and the doctors. She had no time left for herself, no space in which to withdraw. Above all, she dared not define her limits, nor express her needs, for fear of losing the love she needed so desperately. She satisfied her need for acknowledgment by being unfailingly devoted and generous. Now, however, she had come to a point in her life where she had to choose between the satisfaction of giving herself unstintingly to others and the satisfaction of attaining a certain freedom of action. Since the price she paid for her devotion was acute anxiety, Victoria decided to create some space for herself in her life. In order to do so, she needed to impose certain limits on her entourage. The results were disastrous. Accustomed as they were to "using" her whenever they needed to, her husband, her children and her friends were shocked when she began to establish limits and make decisions.

The invadee has a great deal of inner work to accomplish before he can leave his pattern behind, for he has to tackle the whole issue of acquired rights. As he lets himself be invaded by others, he progressively hands over to them the power to control his life. Once he withdraws that right, they inevitably react with outrage and rejection. In other words, he has to accept the fact that breaking free from his pattern will entail the loss of certain relationships. And this is precisely what makes it so hard. Since the invadee has let himself be invaded in the first place because he couldn't bear to lose the other, he must accept rejection in order to free himself from his pattern and he needs help in order to accomplish this.

There comes a time in the invadee's life when the need for space and freedom becomes a matter of survival: the pattern has got to go. Without freedom, he is tormented by anxiety, he suffocates, he loses the will to live. At this point, on one level, the invadee is almost dead. Struggling to extricate himself, he pays for his renaissance with the loss of relationships he held dear. However, if he chooses to die in the eyes of the other in order to be reborn in his own, then fulfillment of his fundamental needs will come easily. Freedom is one of mankind's greatest needs; for centuries, human beings have suffered and died for it. Being physically free, however, is not enough to ensure our happiness, for mental freedom, the freedom to be oneself, to choose to share one's personal space and to define one's limits is just as vital.

Unless we have that inner freedom in our dealings with others, we cannot really have satisfactory relationships. One single relationship based on freedom is worth a thousand based on dependence and self-abasement. Being free means being capable of making choices and accepting the consequences of our decisions. It means being capable of establishing limits and setting the boundaries of our mental, physical, ideological and professional space. Being free also means respecting the limits and the territory of others. It means asserting our right to be different without imposition, and respecting the differences of others. Being free means setting our priorities and acting upon them. It means being able to give without expecting anything in return and receiving without feeling indebted. Finally, being free means accepting responsibility for what we experience and for who we are, and refusing to take responsibility for what others experience.

This freedom is precisely what makes human relationships so wonderful. Those who discover this find it impossible to be satisfied with relationships that foster an unhealthy dependence. Given the choice, people will consistently choose to discard suffocating relationships in order to acquire healthy, creative, propulsive ones which encourage autonomy. This choice, in fact, was a significant factor in making me what I am today. All my life, I had given others power over me, letting them invade my mental, physical and professional space. I let them do this without really opposing them, because I was afraid of losing their love.

One day, however, I realized that I no longer had either love or respect for myself. Because I wanted other people to love me, I was completely denying my own needs and emotions and failing to set my own limits. This left me with a profound feeling of emptiness, and an inescapable suffering. Specific instances of invasion occurred, and I decided to risk defining some limits. I even decided that some very important relationships would have to be sacrificed. The decision to put myself first, to respect myself, did not come easily, but the changes it brought about in my life were and are priceless. Thus one of the most painful periods of my life was also a pivotal one, leading to a veritable renaissance. Since that day, I have never lost touch with my inner strength and creativity. I remain convinced that, had I not made that fundamental choice, I would never have come to be founder and director of the counseling center, never have been able to successfully run a school for more than 550 adults, nor organize the teaching and training of some 45 trainers, group leaders, research directors, supervisors and regulators.

I am convinced that the reason I knew how to pick responsible, competent individuals to work and be friends with was that I decided to put myself first and to act with self-respect by defining my own limits. My relationships with colleagues and acquaintances are honest; they are based on the fact that we share our experiences in a responsible manner and respect one another and ourselves. Within our relationships, we strive for total independence and complete freedom.

The stages of this inner work, some of which are more difficult than others, that lead us toward freedom also apply to demystifying the patterns of the judge and the offender.

4. The judge and the offender

The patterns of judge and offender are complementary in the sense that the judge is also an offender, and vice versa.

In an attempt to escape from his problems, disappointments and suffering, the judge projects them onto others through arbitrary judgments. He takes no responsibility for his feelings because he has guilt about his emotions and because he is afraid of them. Instead, he makes others responsible for every unpleasant thing that happens to him.

This pattern is established fairly early in an individual's life, and is formed in the following manner: when those who are in charge of raising the child are not in touch with their own emotions, they tend to judge the child often and harshly, making him feel guilty and teaching him to view himself in the same harsh light. So, he becomes very hard on himself, but also displays an obsessive fear of being judged by others, against which he defends himself by becoming their judge. Figure 3.12 illustrates the judge pattern.

Figure 3.12

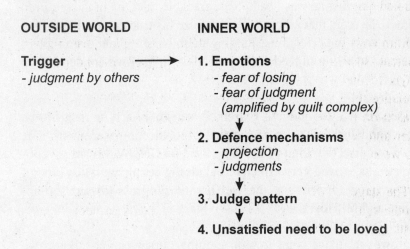

As with most other patterns, the one illustrated above originates in an unfulfilled need for love. For, as we have seen, the child's self-esteem and behavior are shaped by the desire to please those who raise him, in order to avoid being judged, rejected or unloved. Because his actions are consistently motivated by the need to please others and be loved by them, he has no idea who he is or what he wants. When others judge him, he not only feels "bad" and guilty, but also rejected. In this sense, the judge is also an offender and an abandonee.

Anyone whose life is marked by this pattern will display a tendency toward inhibition and live in constant fear of being, doing or saying anything that will bring judgment down upon him, either from himself or from others. This fear considerably restricts his sphere of activity and the scope of his creativity. His attempts to deal with his fears take the form of arbitrary and misplaced judgments, for which he is naturally rejected. He judges others in order to protect himself from the pain of being judged and rejected by them, unaware that his attitude brings him the exact opposite of love and acceptance.

The judge is not in touch with his inner self. We feel ill at ease in his presence because he cannot acknowledge his fear of being judged, but suppresses it, and projects it onto others. Having been taught by his upbringing that he was "bad," disagreeable, lacking in the required attributes, he fears that others will recognize his true nature. He cannot accept his own imperfections, judging them harshly, and even though he is afraid of being judged, he is merciless in his own condemnation of the flaws and weaknesses of others.

Deep down, the judge is extremely sensitive, and he needs to be accepted and listened to in a way that precludes any judgment. The creative nondirective kind of listening used by CNDA-trained psychotherapists has proved very effective in helping people with this kind of pattern to stop condemning themselves and progress toward self-acceptance and self-love.

However, if we want to stop judging ourselves and others, we must make contact with people in authority whose attitude differs from that of our parents and teachers and does not load us down with guilt. When we work with a therapist or teacher who accepts us as we are, without judgment, who helps cultivate our nascent self-love and progressively eradicates our guilt, then we can throw off the yoke of fear and judgment that prevented us from being truly alive.

This shared feeling of guilt is what creates the bond between the judge and the offender. Ensconced behind a wall of judgment, the judge protects himself from his own guilt by making others feel guilty. Inevitably, he attracts a partner who harbors a guilt complex similar to his own, who is inhabited by an offender pattern.

Lack of self-confidence causes the offender to simultaneously take responsibility for other people's problems and protect himself from it by self-punishment.

Like the judge, the offender was made to feel guilty by those who raised him and, like the judge, he learned to think of himself as bad. To defend himself against those negative feelings, he avoids standing up for himself and punishes himself. His unconscious or unacknowledged goal in this is to punish the other and transfer his own guilt onto him. The only difference between the patterns of judge and offender, then, lies in their defense mechanisms. The former uses judgment to protect himself, the latter self-punishment. In both cases, however, there exists an enormous need for love and an intense fear of rejection and judgment, as well as a well-developed guilt complex. There is a fairly close connection between this set of complementary patterns and the bully/victim duo: the judge and the bully both condemn, and the offender hides and punishes himself, just like the victim.

The phenomenon of self-punishment becomes a key element in the offender's pattern. This defense mechanism is responsible for earning him the judge's condemnation, which he accepts. However, in an indirect way, he is himself a judge because he uses his self-punishment to punish the other. This subtle maneuver reinforces the judge's guilt; he, in turn, continues to defend himself against this feeling by judging his partner, which increases the offender's guilt. Thus, a neverending cycle is established, maintaining a state of mutual dependence and dissatisfaction.

The cycle cannot be broken until the dissatisfaction of one of the partners becomes unbearable. This is what happened in Sandra's case. When she decided to go into therapy, she was unaware that she was punishing herself. She did know that she felt overwhelmed by the constant condemnation of Dorothy, who had been her lover for six years. In therapy, Sandra not only came to understand how she had been encouraging her companion's judgments, she also discovered how her resulting defense mechanism manifested itself. If Dorothy accused her of always coming home late, she decided not to go out any more; if Dorothy thought this or that outfit too provocative, she returned it; if Dorothy criticized a particular program Sandra was watching, she would turn the television off and go to her room; if Dorothy thought her golf swing needed work, she would storm off to the clubhouse for a beer. Eventually, fear of being either rejected or made to feel guilty prevented either of them from communicating.

Shaking off a defense mechanism is not easy, since it intervenes spontaneously in the mental process as a means of protection against suffering. For Sandra, putting an end to self-punishment meant confronting her sense of guilt and her fear of being judged and rejected. It is not easy to replace defensive self-punishment with responsible self-expression. The risk, of course, is that of being rejected because of the emotions one expresses. Moreover, self-expression requires that one be sufficiently in touch with oneself to be aware of one's emotions in the first place. In Sandra's case this would have proved difficult, since her defensive attitude had cut her off from her emotions, of which she was both afraid and ashamed. Breaking out of this behavior pattern starts with self-awareness and continues with self-acceptance and self-love. This is the process that will teach us how our psyche works, and give us the means to improve our personal lives and our relationships. It is also the process that can unravel the complementary patterns of the missionary and the disciple.

5. The missionary and the disciple

The term "missionary" defines the pattern of a person who shields himself from his emotional experiences with introjected principles and beliefs, which he uses to dominate others, by presenting them as absolute truths.

The missionary cannot countenance any truth outside of his own. This explains his need to "convert" those who do not share his views. He feels he is more advanced and better than other people: better, for him, being the ability to adhere to the principles and beliefs he espouses. Convinced that his "truth" can save others, he judges and even mistrusts those who do not receive it.

The person with this pattern may be found in social, political, intellectual and spiritual circles, but wherever he is, the missionary can be recognized by his remarkable ability to present his beliefs or loyalties in a persuasive manner, and to publicly scorn everything else. This psychological type is possessed by a need to sway others, a need to acquire power. Since he is, of course, in possession of the absolute truth, he feels entitled to exert an astonishing degree of influence over others, both directly and indirectly. When he was being brought up, he was himself a victim of introjected principles and beliefs, and so in his adult life he works on impressing those same beliefs on others.

Generally speaking, the missionary comes from a family where the parents raised their children according to their own introjected ideas. The children are taught to respect the same rules that guide their parents, regardless of whether or not those rules are actually suitable for them as individuals. These ideas, whether of a religious, political or social nature, are therefore imposed as indisputable truths on the children, who must make their thoughts, feelings and actions conform to them. In the end, however, the ideas are grafted on rather than truly integrated. They prevent the child from getting in touch with himself because they are based on a principle of standardization. Everyone whose behavior is guided by those principles will tend to think and behave in the same manner. Rejecting such truths, when those who raised him believe them to be the only valid ones, means laying himself open to rejection and insecurity. Because the child is used to modeling himself after externally imposed beliefs, he needs a rigid framework for his thoughts and actions. For this reason, such people leave one school of thought only to sign up for another. Since they are not at all in touch with themselves, nor used to thinking about what is suited to their needs, they unquestioningly conform to prefabricated belief systems that guide and direct them.

With this in mind, it is easy to see how the missionary is also a disciple, for both are, essentially, people who are cut off from themselves, whose sense of power and importance comes from adopting and conveying the introjections they claim are absolute truths. Both patterns, in fact, are born of the same mental process (see Figure 3.13).

Figure 3.13

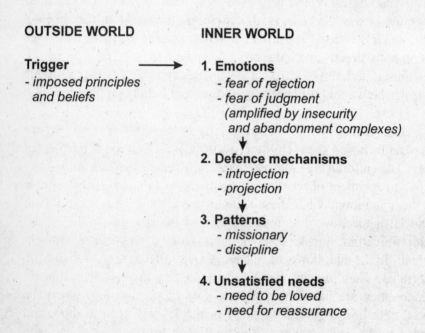

As in other cases, the child adopts a missionary or a disciple pattern to earn his parents' love. He bases his attitudes and behavior on the principles and beliefs they impose on him, without ever determining their suitability. As best he can, he patterns his life on the model they propose, hoping to avoid their judgment and rejection.

Because he cannot direct his life according to who he is, he grows up depending on leaders. In fact, he doesn't know who he is, or what his needs are, because he has never got in touch with his feelings.

The problem of individuals believing themselves to be missionaries is a worldwide phenomenon. Indeed, entire peoples, convinced that their philosophical or religious belief is the only road to truth, regularly set out to convert others to their cause.

Is this to say, then, that all religious and political leaders are unnecessary and should be prohibited? Does it mean that all beliefs and schools of thought ought to be rejected? Far from it. There is a problem, but it should be addressed in another way. The various trends of thought in the world constitute a resource from which we may all draw inspiration. They teach us to respect other people's differences and to open up our minds. Learning about other schools of thought can help us define ourselves, help us find our way. At different stages in his life, man needs a master or guide to discover who he is and where he is going. However, when he denies himself in order to follow the leader and his thought, he is guilty of introjection, of accepting values and beliefs regardless of whether they conform to who he really is. Then he loses his own volition, swayed by external forces like a weathervane. He becomes a soulless disciple, with all his differences smoothed away; an automaton who repeats what he has been taught and who uses those truths to impose uniformity on his fellow men.

Of course, nobody becomes a disciple without some degree of personal responsibility. Breaking out of his pattern requires that the individual's inner work be geared toward self-discovery. This is the only way he will be able to distinguish between what is suitable for him and what is not, the only way he will be able to establish the points where he and the school of thought he espouses meet and diverge. In this event, and in this event only, he will be able to follow his spiritual, philosophical or psychological beliefs in a free and propulsive manner. Otherwise, he becomes a disciple/missionary for principles that mold him into their image, regardless of his inner state.

Teenagers have a particular problem with introjections. Their attempts to shake them off are often at the root of the adolescent "tantrums" that strike such terror in a parent's heart. Since the teenage years are a time in which the adolescent tries to assert his true self, it is perfectly natural that he should also want to shake off the introjections imposed by his upbringing. At this period in his life he often finds himself in a pitched battle with those who raised him: they want to continue imposing their values, principles and beliefs, and the teenager wants to "discover himself," no matter what the cost. Unfortunately, this battle often ends with a clear winner and an even clearer loser. Whether the parent or the teenager emerges victorious, the results can be harmful for both parties. During my years as a high-school teacher, I saw many rifts develop between parents and their teenage children, because of power struggles over the subject of values and beliefs.

On this subject, I recall the story of Janine, a shy girl who was universally rejected at school. Her hairstyle and clothes were completely unfashionable and, because of this, all the other students made fun of her. Once we realize how intensely a 14-year-old girl can feel about her body, we can understand how much their taunting must have made her suffer.

From a teacher's point of view, integrating an "outcast" like this into a group is more difficult than helping a young offender. Generally speaking, one cannot help a teenager unless one first meets with the parents. Janine's family lived in the country, and only came into town on Fridays and Sundays to buy groceries and go to church. They were intent on raising their daughter according to the same principles and demands that had shaped their own lives. Anyone who knows about the general feeling of liberation that occurred in Quebec in the 1960s will understand the difference between parents who hadn't "moved with the times" and their adolescent children. Janine's parents had decided that, cost what it may, their daughter should not take part in the general "depravity." They forbade Janine to go out in the evening or to have anyone over to visit. At any rate, she didn't have any friends, and everyone who knew her called her "stupid," "dumb" or "thickheaded."

At first, I wasn't sure how to help Janine. Thanks to the interest I showed in her, she became excessively attached to me, regularly writing me love letters which she gave to me before class. Her attitude bothered me a great deal, because I was unable to prevent her overstepping my limits. The more attention I gave her, the more she clung to me. I needed to find a way to integrate her into the group so that she would be less dependent on me. Finally, I hit on the idea of suggesting that the students present a written self-portrait of themselves to the class, in which they would recount their life experience, relationship with their parents and feelings with the other members of their group or class. I stressed the verbal presentation aspect of this exercise, and emphasized that the students should be as honest as possible. My intention was to create a situation in which Janine would feel free to express her suffering. When I met with her before class, I strongly encouraged her to participate in the exercise, and to tell her story as she perceived it, which she did.

It must be said that Janine was ashamed to reveal the details of her life to her classmates. At school, she had expended a considerable amount of energy hiding them, and presenting an image of herself that had no connection to reality. Teenagers, however, can always detect a facade. If she wanted to be liked, Janine was going about it the wrong way.

Because she trusted me, Janine agreed to go through with the exercise, and confided in her classmates those things that she had always hid from them: the pain of rejection she suffered in class and the pain caused by her parents' reactionary mentality. She succeeded in talking about her situation without laying too much blame on others. Instead, she tried to ask herself how she could change it for the better.

Revealing her true story brought unexpected results: just as teenagers can be ruthless in some ways, so they can be supportive in others. She was both relieved and encouraged by her fellow students' positive reaction.

Following this exchange, things improved visibly for Janine, at least at school. She no longer presented a persona to the others, which made for more genuine relations between her and her classmates. She realized that hiding her true self in the hope of being liked had only earned her rejection. All she had to do to win was become herself. As the others began to accept her, her self-esteem grew, and she learned to assert herself and find her own niche within the group.

However, the changes that were taking place at school got her in trouble at home. As far as her parents were concerned, she had gone from being submissive to insolent. I finally had a chance to meet her parents for the first time after the report cards were sent home.

At first they were very defensive and dogmatic. However, they loosened up when I made it clear that I was interested in helping their daughter, whose marks were, frankly, terrible. During that meeting I learned a lot about Janine's background, and many things became clear to me. When her father had married her mother, she was already two months pregnant, a fact they had always hidden from Janine, who believed she had been born prematurely. More or less rejected by their respective families, her parents had moved to the country, where they lived quietly on a small farm, hoping to hide their shame and their sin. They had both suffered so much that they would do anything to protect their daughter from going through the same thing. This is why they had tried to restrict her freedom as much as possible. Because the principles on which they raised her were born of defensive introjections rather than being an expression of their true selves, they broke down the relationship they wanted to establish with their adolescent daughter, instead of building it up. I suggested that they tell Janine what they had told me, and explain to her why they were imposing these limits, which were the source of so much strife. I suggested that they speak to her of their pain and their fears. When parents speak honestly to their children, whether toddlers or adolescents, about their emotions and experiences, it is surprising how much closer it brings them. I do not think that Janine's parents did open up to her, but I know that they became less hard on her.

Painful experiences of being judged and rejected can cause us to introject principles, values and beliefs that are potentially harmful, but understanding their origin can lead to self-awareness, self-acceptance and self-love. Through these, we become more open to the differences of others. As I have said before, there is no such thing as an absolute truth. There are only unrecognized fears, from which the missionary and the disciple protect themselves to avoid the suffering of not being loved. Our inner work helps us to understand that other people are just like us in that their happiness doesn't depend on any received truth; they just need to be loved. The drive to indoctrinate others maintains both the missionary and the disciple in a state of dependence, and destroys their relationship. The same state of mutual dependence unites the savior and the protégé, whose patterns form the topic for the next section.

6. The savior and the protégé

The savior pattern is one of the most common among human beings. One of its characteristic features is the compulsive need to protect, spare and take care of others to prevent them from suffering.

This kind of pattern can be observed in many parents, psychotherapists and teachers, who choose to behave in this manner in order to protect themselves from their own feeling of powerlessness and from the suffering it brings. When the savior has to stand by and watch others suffer, knowing he is powerless to help them, it hurts him. So, to escape his own suffering, he attempts to diminish or cover up the other's pain by protecting or mothering him.

On closer inspection, we realize that the savior's attitude is actually based on projection. His attempts to relieve the other's suffering are actually aimed at easing his own pain: it is not the other he wants to spare so much as himself. But why is he so caught up in the suffering of others? Why does it disturb him so much?

At an early age, the savior was made to feel responsible for the suffering of his brothers and sisters, or even his parents. When someone else was sick, hurt or unhappy, he thought it was his fault. The underlying feeling in the formation of this pattern is a strong sense of guilt. Thus, feeling guilty and responsible for the suffering of others, the savior will do anything in his power to diminish or even prevent that suffering, simply to protect himself. He involuntarily falls into this behavior pattern whenever he is confronted with a crisis or a hurt or unhappy person, even if he is not directly involved. Fearing the suffering caused by the others impending unhappiness, he may even go so far as to take charge of someone to prevent possible future injury.

This is precisely what Lawrence did with his brother Paul. Lawrence was the oldest of seven children; Paul had just started university. When he and his brother moved in together, Lawrence immediately took his younger brother under his wing, not only looking after all his physical and material needs, but taking responsibility for all his emotional problems, and for his difficulties at university as well. Whenever his brother was upset, Lawrence became even more attentive and affectionate, showering him with good advice, just as he had seen his mother do with his father. And just as she had done, too, he shouldered the burden of everything that happened to Paul, everything he experienced. In the face of this mothering, Paul reacted as his father had done: with impatience, ingratitude and outbursts of anger. This frightened Lawrence, who retaliated by increasing his protectiveness and mothering, and also voicing guilt-inducing complaints. By this point, their relationship was definitely caught up in a vicious circle.

Children from the same family often end up with the same complementary patterns as their parents. Because the children identify with their parents, or are unknowingly influenced by the methods of those who raise them, the relationships they build with one another are based on the way their parents interacted. Lawrence, who identified with his ailing mother, had fallen into a savior pattern. He was the oldest son, and had grown up with the pain of seeing his mother habitually ill, of feeling obliged to do the impossible to shield her from her frequent, not to say permanent, indispositions. When his attempts to protect her and take care of her failed, he assuaged his guilt by becoming even more attentive. Lawrence truly felt that he was responsible for his mothers ill health, of which she never ceased to remind him during her plaintive ramblings. His guilt was so omnipresent that it overpowered his own needs, desires and emotions, preventing him from being attuned to himself. For example, he was completely unaware that he was just as melancholic as his mother, and that this aspect of his personality irritated his father and brother intensely, provoking them to anger and rejection. In CNDA-directed therapy, Lawrence was able to see his actions for what they were. He discovered that, in addition to being a savior, he was also a victim, the two being often indistinguishable.

This chain of events occurs frequently among those with a savior pattern. Generally, the savior does not realize that he is saving the other to save himself, that he is really the one who needs help and who needs to pursue his inner work in order to be released from responsibilities that are not his.

In savior/protégé relations, the savior is generally a loser, because the help he extends to the other is actually meant to protect himself, and is thus ineffective. In fact, it unconsciously suggests to the other that he is either unable to find any solutions to his own difficulties, or else is too weak and ineffectual to implement them. The savior's attitude is thus responsible for undermining the protégé's self-confidence, maintaining him in a state of dependence and insecurity.

Another serious consequence of one person's adopting a "saving" attitude toward another is that lack of truth and genuine expression distort their relationship. The savior's conscious goal in shielding his partner is to prevent his partner's suffering. However, his unconscious goal is to protect himself from his own fear of losing the other. Basically, then, underlying this pattern is an unfulfilled need for love. In order to keep the other's love and avoid rejection, the savior automatically shields and protects the other. Thus we see a clear link between this pattern and that of the abandonee. In looking after the other, the savior is denying his own needs, and this unwitting lack of integrity leads to the loss of the very person whom his "mothering" was intended to keep close.

This is, more or less, what happened to Mario. Over the years he had lived with Angela, he never told her what he felt, to avoid wounding her sensitive and impulsive nature. Also, although he couldn't bring himself to admit it, he was afraid she would react angrily to the way he felt. So, to protect himself, he kept his troubles, fears and limits to himself.

Angela had a very strong sex drive. Mario spared no effort to satisfy her, because he didn't want to disappoint her, but mainly because he felt guilty when she was frustrated. In doing so, he failed to take his own limits into account. He didn't realize that by not being honest with Angela, he was creating a gulf between them. He didn't realize that he was not being true to himself, and that his relationship with the woman he loved was based on an inability to express his feelings. They grew further and further apart until, finally, Angela left Mario, saying bitterly that he had only ever loved her for her body. The injustice of this accusation stung him deeply. In fact, it was the suffering brought on by this separation that led Mario into therapy. He was shattered that Angela could feel that way about him, after all he had done to satisfy her. Listening to him, one would have thought he were the victim of a heartless, soulless bully. While in CNDA-directed therapy he discovered how his savior pattern had brought about the breakup, and he became aware of and accepted his responsibility for it. This was, in fact, the only way to avoid re-establishing, in his next relationship, the same protective system he had fallen into with the previous three. He was also able to use this discovery in his relationships with his four children, all from different mothers, whom he adored but had a tendency to overprotect. Unless Mario wanted his children to abandon him the way their mothers had, he would have to work on his pattern. And abandon him they would have, since the overprotected child almost invariably rebels against the "mothering" parent, angry at having been robbed of his freedom. The savior pattern, as described by Mario's case, is illustrated below (see Figure 3.14).

Figure 3.14

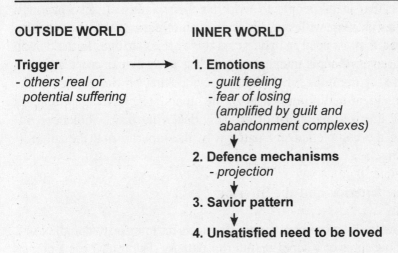

This same mental pattern is reproduced in almost the same manner in the protégé's psyche, as he unconsciously searches for a person to take care of him. Finding such a person is not difficult, as the protégé's apparent weakness suggests that he needs to be shielded from the slings and arrows of outrageous fortune. As a child, those in charge of raising the protégé protected him from classroom brawls and playground squabbles. He never learned to stand up for himself because someone else always did it for him. He attracts a savior because of his dependent attitude and because he projects his own need to be taken care of onto others, thus turning him into a savior as well. To elucidate the complementary attraction of these two patterns, let us return to Paul and Lawrence. As his younger brother's savior, Lawrence did everything to shield Paul from life's misfortunes. When Paul rejected his advice and attentions, Lawrence sulked, making Paul feel guilty and also making him feel responsible for what Lawrence was going through. At this stage, Paul's anger tended to evaporate, and he would treat his brother more kindly, trying, in turn, to protect him. Thus the patterns flipped this way and that, always maintaining their complementary nature.

At this point, it seems clear that a failed relationship is often the catalyst that leads people to work on their pattern. It also becomes clear that dealing with one pattern has an effect on other areas, other patterns, that we need to understand if we are to change. In the human psyche, everything is interconnected. Just as we cannot work with just one part of the body, in isolation, so touching on one aspect of the psychological realm implicates all the others. The CNDA approaches every pattern in the spirit of an individual's intrinsic wholeness, including the complementary patterns of the superior and the subordinate.

7. The superior and the inferior

Generally speaking, people who have an inferiority complex will also show signs of a superior/inferior pattern. The inferior is a person who is profoundly lacking in self-confidence and, because of this, tends to consistently put himself down. This person is a perfectionist, who holds back the product or performance until it is good enough to be unveiled. Since this is so, it is hard for him to translate his ideas into actions, and he often becomes frustrated or withdrawn because he cannot permit himself any kind of mistake, much less failure.

The point of reference for the inferior is never himself, but always others, to whom he compares himself and finds himself wanting. Needless to say, this frustrates him and makes him unhappy. Although he is aware of his talents and abilities, he is unable to develop them because he is convinced that everyone else's work is better than his own. Comparison is, in fact, his downfall. By granting the other disproportionate importance, he loses sight of his own values and creative abilities. Basically, his talents remain underexploited, and he does not live up to his own expectations.

When the inferior was a child, his parents would never take anything less than perfection. They were much more likely to put him down than to encourage and congratulate him. His primary educators compared him unfavorably with his brothers and sisters, his friends, his cousins, and so on. Comparison always has a harmful effect on people because it involves judgments that elevate some at the expense of others. It also has the effect of encouraging performance. The child who is raised in an atmosphere of constant comparison will base his behavior on what others think of him, thus creating relationships based on competition and power struggles.

If I say to a child: "I find your work very interesting; I like it a lot," I am acknowledging his abilities, building up his self-confidence, encouraging him to continue. However, by saying: "I think your work is better than everyone else's," I am making him feel superior, judging him in light of the others and not on his own merits and suggesting, unconsciously, that his worth depends solely on his ability to surpass others. This sort of educational philosophy reserves its praise for the child's performance as opposed to his intrinsic worth. The child raised in accordance with this philosophy will feel worthless unless he does manage to outshine his peers; he will only feel proud of his most outstanding achievements, never acknowledging himself for who he actually is. As he grows up, he will become progressively more insecure.

On the other side of the coin is the child who is made to feel inferior and incompetent through constant put-downs. But whether the comparisons increase or diminish the person's value, the end result over the short and especially the long term is that he comes to believe that his merit as a person resides in winning. Whenever he comes in second, he feels worthless.

Because of the way he was raised, the inferior suffers from a lack of self-love. He grew up believing that if he wanted to be loved he had to be perfect, better than all the rest. As an adult, he is convinced that unless he meets those conditions he will be rejected or lose the other's love. This conviction is a source of great unhappiness. While on the one hand he wants to strive toward perfection because he believes it is the only way to win the other person's favor, on the other hand his need to be perfect and outstanding in everything he does paralyzes him, and prevents him from acting. This dichotomy maintains his frustration, lack of self-confidence and conviction that he is unworthy of another's love.

The best way for a inferior to increase his self-confidence is, of course, to act. But he cannot reach this stage unless he first becomes aware of his psychological process, and is able to accept it (see Figure 3.15).

Figure 3.15

OUTSIDE WORLD

Trigger ⟶
- *comparison*

INNER WORLD

1. Emotions
- *fear of losing*
- *fear of deceiving*
- *fear of failure*
- *fear of making mistakes (amplified by inferiority and sibling rivalry complexes)*

↓

2. Defence mechanisms
- *comparative judgment*

↓

3. Inferior pattern

↓

4. Unsatisfied needs
- *need to be loved*
- *need to be acknowledged*

Because the inferior was raised according to comparative value judgments, he picked up the habit of automatically comparing and judging himself with respect to others, thus inhibiting his actions and ability to assert his right to be different. Actually, he doesn't really know who he is, because he has always used others as a point of reference. Since his pattern leads him to compare himself unfavorably to them, he unconsciously singles out people who appear to think highly of themselves, who place themselves above the common crowd, thus feeding his inferior pattern.

Just like the inferior, the superior suffers from an acute lack of self-confidence, but unlike his partner in the pair, he displays a false attitude of superiority to hide it. Deep down, the superior is a inferior who refuses to accept his true nature.

Because he was made to feel inferior, insecure or worthless by those who raised him, he seeks to protect himself from the suffering brought on by his fears and sense of helplessness by presenting an image that belies his actual feelings. Thus he becomes boastful, even deceitful, in order to make others believe in his abilities.

Like the inferior, the superior is afraid that others will not love him unless he is better than all the rest, so he constantly strives to be "better," using words where actions would not work to his advantage. This is the sort of person who is called a "big talker," because he talks a lot, but does little. His determination to show others that he is kind, intelligent, capable, resourceful, and so on, demonstrates his need to prove to himself that he is worthy of being acknowledged and loved. His insecurity and lack of self-confidence are so great that he overcompensates for them, with words and gestures designed to demonstrate that he can do anything.

It was, in fact, the unpleasant consequences of a superior pattern that brought Marc into therapy. He was then going through his third breakup in less than two years, and found himself unable to maintain the casual attitude he had displayed when the two previous relationships came to an end. A broken and unhappy man, he could no longer lie to himself because he could no longer hide from his deep-seated conviction that he was worthless and unlovable because he didn't love himself.

Marc had attended a lecture on the creative nondirective approach, and had subsequently decided to come and see me. However, he was far from feeling sufficiently at ease to open up completely. I think that the trust he felt for me helped him a lot.

The superior has a hard time allowing others to help him. Since he has adopted his pattern in order to escape his feelings of inferiority in the first place, he finds it painful to show his true self because he is intensely afraid of not being loved. This is why this type of person rarely goes into therapy. When they do, it is because they have come up against a situation in which they experience emotions so intensely painful that they can no longer deny them.

Let me return, briefly, to the importance of the psychotherapist's accepting attitude in helping the client learn to accept himself as he is. Those who are responsible for raising a child should, ideally, be similarly accepting. Since he felt assured that I accepted and even loved him with his lack of self-esteem, his fears, his insecurity, Marc took me more and more into his confidence. This led to the discovery that he had lost his lovers because he was unable to show them his true self.

As we have seen in previous cases, Marc was in the paradoxical situation of someone who pretends to be superior in order to win love and recognition but whose pretense earns him exactly the opposite of what he wanted, namely, rejection.

Although others may be impressed by the superior for a while, they end up being disappointed when they discover his need to prove himself and his total lack of self-confidence. He will not be accepted until he shows his true self, and this cannot happen unless he begins to understand his inner processes. The superior/inferior duo becomes bogged down in unhappiness and misunderstanding because neither one is able to perceive the complementary forces at work: the superior needs the inferior to shore up his fragile sense of superiority, and vice versa. As long as they remain undiscovered, these two patterns inevitably attract each other, as do the set of dominator/dominee patterns.

8. The dominator and the dominee

In order to protect himself from his own emotional frailty, the dominator strives to attain self-mastery, to attain a position from which he can seize power and use it to dominate others.

The person inhabited by this pattern is filled with fear: fear of the unknown, fear of his own vulnerability and fear of his needs, desires and emotions, which he suppresses, to the point where he has no knowledge of his inner world. In fact, it becomes a menace that threatens to engulf him unless he smothers it. And smother it he does, by generalizing, justifying, explaining, intellectualizing or moralizing. To make himself feel secure, he is constantly trying to impose uniformity on others, directing their lives as he directs his own. Above all, he wants to avoid having to deal with the complexity of human existence, so he attempts to trivialize it, viewing it as a sitcom, rife with generalizations that eliminate differences and obstruct independence.

The dominator has a tendency to control, through his defensive attitude, the needs, desires and fears of others just as he controls his own. In this sense, he neither respects himself, nor the right of other people to be different. He could never be a leader because he is far too content-directive. People tend to follow him out of fear or obligation, rather than admiration or love, as they would a true leader.

A leader is someone other people follow because of who he is and the attitude that he radiates; his personality has an unconscious, propulsive and beneficial effect on others. His presence and charisma help them to assert their right to be different, to actualize their potential, to express their creativity. However, when the dominator rises to a position of power, his dominating attitude tends to ignore personality differences, stifle potential and suppress creativity. Contrary to a true leader, the dominator is not a creator but a copyist, who relies on other people's ideas to fuel his attempts at control and to inhibit any expression of feeling. Because he is afraid of them, he expends all his vital energy in containing emotions, both his own and those of others. His attitude engenders subjection, and a lack of confidence.

Because he is cut off from himself, the dominator has a great deal of difficulty building intimate relationships with others. He sees love and affection as emotions that cannot be regulated, and so he is afraid of them. Torn between his urgent need to be loved and his intense fear of revealing his vulnerability, the dominator will see most of his relationships end in dissatisfaction. In fact, his vulnerability is rooted in the suffering he went through as a child, and he is afraid that others will, once again, reject his need for love and ridicule his sensitivity and the "feminine" side of his nature.

This pattern can be observed among a great many parents, and even among some teachers. Robert, who taught history at the high school level, was not well liked by his students, who had nicknamed him "Robby the Robot." Since he himself was not overly thrilled with his job, he confined himself exclusively to the syllabus, regarding as irrelevant any form of interaction and sharing of personal experiences. He knew nothing about his students except their names, their behavior in class and their marks in history. Any attempt to introduce a new element into his frame of reference was ridiculed or rejected. In fact, Robert dominated his students by ridicule, which is how he himself had been dominated by his parents. He came to see me after attending a day-long workshop I organized for the teaching staff at his school. At that time, his stated goal was to deal as efficiently as possible with his proposed career change, asserting extrinsic reasons for his need to take up a different profession. What he was doing, of course, was making the external world responsible for his inner problem. He remarked that, over the past several years, young people were becoming more difficult to control; that they were less attentive, less interesting than they had been in the past.

Thanks to the CNDA, which like the Rogerian approach is centered more on the person and less on the problem, Robert was able to uncover both his dominator pattern and the consequences of that pattern in his personal and professional life. He understood why his wife, whom he loved deeply, had left him for another man.

One particular event in Robert's childhood had proved to be a significant factor in the formation of his pattern: his mother, who had discovered and come to terms with her lesbianism, left his father and went to live with a woman when Robert was only six years old. His father had gone to great lengths to win custody of their child and, having got it, proceeded to influence Robert by ridiculing every one of his actions or reactions that he interpreted as being feminine to prevent, as far as possible, his son from becoming a homosexual. He forced Robert to be "male," and hence rational, at all times. He categorized expressing emotions, taking an interest in the arts and doing housework as feminine; for a male to do those things meant that he must be a homosexual. He worried about the times Robert met with his mother, for though he had once loved her, he now considered her abnormal and even unbalanced.

So, Robert grew up in an atmosphere of domination based on fear. At a young age, he learned to suppress his emotions, needs and desires, and to deny his natural penchant for things artistic. While in therapy, he understood that his need to dominate others stemmed not only from his father's influence, but was also based on an overwhelming fear of his so-called feminine traits which, for him, represented a "threat" of homosexuality.

As Robert gradually evolved over the next two years, he got back in touch with his mother and started studying part-time toward a degree in graphic design. The idea of being gay no longer frightened him because he found his mother to be both strong and sensitive, fragile yet well balanced. His contact with her enabled him to get rid of his prejudices, accept the woman who had brought him into this world, and hence accept his own true nature. When he reached this stage, he left therapy not because he had resolved all his difficulties, but because he felt able to deal with them.

Was Robert gay? Did he give up teaching? Creative nondirective psychotherapy does not concern itself with answering such questions. The important thing is that the client discover who he is, and that his actions be rooted in self-respect so as to increase his happiness and well-being. By bringing his psychological process and his dominator pattern to light, Robert placed his feet squarely on the path to freedom.

As Figure 3.16 shows, the dominator is also a dominee. Self-domination, and his tendency to let himself be dominated, are responsible for his need to dominate others. Thus, he inevitably attracts a person with a dominee pattern, that is, someone who, because he is afraid of his emotions, will dominate himself and let himself be dominated just as the dominator does.

Figure 3.16

OUTSIDE WORLD	INNER WORLD
Trigger ⟶	**1. Emotions**
- ridicule	*- fear of the unknown*
	- fear of vulnerability
	- fear of rejection
	- fear of ridicule (amplified by abandonment complex)
	↓
	2. Defence mechanisms
	- rationalization
	↓
	3. Dominator pattern
	↓
	4. Unsatisfied need to be loved

Based on what we have seen with other patterns, it is not surprising that the dominee is also a dominator: his projective attitude makes him treat others the same way he treats himself. The only way he can break free from this pattern is by becoming particularly attentive to his emotional experiences and by learning to accept the fears that render him incapable of action. However long it lasts, this process must necessarily involve self-discovery if it is to end in liberation.

The last pattern that will be discussed in this chapter is that of the manipulator and the manipulatee.

9. The manipulator and the manipulatee

As with all the other patterns, that of the manipulator and manipulatee develops out of an unfulfilled need to be loved and acknowledged. Let us look first at the manipulator, whose most salient characteristic is his extreme helpfulness, but whose ultimate goal is to make others indebted to him so they will comply with his wishes. The person with this pattern tends to alienate those around him because he robs them of their freedom.

The manipulator's need for love and attention is so overwhelming that it spills over into his perception of others. Believing his partner to have the same need as he does, he lavishes such attention on him that he makes him feel trapped. The manipulator acts in such a way as to become indispensable, so that those he has chosen to love will become dependent on him, assuring him of their unconditional loyalty. He expects acknowledgment, acceptance and love in return for his efforts on their behalf. This is the unending cycle that the complementary patterns of the manipulator and the manipulatee get caught up in: the former gives endlessly to ensure the other's love, while the latter cannot help accepting because to refuse would seem ungrateful. "If I give you my all, you must give me all of you in return"; "I can't say no, because you are so good to me." Thus the pair enters into a state of mutual dependence, with each partner responding to the other's urgent need to be loved.

However, although their relationship may appear well balanced, it inevitably breaks down when the desire for love and the thirst for freedom become mutually exclusive. In the manipulator's case, he becomes trapped by the very dependence he has created in the other, torn between his need for the other and his need to establish his own space. However, although he may want to be free himself, he does not wish to respect the freedom of those he loves. Therefore, he oversteps their limits and infringes on their territory. In this sense the manipulator is also an invader, who feels that his generosity gives him the right to intrude upon the other's space.

The manipulator's *modus operandi* is extremely subtle. To illustrate his mental process and the behavior it gives rise to, let us consider the story of Rose. She was 38 years old when she first arrived in my office. As a high school principal, she came to consult me in my capacity, not as a psychotherapist, but as an educational specialist. She wanted my help to motivate her teachers and make them more committed to the school. As I listened to Rose, I was unable to separate the educationalist in me from the psychotherapist. In fact, I remain profoundly convinced that there is a significant overlap between the two. From what she said, it became clear to me that certain teachers fell short of her expectations. This sort of attitude is characteristic of manipulators: they define specific conditions for their relationships with others, and they have difficulty accepting that these conditions might not be met. When they are not met, the manipulator's overt reaction is to become even more attentive and generous. However, his underlying intention is to force the other to comply with his demands. In keeping with this pattern, Rose's generosity, helpfulness and incessant compliments were aimed at getting "her" teachers to fulfill her expectations.

Compliments are a favorite weapon in the manipulator's arsenal. Since we, as humans, need to be "built up," we tend to feel enormously grateful to those who acknowledge us in this way. There is, of course, nothing wrong with giving this sort of positive feedback. The problem with the manipulator's praise is that he uses it arbitrarily and insincerely. Used in this manner, a compliment is less a way of acknowledging the other's worth than a systematic method of manipulation, deployed often unconsciously to earn love and recognition, whatever the cost. He builds on his compliments with presents, favors and his unfailing helpfulness. Since he is not entirely conscious of his motives in this regard, he fails, just as Rose did, to understand why the people he "serves" are not eternally indebted to him. Too caught up in her emotions to see how she was responsible for what was happening, Rose accused her teachers of ingratitude instead, believing herself to be the victim of egregious injustice. In fact, although they had fulfilled her expectations during the first few years of her appointment, they had become progressively more and more indifferent to their principal's methods of manipulation, taking advantage of her generosity without feeling obliged to repay her in any way. Helpless in the face of this indifference, Rose desperately hunted about for another means of bringing them under her thumb. Instead of providing her with these means, the process she initiated with me led her to discover her behavior pattern and the psychological processes behind it (see Figure 3.17).

Figure 3.17

OUTSIDE WORLD

Triggers ⟶
- *indifference*
- *non-acknowledgment*
- *rejection*

INNER WORLD

1. Emotions
- *fear of the losing*
- *fear of rejection*
  (amplified by abandonment and insecurity complexes)

↓

2. Defence mechanisms
- *blaming*
- *accusation*
- *criticism*
- *projection*

↓

3. Manipulator pattern

↓

4. Unsatisfied needs
- *need to be loved*
- *need to be acknowledged*

At both the personal and the professional level, the manipulator tends to associate with manipulatees, that is, people whose need for love and acknowledgment is fulfilled by the sense of importance they feel when someone else looks after them. The manipulatee, who has an insatiable thirst for love, is infinitely grateful to anyone who pays attention to him. Because, like the manipulator, he suffers from an abandonment complex, he will belittle himself, deny his own needs and his right to express them, and let himself be used, all to avoid losing the other's love.

Alicia's story was proof, for me, of just how far a person with a manipulatee pattern can go to avoid losing a partner's love. Born into a family torn apart by constant conflict, she left home at the age of 15 to become a dishwasher. The pub where she worked was a hangout for substance abusers and people on social assistance. One of the regulars was Jeff, who was twice Alicia's age, but became the first person to ever take the time to listen to her, look after her and acknowledge her. During the first few months of their relationship they spent many enchanted moments together. Alicia's feelings for Jeff were a mix of eternal gratitude, infinite love and blind faith. He was so kind, so generous that she forgot his dubious attitudes, his strange friends, his alcoholism and his reticence with regard to certain aspects of his life. He got her hooked on drugs, then pushed her into prostitution. She always did whatever he asked, in spite of her fear and disgust. First, because she didn't want him to leave her, and second because she was so grateful for everything he had done for her. By the time she was 20, she was trapped in a seemingly hopeless situation: for her, giving up prostitution meant losing the only person who had ever loved her but who now controlled her through fear.

Unfortunately, Alicia didn't stay in therapy very long because her fear prevented her from breaking out of the trap she had fallen into. Her story definitely presents an extreme example of the manipulatee pattern. Nevertheless, it is important in that it shows us how and why such individuals come to subordinate their whole lives to their desire to keep the love of others.

Thus we see how the unfulfilled need for love is at the root of all the patterns we have looked at. Does this mean, then, that the parents who denied their children that love are responsible for their patterns? I do not believe so. Although, as children, we integrate such patterns unconsciously, as adults, we alone can make the conscious decision to get rid of them. By making others responsible for who we are and what we do, we deprive ourselves of the ability to make that decision.

Since a pattern is a type of behavior that is completed and complemented by its opposite, is it necessary to work it out as a couple? The CNDA believes it is important for each partner to begin by working out his own pattern, by understanding and demystifying his own psychological processes before tackling the impact these have on the relationship. Partners can choose to go through this initial stage in the therapeutic process either individually or as a couple. The very act of dealing with the pattern implicates all the psychological processes that contributed to its formation; it means uncovering one's fundamental needs, learning to listen to one's fears, desires, emotions, and using them to combat dissatisfaction. Dealing with the pattern also means becoming aware of underlying complexes and defense mechanisms, and in the end it means understanding what makes people act in an involuntary and frustrating manner.

Trying to work out a pattern merely on the behavioral level is like trying to cure a headache with painkillers. Some of the symptoms disappear, but the real problem has not gone away, and will reappear in one form or another. Conscious of this, the CNDA takes into account our psychological world, in all its subjectivity and subtlety, and how it is affected by external reality. The two realms do, after all, act upon and influence each other. Stimuli of a mainly unconscious nature are given off by our entourage and impinge upon our psyche. The way we react to these stimuli on a behavioral level is dictated by how they affect our inner processes. And the reverse is also true: a person's inner processes, his way of perceiving emotional experiences, unconsciously influence his entourage. As far as the individual is concerned, the end result of this mutual influence is neither discernible nor quantifiable because it is channeled first and foremost through the emotional experiences of the parties involved. It calls forth all the mind's resources, making it react according to its conscious or unconscious inner experiences.

With this in mind, it seems fair to say that one cannot draw conclusions or make judgments based merely on the observation of a person's behavior. Hidden inside the psyche is a wealth of contributing elements that no educational or psychotherapeutic approach can afford to ignore: elements such as the person's needs, desires, emotions, feelings, defense mechanisms, complexes and even insights, which can all direct his actions. All these elements, though they are presented separately in this book to satisfy the need of the rational conscious for order, actually overlap and are constantly influencing one another. As Jung has rightly observed, there is a considerable share of irrational and unquantifiable elements in our human makeup, making it impossible for anyone except the person in question to define, label or interpret them. It is precisely this irrational component that makes him unique. It makes him the only one capable of finding the answers to his questions, the solutions to his problems because, along with the rational element, this component provides the impetus for the individual's drive toward autonomy and self-actualization.

According to the CNDA, whether one is involved in a helping relationship as a parent, teacher, or professional in the field of physical or mental health care, one has to be able to help the child, student, client or patient see himself clearly. One has to be able to help him understand his inner workings so that he can regain control over his life, and so that, thanks to that understanding, he can look within to find the answers to his problems. Consequently, his nascent self-love, without which no lasting change can take place, will begin to flourish. This self-love is both the foundation and the goal of evolutionary psychotherapy, which will be discussed in the next chapter.

CHAPTER 4

RESPECT FOR THE PROCESS OF LIBERATION AND CHANGE

The CNDA's therapeutic process of change is creative and nondirective because it is centered on respect for the way an individual's psyche functions and for his own, unique rate of growth. It is an initiation in the sense that it leads to the death of the persona and the renaissance of the person. Changing with the CNDA means becoming more and more genuine, discovering one's personal criteria for happiness and satisfaction. It means working toward unearthing the person buried under the characteristics of the introjected persona, and exploiting all one's dimensions without favoring one at the expense of another. Most importantly, it means finding and exploring one's true nature.

For all these reasons, and more, the CNDA's psychotherapeutic process of change does not concern itself with resolving problems *per se*, but with the attitude of the helpee toward those problems. The attitude is a faithful reflection of both the entire person and his unconscious psychological functioning, precisely because it cannot be controlled. For this reason, working on the helpee's attitude means giving him more inner strength to face his difficulties. The psychotherapist's work follows the rhythm of the helpee's growth in this respect. This rhythm leads the helpee through certain stages which, if real change is desired, should be neither evaded nor skipped over. The stages presented in this chapter constitute the seven-step process of change; they are the key to our liberation, our renaissance and our innermost transformation.

On a more practical note, let me say that any helpee, no matter who or what he is, must go through each one of these stages in order to attain the fulfillment, the self-actualization and the self-love he desires:

A. Awareness
B. Acceptance
C. Responsibility
D. Expression
E. Observation
F. Choice of protective mechanisms
G. The shift to creative action

Before we begin, we must understand that using these steps to help us through a problem or difficult period will sooner or later inevitably bring about change and fulfillment. However, the process will fail if one or more of the steps is avoided or skipped over.

Generally speaking, when people have a problem they try to solve it as quickly as possible, often through external changes in their behavior, like Juliet did. Over the years, her mother had acquired the pattern of a victim who constantly complained about her husband's attitudes and reactions. Juliet, who loved her mother and wanted to protect her, unconsciously decided when she was quite young that she would provide a more amenable male presence for her poor mother. So she concentrated on developing all her masculine qualities as much as possible. By the time she was 20, her appearance was distinctly masculine and no boy showed the slightest interest in her, which brought her a great deal of suffering. At 23, she went into therapy for the first time. Her psychotherapist strongly recommended that she wear skirts instead of pants, that she let her hair grow and start to use makeup. Juliet really wanted to have a lover, like her older sister Anne had, so she followed her therapist's advice. However, because her "disguise" made her feel ridiculous and artificial, her attempts ended in failure. She stopped seeing her therapist and, one year later, came to consult me. At that point, she finally understood and accepted why changing her appearance and behavior had not brought her any satisfaction. She realized that the unconscious choice she had made so long ago had won her her parents' love, particularly that of her father, who had always wanted a boy. Thanks to him, Juliet had become a first-rate hockey, baseball and football player.

Her attempts to make herself look more "feminine" touched her unconscious fear of not being loved. Because her choice to become a boy had been geared toward earning her parents' love, she was unable to back down from it without recognizing and accepting her need for love and her fear of losing that love. In fact, she was unable to change any aspect of her behavior without realizing that her masculine persona was actually a defense mechanism that she had unconsciously adopted to protect herself from that fear. This recognition and acceptance of herself were necessary pre-conditions for long-lasting change; without them, change was artificial and essentially short-lived. Understanding the way her psyche functioned and following the other steps in the process of liberation, allowed Juliet to work on not just her difficulty with men, but on all her relational difficulties, including those with her parents. Juliet had always felt an intense need to be loved, to the point where she would deny her own feelings, to please others. Her therapist's suggestion that she should change her behavior contained, for her, the unconscious suggestion that if she wanted to be loved, she would have to conform to other people's standards rather than to her own, just as she had always done. However, by approaching the problem on a psychological rather than a behavioral level, by concentrating on the way her psyche functioned, I was helping her to regain control over her life. The individual concerned is the only one who can find the solution to his problems; his own inner resources are all he needs to employ. The job of the creative nondirective process is to enable him to find and use those resources through the use of the seven steps, each of which will be discussed in detail in the following section.

A. AWARENESS

Awareness can be defined as the faculty of being conscious of the self, or as that state in which the individual knows himself for who he is, and is thus able to properly distinguish himself from others.

Self-awareness really is the first step in the process that leads to liberation and change. Without it, transformation simply is not possible. Nor is this a modern idea: over two thousand years ago, Socrates had already encapsulated it in his dictum "Know thyself."

This self-awareness should come about gradually, and in successive stages. As envisioned by the CNDA, this is essential for self-actualization or for helping others achieve this goal. For, in truth, the greater our understanding of ourselves, the greater our understanding of the world. In other words, unless our knowledge of the outer world is informed by what we know of ourselves, we are left with nothing more than disembodied, non-integrated knowledge.

The education we get at school, based as it is on the acquisition of intellectual knowledge, of ready-made principles and beliefs, leaves us with a head full of facts that do not prepare us to face life. Millions of people leave school with only a hazy idea of how to survive in the jungle of human relationships. They find their way through it by copying other people's behavior or by unconsciously adopting defense mechanisms that provide only short term equilibrium. The sad reality is that most people use self-denial as a reliable emotional tool.

As far as relationships are concerned, they try to conform to the stereotypical image of an ideal worker that is implicit in the business world. When they meet, they ponder their actions, weigh their words and make sure their behavior does not deviate from the norm. They have to do this, because they are not ready to deal with their inner complexity and state of flux. They know a lot about their work, but almost nothing about themselves. Their emotions become a labyrinth, which they refuse to enter because it constitutes a dark and frightening world that follows them wherever they go, a world they cannot understand and yet which, unbeknownst to them, influences them.

Preparing individuals to deal with life means first and foremost teaching them to know themselves for who they are and second, teaching them to respect their own right to be different as well as others', within the context of their interpersonal relationships. Without these basics, man will remain a soulless being who conforms to other people's standards and who reacts involuntarily to everything that happens to him. Thus, he loses all control over his life.

Self-knowledge really is a basic ingredient to any kind of learning. An awareness of who we are should be at the foundation of any educational method. To start with, we should acquire the habit of listening to our emotions. Learning to be attentive to what is happening within is not necessarily easy: instead of encouraging this, our educational methods generally advocate stifling our emotions, thus sharing in the formation of patterns that make our relationships superficial and unsatisfying.

Learning to be attuned to ourselves implies that we recognize the necessity of paying constant attention to our malaises as well as to our well-being, both psychological and physical. Instead of delivering our hearts and our bodies into the hands of specialists, and passively waiting for them to deliver the miracle cure, our self-awareness teaches us to take control of our lives. Not that we no longer need others; rather, instead of transferring all responsibility for our well-being onto them, we become the principal agents of our own healing.

When we are attentive to ourselves, we are aware of all the stress and tension in our body as well as all the feelings and sensations that make up our emotional experiences. A lack of attentiveness in these matters can cause us to develop some very serious psychological and physical disorders. By ignoring what is happening within, particularly in the realm of the emotions, the individual has to resort to automatic defense mechanisms to fend off the suffering that is at the root of his illness. Not only are these mechanisms often ineffective, but they also use up a considerable amount of his creative energy. So, when we ignore what our bodies and emotions have to say, we are depriving ourselves of the energy we need for self-creation and self-actualization, and all our efforts are basically counterproductive. However, when we begin to listen, this marks the point at which we begin to take charge of our lives, and which leads on to freedom. For those of us who are not accustomed to it, looking within may signify coming face to face with chaos and nothingness. The inner realm of feelings, of emotions and desires is so complex and so laden with meaning that it is hard to pinpoint the specific source of our problems. Be that as it may, the first step along the road to self-awareness consists of recognizing the undefined turmoil that occasionally wells up within us. This act of recognition lights up the labyrinth that previously lay shrouded in darkness, and helps us feel secure. We dare to enter: to identify, as we delve deeper, our needs, emotions, complexes, patterns and defense mechanisms, to discover how our psyche functions. Along the way, we become aware of what resides within us, what makes us the people we are, on both a physical as well as a psychological level. Thus we acquire the elements that enable us to take charge of our lives.

Recognizing our disorders and our well-being, both psychological and physical, leads to self-awareness. This is the first, and most important, but by no means the only stage in our transformation. We cannot free ourselves from our pain simply by becoming aware of it, nor even by recognizing its source. Similarly, merely discovering our patterns and finding out how they influence us is not enough to eradicate the pain they cause us. Awareness provides us with additional information that we can use in our inner work, but to stop there would be like opening a door and staying on the doorstep. By entering, we initiate the next step: acceptance.

B. ACCEPTANCE

Self-acceptance is an absolutely essential step in the process of transformation. However, it is a difficult if not impossible one for many people to take, because they are firmly convinced that they are "bad."

Accepting himself in his true nature is not easy for someone who expends a great deal of energy hiding behind the persona that represents the person he would like to be. Fear of being judged and rejected is the primary motivating factor here. In order to be accepted by his entourage, a child will become what those who raise him want him to be, and not what he is meant to be. He discovers at an early age how a feeling of shame and inferiority inevitably follows whenever he reveals that part of himself that is deemed unacceptable by others. To avoid this overwhelming feeling, he obeys the explicit or implicit demand to conform, thus denying his true personality.

Most people who go into therapy or strive for personal growth do so in the hope of freeing themselves from certain ways of acting or reacting. They pass from one kind of therapy or from one school of personal development to another only to find themselves, at the end of the road, more burdened-down with defense mechanisms than they were to start with. They are frightened of what lies within, so they try hard to ignore it. However, this merely serves to cut them off from their emotions, making them insensitive to suffering. In the long run, these blocks can lead to serious physical, psychological or relational problems, which the person is completely unable to deal with.

Many of my clients fit this description perfectly; they arrive in my office expecting me to show them a magical means of freeing themselves from their emotional nature, their lack of openness, their jealousy, anger, intolerance, passivity or sensitivity. Jules is a case in point. Because of his upbringing, he had developed a sibling rivalry complex that caused him to feel intense jealousy each time another person was praised in his presence. He had spent his life denying this dreadful feeling, which had contaminated all his close personal relationships. After trying several different "personal development centers," he had learned a variety of different methods involving rationalization, positive thinking, self-assertiveness and so on. These had, however, produced only short-term results, and in the long run had failed to free him of his jealousy. The more he fought against it, the greater it became.

When we fight against ourselves we fight against what emerges from our emotional labyrinth, and we end up right where we started, but with less energy. Jules was quite surprised when I pointed out that he was not trying to accept his jealousy. How could he accept the monster he had been fighting against all these years? He didn't want to accept it, he wanted me to extract those aspects of his personality that were making him suffer. *The CNDA does not deal in extraction, but in transformation through acceptance.* As long as Jules refused to accept his jealous nature, he was fighting against himself. He became, in a way, his own worst enemy, because part of himself was waging constant war against another part. These inner battles pitting the person against the persona can last a lifetime. It wasn't until Jules was able to accept his jealousy as part of his real personality, rather than as something abnormal or bad, that his vital energy returned, enabling him to create a self with who he was.

Man must live his life based on who he is, not on who he thinks he should be.

Why did Jules refuse to acknowledge that part of his nature? Quite simply because, as he was growing up, he had been unequivocally judged and rejected each time he had manifested any signs of jealousy. He learned at an early age that, if he wanted to win the love of his parents and any others involved in his upbringing, he would have to crush this manifestly horrible and distasteful feeling. He had come to regard his jealousy with unspeakable shame, which greatly increased his suffering, since in addition to struggling with the feeling itself, he was deeply humiliated by the very idea that it might be noticed by his entourage. This is, in fact, a difficulty experienced by all those who cannot accept a part of themselves.

Once we pass through the acceptance stage, we give ourselves the right to be who we are, with all our strengths and weaknesses. Recognizing our weaknesses helps us to recognize our strengths, and use them to create a new self. Recognizing our weaknesses means learning to live with who we are rather than fighting against ourselves. When we fight against who we are, we are trying to reject certain characteristics that are inherent to our personality. A person who rejects himself is likely to reject others, and in turn be rejected himself. By accepting himself, on the other hand, he learns to respect his intrinsic wholeness, and to have respect for others, for what they are and not for what he wants them to be, while still staying within his own limits. Until we accept ourselves as we are, with all our needs, emotions, complexes, defense mechanisms and patterns, we cannot use our inner selves for growth and self-actualization. All too often, a person will spend his life making futile attempts to transform himself into an ideal, thereby hoping to escape judgment and rejection. These attempts are actually a way of judging himself unsatisfactory, of finding himself wanting. In this manner, he cuts himself off from the source of creative energy that is the wellspring of inner transformation.

It is strange but true that the only way to achieve lasting change is to stop changing and become the real persons we truly are. We can do so by shaking off all the principles and beliefs that have prevented us from being ourselves. We must stop handing control of our lives over to other people and acquire, instead, an unconditional respect for ourselves. The persona that has got us in a stranglehold must die, so that the person can be reborn. Through this rebirth, we become transformed, in the sense of achieving our true nature. When we change, we begin to move with the current of vital energy that inhabits us and that constitutes our very being. We learn to consistently put ourselves first, rather than making our lives conform to the expectations of the world. We learn to live with what we are. Put simply, before we can change we have to accept ourselves. There is no other way.

This is what Celine discovered when she came into psychotherapy, after having spent most of her life struggling with her lack of self-discipline. She was never on time, couldn't fulfill her obligations and was hopelessly disorganized. Because of her marked insecurity, the concept of other people's territory and limits was completely foreign to her. Her problem, as she perceived it, was that all her efforts to become more organized ended in failure. Because she had been raised by an extremely authoritarian and self-disciplined father, her lack of organization made her feel unhappy and even abnormal. She was therefore constantly trying to hide it, either through lies or manipulation. In fact, she had perfected these methods to the point where they even worked with her father, occasionally allowing her to mollify and even disarm him. At the age of 29, Celine came into therapy because the lack of trust that others showed for her hurt her deeply and reinforced her feeling of insecurity. Before she could perceive her many strengths, she had to accept her psychological processes, that is, her intense need to be loved and acknowledged, her abandonment and insecurity complexes, her fear of being judged and rejected and her lying and manipulation, which she used as defense mechanisms. Until she passed through that stage, she would be unable to recognize that she was in fact flexible, open, generous and helpful, and that her gentleness and sensitivity helped her to make a great first impression on people. Nor would she be able to exploit her creativity, which her lack of self-discipline prevented her from developing.

In the end, Celine was able to change because she accepted herself. The biggest stumbling block to total self-acceptance proved to be her "natural" tendency to lie. However, when it became clear to her that she used lies as a defense mechanism to avoid losing other people's affection, she was able to accept that tendency, all the more so, because she realized that it was essentially counterproductive.

Only by accepting ourselves can we begin to build our lives, using both our positive and negative energies. This goal, and that of learning to live with ourselves, can only be achieved by passing through the stage of responsibility.

C. RESPONSIBILITY

As we have seen, transformation starts with awareness, and acceptance, of our fundamental characteristics. However, these two steps, essential though they are, cannot bring about the metamorphosis we seek unless we can learn to take responsibility. I have already indicated that responsibility is the foundation of the creative nondirective approach. I now wish to add that it is an indispensable pre-condition for change. Quite simply, a person cannot be reborn unless he has the ability to take responsibility for who he is and what he does. Let us examine, then, the importance of self-knowledge and self-acceptance to the process of assuming these responsibilities.

Let me repeat that responsibility is the ability of an individual to take control of his life, to assert himself and to attain the highest possible level of self-actualization.

Anyone who makes others responsible for what he says, does or experiences is denying himself the satisfaction of one of our most basic needs as humans: the need to be free. For when we make others responsible for us, we are in effect giving them power over our lives. When we make ourselves dependent on them, change becomes impossible. Instead of looking within for the source of our anxiety, thus equipping ourselves for our own transformation, we unload the responsibility for all our sufferings onto others. When a person does this, he either turns into a victim who is always trying to change the other or, when the other will not change, into a victim who accuses, criticizes and rejects. This is an almost universal behavior pattern, and it spells disaster for any change or positive transformation. In fact, it can only lead to disappointment and frustration.

Assuming responsibility, on the other hand, puts us on the road, the only road towards autonomy. The story of Melissa illustrates my point.

Melissa expected a great deal of love and affection from her relationship with her partner. Unfortunately, they had grown apart over the years, and the resulting coldness left her sad and dissatisfied. She accused her lover of being impassive and insensitive, thereby driving them even further apart. In CNDA-directed therapy, Melissa realized that in order to satisfy her needs she was trying to change her lover rather than herself. Her need for love and affection did not disappear with this realization, but it did help her to take responsibility for her needs rather than trying to foist it off onto someone else. Thanks to her newfound responsible attitude, she discovered, among other things, why she had been unable to satisfy this fundamental need herself: torn between her deep-seated need for love and affection, and her fear of having to give too much of herself in return, she had been sending her partner a hidden message. Although she had never realized it before, her fear made Melissa herself somewhat cold and distant: in fact, she was unable to make a complete commitment to her partner, even though she was deeply in love. Unless there is full commitment on both sides, true love will slowly disappear. Melissa realized that she wanted to stop this process, but that in the past she had been prevented from giving herself completely to her relationship for fear of ending up lost and abandoned.

Close inspection of Melissa's case leads us to conclude that by taking responsibility for her own need, she was able to discover how her own unconsciously motivated behavior was sabotaging her search for fulfillment. As she became aware of and accepted her psychological processes, she discovered that the real means of attaining self-fulfillment lay within. We become responsible when we are able to look within for both the source of and the solution to all our problems. And this ability is born from and nurtured in the parent/child relationship. Unfortunately, this relationship is often responsible for outbreaks of what I call "victimitis", a chronic illness that causes the child to systematically blame others and his parents in particular, for every unpleasant thing that happens to him. It is certainly true that the way a child is raised will have an enormous influence on his psychic structure, since he is by nature flexible and easily influenced. He learns at an early age what to say and do in order to be loved. However, even when we take into account their principles and beliefs, their limits, weaknesses and the baggage they acquired from their own upbringing, we can still say that the parents of this world raise their children as best they can. In other words, the upbringing parents give their children comprises the best they have to give, considering their complexes, inhibitions, defense mechanisms and behavior patterns. Parents cannot guarantee that they will shield their child from all the evils in the world, and it may well be that one day, when the child is grown up, he will go into therapy and realize that his behavior has been and still is dictated by the way he was brought up and not by who he really is. In the final analysis, parents are responsible for their own problems, but not for their children's. They are not perfect and so they may have made mistakes. However, although they are responsible for how they experience the fallout from that mistake, they are not responsible for what their children experience.

I am well aware that I am entering dangerous waters here. It is easy to unload the responsibility for all our suffering onto our parents, to reproach them for all the unpleasant things that happen to us, but where does that lead us? What is the use? What sort of satisfaction do we get out of continuing to blame others for all our unhappiness? This sort of attitude only encourages resentment, and deprives us of the ability to change anything in our life.

Dealing with our problems in a responsible manner means accepting the way we have turned out and taking charge of our own transformation, by trying to find out who we are. Being responsible means ensuring that the person we truly are can be brought forth, out of the persona that was created by our introjections. And, paradoxically, this renaissance cannot take place unless we completely accept the persona that is such an integral part of us. Once we acknowledge the persona, once we accept it without judgment or condemnation, once we learn to live with it, then and only then can the person be himself. This, in fact, is how Oscar managed to find inner peace.

Because he was afraid of losing his parents' love, Oscar had adopted an invadee pattern that caused him to passively accept every form of invasion. He grew up and got married in the same little village, ending up almost completely surrounded by his own family and that of his wife, to the point where he no longer felt at home in his own house. People came and went as though it were Grand Central Station, borrowed his belongings without asking, often never returning them, and showed up at any time of the day or night to ask for a favor. True to his pattern, Oscar never said a word. When he first came to consult me, I could clearly see the anger and resentment he had been harboring for years, but that he had never dared express directly for fear of shocking people or being disliked. He criticized and condemned his brothers and brothers-in-law but did nothing to earn their respect. In fact, Oscar was not acknowledged as he wanted to be. The need to be recognized often nurtures our ability to earn respect, or to make others acknowledge us. But Oscar, instead of cultivating that ability, went in the opposite direction, letting himself be invaded at every turn, which was, of course, counterproductive. Initially, he had tried to live with the tolerant persona he had created for himself, and he had witnessed firsthand just how much this foreign element in his nature could make him suffer.

Taking responsibility for his problem involved seeing how he attracted this invasion, this lack of respect that caused him so much suffering. Learning to take responsibility meant trying to ease his suffering from within, rather than unloading responsibility for it onto others. This was extremely difficult for Oscar, because it aggravated his fear of not being loved. In order to complete this step, he had to decide to put himself, rather than others, first. Also, he had to accept the fact that if he respected himself, he would indeed lose other people's love and acknowledgment.

Learning to take responsibility for one's life is always a painful process because it necessitates learning how to put oneself first. This learning process is difficult for two reasons. First of all, we have introjected the notion that it is selfish not to think of others first. However, it seems self-evident that we cannot be truly helpful, cannot truly love others unless we are attuned to ourselves and to our fundamental needs. We cannot possibly be useful to anyone unless we first look after our own needs. The second reason why learning about freedom is so difficult is that when we become responsible, there are some things we have to give up: responsibility does lead to freedom, but we must pass through loss on the way. Being free means being able to choose, and in every choice there is something gained and something lost. If we cannot choose and accept the concomitant loss, then we will never be free. Accepting loss is always the most difficult step to go through in any process of growth and transformation.

Oscar had to choose between perpetuating his invadee pattern, or defining his limits so that others would respect him. He made a responsible choice, which inevitably entailed a great deal of loss. Almost everyone in his family and circle of acquaintances criticized and rejected him for his changed attitude toward them. However, in the long run, he gained self-respect and self-love, and through these, freedom as well. By asserting himself according to his needs, he finally won the respect and recognition he had always wanted. Taking responsibility really is a significant step toward renaissance. Unless we realize how we are responsible for our sufferings we cannot be free. However, this realization must be followed by step four in the process: the ability to express our feelings.

D. EXPRESSION

This section will deal primarily with verbal expression, the kind used most frequently for all interpersonal communication. All too often, though, the words we speak to one another are impersonal and deal with everything except ourselves. Human beings tend to either avoid expressing their emotions, or else say the opposite of what they feel, in order not to hurt or displease others, so as not to be judged or rejected by them. This non-expression of our feelings is the main reason why so many relationships are unsatisfying, and why they end in failure.

But why should it be so difficult for people to talk about themselves, and to tell others how they feel about them? Why are we so afraid to say, to speak, to communicate what we feel and who we are?

Expression is the fourth step in the CNDA's process of change, and it is vital that it should rest on what has already been acquired. For if we express who we are without really knowing ourselves, without really accepting our weaknesses as well as our strengths and without taking responsibility for what we feel, we may well lapse into the kind of defensive expression that attacks, hurts and condemns. This type of expression almost always gives rise to disputes, and so people tend to shy away from it in fright. The kind of expression that is born of self-acceptance and responsibility, on the other hand, will always bring people closer together. We must recognize that acquiring unconditional self-acceptance and the ability to take responsibility is a long, drawn-out process; creative nondirective psychotherapists also have to go through these steps as a fundamental part of their initial training.

Learning to express ourselves in a responsible manner means taking responsibility for our own emotional experiences and refusing to burden ourselves with those of other people. The source of all our problems lies within us. If we react negatively to this or that external trigger, it is not the trigger but our psychological processes that are involved. Responsible expression maintains interpersonal ties rather than breaking them, because it loosens the disruptive hold that non-expression has over the relationship.

Why is non-expression so destructive? Quite simply because whatever is kept silent in a relationship does not disappear but remains present, emanating from one or the other partner through his unconscious attitude. This can represent a significant emotional tension for both partners, and will inevitably create a rift. As it gets progressively wider, the rift renders all communication impossible, for the relationship will simply have disappeared.

Most of the time, relationships are born when emotions and happy feelings are expressed and shared. Similarly, they die when unpleasant feelings are not communicated. Rather than expressing what he feels, the individual might remain silent; he might say what he thinks the other wants to hear, or else he might vent his feelings through criticism or accusations, which he levels at a third party rather than at the one concerned. Whichever way he chooses, he ends up sending two contradictory messages: the unconscious one conveyed by his attitude, and the conscious one conveyed by his words and actions. This makes communication impossible, it makes the other insecure and destroys any trust or love in the relationship. Double-sided communication tends to make people feel powerless and hence insecure, and this prevents them from renewing contact with others. This is why I have stressed the importance of awareness, acceptance and responsibility to genuine self-expression. Without them, the messages that partners convey cannot possibly be explicit or harmonious.

Many people believe that only those words that convey pleasant experiences can be considered harmonious, but this is not so. In order to create harmony in a relationship we must be genuine, whether this means conveying pleasant or painful emotions. Most people who hide their unpleasant feelings do so to keep the peace, but they are unwittingly creating total chaos in their relationships.

Does this mean, then, that we should always share all our emotional experiences, no matter when or where they occur? I do not believe so. Choosing not to become involved with just anyone constitutes a healthy means of self-protection. You may decide not to become involved with someone because you do not trust them, or because you have nothing in common with them or simply because you do not wish to expend time and energy on a commitment that doesn't interest you. In other words, we can make a conscious choice as to who we share our emotional experiences with, whether it be at work, within the family or elsewhere. On the other hand, for those who occupy a special place in our lives, whom we love and who are important to us, the question is not whether or not we should say what we feel, but rather how and when we should say it.

We learn the "how" in steps two and three, through self-acceptance and responsibility. The "how" includes self-respect, self-knowledge and self-love, an ability to stand up for oneself and for one's rights without being harsh on oneself. The "when," on the other hand, comprises the ability to respect the other, thus establishing a congruence/empathy dialectic or, if you prefer, a dialectic of self-respect vs. respect for the other. We must always remember that congruence and self-respect are essential pre-conditions for empathy and respect for the other.

In our close personal relationships, it is essential that we express ourselves, that we tell the other, as genuinely as possible, what we are feeling. Unfortunately, it is not only the panoply of fears (as discussed above), but also their power and pride that prevents people who love each other from sharing their grief and pain. The love in many relationships has been destroyed by power struggles, and the relationships fall apart. This is precisely what happened to Joan. She and Larry had been deeply in love for several years, but she felt, to her despair, that their relationship was slowly disintegrating. In fact, they had entered into a power struggle that was completely distorting the reality of the situation. In spite of her intense feelings for Larry, Joan never gave any sign of love or affection, claiming that she would feel humiliated by such a display of vulnerability. So she kept all her feelings to herself, in this and in all her close personal relationships. Whenever she and Larry quarreled, she repressed and denied her emotions, and kept her head high (so to speak) to avoid revealing that she had been hurt or affected in any way. She considered her vulnerability to be a weakness and was convinced that, should Larry find out about it, it would give him overwhelming power over her. She was only able to voice her emotions when the other had first expressed his, and even then, only sparingly, and with great caution. Her attitude revealed a need to control her emotions, but also a desire to exert power over others: the kind of power we get from learning other people's secrets, but not sharing our own.

In CNDA-directed therapy, it became clear to Joan that she had adopted this defense mechanism to protect herself from the fear of not being loved for who she was. She was afraid of showing her vulnerability, her need for others. Since she could not accept that aspect of her personality, she believed that others would judge and reject her for it.

Power games inhibit genuine expression of our emotions, creating coolness in the relationship. In any personal relationship that we hold dear, we must go beyond the struggles for power and the fear of being judged and rejected, and try to express our actual feelings, for this is the only way to get close to those we love. If what one partner expresses ends up driving him and the other even further apart, what he said must have been either defensive, or else have indicated his perceived need for a healthy distance. In any event, when we express our emotions, we may well be hurting the other's feelings. The most difficult part in this kind of expression, is to cope with the other's emotion. A genuine separation based on mutual understanding is far better than an unsatisfactory relationship poisoned by non-expression.

Self-expression that is based on acceptance and responsibility liberates us and draws us closer to others, while fostering an atmosphere in which our fundamental needs for love, acknowledgment and affirmation can be satisfied. This is another step in the process of change, and it is followed by observation.

E. OBSERVATION

It is difficult if not impossible to change overnight. The death of the persona and the renaissance of the person may occur fairly rapidly in some cases, but in others the transformation takes much longer. The creative nondirective approach operates by respecting each person's individual rate of progress. As individuals passing through the stages in the process of liberation and change, we also need to respect the rate at which we can evolve toward greater well-being. Also, we have to accept our personal criteria for happiness and satisfaction. Basically, the end result of the transformative process should be for us to discover how we want to be happy.

For hundreds, even thousands of years, philosophers from every school of thought have tried to discover the secret of happiness. However, this much-sought-after inner state of well-being, contentment and profound satisfaction cannot be achieved by using some universally applicable magic formula; each person must attain it in his own way. In this sense, psychotherapy and education in its larger sense have the same goal: that of helping the person to find his own personal criteria for happiness in general, and more specifically to discover how and when he achieves those instances of well-being that are characteristic of his kind of happiness. Where one person is happy in contemplation, the other enjoys action. One may choose adventure, the other stability. One likes the peaceful countryside, the other loves the turbulent city life. One finds fulfillment in having many relationships, the other prefers solitude. Happiness, in fact, has only one essential ingredient: non-defensive self-respect. It does not come without a cost, and it is never here to stay. The death of the persona involves fear and suffering, yet this is a stage we must go through in order to attain happiness. Happiness, then, is like freedom: we progress toward it one day at a time.

I am a firm believer in happiness. After having tested my theory on myself over decades, I believe that the inner state of completion is something that one experiences more frequently and for longer periods, the further one travels along the long and tortuous road that leads to the heart of the self. Along the way, the road passes by discovery, acceptance and self-love. Freeing oneself from pre-conceived notions imposed by the persona in order to find one's own true nature is the only possible path to freedom. I will admit that this is difficult, for habits and patterns represent what we know, what makes us feel safe and secure. Breaking out of them means facing up to the unknown that inhabits each one of us. Overcoming fear, then, is an important step in any process of change, and unless we can accomplish this, we will never attain the true center of our being, from which the purest kind of happiness springs. Evolving means facing up to our fear of loss, rejection, solitude, judgment and ridicule, our fear of losing control, of emotion, of the unknown, and even our fear of madness and death. Evolving means adhering to our individual rate of change, daring to listen to our fears, until we can enter the very heart of the self. And there is no other way to accomplish this than to become aware of our fears and to accept them in a responsible manner.

At this time in the growth process, a period of self-observation is called for. Merely becoming aware of our inner make-up, accepting it and expressing it in a responsible manner is not enough to ensure a definitive renaissance. Each discovery opens the door to yet another, making self-exploration a neverending process. Knowing and accepting our need for love, our fear of losing the other, our abandonment complex and our defensive repression are not enough to break out of our psychological processes and acquire more productive behavior patterns. Self-knowledge and self-acceptance are essential to the process of change, but an ensuing period of observation is indispensable.

When we observe ourselves, we watch ourselves falling into the same behavior pattern, we see how we function on a psychological level. Knowing and accepting the persona does not automatically usher in the person. Merely distinguishing our "true self" from our "false self" as Winnicott (1980) has called them, does not make the latter instantly vanish, leaving room for the former to blossom. Discovering and accepting our needs, our fears, our complexes, our defense mechanisms and our behavior patterns cannot lead to growth and change unless we can observe who we are in a non-judgmental fashion, unless we can watch as we experience our unsatisfying patterns, unless we can see ourselves falling into the same traps, reacting to the same kind of triggers, blocking the same needs because of the same fears, and adopting the same defense mechanisms, here and now.

For example, even though Helen accepts the fact that she judges, criticizes and blames others, and knows that she does this whenever she feels frightened of being judged, rejected or not loved, she continues to criticize and be afraid. The defense mechanism will continue to intervene automatically, each time the fear becomes apparent. Although knowing and accepting the way we function does not change anything of itself, it does allow us to use our observations as a means of understanding when and how we enter into psychological functioning of dissatisfaction, and how we can make them more satisfactory.

I wish to make a clear distinction here between observation and mental separation. I believe that mental separation is a means of defending oneself through rationalization, cutting oneself off from all emotion in a given situation. Observation, however, is not defensive. For this reason it is very difficult to carry it out in extremely emotional situations. In fact, observation is a non-defensive, intellectual operation which generally follows an emotionally charged period of anxiety, anger, grief or fear. It is a way of analyzing our psychological functioning in light of past discoveries and with the expectation of yet more enlightenment to come. It is a regular occurrence in psychotherapy and consists of using unsatisfactory situations to pinpoint the various aspects of our psychological functioning that have made us unhappy. Often, when a person is having difficulties, he will solve his problems by reinforcing his defense mechanisms, or else by changing his behavior, without ever searching within for the root of the problem. Undertaking a period of observation is extremely demanding, but it is so rewarding that the process of change would suffer greatly if it were not included. It is up to the parents, teachers and psychotherapists to help people observe themselves and analyze their psychological functioning in order to acquire effective skills for satisfying their fundamental needs. A global approach should encourage the individual to use the left side of the brain and the neocortex in his process of growth and change.

By replacing the cult of reason with the cult of spiritual intuition, man runs the risk of throwing the baby out with the bathwater, and of missing an important step in his process of change: namely, that of observation. This period of self-analysis which can run to lesser or greater lengths, depending on the person, opens the door to change and happiness. It does so for the simple reason that it allows us to pinpoint our defense mechanisms, replacing them with protective mechanisms that make it possible for us to be at peace with who we are, instead of trying to extract from our psyche certain integral elements that we refuse to accept.

F. CHOICE OF PROTECTIVE MECHANISMS

Protective mechanisms are freely and consciously chosen by the individual to protect himself from psychological suffering and ensure satisfaction of his basic needs.

Protective mechanisms differ from defense mechanisms: the latter is an involuntary, unconscious trigger set up by the psyche in order to protect the individual from fear or suffering. A protective mechanism, however, is adopted by the individual following a conscious process of responsible self-acceptance, and observation of the way his psyche functions. Whereas the defense mechanism is set up by the psyche to escape from the emotion, the protective mechanism faces up to it (see Figure 4.1).

Figure 4.1

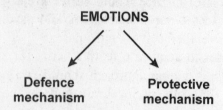

The disadvantage of defense mechanisms is that they trap the individual, sapping his vital energy, and possibly destroying his relationships, although they are useful in the sense that they do indeed protect him from suffering or from his fear of suffering. To do away with them completely would leave a person naked and defenseless, at the mercy of the outside world. Living without any kind of psychological protection in this world of power games means depriving oneself of any chance for actualization and happiness. The goal of the creative nondirective psychotherapist is not to make the person get rid of his defense mechanisms, but rather to help him become aware of them, accept them and take responsibility for them. When the defense mechanism is acknowledged, the relationship is restored and communication becomes more satisfying. For me, there is an enormous difference between protection and defense. In psychic terms, when man sets up defenses to protect himself from his emotional response to the outside world, it is done unconsciously. Protection, on the other hand, is a conscious activity undertaken out of respect for his inner world. The protective mechanism chosen by the individual necessitates a degree of familiarity with his psychological functioning, and the ability to accept them in a responsible manner, such that his process of dissatisfaction may become more satisfactory.

To assist our understanding of how the protective mechanism contributes to the process of freedom and change, I will borrow the mythological image of the labyrinth and the Minotaur. The average person sees his psyche as a darkened labyrinth. His erratic progress through it is dictated solely by his reactions to external events. Thus he ends up going around in circles, coming up against the same dead-ends, both internal and external. He doesn't really know where he is going, and is primarily concerned with avoiding the Minotaur, that terrifying monster which represents everything he fears most, and which he has never dared to confront. His fear of confronting the Minotaur prevents him from surmounting the obstacles in his path, and also prevents him from walking unhindered in the most beautiful and enlightening pathways of the self. The object of the CNDA is to shed light on the darkness, to help the individual find his Minotaur and see what he looks like. Actually, the light comes from the person's awareness of how his psyche functions, as fostered by the CNDA's evolutionary philosophy. When he sees and accepts his fears (the Minotaur), his defense mechanisms, his patterns and his unsatisfied needs, he already has the skills necessary to take control of his life. During the initial stages of the process, the helpee realizes that he has been bypassing or fleeing his fears and other emotions, that his defense mechanisms have been preventing him from satisfying his basic needs. After a sometimes fairly lengthy period of self-observation and inner work, he finally gets to the point where he can find sufficient inner strength to confront the Minotaur, with well-chosen protective mechanisms firmly in place.

In order to illustrate the difference between the process that does not satisfy fundamental needs and the one that does, thanks to protective mechanisms, I have drawn up figures to represent the mental cycle inherent in each of these processes (see Figures 4.2 and 4.3).

Because he feels that his mother neither loves nor acknowledges him, Jack's need to be loved and praised is not satisfied. He therefore experiences intense grief and pain, and even anxiety, all the more so since these emotions are coupled with an abandonment complex. To protect himself from his pain, he runs away (figuratively speaking) each time a conscious or unconscious trigger, no matter how minor, makes him relive the feeling of rejection he finds so painful. Thus he remains trapped in a recurring psychological functioning of dissatisfaction which fails to satisfy his fundamental needs.

Figure 4.2

THE UNSATISFACTORY PROCESS

OUTSIDE WORLD	INNER WORLD
Trigger ⟶	1. Unpleasant emotions
	↓
	2. Defence mechanisms
	↓
	3. Patterns
	↓
	4. Unsatisfied needs

One day, however, Jack may become aware of his process. He may be ready to take responsibility for the elements inherent to it, accept them and express them. He may decide to adopt an attitude of observation and analysis vis-a-vis his psychological functioning. If he does, then he will soon realize that, each time he comes up against a painful situation, he will know how to implement protective measures that will allow him to satisfy his needs, and to discover that inner state of well-being that I call happiness. Figure 4.3 illustrates how the cycle unfolds.

Figure 4.3

OUTSIDE WORLD	INNER WORLD
Trigger ⟶	1. Unpleasant emotions
	↓
	2. Protective mechanism
	↓
	3. Satisfaction of needs

Figure 4.3 shows how the cycle of the recurrent process of dissatisfaction can be broken when, thanks to a protective mechanism,

the individual's need is satisfied. But how exactly does the protective mechanism deliver satisfaction of this need?

Adrienne had an abandonment complex that caused her to suffer acute jealousy every time she and her lover were in the company of other women. The fact that her lover, Paul, was very sociable and even seductive increased Adrienne's feeling of insecurity and her consequent unhappiness. When she came to see me she was considering leaving him because, except when they were alone together, her suffering was too much for her to bear. Even so, she was deeply in love with this man, who never failed to charm her. After having gone through the steps of awareness, responsible self-acceptance and observation, she came up with a means of protecting herself from the sorrow that had initially led her to consider leaving Paul. Her method of protection was to make an explicit request of the man she loved, and run the risk that he might refuse what she asked. If she hadn't face up to her fears (the Minotaur), she would never have been able to do this. In clear, unambiguous terms, Adrienne told Paul that she needed attention and emotional security, that his seductive behavior with other women hurt her a great deal and that she was afraid he would stop loving her and she would lose him. She acknowledged the charming and seductive side of his nature, and the fact that he liked female company; she didn't necessarily want to change him, just protect herself from the pain brought on by her abandonment complex. Her explicit request consisted of asking him to show her, when he was in the company of other women, that she was his favorite, the one he had chosen to spend his life with. All she needed to reassure her was a wink, a conspiratorial look, a thoughtful act, a tender gesture or a whispered word of love. Paul, who really loved Adrienne and was committed to their relationship, agreed wholeheartedly.

Thus we see that Adrienne's explicit request helped her to find renewed satisfaction for her fundamental needs, and to take part in social or informal gatherings without feeling threatened. At this point, I feel obliged to emphasize that one cannot possibly choose appropriate protective mechanisms unless one has first completed the work called for in the preceding steps. How could Adrienne have expressed her fears, needs, and opposition clearly and in a responsible manner, if she had not become aware of them and proceeded to accept them?

There are, then, a number of resources we can employ in a conscious manner to protect ourselves from our suffering, while still maintaining respect for who we are. I will single the following out for individual attention: the explicit request, seeking verification, choosing our entourage and environment, demarcating territory and setting limits, creating new experiences and transforming expectations into goals.

I feel I have to repeat that, before anyone is capable of choosing an appropriate means of protection, he must first be aware of his psychological functionings, accept them in a responsible manner and have observed, however briefly, his recurrent, unsatisfactory behavior patterns. For an individual to choose and set up his means of protection indicates that he is ready to overcome his fears and accept loss. In fact, I remain profoundly convinced that neither evolution nor freedom is possible unless one does accept the possibility of loss. Loss is implicit in all our choices, and what is life made up of but choices? Until we are prepared to take the risk of losing something, we are not, in any real sense, either alive, happy or free. The job of the protective mechanism is to encourage the individual to learn self-respect, freedom and creativity. I have described each one of these mechanisms in detail, for I feel their importance cannot be overstated, all the more so since they constitute a new thrust in psychology and in child education.

1. The explicit request

We rarely use requests as a form of protection, and when we do, they usually don't work out. Many people consider requests to be synonymous with dependence, feeling that asking is similar to begging, or fishing after something. They pride themselves on the fact that they don't need to rely on anyone, that they can get along fine by themselves. In doing so, however, they cause themselves a great deal of suffering because their fundamental needs for love, affirmation, acknowledgment and security are frequently left unsatisfied.

Dependence is an inner state made apparent through our attitude. Thus, it is not the request itself that reflects our dependence or lack of same, but rather the underlying intentions and feelings of the person who makes it. When he makes it in a manipulative or arrogant manner, the request becomes counterproductive, for when it is an order in disguise, one that brooks no refusal, it maintains dependence. In that case, the request is not a means of protection, but rather a distorted defense mechanism, a means of exerting power over another person. The request must be both clear and explicit, and it must implicitly respect the other person's right to grant the request or refuse it. If so, it is a valid means of protection; if not, it will only foster alienation. This is why most people prefer solving their own problems to losing their freedom by unconsciously making requests that contain a hidden message. The interaction between John and Louise illustrates my point. One day John, who doesn't have the car with him, asks Louise if she would mind driving him home after work. However, because he is not prepared to be turned down, the non-verbal message that accompanies his words actually undercuts them, depriving his request of any degree of authenticity. When faced with such a request, Louise, who has unconsciously picked up on the order implicit in what John says, responds in turn with her own hidden message. In other words, she conveys a conscious verbal message and an unconscious non-verbal message that reflects her real feelings and intentions. Each person's hidden message is revealed below:

John:

Verbal message: Would you mind driving me home after work?

Non-verbal message: If you don't, I will feel rejected. I will get upset, and I'll never ask you for anything again.

It goes without saying that requests containing a hidden message create ambiguous relationships and make people feel trapped because, unfortunately, they tend to elicit responses that are equally two-sided such as the one below:

Louise:

Verbal message: Of course not. It's my pleasure.

Non-verbal message: Oh no! Not again! I wish he would stop bothering me like this.

Why are their messages not clear? Quite simply because they contain unexpressed fears, particularly the fear of rejection and the fear of loss.

Basically, then, we have a choice: on the one hand, there are the things that are not expressed, which lead to frustration; there are the alienating things (such as John's request) that are expressed and that often hide a fear of being turned down, which many people interpret as rejection. On the other hand, there are the things that are expressed, that prove liberating for whoever makes the request, and that allow the other the freedom to grant or refuse it. We cannot use requests as a means of protection unless we make a conscious choice between the two. Thus, our requests become liberating when we can move beyond the fear of being turned down or of bothering the other, the fear of rejection, judgment, criticism, ridicule or loss.

We cannot use the protective mechanism until our previous progress has brought us to the point where we can discover and accept the fears that dwell within each one of us and that prevent us from satisfying our fundamental needs. By choosing not to voice any requests, or by making alienating ones, we can never overcome our fears. We succeed in bypassing them, but never in satisfying our fundamental needs. Quite the opposite, in fact, because these two courses either create rifts between people, or else build bridges that are merely fragile structures, ever ready to break apart. We have seen how explicit requests can respect the other's right to react as he chooses, but how can they provide satisfaction of our psychological needs?

When the request is clear and explicit, it provides a feeling of security. Let me illustrate this statement by telling you Henrietta's story, which I found resembled that of many women heard in therapy. Henrietta's need for sexual satisfaction had been much stronger during her first year of marriage than it was when she came to see me: over the years, it had slowly diminished until it was almost non-existent. Marco, her husband, felt so threatened by this that he had started talking about seeing someone else unless she changed her ways. Henrietta felt torn between her fear of losing the man she loved and her lack of desire, and it was this that led her into therapy. In addition to her intense feeling of helplessness, she felt acute guilt, coupled with a profound lack of self-esteem. She was sure that she loved Marco; why, then, was she so uninterested in sexual contact with him? In therapy with me, she discovered that the sexual side of their relationship had been based on hidden messages from the start. During their first year of marriage, she had never turned down Marco's advances for fear of disappointing him or losing his love. Although she was not always in the mood when he was, she pretended to reach orgasm, and intimated that making love with him was a total turn-on for her. This was her way of trying to satisfy her need to be loved and acknowledged. Marco, for his part, thought that his wife had a strong sex drive. Although he would have liked to make love less often, he stepped up his advances and worked on his performance, all so he could satisfy her.

Why were Henrietta and Marco unable to respect their actual level of desire? Because they were afraid of losing the other, of course, but also because they needed love and acknowledgment. This is the trap that the mental process of dissatisfaction unfailingly represents: in order to satisfy a fundamental need and bypass their fears, people will defend themselves by lying and deceiving their partner. However, as with Henrietta and Marco, these defense mechanisms, which are used involuntarily and unconsciously to protect them from their fears, actually bring them the opposite of what they desire.

Is it possible to pick up the pieces and start over again? Henrietta first had to become aware of her own psychological functioning. She discovered that her need for love had led her to always give in to Marco's advances. Although she was aware of this need, at that point, she was still not able to satisfy it by making an explicit request. One day, over dinner, she started making vague generalizations that were intended to convey her needs: "These days, there isn't much affection or tenderness in the world. Perhaps you and I could find a way of bringing love to those unfortunate ones who have never experienced it."

To Henrietta's despair, Marco showed little interest in this little speech. In therapy, she realized that she had never been clear with him. She had always made her requests in a roundabout manner, and then criticized him for not having understood them. She came to understand that, during her first year of marriage, she had tried to satisfy her need for tenderness through sex, but had ended up with more than she had bargained for: where Marco was concerned, she was incapable of showing or receiving any kind of affection because she was afraid of the sexual contact it would inevitably lead to. Through this experience, she discovered the importance of being explicit and of making specific requests, such as: "Marco, tonight I would like us to be tender and affectionate with each other without making love."

This sort of unambiguous request eliminates frustrated expectations and futile performances. By behaving in this manner, Henrietta was able to specify what she needed, without increasing her guilt or diminishing her self-esteem.

Parents and children are often caught in the net of ambiguous demands. All too often, parents are vague when they ask their children to do something, and this leads to frustration, and sometimes open conflict. When she began her therapy, Charlene, a mother of four teenagers, couldn't hide her exasperation as she told me her problem. She felt as though her children, and even her husband, treated her as though she were a maid. Nobody seemed to understand that she was tired of doing all the work herself. I don't know how many people I've met over the years who hoped, as Charlene did, that their needs would be understood. "Can't you see I want you to help me?" they say. Charlene's expectations were not fulfilled because she either didn't ask for what she wanted, or else did so in a roundabout manner. Nobody, no matter what the situation, should be obliged to guess another person's needs, nor can he know where he stands when asked to deal with hidden or indirect requests. Only clear and explicit requests lead to satisfaction. Thus, Charlene would not see any change in her situation until she made it clear to her husband and children what she wanted them to do. Instead of bemoaning the fact that her family didn't understand her, or undertaking halfhearted task-sharing initiatives, she simply asked her husband to do the shopping and her four children to take turns doing the washing up, giving each of them a duty-day. As well, she asked them to spend part of every Saturday cleaning their room: vacuuming, dusting, changing and washing the sheets. To her great surprise, her family was delighted with her requests, especially the children, who had become tired of their mother's constant complaints and now felt liberated and more secure.

A clear and explicit request constitutes an effective means of protection against the insecurity engendered by hidden or ambiguous messages. It fosters satisfaction of fundamental needs. If it is not alienating, it provides a feeling of security and, in case of refusal, it allows people to know where they stand, and change that stance, rather than harbor frustrated expectations. Making an explicit request that respects the other's response means showing self-respect and equipping oneself with the tools for self-fulfillment.

Depending on the situation, other protective mechanisms can also lead to satisfaction of one's fundamental needs, and verification is one of these.

2. Verification

The term verification refers to the act of inquiring about other people's real feelings and intentions in order to see whether or not they correspond to the scenarios we invent and which we all too often use as a basis for interpretation. Too many people grow apart from their loved ones because of a simple misunderstanding that has not been cleared up. The advantage of verification is that it makes situations clear and allows people to be in full possession of the facts when they make decisions. As with all protective mechanisms, it requires the ability to overcome one's fears, such as the fear of knowing the truth or the fear of rejection. However, the sense of well-being brought on by the security it engenders makes it a worthwhile tool, to be used frequently. For most of us, nothing is more unbearable than an ambiguous situation. It is better to know the truth, even though it may be hard to deal with in the short term, than to stagnate in a state of insecurity brought on by doubt. To verify is to free oneself, and find satisfaction for one's basic needs.

Interpretation causes a great many problems in people's relationships. What often happens is that a person will interpret the words or behavior of those in his entourage and invent fictitious scenarios based, of course, on his own perceptions of those people. Interpretation, as we have already seen, provides more information about the interpreter than the interpretee.

In interpersonal relationships, interpretation distorts communication, and over a period of time creates either distance or outright dispute. This is more or less what happened to Gerard. A significant factor in his story was his highly developed abandonment complex, which made him interpret every delay, every lack of attention as rejection. In his relationship with Lilith, he created a number of fictitious scenarios that eventually led him to leave her. Around this time, Lilith was going through a crucial period in her professional life. Although at the time she was a training officer in a large company, she had begun a course in business administration at university in order to accept a management position that had been offered to her several months earlier. In addition to her regular day job, her on-the-job training required many hours of overtime. Also, two evenings per week and two weekends per month, she attended business administration and marketing courses. Her work, studies and projects took up almost all her time, leaving very little for her relationship with Gerard. For her the situation was difficult but she was able to resign herself to it, knowing it was temporary.

Gerard saw things quite differently. When Lilith first told him that she would have to leave work at 6:00 P.M. instead of 4:00 P.M. two nights a week, and that some evenings and weekends she wouldn't be around at all, he understood the situation and congratulated her, but kept his feelings of anxiety to himself. It wasn't until he actually began to feel her absence that his suffering became more acute. Instead of telling Lilith that he felt abandoned, he began to imagine that she didn't love him anymore, that she had a lover and that she was going to leave him. Moreover, he interpreted her every word and gesture in such a way as to confirm his doubts and fears. When she came home later than expected, when she said she would phone him and then forgot, when she didn't want to make love because she was too tired or when she wanted to stay in and rest on their usual night out, all these things were proof for him that he was right and that she had indeed stopped loving him. Thus, one Sunday, when she came home after a weekend course, tired but happy, she asked him:

She: So, did you have a good day?

He: You're never here. You're not interested in me. Our relationship isn't important to you any more. You treat me like dirt. I'm fed up with all your silly excuses for going out.

She: What excuses?

He: I've been watching you, and I know that it's not really courses and work that are taking up all your time.

She: What do you mean?

He: You can't hide it from me. You're seeing someone else. You don't care about me anymore, so why should I hang around like an idiot? I'm leaving. Goodbye!

And he left, without even giving her a chance to reply.

This sort of thing happens fairly often. Instead of verifying with Lilith whether or not his fears were justified, Gerard created all sorts of imaginary scenarios that he came to believe implicitly. Since he had lost touch with external reality, he interpreted all Lilith's actions in light of what his own inner fears made him experience. However, we must remember that the intensity of his fears did not depend only on the immediate trigger, but also on the suffering that trigger brought back to his unconscious memory, suffering caused by a real abandonment situation he had experienced in the past. Since the unconscious, as we know, is the storage center for our emotions and feelings, it retains not the past event itself, but rather the emotional experience that was associated with it. Thus, when a present situation makes the unconscious relive past suffering, it automatically transfers those negative feelings and emotions onto the new situation, without considering its different implications. The danger of this process is, of course, that it will lead the person to interpret incidents based on his own internal processes rather than on external reality, and on his relationship to the past rather than to the present. This is why it is so important for us to be aware of our psychic functioning, so that we can eventually replace interpretation, which is an unconscious defense mechanism, with verification, which is a conscious, protective one.

Let me tell you about Jerome, a young man who came to one of my training courses. One day Louise, one of the participants, said something to him that he took for rejection and ridicule. This young lady, whom he had initially rather liked, had said: "You remind me of a time in my life when I was very unhappy, and that makes me feel uncomfortable." Jerome was deeply disturbed by these words, and took them as a wholesale rejection of himself as a person. Feeling that Louise neither liked nor acknowledged him, and convinced that she was avoiding him because she didn't return his interest, he decided to ignore her. Nevertheless, he was possessed by a desire for vengeance that upset him a great deal. He came to see me after the fifth class, and told me about his past. It goes without saying that I listened attentively to his story; I learned that his mother had given him into the care of his grandmother when he was still very young. Every two weeks she would return to pick him up, and he would spend the weekend with her and her lover. He dreaded those times because he was forced into the company of a man who rejected, judged and ridiculed him openly and with apparent pleasure. He came to hate his mother's partner with a passion, longing to find a way of taking revenge on him, and also on his mother, who took no action whatsoever to protect him from the hostility of this man. I suggested that Jerome verify with Louise if his interpretation of her behavior was well founded. He refused, saying that she wasn't worth the effort. However, the next day at break, I noticed that he and Louise had retired to the far end of the room and were deep in conversation. When break was over, they sat side by side, and Jerome shared his joy and satisfaction with the group. He conceded that his interpretations had no basis in external reality, but were based on his fears. In fact, Louise had felt uncomfortable with him precisely because she was attracted to him. However, she had been afraid to acknowledge this feeling for the simple reason that he bore a strange resemblance to her former lover, with whom she had just gone through a particularly painful separation.

The fact that Jerome chose to verify whether his fears were justified brought him and Louise closer together, whereas their interpretations concerning each other had driven them apart. Jerome's choice forced him to deal with his fear of rejection, for protective mechanisms necessarily imply an ability to overcome one's fears. However, another of their features is that they encourage one to progress toward inner freedom and creativity.

The fields of child education and psychotherapy are, unfortunately, also rife with interpretation. Unaware that they are projecting their own inner world onto the helpee, a great many parents, teachers and psychotherapists end up showing a lack of respect for the child's or client's frame of reference. The following dialogue is between a therapist and a female client.

Client: Sometimes I feel trapped, because I can't stop trying to figure out what other people think of me. I suppose I'm afraid of being judged. Often, I feel useless, like I'm just not worth anything.

Therapist: You don't feel you are loved by those around you.

Client: I don't know, really. Maybe. (Silence). Well, yesterday at work my boss offered me a promotion, but I refused it because I was afraid of letting him down. I was afraid I would fall flat on my face and my colleagues would laugh at me.

Therapist: You think your boss doesn't understand you, and that your co-workers don't appreciate your work.

Client: I've always found my boss very empathetic, and my co-workers tell me almost every day how impressed they are by my work. I'll have to think about what you just said. Do you think it's possible? It seems to me that . . . (Silence).

Therapist: You always want others to love and praise you. This is what motivates you to work hard.

RESPECT FOR THE PROCESS OF LIBERATION AND CHANGE

Client: It's true that I want to be loved, but I don't feel motivated at all any more. I only feel afraid, and I'm always tired, because I expend all my energy on being perfect. I'm afraid that if I don't, others will think I'm incompetent.

Therapist: You're afraid your boss will think you're incompetent and fire you.

Client: I never looked at it that way before. Do you think I could be fired for that? I always feel as though I'm inferior, and I'm always surprised when I do well at work. Something is wrong here, but I don't know what.

Therapist: You find it hard to trust other people.

Client: Do you really think so? Now I don't know what to say anymore. (Silence). Maybe you're right. I know I don't have much confidence in my abilities, and I always hang back so that I won't be noticed. But I would so much like to be more aggressive, more sure of myself. Do you think it's because I don't trust other people?

Therapist: You would like others to notice you, pay more attention to you.

Client: (Silence). I admit I feel kind of lost here. I always thought that I hung back because I was afraid of being judged by other people. I didn't know that I wanted them to notice me. I feel as though I'm caught in a trap.

Which trap does she mean? The trap of being judged by others, or that represented by the therapist's interpretations? Either way, the latter's tendency to interpret his client's feelings distorts the inner work she is trying to accomplish. She ends up going round in circles, feeling more and more disoriented. Interpretation is a trap that can lead, as we have seen, to utter confusion and sometimes even disputes. Is there any resolution?

First and foremost, it is vital that we be aware of our psychological functioning, and that we realize what feelings or what fears are at the root of our tendency to interpret. It is obvious that the therapist in the preceding dialogue is not basing his statements on what the client is saying. He is, in fact, concentrating only on himself; the need to be noticed, loved and praised is probably his own. It is extremely important that he get in touch with himself, so that he does not project what belongs to him (that is, his own needs) onto the client.

As with all the other protective mechanisms we have seen, making verifications requires that we overcome our fears. Although they are important in that they help us refrain from creating imaginary scenarios that deform reality, they are not always easy to put into practice, as is also true for the next protective mechanism: the choice of entourage.

3. Choice of entourage and environment

While he was doing research into suggestology, Lozanov discovered and proved that a person's entourage has a significant impact on the way he functions. People's attitudes act as stimuli, impinging on the other's unconscious and creating propulsive or destructive forces within the psyche. Michel Lobrot made his contribution to this area of study in the 1970s, by proving the paramount importance of parents and teachers to a child's development.

Unconscious influence is a universal phenomenon, and it plays a crucial role in our human development. As evidenced earlier in this book, there can be no doubt that man is influenced by his entourage. If the attitude of those who raise him primarily conveys feelings of love, trust and respect, he will grow up at peace with himself; the satisfaction of his basic needs will have a propulsive effect on him. If, on the other hand, he grows up surrounded by feelings of hatred, violence and revenge, he will inevitably suffer the consequences, especially if these feelings are not brought out into the open. When a person becomes aware of this phenomenon, it is vital that he find people who will have a more beneficial effect on him, an entourage that favors actualization and assertiveness, that allows him to exploit his creative potential. It is equally vital that he escape from an entourage that makes him feel troubled, inferior or defeated.

Does this mean, then, that our entourage is entirely responsible for who we are and what we feel? I do not think so. As we have already observed, there are certain areas of excessive sensitivity within the human unconscious that arise from strong emotional reactions to past events. It seems obvious that if the attitude of the people in our immediate entourage constantly brings back to us, albeit unconsciously, the memory of that past suffering, then it will cause us psychological pain, and inhibit our ability to act. The family, because it is generally the arena in which our areas of great sensitivity are formed, and where they are constantly stimulated, is all too often the primary cause of psychological problems in its members. For this reason, sooner or later, the child should leave the nest in order to escape the influence of these stimuli, which in certain cases maintain him in a state of dependence, insecurity and inferiority. Ideally, he should move on to an environment that, rather than acting on and thus maintaining his sensitive, even pathological areas, will stimulate his creative potential. Anyone who finds an entourage whose attitude activates his creative reserves rather than opening his psychic wounds will discover his inner forces, develop his self-confidence, increase his ability to act, and overcome more and more of his fears until he finally reaches a point where each day brings greater self-actualization.

Changing our entourage may sometimes imply changing our environment: the location of some or all of our activities, whether personal or professional. However, human beings are afraid of change, and this fear of the unknown will prevent a given individual from escaping from an environment in which he is imprisoned. Unless he overcomes this fear, he will stagnate in his own psychological suffering. Slowly, his soul and heart will die. Even so, leaving the security of what he knows for the insecurity of the unknown is extremely difficult. It involves a risk, but choosing to take a risk also means choosing to live. He should look with hope to tomorrow, for he is risking just as much by staying in a situation where he is unhappy as he is by moving to an unknown one. In some cases, a change of environment may involve taking on new challenges, being open to new influences, exploring new potential, making new discoveries and creating new hope. There are, however, two necessary preconditions to all of this: a readiness to change and an ability to overcome the fear of the unknown that so often hinders our free choice.

On a personal note, I believe one of the greatest opportunities for growth of any kind that ever came my way was the change in entourage and environment that I experienced when I spent three years in Europe, and that I experienced again, perhaps to a lesser degree, when, upon my return to Canada, I settled in Montreal rather than going back to my home town. These were big risks for me, but they were also a driving force that opened the gates to life and liberty. It goes without saying that I did not take those risks blindly, in order to run away from something, but rather knowingly, impelled by a deep-seated need for change, liberation and progression.

All this, however, does not mean I am advocating running away whenever there is difficulty or conflict in our relationships. I wish to distinguish here between flight, which is a defense mechanism, and choosing our entourage and our environment, which is a protective mechanism. We may choose to stop associating with certain people because, in spite of our efforts, whenever we are with them, we feel the same dissatisfaction, the same urge for self-effacement, the same constant uneasiness. Fear of loss, solitude, abandonment and judgment are generally what keeps a person in this painful state of dependence. Impelled by chronic fear, he inevitably puts the other first, rather than himself. For him to actively choose his entourage, then, he has to overcome these fears, and also agree to "lose" the other so he can "find" himself. Let me add that this is not an easy thing in our society, where most people have introjected the notion that we must put others first, in an atmosphere of universal and reciprocal love, where we have no enemies. This is the paradoxical heritage of a religion that preaches love, but that is based on an eternal fight between Good and Evil, between Christ and Satan.

In addition to putting ourselves first and overcoming our fears, choosing our entourage means we are breaking free from that which our education has grafted onto us and that prevents us from being truly alive. One of the most significant rites of passage man goes through in his lifetime is the stage during which he learns to act for himself rather than for others. The point at which we stop being motivated by the desire to please others, and no longer make ourselves believe we are acting for their good, marks the beginning of the persona's death, and the birth of the person; it is the start of our liberation.

By choosing our entourage, we free ourselves from useless burdens, from cumbersome barriers and negative energy. Above all, we break away from our restrictive introjections, our paralyzing fears. If our choice really is a means of protection, it will lead to well-being. However, it should not be made out of revenge, or in an atmosphere where we criticize, blame or reject the other, but rather in an atmosphere of love and respect. Instead of putting up with the people around us, it behooves us to choose them, whether they be friends, family members or co-workers, so that our entourage will be beneficial to us. When we act in this way, we break out of our victim pattern to take control of our lives. I believe that this protective mechanism is essential to our evolution as human beings, for he who is strong enough to choose a propulsive, healthy entourage and environment also has the strength to create his life, to create his own self. True self-actualization and happiness will remain forever beyond our grasp unless we can make that choice. Power struggles, the need to prove oneself, domination, unhealthy competitions, these have no place in a propulsive entourage. Such an entourage encourages people to assert their differences and exploits their creative potential, through implicit respect: for oneself, for others, and for one's territory and limits.

4. Territory and limits

The ability to clearly demarcate our territory and define our limits is in direct proportion to our ability to define and assert ourselves. Without boundaries, we have no identity, and cannot assert our differences. In the end, our territory is nothing more and nothing less than ourselves, so having our territory invaded means being invaded in a personal sense, stripped of dignity and respect. By failing to acknowledge his own territory, a person feels he is nobody, that he has no importance.

The need to be acknowledged is indeed crucial to one's sense of self-respect. When my territory is invaded, I am not acknowledged as a person, and this can have serious consequences for me.

What exactly does the idea of territory imply? According to the International Society for Interdisciplinary Research in Communication, or SIRIC (1982, p. 283), it includes "my geographical space," that is, my room, my living space, my furniture, my home; it also includes my time, the way I organize my appointments and stick to my schedule. My territory is also made up of "my body, my health, my life and death," "my job in the company where I work, as well as all the supplies I need to perform it: my desk, my files, the equipment I use every day." My territory refers to my name, my "acquired knowledge and experience, my successes and failures," and it also comprises "my ideologies and beliefs," "my lifestyle, my daily choices" and "my money, my car, my possessions" that I may choose to lend to others, if it suits me. Finally, my territory includes "my commitments and responsibilities" (but not those that do not belong to me), "my social circle, my friends, my mail, my clothing and the way I cut my hair."

The loss of one's territory, or the failure of another person to respect it (SIRIC, p. 285) can have serious implications, for loss of territory entails loss of autonomy, of freedom of action, of psychological and even physical health and of the kind of aggression necessary for sheer survival. I would add that, given the numerous disputes born of neverending frustration, loss of territory also leads to a breakdown in communication and, eventually, failed relationships.

Merely defining our territory, however, is not enough; nor is it enough to know what it comprises. The most difficult and critical step is to set clear and precise limits. These constitute an important means of protection, for setting and enforcing them satisfies all our fundamental needs: the need to be loved, acknowledged, listened to, accepted, and made to feel secure, as well as the need to assert oneself, to create and to be free.

Every human being on this planet has the urge to live, to exist. Everyone wants to be acknowledged by others, to have his own niche, territory, and space in which he can exist. Because he is surrounded by others, he must demarcate his territory precisely. If the boundaries of that territory are not clearly marked, he will be invaded, giving him a feeling of futility. This feeling can become so overpowering as to lead to annihilation, to dissociation of the self. To feel that one does not exist is a form of psychological death.

I cannot emphasize enough how important a person's territory is to his survival. It is also a crucial factor in his relationships with others. When he can command respect for his territory, he can also command respect for himself as an individual. People tend to love and acknowledge those who assert themselves because they are vibrant and because they make us feel alive. Being alive means asserting oneself, establishing one's territory and setting one's limits.

In the context of interpersonal relationships, the ability to establish one's territory and to respect that of others creates an atmosphere that is conducive to communication because each person is loved and acknowledged, his right to be different is upheld, and he feels free. The thing that prevents us from being free is the same thing that prevents us from demarcating our physical and psychological space: our inability to get in touch with our feelings, to respect our needs and to acknowledge our fear of loss, rejection, judgment or conflict. These are the fears we must overcome if we wish to implement this particular protective mechanism. In order to achieve this, however, there are certain basic concepts we must learn. I will therefore interrupt my description of this protective mechanism to briefly look at the notions of invasion, life goals, priorities and discipline.

a) *Invasion*

Unless he can overcome his fears, man will lose his freedom and the acknowledgment of others because he will never be able to prevent others from invading both him and his possessions.

Invasion, as we have already seen, is the main reason why wars are fought. Basically, it is a conscious or unconscious means of exerting power over others, and shows a lack of respect for them. It robs people of their freedom, no matter which side of the fence they are on: whether they are the "invader" or the "invadee," they are not free.

If a person wishes to become the master of his own destiny, he must work out his invader or invadee pattern, for he cannot satisfy that urge to be free, creative, loved and acknowledged unless he implements protective means, and they require self-respect and self-acknowledgment. Only self-respect will enable him to speak the words and take the initiative that will prevent his territory from being invaded, and that will take away from others the power they have been wielding over his life. He does not have to fight with others in order to occupy his own rightful place; instead, he oversees his own inner combat, one between his need to exist and his fear of loss. By defining his territory, and setting his limits, he will emerge the victor in the sense that he will have sufficient self-love to put himself first, to respect his fundamental needs even at the risk of losing, being judged or being rejected.

How do we know what our limits are, though? Obviously, before we can integrate this protective mechanism into our lives, and before we can be ready to use it, we have to go through all the previous steps indicated in the process of change. So, before we can know our limits, we must first become aware of who we are, and particularly of how our psyche functions. This will enable us to define our life goals.

b) Life goals

When we set out our life goals, we must ask ourselves the following questions: "What do I want to accomplish over my lifetime? What is my mission in life?"

It is extremely important to come up with specific answers to these questions, because they will allow us to define our territory and our limits, and help us to avoid becoming fragmented; if we have set our own goals, we will not let ourselves be guided by events, or other people. However, if we have no idea where we are going, it is easy for us to spend our lives being drawn down this road or that one, as dictated by events or the needs of others, and end up getting nowhere. By setting life goals for myself, I am choosing my own road, on the basis of what I want to become.

I am a firm believer in the saying: "Heaven helps those who help themselves." Merely waiting passively for "heaven," or others, to help them turns people into human puppets, pulled and jerked this way and that by the world around them. Man's relationship with God involves reciprocal collaboration toward a common goal: the actualization and ongoing creation of the world. This collaboration necessarily implies that man will do his part, that he will act, and take charge of his destiny. By being in control of his life, by using the appropriate resources, he is enabled to create himself, and to go on from there to help others, with God's help.

Setting life goals for myself means directing my actions toward a specific goal. If this goal in any way involves my own creation, and the creation of the world, I shall be unable to attain it unless I can boldly confront the obstacles in my path and not let fear hold me back. My ability to overcome these obstacles is commensurate with my determination to achieve the greatest possible degree of self-actualization. The obstacles also constitute a testing ground, in the sense that if I conquer them, I will emerge stronger, more self-confident, with a richer inner world. He who knows how to transform obstacles into guiding lights can watch as fear and suffering diminish making room for faith in oneself, in others and in life itself. Vanquishing the obstacle means choosing to live one's life more intensely, with more energy and greater love. This on-going choice necessarily involves adhering to our territory and our limits: when, in spite of the obstacles that rise up before us, we never falter from the course set by our life goals, we are consistently putting ourselves first, we are directing our own lives and, above all, we are confident in our ability to create ourselves and, consequently, to create the world. For when, as an individual, I create myself, I bring to bear on others the unconscious influence of my own actualization. This contribution is a subtle one; pride, and the need to prove oneself or to excel, have no part in it. On the contrary, it is informed by inner actualization based on the ability to surpass oneself and to respect one's differences.

How does one go about choosing life goals? I choose them by imagining myself at the end of my life, and wondering what things I would like to have accomplished in the spiritual, affective, social, intellectual, professional, physical and material fields. Although each of these dimensions is important, they need to be worked on concurrently; if one is singled out at the expense of the others, then problems arise.

When I teach courses on the concept of change, I always ask the students to envision what they will have accomplished in all these categories by the end of their lives. These possible future achievements then become their life goals, the objectives they wish to attain. Moving from theory to a concrete example, let me tell you about Jon. He was 36 years old when he did this exercise with me: he was married, the father of three children and a manager for a store that sold building materials. These were the goals that he set for himself:

- *Spiritual dimension:* Be able to get in touch with the "sage within" on a daily basis.

- *Social dimension:* Become mayor of my district.

- *Intellectual dimension:* Improve my qualifications in administration, and particularly in marketing.

- *Professional dimension:* Own a chain of stores specializing in building materials.

- *Physical dimension:* Be able to enjoy food, sex and sensual pleasures in a balanced way and be physically fit and active.

- *Material dimension:* Reach an annual sales figure of $2 million.

These life goals may be adjusted throughout the course of a person's life. However, the knowledge of where he is going allows him to use his resources to follow that course; his choice of personal priorities constitutes one of those resources.

c) *Priorities*

Once we have set our life goals, then of course it is easy to demarcate our territory and to specify what our limits are. However, this step becomes even more satisfying if we can learn to establish our priorities. To do this, we must determine the comparative value we place on the various elements that make up our lives: spouse, children, relatives, friends, work, leisure time and holidays, material possessions, plans, our personal development in a physical sense (health), an intellectual sense (studies, thirst for knowledge), and in the affective, social, spiritual and creative senses. By reflecting on these elements, we may realize, for instance, that our children are vitally important to us, yet that we almost never spend time with them because we are too busy responding to external pressures. Or else we may become aware that we let ourselves be invaded by our work or our family, and that we don't make time in our lives for what really interests us. Such realizations help us to learn more about our needs, and to establish our limits accordingly; this way, we can take control of our lives, and others will respect us.

In a purely practical sense, thanks to these realizations, we should be able to divide up our time based on the priorities we have chosen, and not based on our reactions to events. The agenda is a useful tool in helping us manage our time more efficiently but, unfortunately, we tend to use it for business purposes only. In my opinion, we should use it to allocate time for our spouse, our children, and ourselves, too. If we don't, chances are we will feel overwhelmed, and frustrated by our inability to "find time."

All these skills involving self-respect and self-actualization, essential though they may be, will have no noticeable effect on our lives unless we bring a sense of organization and discipline to bear on it.

d) *Organization and discipline*

I am not exaggerating when I say that discipline is the most important criterion to self-actualization and satisfaction of our fundamental needs. In my various careers as a teacher, psychotherapist and group leader I have observed that people who lack discipline suffer a great deal from this. By teaching our children and our students about self-discipline, we are showing respect for the natural way the brain functions. Second, we are giving them a sense of security. Finally, we are equipping them with a basic tool kit for self-creation and self-actualization. Discipline allows a person to follow through on the goals he has set, to stick to his priorities and to conform to his daily schedule. Discipline is what encourages him to demarcate his territory and establish his limits.

In many cases, however, parents and teachers are prevented from teaching those in their care how to be self-disciplined or how to set their limits because their own lives have no structure, and are at the mercy of events imposed by the outer world. For example, many parents find the task of raising their children difficult, if not wearisome, and this can be aggravated by a lack of discipline. A family that lacks discipline and structure can easily fall prey to conflict, frustration and dissatisfaction. Territorial boundaries are not respected because they are not defined.

Valerie was 28 years old when she came to see me; it was her first visit to a psychotherapist. She was finding the job of raising two young boys, aged three years and ten months respectively, to be a difficult one. She felt that motherhood had enslaved her, that she had no freedom and no life of her own. Her two young boys took up all her time, both day and night, to the point where she began to regret her decision to have children. After all, she had given up everything for them: her career, her leisure time and even her friends, whom she no longer had time to see. Valerie was a textbook case of a mother who sacrifices everything for her children and then makes them responsible for her frustration and the choices she has made. Raising children is not meant to be a painful task, but a source of profound joy. If this is not the case, we need to ask ourselves some serious questions. Of course we should spend time with our children, but we should also set limits on that time, so that we have some left over for ourselves.

Valerie realized that her feelings of guilt and her endless introspections on the subject of how she raised her children had left her out of touch with her own needs, and unable to define any personal limits. Parents who do this unwittingly make their children insecure; they become more and more demanding, but are never satisfied. For parents, the most difficult thing about limits is not setting them but enforcing them. This is where discipline comes in. Children can generally understand the correlation between limits and consequences when they are presented in the form of a choice:

- You can sit down to eat, or you can leave the table.
- You can play in the yard, or you can play inside.

This way of phrasing things teaches the child to make choices, and to accept the consequences of his choices, as long as the parent enforces them. In other words, if the child goes outside the yard to play, he has made a choice, and he must accept the consequences of that choice, that is, be brought inside, even if he cries, screams, or stamps his feet.

A good educator is someone who, once his limits are established, knows how to have them respected. However, this task requires that the educator be able to overcome his own fears: fear of being judged by "others," fear of being unloved, fear of being wrong. The results are infinitely rewarding; it develops the reliability, sense of discipline and security that are necessary for harmonious self-development.

Unfortunately, the quasi-radical changes that rocked Quebec in the 1960s were founded on values that had to be discarded because, in many cases and in many different settings, the concepts of organization and discipline were neglected. I say "unfortunately" for discipline really does supply structure for our human existence; it is the directivity provided by the container. Without it, we can easily lose sight of where we are going, as Leonard's experience so clearly shows. His mother abandoned him shortly after birth, and he was lucky enough to be placed with a good family. Although his adoptive parents loved him, they were disorganized, and could not provide a structured environment. Thus Leonard grew up with the pros and cons of a "laissez-faire" upbringing. I met Leonard when he was in Grade 9, and instantly felt drawn to this intelligent, likable boy. Unfortunately, in spite of his ability, Leonard did not do well at school, and this lowered his self-esteem and caused him a lot of suffering. Since he had no self-discipline, he was simply unable to set himself regular study hours at home. He told me that he was lazy. This is, in fact, a common misconception among people who are disorganized or who lack self-discipline.

When discipline has not been taught at home, it tends to take longer to learn, and the person's progress must be accepted as proceeding in stages. We may introduce discipline into our lives, and then organize our daily routine. This may sound like an arduous and stifling task, but once begun, we quickly realize that it actually gives us more free time, and leaves us more satisfied at the end of each day. Organizing our lives does not only mean planning our work time, it also means arranging our leisure activities, our rest or our periods of unstructured time. Bringing discipline to bear on our lives means, quite simply, making sure that we get what we really want out of it, rather than submitting to circumstances that are not of our choosing. It means giving ourselves the power to set the limits that will allow us to follow the route that we have chosen. When we are able to consciously single out this protective mechanism by confronting our fears, we automatically take charge of our lives.

Knowing how to make explicit requests, how to go beyond our imaginary scenarios by seeking verification, how to choose our entourage and our environment, how to demarcate our territory and establish our limits are all, as we have seen, valid protective mechanisms. Let us now turn to the next one: the ability to create new life experiences.

5. New life experiences

Because of the way his brain is constituted, man needs rituals, discipline and a certain kind of routine. However, he also needs change. If his life is overritualized, if there is no room for novelty or the unexpected, then his evolution will be slowed down, and maybe even brought to a halt. Instead of marching ahead, he will be sucked back into the closed system he created to make himself feel secure. If he does, his behavior will continue to play out the defense mechanisms that cause him pain and the relational patterns that make him unhappy.

Man needs to feel secure. But if, in order to satisfy that need for security, he fails to fulfill his needs for self-affirmation, creation and freedom, his life will become unbalanced. Satisfying one need at the expense of the others leads to feelings of being trapped, stifled. True happiness comes from the satisfaction of all the fundamental needs, not just one. Thus it is crucial that man find a balance between structure and self-discipline on the one hand and change and the unexpected on the other. Without innovation and variation, evolution is not possible. Instead, we become bogged down in dissatisfaction, frustration, disappointment and regret. By leaving room for change and the unexpected, we open the doors to creativity and freedom, and enhance our zest for life.

If he really wants to stop wallowing in a routine that emprisons him in feelings of dissatisfaction and that keeps him paralyzed with fear, man must make a conscious choice to experience new things. When he constantly repeats the same experiences, he is not providing his psyche with any new information. This makes it rigid in the way it functions, and it becomes more difficult to implement psychotherapy to render his inner world more flexible.

It is, if course, impossible to make that choice to experience new things unless we are able to overcome certain fears, such as the fear of the unknown, of failure, of mistakes, of ridicule and of judgment. We cannot be truly free until we have confronted that monstrous Minotaur that prowls our psychological labyrinth. The success of this step, however, depends on the completion of the previous steps in the process: that is, awareness, acceptance, responsibility and observation.

Implementing this particular protective mechanism, the one that deals with new life experiences, means really taking charge of our life and no longer simply waiting for people or events to hand us experiences that often are not to our taste. Because the protective mechanism is used consciously, it allows us to actively choose rather than passively submit. Also, it makes us sufficiently open-minded and flexible to confront unexpected situations without being overwhelmed, or becoming unbalanced in the way we function.

Fear of change keeps people trapped in the past, whereas their natural inclination is to push ahead into the future. Routinely and incessantly experiencing the same things, with no room left for variety, is contrary to the very essence of life itself. When we fall into this trap, we are damaging ourselves, and this is just what Ezra was doing. He was very depressed when he came to see me; he had hit rock bottom. All the signs were there: a feeling of helplessness and despair; a total lack of interest in his surroundings and for his friends and family; inability to commit himself or fulfill his responsibilities; no motivation with regard to sex, personal well-being or physical appearance; chronic guilt; profound conviction of his own lack of worth; negative self-image and lack of confidence in his own potential; intense sadness; a self-destructive tendency; lack of motivation; propensity to dramatize and exaggerate; longing for death, difficulty communicating; a tendency to project an image of well-being to conceal his illness; and difficulty making any kind of effort to help himself.

Ezra stayed in therapy for almost two years. During that time, he went through all the stages in the process of change. As he did so, he made some surprising discoveries concerning himself, and concerning his psychological functioning. His greatest revelation, however, came when he discovered his insecurity complex. He realized that, at the age of 30, he had organized his life in such a way as to rule out the possibility of anything unexpected happening. Every action in every day was thought out, planned, structured, ritualized, and had been so for many years. He had never moved out of his parents' home, so had few responsibilities, and spent his day following the same timetable: get up, eat breakfast, go to work, come home, eat dinner, watch TV, go to bed, and so on and so forth. At work he had steadfastly refused to be promoted, but had kept the same operator's job he had when he started. He confined his close personal relationships to his immediate family, and almost never went out in the evening, except to go and visit his sister, who lived not far away.

Was Ezra mentally deficient or abnormal? Not at all. He had enormous emotional blocks that he maintained through constant contact with a castrating and domineering mother and a feeble and self-effacing father, with whom he was forced to identify because he hated his mother. Before coming into therapy, he would never have admitted to such feelings. It was difficult, not to say painful, for Ezra to make even the smallest changes in his life, for this meant challenging his mother's authority, and this had an extremely destructive effect on him. By the time he left psychotherapy, he had moved out into an apartment by himself, subscribed to a series of classical music concerts, asked for a promotion and promptly received one, and even got in touch with a dating agency in the hope of finding a possible companion, but these changes did not come easily. He had fallen into his former monotonous routine because his mother had discouraged all his previous initiatives, saying that he wasn't capable, that he wouldn't succeed, that he would be unhappy, and so on and so forth. Like in a nightmare, these fears were suffocating him, yet when he tried to run away, he found he couldn't. When, at the advice of his sister, he came into therapy with me, he kept it secret from his mother, and used the pretext of overtime at work to explain why he sometimes came home late.

When we create new situations and new experiences for ourselves, we are giving ourselves a wealth of opportunities for ongoing rebirth and unhoped-for discoveries. For it is only by experiencing new things that we can exploit our hitherto latent potential. Also, by placing ourselves in the path of new experiences, we discover our strength, our ability to go onward and upward, to unlock the secrets of unlimited creativity. By having new experiences, we bring to fruition our talents, and all our inner riches that, all to often, are kept dormant by our fears. Having new experiences means cultivating a taste for adventure, a desire to beat one's personal best that can do wonders for one's self-confidence.

As long as our search for new experiences is not undertaken out of a desire to flee the old, but rather out of respect for the natural inner urge to push on, to advance and to grow, so that we can be proud of ourselves and happy to be alive, then it will assist us in our process of change. Moreover, this step will be that much easier to accomplish when we can transform our expectations into goals.

6. Transformation of expectations into goals

Expectation is one of man's greatest sources of suffering. He waits for something to change, for something nice to happen, for his loved one to come back to him, for the "others" to get moving, for the silver spoon to appear and, as he waits, he is doing himself incalculable damage. The whole world over, people expect and wait in vain.

Waiting is the opposite of taking responsibility. When I wait, I am using a form of passive power to try and change the outer world but, paradoxically, I am at its mercy. If we were to spend all the energy we waste trying to change others on trying to change ourselves, there is no doubt that we would all find the satisfaction we strive for. The "others" are not responsible for our needs and our expectations; like us, they are only responsible for their own.

When we are in a waiting mode, we stagnate. No one should grant others the power to try and change them. To truly love ourselves is to transform our expectations into goals so that we can regain control of our lives.

Religion has taught many of us to expect everything from God, from people in authority, and indeed from anyone around us to whom we relinquish power. This passive attitude maintains us in a state of frustration and disappointment and, consequently, fosters such defense mechanisms as criticism, interpretation and judgment.

The real reason why we wait, though, is fear. We wait because we are afraid of acting and especially of the consequences of our actions. This is what kept Camille in a dead-end relationship for years. She was in love with a man who treated her like dirt: when he wanted her, he promised her the moon, and when he was tired of her, he threw her aside like a rag doll. During those periods of rejection, she went through hell. She hated and despised him, but even so, deep down she hoped that he would come back to her. Camille had so little self-love that she had given her lover complete control over her life. When she came to see me, she had just split up with the same man for the eighth time in three years. She was a broken woman, and yet in spite of her almost unbearable pain, she still wanted him back. She was waiting once again, this time in a state of near despair.

Camille's problem obviously went too deep to be dealt with on a superficial level. She had a highly developed abandonment complex, which made her fear rejection above all things. Thus, in all her relationships, but particularly in those with the opposite sex, she totally denied her own needs. Since she rejected herself, she was rejected by others. Her fear and her expectations brought her exactly the opposite of what she had desired: instead of being loved and respected, she was rejected and abandoned.

After having gone through the steps leading to liberation and change, Camille decided to confront her fear by transforming her expectations into goals. Her first goal was to acquire enough self-love to be able to fulfill her fundamental needs. Since her relationship with her lover was basically painful and unsatisfying for her, and since his company significantly undermined her self-esteem, she decided to call it quits with him. She had definitely made up her mind, and this made the break-up that much easier, because she turned away from the past and looked to the future. In fact, she changed her whole lifestyle: she became much more active than before, took an interest in dance, started a jazz ballet course, planned a holiday abroad and went out regularly to the movies, the theater or other spots around town. Unwilling to let Camille go on her own terms, her former lover made several attempts to win her back, but she stood firm. This was not easy for her, but she was strengthened by the several months she had spent in therapy. She had definitely decided that she would put herself first, and no longer let herself be dominated by fear.

When we transform our expectations into goals, we are giving ourselves the impetus to act. In my opinion, this is something parents and teachers should be teaching children how to do. Each time I start a course, a workshop or a day-long seminar, I tell the participants what the syllabus will be, and I state clearly that I will not take responsibility for their expectations. Since I have explained the program's layout and underlying philosophy, they are well acquainted with them both. They can set their own personal objectives, and figure out how they will attain them through what is offered. In other words, I come with who I am and what I have to offer, I present it clearly and unambiguously, and I do not try to conform to the participants' expectations. Indeed, I suggest that they transform their expectations into goals, so that they can get what they need out of the course. When people want me to change the content of the program so that it meets their needs, I suggest that they either look for what they need in what is offered or, if the program really doesn't suit them, that they simply withdraw. They thus become both active, and responsible for their actions. If they stay in the course, they are no longer passively waiting, but actively participating and committed, which is, in fact, the only way to get anything out of life.

As with all the protective mechanisms we have looked at, the one that consists in transforming our expectations into goals allows the individual to take control of his life. But he cannot go through this stage in the process leading to liberation and change unless he has been able to overcome the fears that keep him in a state of passivity. The turning point in the therapeutic process or in the individual's evolution toward greater well-being occurs when the helpee is ready to confront the Minotaur in his labyrinth.

If the previous steps have allowed him to see clearly along the pathways of his psychological labyrinth and to locate the Minotaur, the monster that represents everything he fears most, then the final stage in the process of change, that at which he starts using his protective mechanisms, is what makes him free, because it motivates the individual, moving him out of his habitual unsatisfactory behavior patterns. However, in order to go through this stage he must confront his Minotaur, and deal with those fears that, up until then, had always prevented him from making any progress. Because of this, the final stage really is the most painful and the most difficult to go through.

Some people have stayed in this stage for years, thinking that they would never get out. However, we must not forget that although it seems to be the darkest and most terrible path of the labyrinth, it is also the one closest to the exit. When we finally get out, after having challenged our fears and won, we will bring back nuggets of gold; symbols of self-love.

There is always a certain risk involved in confronting our Minotaur: the risk that we will lose something, be judged, abandoned or ridiculed. However, this is the risk we have to take in order to find self-love. We have to pay for the freedom and happiness that self-love bring, with the possibility of losing others, but it is better to lose them than to lose oneself. Indeed, we should always be ready to take that risk, for it is the only possible road to freedom, creativity and love.

If this book has anything to give you, I sincerely hope it would be encouragement in your own inner work, as you strive to know and accept yourself, so that you can then move on to confront your fears on a daily basis. Only then will you be reborn, and be able to discover your sole *raison d'être* on this earth: love. Until you have enough self-love to put yourself first in every situation, you will not learn what it is to love others. Love is the only act that creates both the Self and the world.

G. THE SHIFT TO CREATIVE ACTION

Why is this last stage included in the process of change? Because creation is the final outcome of that process. When I have succeeded in facing up to my fears and in taking control of my life, I enter the stage in which I create myself and my life, and in which I create the world. The more I "create myself," in the sense that I ascribe to the term here, the more I assert myself as a creator. And each one of my creations is a personal contribution to the evolution of the world and of the human race. Thus I participate in the work of creation.

RESPECT FOR THE PROCESS OF LIBERATION AND CHANGE

Now that I have tamed the Minotaur, the energy that I spent on defending myself from my fears has been liberated. Since my creative potential is no longer imprisoned in my unconscious, bound by my fears, this is the time for me to exploit it to the fullest.

Let me emphasize, however, that I cannot become a creator unless I have first created myself by taming the Minotaur. If I do not face up to it, I remain a mere copyist. I may succeed in a material sense, but my success is not creative either for myself or for the world. The struggle never ends conclusively, however. Fears rise up again, and my ability to participate in creation depends on my willingness to confront them. However, each victory I win over them gives me greater confidence in myself, in my strength and in my abilities. Each victory takes me one step further along the road that leads to self-love. The confrontations become progressively less painful, because the knowledge of past victories and the memory of past suffering urge me on toward renaissance and creativity.

This ultimate stage in the process of change is crucial to the CNDA. It is psychotherapy's final goal, the outcome toward which the whole growth and transformation process is geared. It is at this point that the nondirective approach becomes creative, and this is why it is not possible to speak of the CNDA without mentioning its creativity aspect, which alone ensures a person's true renaissance.

Going through the stages in the CNDA's therapeutic process, which leads on to freedom and change, means truly following the pathway of transformation toward love and happiness. We deal in neither magic nor miracles here, but rather, nothing less than the well-earned reward for long, drawn-out inner work, informed by acceptance and responsibility.

To love ourselves, then, we need to confront the fears that prevent us from satisfying our fundamental needs. To love ourselves means having enough self-esteem to know that our happiness is worth the price of loss.

CHAPTER 5

RESPECT FOR THE DIFFERENT TYPES OF INTELLIGENCE

A. DISCOVERY OF DIFFERENT TYPES OF INTELLIGENCE

The CNDA-centered helping relationship is above all founded on the psychotherapist's personal and professional education and more particularly his profound knowledge of himself, which leads to love for who he is. It also necessarily comprises deep respect for the human person. The creative nondirective helper never ceases to learn greater respect for the operation of the brain and of the psyche, both within himself and others, as I have described them, and also greater respect for each individual's natural rate of evolution.

Respect for oneself and for others does not end there, however: the CNDA-trained helper also learns awareness of and appreciation for the different types of intelligence and approaches to learning represented by each of his students or clients, as well as their ways of perceiving and understanding the world around them.

This examination of different types of intelligence follows my own experimental research, conducted first during my years as a teacher and later on in my career as a group leader, educator and psychotherapist. During the 19 years I spent teaching high school, I invested a lot in my relationships with my students, both in class and during various kinds of extracurricular activities. I observed my students, communicated with them, and sometimes communicated with their parents. I also recorded and played back several of the classes I taught, and regularly kept a diary of my reflections, factual comments and questions, the better to assess my experiments, study the reasons for my successes and failures, and search for solutions. When I became a psychotherapist, I continued this practice after each session.

Thanks to this unstinting research that came to be part of my personal relationships with students and with clients, I learned things that helped me discover ways to motivate my students, as well as ways to help people find their own solutions and their own paths, out of respect for their true selves. I deduced, from my observations and personal experiences, that behavioral difficulties, mental problems and psychological learning blocks all stem from two fundamental, interrelated causes: lack of love and lack of motivation.

1. Lack of love

In previous chapters I have extensively discussed the importance of the emotions in helping relationships and in children's upbringing. In my professional life, love for my students and clients has always come first. I also realize, today, that as I love myself more and more, my ability to love others is that much greater. I am profoundly convinced that my work with young people and adults alike owes its success to the sincere, deep love that I bring to them, and to my unshakeable love for my own work and for myself. Thanks to this atmosphere of love, I have often had the emotionally fulfilling experience of seeing people literally come back to life. And it is precisely that love that is the basis for motivation.

2. Lack of motivation

Love is the key to motivation, as long as it respects an individual's right to be different, acknowledging people's particular interests and ways of seeing the world. But how do different people perceive reality?

This is exactly the question that led me to make significant discoveries about the ways my students learned. I realized that if my classes were filled with intolerant, apathetic slackers, then the fault lay in the type of teaching I was providing. I did not respect my students for what they were: that is, I failed to properly take into account what they were feeling in the here and now of the classroom situation, their skills, life histories, ways of learning and interests. By re-examining my own methods instead of blaming my students for my problems, I was able to conduct this research to my own satisfaction.

I had to find a way of getting my students to be as interested and involved as possible. Motivation was one of my main preoccupations, and indeed it has taken on paramount importance in the CNDA. The positive impact of the approach depends to a large extent on the ability of the helper (parent, teacher, or psychotherapist, as the case may be) to respect the helpee's individual nature and motivational need, which are rooted in his early childhood experiences. When a child reaches school age, for example, he already has an emotional past, his own personal history. Being highly impressionable, he has already learned a great deal. The unconscious influence of his entourage and environment has helped cultivate well-defined interests, ways of learning, language forms, attitudes and abilities within him, all of which set him apart from other children the same age. The social standing of his parents, their friends, their world views, values, principles, beliefs, fears, defense mechanisms, attitudes toward their children and each other, the types of employment held down by the father and mother on the one hand, and on the other, the extent of their "permissiveness" with respect to the child, the gender of the child, his rank within the family. All these factors have an influence on the child's ways of perceiving and acting, as well as on his level of motivation.

To all these influences must be added those of the environment: the city neighbourhood or village, the apartment or house in which the child grows up, the park or field he plays in, the furniture, décor and colors that surround him, the toys he gets as presents or builds himself, the games he learns or invents, the interior and exterior spaces he can occupy and make use of. Taken together, these factors mold the child's character.

The child is already a whole universe unto himself once he starts school, and he continues to learn and discover things outside formal educational settings, finding his own ways to satisfy his needs and respect his tastes.

What does school do with this experience? Most, if not all, of modern educational theory is concerned with the problem of motivation. It is by now a time-worn theme that has been dealt with from several perspectives, notably from the outside, in the form of changes to structures, programs and methods, some of which have been less satisfactory than others.

Since motivation is defined as the action of the conscious or unconscious forces that determine an individual's behavior, it follows that in order to motivate someone, one cannot act on his behavior from the outside using external means; one must work from the inside, on the internal forces governing that behavior, using means that respect the person's true nature. And those means cannot be found unless one first observes the individual in order to seek out his points of reference.

I do believe that most educators are aware of how important it is to motivate students, and that the majority of psychotherapists know the importance of motivating their clients to go through the stages of growth and healing. In a society that is caught up in the "learning for the sake of learning" mindset, everyone knows about it, but very few act upon that knowledge. How can a teacher find the means to motivate each one of his students if in his own education he was poorly motivated, if his competence is assessed in terms of how well his students regurgitate facts learned by rote at exam time, if in order to win the esteem of some of his superiors he takes on attitudes that do not belong to him, if in order to gain the protection of his union he rebuffs any potential friendship with senior administrators and avoids any "overzealousness," or if, to avoid excessive complaints on the part of parents, he conforms to values that are not his own? Put simply, how can educators respect their students when in many cases they do not respect themselves?

And yet it is essential for the educator who wishes to facilitate his students' learning processes, and for the psychotherapist who wishes to encourage his clients' evolution, to be sensitive to their modes of reference, to the way they function, and to their interests and the means they use to satisfy them.

My constant desire to respect individual differences has led me to the realization that there are many different types of intelligence among helpees, whether in educational or psychotherapeutic settings.

As soon as we define intelligence as the ability to acquire and retain knowledge (*Webster's Ninth New Collegiate Dictionary*), it becomes important to acknowledge, as parents, teachers, therapists and so on, that there are as many different ways of perceiving the world, and therefore of knowing, understanding and learning, as there are people in it. It is possible, however, to group them into three specific types, without losing sight of the fact that none of these can exist in its "pure state."

B. TYPES OF INTELLIGENCE

Not all human beings possess the same kind of intelligence. I have observed, from systematic research spread over more than 25 years spent as a teacher, trainer, group leader and therapist, that, based on the different modes of learning and of understanding reality, three types of intelligence can be distinguished in all human beings: speculative intelligence, practical intelligence and intuitive intelligence.

If the helper is to reach his students or clients, it is essential that he respect their different types of intelligence: only by recognizing the helpee's modes of perception can the parent, teacher or therapist intervene in a nondirective manner. In other words, one doesn't enter a house through any door but the owner's.

I have three specific descriptions for people, each relating to their particular way of learning. Those whose intelligence is speculative are "rationalists," those who display practical intelligence are called "pragmatists," and those with intuitive intelligence are "esthetes."

Before detailing the distinguishing features of these types, I must make clear that this classification must be viewed only as a "bridge" for reaching clients or students. Pigeonholing or labeling individuals in this way is extremely harmful; far from stimulating their progress, it may well slow or block their evolution. This classification should thus be seen merely as a way for the helper to understand the helpee and respect him for who he is.

Helpers wishing to respect the ways in which helpees understand the world must be aware that the characteristics of each intelligence type are part of each individual's potential, and can be developed at any given moment. Indeed, the "pure" type does not exist. And yet, based on his genetic baggage, his upbringing and the factors that have influenced him and his mental state, each of us has developed features more characteristic of one type than of the other two.

There is, however, one basic and indispensable rule here, and that is to never allow prejudices for or against one or another of these types of intelligence to develop. These will inevitably lead to judgments, and thus have a negative effect on helpees, belittling their strengths and preventing them from evolving in any way. That said, there are great advantages to being aware of the different types of intelligence. Besides helping us to respect the helpee's interests and his ways of perceiving things, they enable us to foster awareness of the strengths, skills and talents inherent to each type, to stimulate respect for individual differences and for limits, to facilitate development of all the resources of a given individual or group, to encourage the complementary nature of exchanges, to emphasize the acknowledgment and development of individual skills, whatever they may be, to ensure openness and acceptance of the self and of others, and to cultivate a taste for education, in the sense of research and self-discovery.

With this spirit of openness in mind, I will now give a detailed description of each of these types of intelligence.

C. RATIONALISTS

1. Intellectual characteristics

Rationalists are usually cerebral types, characterized by an analytical mind and speculative intelligence. They are logical, thoughtful, methodical and structured, possessed of a great ability for mental concentration and undaunted by abstraction. They are intellectually curious, and when it comes to affairs of the mind they are organized, disciplined and hardworking people. Their desire to enrich their knowledge and their rational understanding of reality translates into a constant and regular work schedule. Their preoccupation with success in whatever field they may enter makes them perfectionists: conscientious, persevering, even provident. Few rational details escape them; thanks to their ever-attentive and serious minds, they are able to complete lengthy and exacting intellectual assignments and achieve long-term goals. They usually meet all their deadlines, and in school fulfill all their course requirements. Most are masters of abstract research and information analysis. Lucid, sensible, filled with ambition and, often, a competitive spirit, they demand much from themselves and are indefatigable when it comes to abstraction, intellection and cognition.

2. Affective characteristics

Rationalists are for the most part highly sensitive, emotional individuals, but who are deeply afraid of their emotions and protect themselves from them through rationalization and repression. They know how to keep their reactions in check, to stay in control of their emotions, which they see as dangerous. Unfortunately, this tends to make them cold, distant and not very forthcoming in expressing their feelings; they are extremely reserved and cautious in this regard. When people around them react spontaneously or emotionally, and show affection, they feel irritated, even attacked, for they are unfamiliar with this aspect of their own psyches and therefore afraid to seek it out among people in their entourage. They will even go so far as to view emotionalism as a human frailty that must be tamed, denied and overcome in order to succeed. For them, the world of emotions and feelings is an unreliable one that can be a barrier to the success of their future projects. Since the rationalist needs to feel secure by directing everything according to reason, he will tend to flee or even reject his affective dimension because he cannot control it; his emotions are so intense that he unconsciously chooses to crush them by letting reason reign supreme. Since the affective dimension constitutes the heart of the psyche, however, his hyperrational defense system will never succeed in destroying his sensitivity and the power of his feelings. Rationalists, who need affection and love more than anything else, often end up rejected and alone as a result of their defensive attitudes. They can also suffer from serious long-term psychological or physiological problems.

Helping a rationalist at the affective level means first of all respecting the way in which he apprehends exterior and interior reality. It is thus important that the helper accept this type of person's need to become aware of what is happening within him, and that he respond, through his accepting attitude, to the helpee's need to understand and to learn. In order to impart a sense of security and of respect, the psychotherapeutic approach must, at least in the beginning, be informed by reason, emphasizing information and verbal exchange, and hence fostering the helpee's awareness of how his psyche functions. The numerous methods that revolve around catharsis (emotional discharge) and non-verbal communication are not only threatening for rationalists, but they also run the risk of rendering them unresponsive to all other psychotherapeutic processes. By taking the nondirective approach with rationalists, the helping person is showing respect for their nature, their physical and psychological functioning and their individual rate of progress. Otherwise, the psychotherapeutic process will be a power-based relationship, and not a helping relationship.

3. Relational characteristics

Because they are so adept at controlling their emotional world, rationalists have great difficulty with their relationships, especially when it comes to making the required emotional investments. They are fairly individualistic and prove to be extremely selective and critical in their choice of relationships. They are often loners who have trouble in group situations, whether at the professional or social level. The fact that they prefer working alone to being part of a team explains why, in psychotherapeutic settings, they are more likely to choose individual rather than group therapy. In fact, even in a group situation, the rationalist is alone. If he is forced to work with colleagues, he has trouble delegating work to them because he is obsessed with results. He is demanding of himself and will not settle for mediocrity, and so he will always try to direct others in not-so-subtle attempts to reach the performance level he seeks. This is why teamwork upsets and disturbs him so. If he cannot manage to direct the other members' work according to his own perspectives and requirements, he will step in and attempt to complete the entire assignment himself. In this case, he experiences a feeling of unfairness that reinforces his contempt for teamwork.

The rationalist's difficulty in expressing his feelings and his obsession with success are such that he has problems sharing, exchanging, negotiating and communicating. He is aware of the fact that in order to succeed, in a broad sense, in society, he must work; he is therefore determined to reach whatever professional goal he sets for himself, no matter what the cost. For him, results are everything, and for this reason he is ready to take difficult and unpleasant routes on the way to that goal, at the expense of his relationships. Indeed, this type of person displays a tendency toward power, which is, for the most part, nothing more than a means of defense, one that renders his close personal relationships extremely unsatisfying. Since he constantly keeps his own emotions in check, he tends, through projection, to do the same with other people's emotions because he is afraid of them, with the result that communication on an emotional level becomes impossible. Unless he concentrates on inner work and on taming his emotional world, his personal life will end in either chronic dissatisfaction or failure.

4. Reference points

For a helper to reach a rationalist, he must be attentive to his interests, to his way of seeing the world, and to his specific reference points. Rationalists will only trust those who are competent, who possess adequate intellectual knowledge in their particular field, and who are able to answer their questions with clear, structured, irrefutable theoretical explanations. Such cognitive, intellectual referents give rationalists a sense of security, because they find themselves at ease, on familiar ground. We have seen, in my earlier study of how the brain and psyche function, how important a sense of security is; we cannot help people without first instilling it. Respecting people for who they are is one of the best ways to achieve that security. Once he feels secure and completely trusts the helper, the rationalist will be able to transcend his usual reference points and progress toward self-awareness. Here we see how vitally important it is for any helper to exploit all aspects of himself to the fullest in order to be able to approach any human being with respect for who he is. This insistence on multidimensional self-development is a major part of the training for creative nondirective therapists. The key for the helper who wishes to attain maximum self-actualization, and also be in a position to properly approach each of his clients or students out of respect for the way they function, is to develop his speculative, practical and intuitive intelligence as much as possible. Only in this way will he be able to use all his skills and help others to use all of theirs.

5. Skills

The skills possessed by rationalists are mainly intellectual in nature. Such people know how to structure their thinking and are good at clarification of ideas, analysis, discernment, nuance and precision. They easily grasp the proper meaning of concepts, which allows them to clearly define, compare and classify them. Rationalists have a gift for thinking, organizing and expressing ideas, and for theory, abstraction and objectivity. They are workaholics who don't watch the clock, and who more often than not succeed impressively, thanks to their efforts and great ambition. With their talent for intellectual research, analytical theory, logically structured plans and methodically thought-out projects, they make great contributions to the progress of science and technology, and of knowledge in all fields, especially if they draw inspiration from reality and work closely with people who know how to translate their ideas into practical action. For though rationalists have a gift for concept, they are often out of their element when it comes to practical application. Their skills remain disconnected from reality unless they make the effort to adapt their abstract ideas to real life. I am thinking here of people who develop educational programs without ever having set foot in a classroom or taught, and those who make laws that affect the poor yet have lived all their lives in luxurious surroundings. The ability to conceive, to structure one's thoughts is extremely valuable if one is to go from "thinking for knowing" to "thinking for being"; this is probably the rationalist's biggest stumbling block.

6. Difficulties

The rationalist is above all an intellectual, and so he has difficulty accepting his sensitivity and developing a sense of practicality. Because he is more at ease with abstract concepts than with concrete reality, he often tends to put himself above others and to use the resources of his intellect to lay claim to the power of truth. He has difficulty acknowledging the value and importance of other types of intelligence, which means he will use pragmatists and hold esthetes in contempt. Furthermore, since his life is as ordered and disciplined as his thinking, he is often disturbed by the unforeseen, by change and by spontaneity, and this prevents him from enjoying the present. As we have seen, his greatest difficulties lie in relationships. The incoherence and illogic of feelings make him very uneasy, and the expression of emotional experience leaves him feeling anxious or threatened; therefore he retreats into his world of rationality, cutting himself off from genuine communication. Finally, since the rationalist devotes enormous amounts of time to mental considerations, usually to the detriment of his physical health and well-being, he faces, from a relatively early age, the threat of physiological problems that may be quite serious.

The only way for the rationalist to achieve the balance he seeks and satisfy his fundamental needs is to exploit his potential on every level: intellectual, affective, physical, relational, spiritual and creative.

7. Ways of perceiving and learning

Obviously, the rationalist perceives the world via thought and reason, and so any helper must first respect that *modus operandi* if he is to reach this type of client, hold his interest and gain his respect. Any type of analytical work, abstraction, study, intellectual research, anything relating to the rationalist's need to know and understand, may be of use in education or psychotherapy to attract the rationalist helpee's interest and progressively lead him into the multidimensional approach, opening his mind to other ways of learning and perceiving the world, to other sides of himself. Traditionally, educational methods have been based on the ascendancy of rationalism and intellectualism, and therefore rationalist students have always done very well in school. They are interested, encouraged, and praised by the system. School, at least the way it currently exists in most settings, is made for them, and intelligence tests are designed with this type of student in mind. Hence the "intelligent" label conferred on such students from their earliest years of schooling. In most cases, these students are those who persist and whose studies are the most advanced, which is not at all the case with people who display the other types of intelligence.

Helping rationalist people requires that the helper exploit his own intellectual dimension to some extent and also accept the helpee non-judgmentally, by loving and having faith in him.

I will conclude my examination of the rationalist type by looking at two examples, one from my experience as a psychotherapist and the other from my experience as an educator.

8. Psychotherapeutic case study

As a therapist I have worked with rationalist people on many occasions. One such person who comes to mind immediately is Martina. She came to see me on the advice of her doctor, because she could not stop mourning her husband, who had died of cancer some months earlier. She had retreated from the world to suffer her grief in solitude. Impassive and withdrawn, she kept her extreme pain locked up inside her, trying to avoid the subject whenever it came up, or else responding in a completely rational manner. In fact, Martina had never been one to talk about herself or her feelings to anyone. Only Andrew, her late husband, had been able to open a small window onto her inner world.

In fact, Martina had originally gone to see her doctor because of a fairly serious physical ailment: she was experiencing severe stomach pains without any discernible physiological cause. Her doctor advised her that psychotherapy was the only solution under the circumstances, but she had a profound fear of therapy and had little faith in its benefits. Had it not been for her persistent ailment, which she could not cure by medication, Martina would never have come to see me.

I perceived Martina's rational nature right from our first session together. She spoke in a detached manner, analyzing the facts, and explaining and interpreting each element of her story, almost as if she were relating another person's experience. Obviously, leading Martina toward a catharsis was out of the question: she probably would have lost all trust in me. I had to accept her for what she was and show respect for her rational way of operating. I began by explaining the approach I planned to take with her. I also tried to rephrase her statements based on her internal way of operating rather than on the emotions she was holding in check. As a rationalist, the last thing she needed in the early stages of her therapy was an emotional discharge; rather, she had to understand what was happening within, which she had never wanted to see.

The rationalist moves toward growth via awareness and understanding. By leading him down a path that is not his own, we run the risk of setting his defense mechanisms in motion and thus preventing him from taming the emotional world that frightens him so. The rationalist needs to apprehend his fear of his psychological realm and understand what is going on within before he can let his emotions free and experience them. By respecting that need, we give him a sense of security, which he must have if he is to trust others as well as himself. This said, the therapist should know that it is not necessary for the rationalist to go through a cathartic emotional experience to progress toward well-being; the therapeutic process can occur at the level of understanding first, and then, by maintaining the relationship between the helper and the helpee, the latter will gradually learn to feel what is going on inside him and express it. Before he can feel, though, he must understand.

Martina, for example, did not undergo a catharsis during her therapy, but she nonetheless got in touch with the emotions inside her and expressed them. She also learned to distinguish feeling from reason and see how, throughout her life, she had denied her emotional side and fought against it through rationalization. Martina came out of therapy extremely satisfied. The suffering caused by abandonment and absence did not disappear completely, but she knew what she was experiencing and understood what was hurting her.

9. Educational case study

Right from her first year in school, Elizabeth had been the very best student in her class. She succeeded brilliantly in all subjects except art, but this did not bother her too much because her father was convinced it was a useless course that did not belong in any "serious" program. When she started in my Grade 9 French class, I noticed she had no friends and was terrified of working in a group. She also felt literally under attack whenever any classroom activity required her to step away from the reassuring confines of her intellect. Since my classes were not limited to activities of an intellectual and analytical nature, she would panic each time she had to deal with anything involving the expression of her emotional experience, creativity or spontaneity. She thus had no real appreciation for the class I taught and remained extremely reserved about me personally. Had it not been for the fact that I had a good reputation in my field and that her classmates were all enthusiastic about my classes, she would surely have asked her father to intervene. At least, that's what she confessed to me later. I met with Elizabeth during the first week of school and told her that I had noticed her lack of openness, her withdrawal, and wondered why her participation in some activities seemed so soulless and why she couldn't properly integrate with the group. I told her that I had noticed her interest in and talent for intellectual work and was very impressed by this, but that in order to foster the overall development of each of my students and motivate them, I always included a number of different types of activities in my course. I added that I was aware of her strengths and her difficulties, and that I definitely planned to respect her own rhythm when it came to approaches that did not suit her, and which, moreover, she viewed as useless and substandard. She appreciated my approach, especially my accepting attitude, and this caused her to respect me greatly. A relationship based on trust was born between us. After this first meeting, she took part more readily in all our classroom activities, although she was doing so based on the belief that it was for the good of the others, and not hers. She still went on the defensive if she was called upon to express her personal experiences, and lapsed easily into judgment and criticism.

At a second meeting, I let Elizabeth see to what degree she was giving others power over her when she made them responsible for her discomfort. After that, each time I sought her out to provide an explanation for the way she operated or to give her some information on human psychology, she was very receptive and did not display an attitude of rejection. She needed to understand, in order to tame the world she had always held in contempt because it frightened her. The time I gave her to fulfill that need made her feel more secure, and eventually, during a class exchange on the topic of "boy/girl relationships," she talked about her feelings for the first time. Shy and reserved, she had grown up as an only child. Very early on, her father had warned her about boys, and about certain girls whom he considered "lower-class." His rational nature, his upbringing and his lifelong army career had made him a man of principle, who never expressed his emotions and who had brought his daughter up without consideration for the affective side of her nature, rejecting any activity that did not bring about results at the professional level. In Elizabeth's case, therefore, fear of her emotions was linked to fear of rejection; to express her feelings meant losing the love of her father and of others. She quickly realized that the opposite was true, for that first account of her feelings, and subsequent ones, had the effect of bringing her closer to her classmates for the first time in her life. In order to be loved, she had become withdrawn, and had of course ended up with the opposite of what she wanted. I have to admit I was quite touched, in the weeks and months that followed, by the change in Elizabeth. I saw her having fun, laughing and singing, and I saw her making friends. Her transformation did not affect her intellectual skills, which she learned to exploit not only to her advantage but also to help others. This was not a miracle transformation, but the result of an approach that respects the helpee's unique way of functioning and his evolutionary rhythm. These, then, are the rationalist's needs, and they differ to a significant extent from those of the pragmatist.

D. PRAGMATISTS

1. Intellectual characteristics

The distinguishing characteristic of pragmatists is their practical intelligence. All their ideas are geared toward action. They manipulate things the way a rationalist manipulates ideas. They have an extraordinary command of external, concrete reality, which they are able to modify, repair or transform at will. Lengthy intellectual effort is difficult for them, but they can work at practical and manual tasks for hours at a time. They are active, problem-solving individuals who never miss a detail. They are achievers, builders and producers. Usually realists, they are dexterous, clever, ingenious and shrewd. They adore practical experiments, for this is how they learn. In other words, action is their way of seeing the world. Therefore, one cannot contribute to a pragmatist's learning process without placing him in situations involving concrete action. Pragmatists have a gift for trouble-shooting and inventing, are masters of all things practical, and are reliable, diligent, efficient and sure of themselves in their own particular fields.

2. Affective characteristics

Pragmatists are by nature spontaneous and impulsive. Tirelessly focused on action, they express their feelings through gestures, rather than words, as would a rationalist. Indeed, they need to have visual and especially physical contact with others in order to express what they feel. Unfortunately, they often feel obliged to limit themselves to discreet glances and repress their gestures. Whereas, for the rationalist, the impulse to censor his surges of emotion comes from within, the pragmatist is paralyzed by societal norms and by moral principles, even though he tends to reject them. In more permissive settings, he shows his feelings spontaneously through action, fervently and simply. He cannot abide emotional complexities and in fact tends to flee from them through action.

3. Relational characteristics

Professionally speaking, pragmatists are usually quite at ease in their relationships and will readily adapt to all sorts of contexts and people, because they are simple, direct, obliging, flexible, tolerant and somewhat unconventional. Since they appreciate human contact, they enjoy teamwork, especially when it involves action. They are not overambitious, and so are more able to live their lives on a day-to-day basis and enjoy the present. In close personal relationships, however, they sometimes have difficulty with emotionally complex situations. They tend to trivialize emotions, or avoid them through jokes that disrupt conversation and prevent real communication. Since they are neither spiteful nor vindictive, they forgive and forget easily and move on to something new, leaving others alone with their wounds.

Since other people feel comfortable and relaxed in their company, and since rationalists and esthetes need their simplicity and practicality, pragmatists can enter into close personal relationships that are propulsive. However, at the same time as they convey their simplicity and *joie de vivre,* they must learn to demystify the complexities of emotion and reason that are so frightening to them.

4. Reference points

What matters to pragmatists, and this is the key to reaching them, is the present, social life, relationships, action and concrete reality. The pragmatist, because he only feels alive in the present and his day-to-day existence, cannot bear stagnation, and therefore has great difficulty sacrificing the here and now in order to take on a long-term project. "A bird in the hand is worth two in the bush" is an apt motto for him. He enjoys life: every moment is important, and so if he is bored, his immediate reaction is to find something to keep him busy. In school, the pragmatist is usually the type of student who breaks the monotony by being insolent and undisciplined. He needs to move, to act on concrete reality. What interests him is what he can see and touch.

It is difficult, if not impossible, to interest a pragmatist in purely intellectual, analytical or abstract pursuits. He craves concrete things: above all, he does not want to "know" or to "feel" but to "do", to build, to produce. He seeks tangible, effective results in the very short term. Attracted as he is by practical experience, realistic adventure and physical danger, he is able to expend great amounts of energy without tiring. He derives pleasure from his rapport with his body and with other people and things, so this is the only route available for the helper who wishes to reach him.

5. Difficulties

The pragmatist, given his vital need to feel useful and efficient, and his strong urge to act and to see the results of that action, feels uneasy in the world of ideas and metaphysical abstraction, or when faced with the subtleties of the human soul. He feels powerless in such situations, and that feeling of uselessness is difficult for him to bear. As well, he is normally fearful of immobility, silence, routine and constraint as concerns physical space and concrete, material existence. Without the freedom to act, he will wither like a plant without water.

6. Ways of perceiving and learning

To foster a pragmatist's learning process and initiate him into the multidimensional world-view, the helper's approach must revolve around action. Any activity that leaves room for movement, for practical achievement, for "doing," for material order, for teamwork, *joie de vivre* and pleasure will motivate him and open him up to other ways of learning. Since he knows how to live in the present, the pragmatist has no chronic anxieties about what the future will bring, and no regrets about the past, which makes life much more enjoyable for him. He lives life fully and actively. As helpers, we must not lose sight of the fact that for the pragmatist, action and tangible achievement are not simply a means to an end but an end in themselves. Practical work, therefore, will only prove to be an effective way of learning if it is viewed for its own sake, and if it is rewarded in the same way as intellectual effort. The acknowledgment of this truth has not taken root in our school system; far from it. Traditional educational methods, because they revolve around intellectual exercise, are ill-suited to the pragmatist's need for action. When he does work at school, he tends to be motivated less by interest than by a desire to avoid detentions or extra work. The fact that he is not particularly attracted to intellectual effort means that he fears punishment: it deprives him of recess time, and might cut into the time he devotes to practical activity at home. Choosing the lesser evil, the pragmatist suffers the necessary drudgery of classes while waiting for the only worthwhile time of the day: recess.

Since their type of intelligence is neither developed nor praised by traditional methods of schooling, pragmatists are often called lazy, or else labeled as dunces, or intellectually handicapped. The things they do know were not learned in school and therefore are not acknowledged. They also fall victim to utterly destructive remarks from teachers, which ruin their confidence in themselves and in their potential, thus cutting them off from any form of learning and preventing them from evolving at their own pace.

The unfortunate consequence of all this, of course, is that parents of such students tend to believe that their children are indeed not very intelligent and that they will probably have to be content with learning a trade rather than pursuing avenues of higher education. In society, pragmatic qualities are just as undervalued as in school, and so anyone whose work is founded on technical and manual skills is likely to go unacknowledged. And yet, the world needs persons with practical intelligence. This type of intelligence should therefore be praised just as much as the others in educational settings. In almost every case, the individual who chooses to learn this or that trade does so not because he lacks intelligence, but because he respects a form of intelligence that school and society unfortunately do not acknowledge. What people do not realize is that we would all be lost without pragmatists. We need their practical intelligence, their ingenious abilities, their resourcefulness. Until these talents are praised in our schools and given as much credence as those displayed by the other types of intelligence, the world will be deprived of the mutually beneficial nature of exchanges, and a group of people whom I consider to be invaluable to society will continue to be disparaged.

We can see, then, the negative aspects of an educational approach that revolves solely around the exploitation of intellectual values. When the system fails to respect pragmatists' motivations and ways of learning, it cuts them off from the beneficial influence of rationalists, and vice-versa.

We often face the same type of problem in psychotherapy, where the type of intelligence and the interests shown by these kinds of people are not always respected. Our approach to pragmatists must be highly realistic and geared toward action. We must never lead such clients into their intellectual or emotional realms, especially not at the start of their therapy. Because they love to "do" things, we can start by grounding our approach in terms of physical movement, eventually moving on to techniques of expression (drawing, sculpture, dance) that will encourage them to continue with their inner work. Otherwise, they will get bored and feel they are wasting their time, causing them to leave therapy rather than pursue it.

To better define the role of helpers relative to this type of intelligence, let us consider the case of Conrad.

7. Psychotherapeutic case study

Pragmatists make up only a small percentage of clients in psychotherapy. This is because they live in the present and have little interest for introspection, preferring to avoid undue complexities and suffering. If they do wind up in a psychotherapist's or psychologist's office, it is usually as a result of some dramatic event, and more often than not on the urging of some significant other.

Such was the case with Conrad, who came to see me because his relationship with his wife Teresa, who meant the world to him, was deteriorating at a frightening pace. Teresa, who was herself in therapy, had told Conrad that if he did not also begin a process of inner work, she would leave him. Conrad valued their relationship above all else and was ready to try anything to save it, even psychotherapy. This was how he approached our first sessions together. He was convinced he was consulting me to work out his wife's problems, it was she, not he, who was deeply dissatisfied with the relationship. He was quite ready to go into therapy to please her, but couldn't see how the resolution of Teresa's difficulties concerned him.

Being disinclined to question his own behavior so as not to complicate his life, Conrad tended to solve all his problems in a pragmatic and superficial manner. He thus had a hard time understanding what was bothering Teresa, who criticized him for being unable to communicate. Conrad, who was well known for being extremely talkative and sociable, was convinced that if anyone had a problem communicating, it was Teresa, who was more taciturn and solitary.

Making Conrad confront his own responsibility was out of the question. This would have shown a lack of respect for his rate of growth within a procedure he had just barely begun to follow. Knowing that in the process of change, responsibility is preceded by awareness and acceptance, I couldn't make Conrad responsible for something he neither knew nor accepted, and so the first step was to foster self-awareness on his part, out of respect for his *modus operandi*. Knowing that pragmatists need to do things, to touch and handle things, and knowing that Conrad was a carpenter by trade, I suggested that he work with clay. For more than three months, we devoted the first part of our sessions to molding different shapes out of clay, and the rest of them to talking about his creations. In this way, Conrad made unexpected discoveries about himself that enabled him to make remarkable strides. Respecting pragmatists' modes of learning really is the key to their progress, whether in psychotherapy or education.

8. Educational case study

When I met Mike, I was teaching Grade 8 French at a public school. At 17, Mike was three years older than almost everyone else in the class. He had a reputation for being lazy, insolent and stubborn, undisciplined, disinterested and beyond help. I knew that he had always been considered a problem student, so it was important for me to approach him without prejudice and with a positive, accepting attitude. He was the second in a family of four children. His elder sister was considered brilliant: her marks at school were so high that all the teachers called her a gifted student. I had taught her myself a few years before. She was the perfect example of a rationalist. Because of her exceptionally high grades, the family held her in high esteem, in direct contrast to their attitude toward her brother. The youngest child, a girl, was a paraplegic as a result of a car accident, and her parents, given the circumstances, paid special attention to her.

Mike therefore felt undervalued within the family setting and had a lot of trouble finding his niche. At school, he was aggressively unreceptive toward all his teachers, and most of his classmates. During the first few weeks of school, he went along nonchalantly, indifferently, with class activities. I have always imposed one hard-and-fast rule on students, and that is that they must participate in all class exercises. I decided not to question the attitude behind Mike's behavior. My experience with teenagers has taught me that one must never become persistent since this puts the student on the defensive and destroys the atmosphere of trust required for learning. I discovered there is only one solution when faced with apathy, and it involves love, trust, patience and respect for the student's rhythm. In Mike's case, this attitude did both of us a world of good.

Mike attended all my classes. He sat at the back and silently observed everything. Never before have I had such an intense feeling of being watched by a student. In spite of his apparent indifference, I felt he was attentive, not to the content of the course, but to what was going on, and this was what gave me the most hope. And yet, whenever I tried to communicate with him, he would close up, becoming impenetrably silent. I had never questioned him unpleasantly in front of his classmates, and I had never forced him to express himself before he felt ready to do so. Since he kept up this kind of searching silence, I really had no idea how to deal with him. After two weeks of school, I suggested to him that we meet one day during recess. He didn't show up. Recess, to a pragmatist, is the only interesting time of the school day. I therefore made a second attempt to talk to him, this time in a class while the others were working in groups.

During that meeting, I expressed to Mike my desire to help him, while respecting him for who he was. His answer went more or less like this: "No teacher ever gave a damn about what I am, inside. They always thought I was a hopeless student and an idiot. I don't work any harder with you, 'cause I just can't believe you don't want to hassle me the same way the others always did. I think you're playing games with me so you can trap me later on. Anyway, I'm not interested in school and it's not made for me. I like doing things, I like a little action. I want to be a carpenter; I've got no use for math and even less for grammar."

Mike's comments conveyed a lot of different pieces of information. I had to use that information to his benefit, to get him interested and get him to join the group. A few days later, I again met with him, and this time I had a proposition for him: would he help me prepare a class that would introduce the French vocabulary of automobile parts? I told Mike what we would need: a model car, in wood or some other material of his choosing, that could be taken apart. I indicated all the important parts to be included, and I did this using the vocabulary that he knew, that is, anglicisms, so that I would be better understood, and so as to respect his mode of perception. He accepted. The finished work was exceptional, and I praised it highly. Later, we got together again, and I asked him to dismantle his model car for me. Each time he took a part away, I told him the proper French name for it, and after taking apart and rebuilding the car three times, he knew the French name of each and every one. Again, I praised this work highly. If that particular process had not involved action, or "doing," Mike would not have learned as much.

For my work with Mike to be complete, though, he would have to become integrated into the group and acknowledged by his classmates. Since the model car was made of heavy cardboard, I suggested to Mike that he demonstrate to the other students, using the vocabulary he had learned, how they could make their own. Afraid at first of being ridiculed, he finally agreed, and it went very well. He left his model in the classroom for the others to consult, and with his help, they repeated the dismantling and rebuilding operation, using the French vocabulary. In doing practical things, Mike was in his element and felt he was worth something. At the end of the class, I gave the students an assignment to be handed in the next morning so they could all apply the newly learned vocabulary. They had three choices: build a model car based on Mike's, with the parts identified in French (this option was for the pragmatists in the group), draw an automobile according to their own taste in a particular setting, with all the parts numbered and identified on the reverse side (for the esthetes), or define each word of the new vocabulary (rationalists).

This kind of work enabled me to gradually bring Mike into the group and make him more receptive to other class activities. A radical change took place in his relationships with me and his fellow students. He felt happier about coming to school and less rejected.

This shows, once again, how motivation is linked not only to respect for an individual's mode of learning, but also to that person's emotional life. Helpers must never lose sight of the fact that as humans, we need first of all to feel loved before we can be motivated. This belief is born of my personal experience, which I am now going to relate because it was the starting point for my own questions, and my research into the different types of intelligence.

9. Personal experience

For thirty years, my life has been brightened by a love story that I feel is truly remarkable. I was quite young when I first met the man with whom I still share my life today. We lived in the same small town, a few miles from each other, at the foot of a mountain. I was 19 when our love relationship started; François was a year younger. At the time, I was in my third year of undergraduate studies, working toward my certificate in education, and he was in the tenth grade at a private school. He had had to repeat Grade 7 once and Grade 9 twice. Both the principal of the school I was attending and one of my professors warned me against getting involved with him, feeling that the gap between our respective levels of schooling would cause problems. Their admonitions shocked me at first. François was not any less intelligent than I just because he had not done as well at school. I was convinced of that. From that point on, rather than distance myself from him, I got even closer, and came to recognize his learning difficulties as well as his great strengths. I knew at that moment that I had found my perfect complement. He was a pragmatist; I was a combination of rationalist and esthete. We couldn't have made a better team.

After meeting me, François never repeated another year of schooling. He got his certificate in education and became a first-rate teacher, going on to complete a master's degree in education, and later a master's and a specialized graduate studies diploma in clinical psychology, both from the Université de Paris. What was the key to this discovery? I think François' main motivation operated on an emotional level. He was able to move forward because he felt loved, acknowledged and praised for what he brought to our relationship; in other words, his fundamental needs were satisfied. As well, being a pragmatist, he didn't much like studying alone. He needed companionship, needed to be part of a team, in order to work. So we worked together, at least for the first few years; this gave him self-confidence and allowed him to develop his unexplored rational faculties. It was precisely that faith in himself that pushed him toward his graduate studies, in which he succeeded wonderfully.

Today, at the Montreal Counselling Centre, we still work as a team, and a remarkably efficient one at that. The union of our complementary strengths, the profound love we have for one another and the respect in which we each hold the other's territory are what make us a harmonious unit in which mutual trust, inner and outer peace, and the joy of living really do reign supreme.

My relationship with my partner, as well as my personal and professional relationships, have taught me the importance of emotion as a primary motivating factor, and the importance of respecting others' differences. To apply the types-of-intelligence theory without incorporating these elements would certainly lead to failure. A human being, whether in childhood, adolescence or at the end of his life, needs to be loved, praised and made to feel secure. He also needs to be listened to and accepted, and to assert himself in freedom. Unless these primordial needs are satisfied, the theory being explained here cannot be put into practice; this would lead to poor results. Respect for fundamental needs is the basis for any process of learning and growth, whether the learner is a rationalist, a pragmatist, or an esthete.

E. ESTHETES

1. Intellectual characteristics

The word "esthete" comes to us from the Greek *aisthêtês,* which means "one who feels." Because they apprehend reality globally, rather than analytically, as rationalists do, or concretely, as pragmatists do, "esthetic" individuals are noted for their sensory, intuitive intelligence and their remarkable sense of symbolism. They are basically irrational in nature, and are romantics in the most literal sense, as comfortable in the realm of the invisible, the indiscernible, the unconscious as pragmatists are in the material domain. They are dreamers, who create imaginary worlds that they often find easier to live in than the real world around them. Caught between their lofty ideals and the constraints of reality, they often become complex, ambivalent, anxious and secretive. They flee concrete reality for the security of daydreams, where they feel truly at home. Their intellectual lives and relationships with others revolve around the inner world of their imaginations. Their minds are constantly filled with projects, ideas and dreams, but they have trouble lending structure and organization to them, and thus find it hard to bring them to fruition, which tends to leave them frustrated and permanently dissatisfied. They are neither thinkers, nor achievers, but rather dreamers, who rely on intuition.

Esthetes' intuitive potential is vast, and this often helps them see beyond what is immediately apparent. Some of them, however, use this natural skill as a means of wielding power over others, which can be very dangerous.

2. Affective characteristics

Being rather anxious, and quite often affected by an insecurity complex, esthetes are loath to make others privy to their imaginary worlds. They are silent types who, in spite of their "flights of fancy" and their inattentiveness, readily perceive anything having to do with sensations, emotions and feelings. Since they require a high degree of emotional and visual harmony in order to progress without hindrance, they are extremely sensitive to the attitude of everyone around them, as well as to their physical surroundings. Theirs is the most impressionable of the three types of intelligence, and they can be deeply affected by the most insignificant occurrences. For esthetes, a glance or an oversight, a single word or a period of silence can be either positive and progressive, or else negative and repressive. Because of this, they are easily worried or disturbed.

Esthetes are highly perceptive and emotional; they can easily lose themselves in their inner worlds, and as long as they fail to distinguish between what belongs to them and what does not, they will remain constantly and utterly confused. Their sensitivity is so pure, fragile and sophisticated, and paradoxically, so confused, muddled and blurry, that it can only be expressed satisfactorily through non-verbal means, or via the irrationality of imagination and symbolism. This is why helpers, be they parents, teachers or counselors, must look to the world of the imagination when approaching esthetes.

3. Relational characteristics

For those who are not esthetes themselves, at least to some degree, entering an esthete's world is a daunting prospect. It is a realm cut off from concrete reality, an irrational and nebulous world that demands an ability to feel, great respect for the other's reality, and much love. Esthetes usually have few friends, because they generally feel misunderstood, and hence fear rejection or ridicule. Often, their solution is to create imaginary friends according to their perceptions and psychological state. Because their relationships are both imaginary and imagined, they are often disappointed. In their mind they travel to exotic destinations and have wild adventures and love affairs, fully expecting to see their most secret dreams come true. When they do not, esthetes become disconsolate. Even the smallest emotional setback, the slightest rejection or refusal becomes a catastrophe.

Getting in touch with an esthete is practically an art. It requires gentleness, a well-developed ability to listen and to accept, a willingness to help that comes from the inside, and a great deal of honesty with and respect for ourselves; if we express our feelings toward them in a distorted manner, or if our words belie our attitude, they will sense this immediately and withdraw. The key to reaching them without upsetting them lies in understanding that the imaginary realm is their reality; it is what guides their lives and it is the only door we can use if we want to guide them toward new horizons. As helpers, it is important for us to listen to what their non-verbal language and their more-or-less irrational spoken language tell us about them.

Since society in general and schools in particular neither acknowledge nor praise esthetes, some try to gain acceptance and love by presenting a facade to the world. They act in accordance with an image created by their imagination, which they believe to be more acceptable than their actual personality. The same applies to pragmatists. In this case, though, relationships become even more problematic because they end up totally distorted; esthetes thus find themselves completely unable to exploit their resources and abilities. Once again, it is only by accepting their true nature that esthetes can acknowledge themselves; then they can properly exploit the potential of that sensitivity which they rely on to such a great extent, and bring it to bear on the world.

4. Reference points

The esthete's world is the intemporal, the immaterial. They have no concept of time, of standards, of deadlines, of reality. What matters to them are things fantastic, wonderful, extraordinary, unreal or imagined. However, since they are often fairly unsure of themselves, they almost never openly contest the rules that they find so annoying; rather, they get around them or flee them through imagination and distraction. Manual and intellectual tasks are interesting only if they relate in some way to their inner world. They are not interested in the practical aspects of things, like pragmatists, or by the logical order of things, like rationalists, but by their beauty, their intrinsic value, their sensitivity.

"And since it is beautiful, it is truly useful", so said the Little Prince to the streetlamp-lighter in Antoine de Saint-Éxupery's famous story. Esthetes are somewhat like the Little Prince, in the sense that they too see the world through childlike eyes, almost in pictures. An esthete's expression and actualization, then, depends neither on knowledge nor on concrete reality but rather on images, feelings and intuition.

5. Skills

The kinds of skills esthetes have deal with perception and nonverbal, creative expression. They are comfortable with anything having to do with the soul, with feelings, emotions and intuition. They can see beyond appearances. They often play with shapes, colors and words the way children do with stars, endlessly bending, changing and modifying them. Their creative imagination is boundless. In their hands, a flower can become a whole garden, a color a work of art, and a word a poem, as long as they have sufficient inner and outer space available to them. Their extraordinary creative potential is often difficult to tap, though, because they lack discipline and organization. By pursuing their inner work, recognizing their true nature and exercising their creative talents, they can beautify everything they touch and find their true niche in the world.

6. Difficulties

Esthetes abhor violence, vulgarity, noise, excessively strict supervision, analysis and material responsibility. They have a great deal of trouble respecting rules, constraints and limits, deal poorly with conflicts, and cannot easily be forced into any kind of mold. Despite their lack of self-confidence they are, paradoxically, convinced that they have talent and that others do not appreciate them. This is why they spend all their time yearning for that kindred spirit who will truly understand and love them and be ready to discover them, because they simply are not the type to forge ahead in life. They cannot deal with feelings of worthlessness, of not being acknowledged for who they are, of being rejected, though they themselves are apt to reject others.

Rushing an esthete is out of the question when one wants to truly know him and lead him to self-discovery; he will simply become defensive, closing the door to any kind of communication. His highly sensitive nature is at the root of his suffering; because of it, the esthete can easily become hyperdefensive, protecting himself by the use of self-repression or self-punishment, of rationalization, projection or rejection. Inevitably, this adversely affects all his relationships and increases his suffering. He needs the love and acknowledgment of others, but his defensive attitude deprives him of the nourishment that is so vital to his personal development. He requires a calm, loving and harmonious atmosphere in which to make the most of his potential. He also needs time and space. Nature, images, symbols and feelings are important sources of creativity for him. He must feel and sense things in order to understand; indeterminate, imprecise, polysemic or imperceptible things easily give way to the esthete's capacity for imagination and creation. However, his tendency toward escape needs to be counteracted by a modicum of structure and supervision. A complete laissez-faire attitude is unsuitable because esthetes tend to spread themselves too thin, which is why many of them have inferiority or insecurity complexes. They need to explore the creative process to the fullest in order to acquire some measure of self-confidence. The helper should be respectful, encourage and praise the helpee, and ensure a solid framework and an educational process based on discipline, for esthetes cannot create in the absence of these preconditions. They will attain maximum self-actualization only when they are completely free to be themselves, while simultaneously working within an imposed structure.

7. Ways of seeing and learning

An esthete will become interested and motivated if one begins by leaving him alone during his quiet moments, displaying a lot of affection, giving him sufficient interior space, respecting his meanderings and "flights of fancy," and, more importantly, using them to guide him toward creative acts. This is one of the CNDA's fundamental principles; we cannot hope to open others up to new fields of experience unless we do so "through them", through their worries, their needs, their moods. There simply is no other way. So it is with esthetes; educators and psychotherapists must use imagination and creation when dealing with them, so that they may uncover new interests and new ways of learning.

In a classroom situation, where a pragmatist will try to draw attention to himself, for example by "baiting" the teacher, the esthete quietly flees from his surroundings for the tranquility of his interior world. He cannot bear to have the teacher suddenly draw him out of that world by asking him to speak up in front of everyone. It is quite obvious that school in its present form is of little interest to the esthete. Art courses are extremely rare, and many of them are taught from a highly technical or rational point of view, leaving little room for him to express his creativity. As a result, he becomes inattentive, absent, apathetic, alone and silent. Traditional educational methods leave no room for this type of student, whose strengths and talents cannot be measured, and are therefore neither appreciated, exploited nor respected. An educator who cares about motivating all his students must not overlook the esthete's ways of learning and his needs, for his contributions to the group are enlightening and enriching for everyone.

In psychotherapy, esthetes can be approached according to any method that satisfies their imaginary reality. Visualization techniques, waking dreams, working with symbols, stories, dreams and myths, all these are effective tools that will put the esthete at ease. The therapist must also, however, rely on techniques of creative expression, which encourage esthetes to exploit their potential in this domain and to turn their dreams and projects into action. He must help them see what their strengths are, and at the same time recognize their limits. This way they can acquire self-confidence, accept themselves for who they are, and accept others. This is exactly what I did, with great success, in the case of Ronald.

8. Psychotherapeutic case study

Ronald was 18 years old at the time of his first visit. In fact, he had been waiting for the day he turned 18 so that he could leave home and thus escape the unbearable relationship he had with his father. Ronald came from a rather strange family background, his parents were practically polar opposites, and he had always wondered how they could possibly love each other and live together. More specifically, he couldn't understand why his mother insisted on staying with his father. Ronald told me how he detested his father but idolized his mother, because he identified with her. She was a painter, and had passed on her refined artistic sensibility, her unique style, her sense of beauty and her creative talent to him. Like her, he was an esthete, but unlike her, his relationship with his father was one of profound dissatisfaction.

In fact, his father was the perfect example of a pragmatist. A prominent businessman who owned a hardware store, he was a skilled carpenter, with a good head for business and a gift for salesmanship. Since Ronald was his only son, he had wanted him to follow in his footsteps and eventually inherit his flourishing business, but his efforts were in vain. Very early on, a deep rift developed between the two; their interests and personalities were too divergent. Ronald was extremely vulnerable and emotional; his hypersensitivity caused him to feel misunderstood and rejected by his father, who, according to Ronald, belittled his feelings. This is the classic esthete/pragmatist relationship: the former apprehends the world through feelings, emotions and intuition, the latter by "doing" and in terms of concrete reality put simply, they are not on the same wavelength.

In therapy, Ronald discovered something he had never wanted to acknowledge: his parents' deep and abiding love. They complemented each other in spite of their marked differences. His mother, who had no sense of practicality and whose life was totally unstructured, needed his father who, for his part, was a realist who took care of the groceries and made sure the household chores were done. It was he who had built and organized the studio where his wife spent the better part of her time. It was he who had built and repaired Ronald's toys and taught him to ride his bicycle, and later to drive a car. He may have been ill-equipped to deal with the world of emotions, but he had his own way of expressing his love.

By learning more about himself, Ronald became more open to understanding others, most particularly his father. When he discovered his own limits in terms of putting ideas into practice, and his resulting frustration, he came to understand his father's strengths and accept his limits. He had thought his father had been rejecting him, when in fact the opposite was true.

Nondirective creative psychotherapists and educators alike will find that knowledge of the different types of intelligence is an invaluable tool for understanding and approaching clients and learners, and for helping them accept themselves, exploit their strengths while respecting their limits, and respect others' right to be different. Often, acknowledging our own limits is the key to developing a tolerance for others' limits, and to realizing, though it is never easy, that more often than not we are guilty of the very things we criticize in others. In my view, this acceptance of limits is the best way of opening ourselves up to others. Victor's story provides an excellent example of this.

9. Educational case study

Victor's was one of the most touching, and touchy, cases of my teaching career. In my dealings with him, I went outside the course curriculum to focus on Victor himself, as a person. Indeed, I am convinced that it is impossible for a teacher to foster a student's overall development if his task is limited to teaching in the strictest sense.

Victor was 16 when I first met him. Right from the start of the school year, I noticed that he always kept to himself, both in class and during recess. Here was a student who seemed to have no interests, no passion, at least for school. He went about most of his assignments like a robot, displaying no real interest for participation, commitment or communication. It was as if he had retreated into a bubble, to which he granted no one access. When I assigned him an individual activity, he would rush through it and then return to drawing, which seemed to be what he liked most. He would draw everywhere: on his notebooks, in textbooks and even on his desk.

Victor's withdrawn and dreamy attitude as well as his interest in the arts and in creating, which he had displayed from the beginning of the year, told me that he was more the esthetic type than anything else.

I had to find some means to gain his interest and integrate him into the group. My experiences have taught me that it is essential to link a student's interest for the course to his integration into the group, since motivation is inextricably tied to our need for affection, and thus to relationships. One cannot evolve without the other. And without that integration, we get inferior results despite our knowledge of the different types of intelligence. The same is true, incidentally, for any type of knowledge; it has no worth in and of itself. As helpers, we cannot effectively apply it unless we see to it that our students' or clients' needs are satisfied. If the helpee is not loved, acknowledged, made to feel secure and accepted for who he is, then applying even the most sound of theories will lead to only marginal success, or even outright failure. Respect for people's fundamental needs is at the root of all approaches to learning and growth.

In Victor's case, integration did not come easily. His experience confirmed my belief that in education, as in any situation, the learning process cannot be dissociated from the student's psychological experience and physiological state. Teachers must never lose sight of this absolutely fundamental principle.

It took me a long time to realize that the best way to inspire Victor to integrate the course material was to integrate him into his classroom entourage. Even when I suggested activities likely to earn him the praise of his fellow students, which he carried out with great interest, he remained taciturn and kept to himself. Another problem emerged: Victor was regularly absent from school, often for fairly long periods. He always came back with notes signed by a doctor that justified his absences, albeit rather vaguely.

In November, at a parent-teacher meeting, I had a chance to meet Victor's mother and father. They were a simple, working-class couple who showed much understanding and a humanitarian spirit. They had married late in life, and Victor was their only child. When I mentioned the problem of his frequent absences, they began by stating that these were absolutely necessary and unavoidable. They didn't seem to want to say any more. I pressed the point, assuring them that they could count on my complete discretion. Finally, Victor's mother, under her husband's approving gaze, said to me: "Ever since he was born, Victor has lived with an incurable disease that he cannot accept and that he is ashamed of. He feels abnormal, not like the others. He suffers from hemophilia."

I kept talking with Victor's mother, and it was not long before I realized that she felt guilty because she believed she was responsible for her son's condition, and that this in turn had an impact on Victor. In the course of our discussion, she came to realize that the best way to help her son was to accept the reality of the situation without guilt, and to convey that acceptance to him. Only in this way would she be able, through her unconscious influence, to help Victor live with his handicap without wanting to hide it.

My meeting with Victor's parents proved to be a crucial and invaluable event. I saw an immediate and significant change in Victor, and the key to that change was his mother's new attitude. At the beginning of January, Victor was away from school for a week. When he came back, he was using crutches, something he had never done before. To my great surprise and amazement, when his classmates asked him what was wrong, he told them the truth. No one knew of this particular disease, so he explained it and answered their questions. This single experience was more enriching for them than any French class I could have taught.

After that day, Victor's behavior in class changed immeasurably. Obviously, he didn't change overnight into a highly sociable student, but he was comfortable within the group, which allowed him to exploit his creative talent and even to develop it. Once a student feels comfortable in his group, feels relaxed and happy with his peers, and feels acknowledged and praised for who he is, he is certain to develop his potential. And when an esthete is able to express his suffering, his emotions, his imagination and his creativity in an atmosphere of trust and acceptance, his actualization is inevitable.

Helping people according to an awareness of the different types of intelligence can be very useful as long as that awareness serves as a way of approaching them, not of labeling them. This is why I have not developed any sort of test for detecting different types of intelligence. The approach is not meant to be a tool for labeling people, but rather a means of increasing our acceptance of differences, of *modus operandi,* of ways of learning and of ways of seeing the world. The educational or psychotherapeutic relationship must be based on respect for the helpee's fundamental needs and the importance of the helper's own inner work. This is the only route to the crux of people's difficulties, whether in the short or long term. The human relationships we enter into as helpers, and not the interpretation of test results, teach us most about our students and clients and give us a true sense of the multiple facets of their beings. Thus we learn not to define people according to types, but rather to use what we know about the different types of intelligence in order to understand them better, and to open ourselves up to the myriad elements that make every one of us unique, different and incomparable.

This approach, in order to be effective, nondirective and creative, depends first and foremost on the helper's own progressive knowledge, acceptance and love of himself, such that he exploits his own strengths and develops his untapped potential. Each one of us carries the seeds of all three types of intelligence; each one of us could develop all three, if we chose. However, we expend less energy when our self-actualization is consistent with the way we evolve naturally.

It is therefore important that, as helpers, we know ourselves well enough to achieve maximum self-actualization and to choose partners, in both our personal and professional lives, who complement us. As humans, we are made to interact with other humans. Since we are all unique and different, each of us needs others to know ourselves, to exploit ourselves, to fulfill ourselves. Only in relationships can we learn to love ourselves and others, and only in relationships can we learn to be good helpers. We must not lose sight of the fact that the helping relationship is above all a relationship that involves acceptance, acknowledgment and love of ourselves and of others. The theory of different types of intelligence is born out of relationships. As part of the CNDA it fosters relationships, more specifically the helping relationship, as long as it is not applied solely for its own ends, but rather with respect for our fundamental needs and those of our helpees. In this sense, our role as helpers becomes of paramount importance in any educational or psychotherapeutic process.

CHAPTER 6

THE PARAMOUNT IMPORTANCE OF THE HELPER

The CNDA reflects the influence of Lozanov's theory of suggestology in that it sees the helper as being of paramount importance in the helping relationship. In fact, the creative nondirective approach is not particularly concerned with the method or the school of thought employed by the person wishing to help; neither does it revolve around the helpee. Instead, it is chiefly based on the psychotherapist or the educator as a person, considering him to be the most significant element in the helping relationship. By giving the helper a determining role to play in the educational or psychotherapeutic process, the creative nondirective approach is merely acknowledging an already-established phenomenon, one that has existed naturally since the dawn of time and that suggestology itself merely drew our attention to. The phenomenon I am referring to is the unconscious influence of attitude. By emphasizing the helper's role, I am not stressing the aspects of power or domination, but rather the influence he unconsciously brings to bear on the helpee.

The concept of influence is extremely important in the helping relationship, but has unfortunately been neglected in most educational and psychotherapeutic approaches. And yet, whether we are ready to admit it or not, the helper does indeed exert a remarkable degree of influence over his helpees, thanks to the role he plays and the authority it confers on him. In fact, I believe that all educational or psychotherapeutic relationships are based on the helper's influence. The things that a child, a student or a client will retain from his relationship with his parents, teachers or psychotherapist have little to do with what they say or do, and everything to do with who they are and the kind of impression they give. It is the helper's attitude, for instance, that dictates whether the helpee feels at ease with him. The helper's personality, his emotional experiences, his feelings and his intentions will all be expressed through his unconscious attitude, and this can cause the helpee to feel either calm or agitated, serene or anxious, confident or mistrustful, inclined to accept or inclined to reject. If the helper's verbal and non-verbal communication are consistent with one another, and if his attitude reflects sincere feelings of love, acceptance and faith in the helpee, then the combined effect of these factors will be beneficial.

It is impossible for any educator or psychotherapist to radiate this sort of attitude if he is being false, or feeling frustrated or insecure, if he is imitating other people's behavior or if he is forcing himself to conform to an introjected image that bears no resemblance to his actual personality. A positive attitude is genuine, authentic, natural, simple and sincere. It is an attitude that shows love, gives security and praises the helpee. It places the helpee in a receptive state, without which he cannot possibly grow. For whatever words the helper might speak, if he harbors judgments, if he is experiencing unexpressed rejection or feeling a lack of self-confidence he cannot share, the helpee will be aware of his uneasiness, and will not be open to any exchanges with him. This will destroy the state of inner receptiveness that is so vital to any effective process of learning or growth. However, when that state of receptiveness is created by a propulsive attitude that fosters a sense of security, everything that the educator or psychotherapist does to encourage learning or growth will be received and become food for thought. This undeniable yet somewhat surprising truth is enough to give us pause, for it has far-reaching implications. For instance, if the helpee is not attuned to his feelings, he may well let himself be manipulated by the encouraging words of his helper who is, in fact, merely trying to satisfy his own ego by subtly controlling the lives of his students or clients.

Grounding the helper's training on attitude is vital to the process of making his verbal communication consistent with what he conveys non-verbally, and to encouraging the development of the helpee's potential. This final chapter will focus on the primary role of the helper in the educational or psychotherapeutic relationship, and on the problems caused by the kind of therapist or teacher training that concentrates on unintegrated knowledge. It will end with some thoughts on how the principles of the CNDA could be used in training teachers and psychotherapists.

A. THE TEACHER AS HELPER

A teacher is someone who is involved in education in its more comprehensive sense of mental, moral and esthetic instruction. Even if he never goes beyond the course curriculum, he will inevitably influence his students, simply because of who he is. Since schooling is mostly channeled through teachers, it seems important to me that theories of education should stop confining themselves to questions of structures, teaching methods and program content and pay more attention to the teacher as a person. How and what a child learns in school does not depend on purely cognitive and rational input, but rather, as I have demonstrated in preceding chapters, on the emotions. The act of teaching is thus primarily based on relationships, and the factors involved in those relationships determine the students' degree or level of integration and learning. Thus the subject matter ends up being less significant than the rapport between the student and the teacher. And the propulsive nature of this relationship depends first and foremost on the teacher's personality.

1. The teacher, the lifeblood of the education system

Today's schools conceal a sense of sadness and dissatisfaction, that their impressive array of structures prevents us from seeing and reacting to. Much more energy is expended on oiling the wheels of bureaucratic organization than on searching for the deep-seated reasons behind people's lack of well-being: reasons for phenomena like the figurative tearing-apart of the learner or teacher on his first day, the fact that teacher and pupil alike are both robbed of their intrinsic wholeness and their right to be different, the imposition of uniformity, the transformation of their personal truths into a "persona", all this in the name of principles that serve abstract realities, such as society, the department of education, the union, the school board, the church. All too often, the school is a pawn in the hands of the ideological, political, economic and religious powers-that-be. And, while representatives of the various decision-making groups are busy blaming each other for the failures and dissatisfactions demonstrated by the public in general and by the school population in particular, there are any number of teachers who are busy trying to keep their heads above water in the daily reality of the classroom. They have to abide by decisions concerning teaching and educational theory in general that have been made, often without their help, with programs, structures and collective agreements foremost in mind. Indeed, our education systems are run by organizations so complex that it is difficult to find their human face.

There are few tasks as difficult or delicate as that of teaching under such conditions. After all, we expect the teacher to contribute to the development of the student's personality and that he participate in the progress of society in general by granting knowledge an almost exclusive place in the educational process. On an ideological level, we expect the teacher to develop his pupils' autonomy, their initiative and their creativity. But is there any room left for the professor to express his own autonomy, initiative and creativity in the maze of decrees concerning programs and structures, in the plethora of ideological principles he is supposed to transmit? If his wings are tied, how can the parent bird teach his young to fly?

Many teachers today spend a lot of their time on fruitless attempts to reconcile the numerous contradictions inherent in the system, with which they have to deal one way or another in order to satisfy their superiors in the educational hierarchy, the parents, the union representatives and, of course, the students. Thus they are forced to create by copying, innovate by relying on tradition, feel renewed within the routine, evolve through conformity, instruct through repetition and turn our classrooms into assembly lines.

In order to teach in this kind of environment, a person is more or less forced to be either an intellectual acrobat, a champion diplomatic maneuverer, or simply a sponge. It is not surprising that there is a mounting feeling of dissatisfaction, a rising tide of frustration among teachers, many of whom are just putting in time until they retire. I think the time has come for us to ask ourselves some serious questions.

But how can schools give priority to the human being in the morass of bureaucratic and ideological structures that dominate and control them? This is, in fact, the very crux of the dichotomy between theory and practice, between knowledge and being, between ideologies and their application. Ideologically speaking, education should be based on the needs of the learner, and on the development of his full potential. How does one go about looking after those needs in practice?

When he is in school, the child relates not to the various representatives of the decision-making bodies, but to his teachers. His first impressions of what learning is all about depend on those who teach him. In the daily reality of school life, they are the focal point of his education. But what do we do when confronted with this undeniable fact? In the field of education, and in our teacher-training programs, how do we rate the importance of the teacher as a person?

Let me explain myself: acknowledging the importance of the teacher does not mean that he should be made the most powerful person in the educational hierarchy; this would only perpetuate the inequitable distribution of power. What it means is that the teacher should be given the means to fulfill the true requirements of his calling.

How can an instructor adequately respond to a child's needs if he only has a rational, intellectual knowledge of psychology as it pertains to his students? If the teacher's training has concentrated solely on increasing his theoretical knowledge in his particular specialty, and in the fields of psychology and education, how can he possibly, in practice, gear his teaching methods toward the development of the entire person? Is it enough to know how a car works in order to be able to drive it? If we know the techniques of swimming, does that mean that we can swim?

How can a teacher respect the needs of his students if, in his own training, no one ever paid any attention to his needs? How can he contribute to the development of his students' creative potential, and of all their other aspects, if he himself was educated in such a way that his own creativity was never called upon, and that only the cognitive side of his nature was exploited? Again, how can an instructor possibly go beyond the course material if he is only evaluated on his students' intellectual performance, and if he himself was taught to consider knowledge alone as being relevant? How can a teacher who has been trained almost exclusively to develop intellectual knowledge be able to deal effectively with areas of human psychology?

If knowledge is the main value that guides our principles of teacher training, what fundamental difference could there be between a legally qualified teacher and one who is not legally qualified? I'm sure we have all had one of those professors who are hired solely on the basis of their outstanding ability in their field, and who turn out to be excellent teachers as well, even though they do not have a piece of paper to prove it. Does this mean, then, that all one needs in order to teach is a degree in this or that particular field? If this is so, what is the point of teacher training besides making a person legally qualified to teach? Can one become a doctor, a lawyer or even an electrician as easily as various specialists, over the years, have "turned themselves" into teachers? Here is a question that should make us stop and think. If we only expect our teachers to be competent in their given field, what on earth do they need to be trained in "educational sciences" for? And, if we expect them to be capable of passing on that intellectual knowledge, can we truly say that a theoretical familiarity with current pedagogical trends and methods, followed by a few weeks' practicum, is enough to produce a good teacher? I believe we need to ask ourselves: what is teaching, exactly? What characterizes day-to-day school life for the real teacher?

Let me begin by saying that teaching does not mean merely transmitting facts. If it did, the job of teaching could be handed over to computers. Teaching refers to the ability of the teacher to gear his approach to the learner as a distinct person, and to satisfy his fundamental needs. Unless the learner's need to feel free, loved and acknowledged by others, made to feel secure, listened to and accepted are all satisfied, whatever he tries to learn will either not be integrated or else will quite simply be blocked out. Teaching means developing every aspect of the learner's potential, whether it be physical, emotional, intellectual, imaginative, social, spiritual or creative. It also means having a "feel" for interpersonal relationships. Let me assure you that it is impossible to speak of the day-to-day reality of teaching without taking into account the complexity of what the teacher actually has to do to find his way through the tangled maze of innumerable relationships, within which he has to deal both with his own reality and that of others.

A teacher's job description includes more than just keeping up with the latest advances in his field, conveying his intellectual knowledge, studying programs, setting goals for his work, preparing courses, marking assignments, attending meetings, symposia, seminars and refresher courses, not to mention his ongoing attempts to keep up with "new" programs, structures, methods and general and particular objectives. In order to adequately meet the requirements of his calling, a teacher must, first and foremost, be a "people specialist" and a specialist in interpersonal relationships.

This is the real reason why schools are trying to conceal a malaise that will not go away, in spite of all the changes made to structures, methods and programs. The energy expended on these is misdirected, for it would be better spent on making sure that the teacher is given the acknowledgment he deserves.

Until we place the teacher squarely at the center of our children's education; until we acknowledge that he is indeed the very heart and soul of all school learning; until we begin to gear his teacher training toward his own inner work and until we can accept the fact that he must, first and foremost, be a "people specialist" and a specialist in interpersonal relationships, then our schools will continue to be plagued by difficulties and dissatisfactions. The learner as well as the teacher will continue to deliver themselves into the clutches of today's education system, one out of legal obligation, the other out of economic necessity, but neither of them because they feel either happy, satisfied or validated there.

In order to bring satisfactory, effective and lasting changes to our school system, we have to center our teacher-training programs not on knowledge but on the teacher himself, as a person.

2. Teacher-training programs

a) *Training centered on the teacher*

The idea of a teacher-training program centered primarily on the teacher as a person may well seem illusory and idealistic when we consider the priorities inherent in the training provided by most traditional western settings. Be that as it may, this sort of training would be undeniably better suited to the actual day-to-day requirements made on the teacher than is the present kind, which inculcates first theoretical knowledge, and then a practical ability, a *savoir-faire*.

What happens when a teacher, fresh out of teacher's college, comes face to face with the harsh reality of the actual classroom situation? He either hides behind his knowledge, and makes it his main priority, thus impairing his ability to be attuned to his pupils' needs, or else he tries to become a person-centered teacher, through improvisation. In the first instance, his approach does not take the learner's needs, his feelings into account, and this will give rise to dissatisfaction, both on his part as well as on theirs. In the second instance, the teacher will be confronted with some significant limitations for, in fact, it is really not possible to become a "people specialist" in the blink of an eye. Anyone who does so is taking a serious risk and will probably fail to understand, albeit involuntarily, how the human psyche operates, and misjudge his personal rate of growth.

When I graduated from teacher's college and started teaching, I quickly realized that the demands made on me called for more than just knowledge. Every day I was confronted with real people, adolescents who had significant emotional problems. I also had to deal with chronic lack of motivation and, within the classroom itself, with the students' inability to get along with each other. Some students had difficulty functioning in an environment where they felt neither integrated, motivated nor liked, and developed fairly serious learning problems. My intellectual knowledge and my certification were more or less useless in helping me deal with these situations, for which I was completely unprepared. It didn't take long for me to become aware of my limitations and, although I had a certain amount of personal experience listening to, accepting and understanding others, I realized that I needed to approach the daily realities of my job differently. My training continued: not just at university, but also outside the officially recognized circles of educational advancement, namely, with a psychotherapist. I quickly perceived that, the more I learned about and accepted myself and pursued my own inner work, the better I was able to understand and help my students. It became clear to me, then, that becoming a good teacher isn't just a process that involves the intellect; it is first and foremost a process that involves the development of every facet of the self. Unless he undertakes this lifelong learning, a teacher's ability to get involved with his students at the psychological level will remain theoretical and hence irrelevant and ineffective. The teacher cannot truly understand the student unless he has worked on his own attitude, and this attitude is the source of his unconscious influence, which has an inevitable and determining effect on the student/teacher relationship.

The CNDA is not the first approach to realize the overwhelming importance of teacher-training geared toward the teacher's inner work. Others such as Jung and especially Lozanov have come to the same conclusion. Unfortunately, this conviction is not shared by many. Indeed, there are millions of teachers, social workers and parents who are oblivious of the unconscious influence their personalities have on their students, clients or children. Consequently, they are equally ignorant of the need for inner work to enable them to teach, assist or raise. Above and beyond any visible results, all teachers have deep-seated, lasting psychological effects on the children they are involved with. The children pick up on the unconscious messages they receive, whether of peace or violence, love or hate, respect or violation, inner freedom or dependence, autonomy or enslavement, confidence or fear, strength or weakness, honesty or hypocrisy, faith or disillusionment, joy or sadness, and so on. In most cases, the instructor himself is not even aware that he is conveying these messages. They involve feelings and emotions that he is not attuned to because nothing in his training has made him aware of the sometimes irreversible consequences of his non-verbal unconscious influence over others. Also, he is unaware of the messages he is conveying because he has not grasped the importance of self-knowledge, nor understood why he should see himself as the *primum mobile* in instruction and education in its more comprehensive sense.

b) Training centered on inner work

Whether we are aware of it or not, we cannot avoid the phenomenon of the teacher's influence on his students. In fact, it is a determining factor in their education, one that goes much deeper and lasts much longer than the rules of grammar or algebra. It is thus more than important: it is crucial, as Krishnamurti (1987) tells us when he says that "true education starts with the educator as a person. He must understand himself, and be freed from stereotypical ways of thinking. For the kind of person he is will be reflected in his teaching."

We have seen, then, that the instructor's teaching is based more on who he is than on what he knows, and also that his influence on the students is a determining factor in their development. Because of this, the focal point of his training should be, not his particular specialty, although this should be a prerequisite, but rather the study of educational methods and human psychology, as channeled through his own inner work.

Since his specialty has become a prerequisite, the teacher in training can set that part of his preparation aside and concentrate on learning how to convey his knowledge (educational methods), without losing sight of who he is and who he is talking to (psychology). However, his intellectual knowledge in these two areas must necessarily be complemented by his practicum, and he must analyze the results of that practical application of his learning through research. However, even this (that is, knowledge of educational practices and psychology, practicum followed by analysis and research) is not enough because it does not address the most essential element in the whole teaching process: the teacher himself. Neither knowing nor doing have any relevance unless they are channeled through the very self of the future instructor. I cannot emphasize enough that unless the teacher's inner work becomes an integral part of the basic and ongoing teacher-training programs, our schools will not be able to meet their most fundamental objective, namely that of developing well-balanced, autonomous and creative individuals.

Unfortunately, as Jung (1976) so aptly reminds us, "people everywhere hold the real human soul in such overwhelming scorn that anyone who wants to become attuned to it is well on his way to being considered obsessive."

Since current trends in teacher training do not encourage the instructor to pursue his own inner work, those who wish to do so must go outside the regular channels. There is, in fact, an increasing number of teachers who are doing just that; as they practice their profession, they come to the realization that their formal training has not equipped them with the skills they really need. Generally, they begin to doubt their own proficiency, and hasten to supplement their initial training with workshops focusing on group leadership or psychotherapy. However, such "parallel" training initiatives are far from being either recognized or encouraged. According to the prevailing hyperrationalist, conformist, bureaucratic mindset, therapy is the preserve of the mentally ill, the neurotics and the acute depressives. For this reason, those who receive some form of psychotherapeutic training centered on their own inner work are often considered to be weak, maladjusted and psychologically disturbed. The people who follow through with these initiatives have to be profoundly convinced of the ultimate rewards they will reap in order not to be discouraged.

The only possible way that teacher training can affect the inevitable influence a teacher has on his students is to provide him with the kind of training that teaches him to know himself, to accept and love himself. It is precisely this self-acceptance and self-love that he will communicate subtly and unconsciously to his students through his attitude, before he has had a chance to pass on his intellectual knowledge. Unfortunately, the effect of the teacher's unconscious influence on his students is given no credence whatsoever in educational circles.

All too often, those who are well established within these circles will reject those who fail to conform, fear change, have contempt for those who challenge the *status quo*, be close-minded in the face of the differences that distinguish us from each other, refuse to accept emotions and contradictions, hide from ambiguity, uncertainty and anxiety and display a narrow and stifling rigorism that turns its back on change and inner work. In this sort of atmosphere, it is not exactly easy for an instructor to be himself and to work on his self with every means possible, especially those that are less officially accepted. Nor is it easy for him to feel he has the right to get in touch with his emotions, to be irrational. In fact, it is not easy for him to "be," period. However, this is precisely what the person-centered educational approach urges him to do; he is invited to do all this, and more, by an educational approach that considers inner reality, which includes the influence of the teacher's attitude, to be as important as external reality.

As long as official institutions fail to offer programs geared to the actual needs of his profession, the teacher is obliged to continue his training wherever the skills required by his job are provided. He must go searching for whatever he needs to complete his own personal evolution, filling the void created by a one-dimensional kind of training with the kind of inner work that brings out every aspect of his being.

The personal and professional initiatives being undertaken by an ever-increasing number of teachers constitute, to my mind, a very clear message, which sooner or later must get through to the pedagogical powers-that-be. If those teachers who are in the classroom feel a sometimes urgent need to go outside officially accepted channels in order to round out their education through inner work, it is because they understand that teaching is essentially an interpersonal activity. In this activity, the teacher wishes to be not just a talking head that passes on knowledge, but also a real person and a "people specialist."

How should he go about becoming a "people specialist"? How it is possible for teacher-training programs to adequately prepare instructors for their true task: that of being specialists in human relations? Quite simply, by opening the programs up to include time for the teacher's inner work. If our goal is to turn our schools into places that are not just focused on intellectual learning, but also emphasize the student's overall development, places that provide a balanced environment, that encourage autonomy and creativity, then the instructor must inevitably undertake his own inner work. I am well aware that I have to tread carefully here, for many people are going to ask "What does inner work have to do with education?" I believe that everyone who works in the fields of psychological and physical health, and all those who, in the course of their work, are constantly placed in the context of interpersonal relationships and helping relationships in their larger sense, cannot truly fulfill the requirements of their job unless they undertake some sort of psychotherapeutic inner work. I will go so far as to say that inner work should constitute an integral part of the training for every kind of helper: those working in education, medicine and therapy, and all the related specialized fields.

B. PSYCHOTHERAPEUTIC INNER WORK AS PART OF THE TRAINING FOR ALL HELPERS

1. Preparation for self-knowledge

What exactly do we mean when we talk about psychotherapy as a part of the training for helpers? Before I answer that question, let me again define the psychotherapeutic act. Essentially, it is an act that aims to prevent and cure a person's psychological disorders and his behavioral difficulties. Strictly speaking, the role of the psychotherapist is more a curative one, in that he helps the client to find his own ways of freeing himself from his problems and blocks, although this does not necessarily rule out the preventive possibilities of his approach. As for the teacher, I believe that his role is to assist in the prevention of psychological and behavioral problems in his students through an approach that centers on the wholeness of the human person. He does not engage in psychotherapy *per se*, but his approach ought to have a beneficial effect on his students' behavior and on the development of their personalities. Nor can he attain this goal merely by deploying his intellectual skills; it is the kind of attitude he displays and the unconscious influence he has on the learners that will make the difference. Even the most competent teacher cannot imbue his students with psychic balance if he himself has not properly developed all the aspects of his personality and is hence mentally disturbed or imbalanced; the same is true for doctors, psychologists and psychotherapists.

Preventive educational methods that foresee and forestall psychological and behavioral problems, and hence physiological ones, are definitely the way of the future in education. These preventive methods make full use of the teacher's unconscious influence and are based on who he is, as a person. However, these methods cannot take root and grow unless personal growth and inner work are placed front and center in every aspect of teacher training. The same applies in the fields of medicine and psychology of the future.

But why psychotherapeutic inner work, you ask. The kind of training for helpers that is centered on the teacher, the psychotherapist or the doctor as a person must give future practitioners in these fields the means to acquire self-acceptance and self-love and to become acquainted with, develop and improve every aspect of themselves. The helper who neither loves nor accepts himself cannot pass on to his helpees what he is lacking himself, namely self-love, which is the basis for all personal development. Every such initiative must inevitably be channeled through self-knowledge. The helper who does not know himself will unconsciously project his emotional experiences onto his students or his clients and make them responsible for his problems.

It goes without saying that every single one of an individual's life experiences can contribute to his growth and to his inner work as long as he has sufficient self-knowledge and self-confidence to learn from his mistakes. Unfortunately, however, life experiences do not always place his feet on the path of freedom. More often than not, they maintain him in a state of anguish, feed a sense of self-destruction and make him hopelessly confused about himself and his entourage. Thus they reinforce behavior patterns that fail to satisfy his basic needs. His attempts to extricate himself are futile, for in deploying his defense mechanism he actually reinforces the very patterns from which he wants to escape. Thus he finds himself constantly falling into the same types of difficulties, oblivious of the internal mechanisms that lead him there. No matter how much he may want to escape from this vicious circle, he cannot.

However, it is not enough to simply want to change; there is a huge step between wanting something and going after it. Everybody wants to change; everybody wants to move forward. But at the same time, the thought of change in their lives makes people afraid and insecure; it is always easier to see why others should change. Accepting the fact that we have to change means first looking at ourselves with the same critical eye we regard others with, and then searching slowly and ever deeper for inner, rather than external reasons for our dissatisfaction, and for the resources to improve our situation. This is precisely the sort of thing that creative nondirective psychotherapy makes possible. It is a process that brings the individual face to face with himself. It enables him to get rid of the psychological crutches he has been hanging onto for so long, because he is strengthened by self-knowledge and self-acceptance, and by the progressive development of all aspects of his personality.

2. Preparation for the multidimensional approach

The kind of teacher training proposed by the CNDA is one that encourages the teacher's ability to develop every facet of his self. It is designed to prepare the teacher to work toward the goals inherent in this sort of multidimensional approach. Similarly, training programs for psychotherapists should prepare them to approach the helpee in terms of his intrinsic wholeness again, through multidimensional development. Every aspect or dimension of the helper as well as of the helpee, needs to be called forth and developed, whether it pertains to his imaginative, intellectual, spiritual, social, emotional or physical side.

In all too many cases, practicing sports is the only way human beings interact with their bodies. Without wishing to minimize the importance of sports activities, I must say that I consider them inadequate as a means of getting to know, and especially accept, one's body. There are any number of physical education specialists who do not feel comfortable with their bodies and who reject their own physical appearance. Knowing one's body, accepting it and integrating it into one's overall self-esteem does not come easily to many people. However, it is an indispensable factor in the development of self-love and self-acceptance. The body is an important key to one's inner work, something that cannot be ignored without repercussion.

Unfortunately, training programs for teachers and psychotherapists have seen fit to ignore any discussion of the helper's feelings about his sensuality, his sexuality, his desires and seduction in general; the mere mention of such topics is enough to upset or shock people. However, although they remain unexpressed they are nonetheless real, are present in the unconscious attitude of the helper, and influence the helpee. By rejecting and hence symbolically killing the body, the Church did not extirpate it from human relationships. It remained, but in some cases took on twisted and threatening forms. Whether we like it or not, human beings are made in such a way that they need to experience their desires, physical sensations, and seductive urges. Sensuality and sexuality are only "evil" for those who live them out in unhealthy ways. In their true state, they merely represent reality, an integral part of our human nature. And it is impossible to bring up children to be well-balanced individuals by denying that reality. Nor is it possible for simple verbal information on sensuality and sexuality to assist educators and psychotherapists in accepting their physical dimension; what is truly important is their attitude. If they feel good about their bodies, if they know what their physical needs are and how to satisfy them, if they are honest with themselves and others, if they can accept themselves as they are and if they live out their sensuality and sexuality with the proper respect for themselves and for others, then they will exert an unconscious positive effect on their students or clients, even if the topic is never raised. As the helper understands more and learns to feel good about his body, the problems caused by disrespectful and inappropriate sexual activity will progressively disappear, and the helper can assist in developing healthy beings who respect themselves and others.

When we dissociate the physical side of our nature from the emotional one, however, we run the risk of losing our inner balance. Every human relationship, and particularly every helping relationship, needs to give some room to the irrational. As we have seen in the preceding chapters, all our life experiences are informed by our emotions. A helper who ignores a helpee's emotional experiences is missing the obvious. How, though, is a helper supposed to feel at ease with the helpee's feelings if he is afraid of his own, if he is incapable of dealing with his own emotional blocks? At school, the emotions that lie beneath the surface during class lectures and discussions and at teachers' meetings are for the most part completely denied. Emotion is rationalized, and in order to function in this environment, the individual is constantly forced to cut himself off from his feelings. If the teacher feels "fragmented" in this way, he will have a negative effect on his students. If the psychotherapist is cut off from his emotions, his approach will be ineffective because the bonding process between himself and his client, which is so fundamental to his work, cannot begin to take place. His training should therefore emphasize the importance of emotions and emotional experience.

Our emotions are the basis for all our human relationships as well as for our inner work, and I believe that becoming attuned to them should be a priority in teachers' and psychotherapists' training programs, so that they learn to be as much at ease in the realm of feelings as in that of words. To do so, they must bring their own emotions into perspective, and recognize that they are as important as the intellectual side of their nature. They must also be able to perceive how they hide from what they feel by unconsciously using defense mechanisms that, on a conscious level, they refuse to accept and that sever or impair their relationships with learners and others. Finally, they must learn to accept their own emotional subjectivity, and accept the fact that it is the foundation of everything they teach.

I believe that the emotional realm has an extremely important evocative role to play in psychotherapy and in education. Indeed it may well be the single most determining factor in the client's or student's progress or regression, his success or failure; in short, it affects every aspect of his physiological or psychological improvement or decline. I cannot overemphasize the power of suggestion and its concomitant beneficial or harmful consequences as transmitted via the emotions in the educational and psychotherapeutic relationship. Human beings at every stage of life are affected by feelings, not by words.

Conquering his emotional world, for the helper, means opening up the doors to the self and discovering that acceptance of and understanding for humanity are finally within his grasp. It also means accepting the fact that he too has an irrational side. With understanding comes the realization that the mind is not only made up of rational faculties, such as thought, analysis, knowledge and understanding, but that it can also feel, perceive, imagine and intuit. All of these irrational aspects of the mind have been summarily rejected by educational science, and for this reason imagination as well as emotion have been banished from the classroom.

The imagination is often seen as a faculty that disrupts the normal functioning of the rational conscious. The only people who are allowed to give it free rein are artists, those endowed with special talents, the sort of talents they can put to use anywhere but at school. A word of warning, though: the imagination can destroy man just as easily as it can strengthen him. We should examine our imagination in detail before we let it roam free; otherwise, it may lead us to our doom or, at the very least, maintain us in a state of suffering and misfortune. Any training program for psychotherapists and teachers should necessarily include a thorough examination of the imagination.

Imagination is an ideal pathway to self-knowledge, to freedom from emotional blocks; it also acts as a sort of psychic compass by which the teacher can plot out his journey through life. If he accepts his imagination, the teacher can explore his creativity, and plumb the innermost depths of his spiritual being. However, if he denies the realms of his imagination, he is cutting himself off from pleasure, from fantasy, from the creative expression found in music, painting, sculpture, singing and poetry. By denying his imaginary world he is killing the artist and poet that live within him. Man is himself a poem, giving off fleeting, subtle, fragile emanations, each of which is in itself a creation that provides unique insight into his inner world. He is a temple, protected from profanation only by a polysemic mentality; he is an indefinable being, both stable and open to change, mysterious and transparent, different and yet the same, unique and complex. His imagination can open the door to infinity, to freedom. Education and psychotherapy, by putting reason on a pedestal and grinding imagination into the dust, destroy the mind's inner balance; only the union of its rational and irrational faculties can restore that balance and make it function harmoniously.

Psychotherapeutic and educational helping relationships stand in need of those therapists and teachers who can provide the sort of unconscious influence that instills balance, of those helpers who are working on developing every aspect of their selves. This multidimensional approach to the human self is a primary source of evolution and change. Developing one aspect at the expense of others creates inner imbalance; overlooking one means severing an essential part of oneself and denying the importance of man's intrinsic wholeness. Human beings are more than just rational creatures. They are also made up of body and soul, emotions and visions. Any kind of inner work, in my opinion, remains incomplete unless some form of spirituality is attained, and by spirituality, I mean a realization of the symbolism inherent in the divine.

Man and the universe are inhabited by an immaterial, invisible power, whose existence cannot be proven scientifically, but whose presence is nonetheless confirmed by such experiences as interiorization and letting go. Tuning out the defensive rational side of the conscious allows us to tune in to our bodies, our emotions; it also allows us to attain within ourselves unconditional love and immeasurable peace, and brings us to a point where we can enter into the infinite. This experience allows us to get in touch with something indefinable within ourselves, something that reason is unable to explain. True spirituality has nothing to do with dogma or officially sanctioned truths; it is, instead, the result of intense personal experiences of interiorization.

To be authentic, it must be channeled through our bodies, our emotions. If it is not, then "spirituality" becomes nothing more than a defensive attitude, and a means of displaying our power and superiority over others. Sects and religions are only the manifestations and outward forms of spirituality. It is quite possible for a person to be a lifelong member of a certain sect, or practice a given religion, without ever having had a spiritual experience. On the other hand, however, those who have a certain religious affiliation may find that organized worship can help them lead a truly spiritual life.

I myself have a Judeo-Christian background and, along with the majority of people in Quebec, I was raised to be a practicing Catholic. At the age of 25, I renounced the Church because I felt stifled by the need to adhere to religious precepts that seemed, increasingly, to be an aberration. Feeling neither shame nor guilt, I gave up prayer and stopped going to mass or confession. I saw them merely as empty, soulless practices that had no interest for me. My upbringing had taught me that religion was about outward forms, rites, dogmas and so on. After a while my adherence to these forms became problematic because I realized that they had no inner resonance for me. Today, even though my own spiritual life is not connected to any particular religion, I do not reject it. I recognize that religion is a perfectly valid tool for many people to help them get in touch with the divine. No one has the right to judge the means that others use to further their self-actualization. When one enters the realm of the irrational, one is dealing with a person's intensely subjective opinions, and this demands nothing less than the most profound respect. Also, I am well aware that my spiritual path is mine and mine alone, and that while some may have reached a certain level of spiritual experience without the help of sects or religions, others have attained it because of them.

After I renounced the Church, I continued my inner work, continued to develop my physical, affective and intellectual potential through university courses and training in parallel institutions, through life experiences and, most of all, through psychotherapy. I studied educational science and psychology at a fairly advanced level, I worked on my emotional blocks and I stopped being afraid of my sexuality and my sensuality.

All these steps were both revelatory and satisfying, yet I nevertheless felt that there was something missing. Then, an unexpected event took place, a determining event that led me to experience interiorization and letting go in a significant way. I will not go into the details of this experience, but I will say that it led me to the realization that there was another path that I could follow, in addition to that of reason, and that this path could provide me with answers to questions that my rational conscious had been powerless to resolve. Now that I make a point of getting in touch with it on a daily basis, I am firmly convinced that an extraordinary irrational force resides within man. This force can only operate if we abandon ourselves to it, if we agree to let go of our rational self-control. Depending on your beliefs, you can call it love, energy or God, but whatever you call it, it is an infallible source of peace, self-confidence and inner freedom. To experience it, however, you have to have faith. This is unfortunate for those of us who demand rational proof of things, for faith does not come from scientific theories or dogmas; it comes when we experience our inner greatness, which, paradoxically, we can only attain through humility, in the sense of accepting the limits of our conscious minds.

I believe that those who set up training programs for helpers should concern themselves with these things: with the teacher's and psychotherapist's readiness to get in touch with the rational and the irrational, with the development of their imagination, their physical, affective, intellectual and spiritual potential and with their self-knowledge and self-love. Here, and only here, can one see the way of the future in helping relationships. We are moving toward a view of the helping relationship that will put personal wholeness first and that will take into account the determining effect the helper's unconscious influence will have upon the helpee, and how the helper's inner work and his ability to develop every facet of his own self can make that influence beneficial. The helping relationship of the future is one that will have gone beyond experimentation and dissatisfaction to take its rightful place and assume its preventive and curative role with respect to psychological disorders, and its creative role with respect to individuals, helping them to become balanced, autonomous and happy individuals. It will do so because it has given priority not to disembodied learning but to real people, and has recognized that the most important, the most valuable tool in the helping relationship, is the helper himself.

C. THE HELPER AND PSYCHOTHERAPY

Because of the extremely delicate nature of the psychotherapeutic relationship, the psychotherapist needs to fully understand the realm of the psyche so that he can approach it confidently. However, it takes time for him to acquire the many skills necessary to qualify him as a "specialist in helping relationships."

How can he acquire these skills? I do not believe that a person can become a psychotherapist simply because he has learned a lot about psychology and the various trends in psychotherapy, or because he has learned a few counseling techniques, or even because he knows how to administer and interpret different kinds of assessment tests. Having a doctorate in psychology is no guarantee that he will be a truly qualified psychotherapist; nor is the fact of having developed and experimented with a particular counseling technique. In addition to his theoretical learning and practical experience, he must have an in-depth knowledge of himself as a person. Anyone who calls himself a psychotherapist should have mastered these three intimately connected and inseparable elements during his basic training, and be able to work competently, with respect for himself and others.

1. Training for creative nondirective psychotherapists

a) Competence

Training competent psychotherapists means providing them with in-depth knowledge that will allow them to practice their calling in a professional manner. The training for creative nondirective psychotherapists emphasizes the importance of self-knowledge, self-acceptance and self-love. This inner work is not only an essential part of their basic training, but is also carried on throughout their on-going training, for as long as they practice psychotherapy.

For the student in training, this inner work consists in understanding his needs, emotions, desires, defense mechanisms and patterns, and coming to terms with them. It also consists in getting to know how his psyche functions, so that he will not project what belongs to him onto the helpee. Moreover, in creative nondirective training, inner work includes discovering and accepting one's stumbling blocks, to prevent them from interfering with the helping relationship. So, he needs to work out where he stands in relation to judgment, advice, rationalization, power, interpretation, taking charge and so on. The creative nondirective training program does not present these as undesirable elements, that must be banished from one's psyche and behavior; the goal of his inner work is not for the helper to become a robot, and mindlessly conform to an imposed theoretical ideal but, on the contrary, for him to get to know and accept himself as he is. The advantage of this sort of work is that it makes a person judge himself less harshly, and frees him from guilt. Instead of hiding his true self in shame, he can accept himself, and openly acknowledge that, yes, he does indeed have a tendency to judge, project or take charge of others. As I have mentioned before, the paradox of this situation is that, in order to change he is called upon to stop changing, to shake off his persona and learn to live with the person he truly is, without guilt or shame.

The key elements of the inner work that is begun in the CNDA psychotherapist training program are responsibility, respect for fundamental needs, personal discipline, honesty, empathy, congruence, self-love and love for others, and the like. Rather than being presented as absolutes, these important values are presented as points of reference. The helper can begin to determine where he stands in relation to each of these values, and accept where he is in his own learning process, without comparing himself to others or to a disembodied, unattainable ideal.

This fundamental part of the future psychotherapist's inner work, which is the foundation on which the whole creative nondirective training program rests, is supplemented by important parallel studies in human psychology, appropriate techniques and methods for assisting the helpee, analysis of practical application and research.

The program aims at teaching an overall, all-encompassing competence that starts with the helper himself, as a person, and that goes on to encompass theory, practical application and research that are "felt" because they resonate within the trainee's experience. Any theory or method that fails to elicit a response from the psychotherapist remains unintegrated, and will lead him to place his helpees in identical molds that will lead them further away from self-knowledge, rather than bringing them face to face with who they are. Similarly, any technique that does not acknowledge the therapist as a person reduces him to the level of a mere technician. Heedless of this, helpers are constantly falling into the trap of hiding behind their techniques. Just as many teachers rely on their course material to make them feel secure, so many therapists fall back on a particular theory or technique.

There is a great deal of abuse in the area of counseling techniques. Some individuals set themselves up as psychotherapists on the strength of an interesting and apparently effective technique they have become proficient in. Proponents of the CNDA see things in a different light. For them, techniques are tools that the therapist can use, but the psychotherapeutic relationship is essentially channeled through him. As far as the CNDA is concerned, centering a psychotherapist's training solely on techniques and hands-on workshops is as absurd as centering it solely on theories and research. Whether these two elements are developed together or separately, they are of little use to a helper involved in interpersonal relationships unless they are integrated into his experiences, his senses and his emotions.

In my opinion, the psychotherapist is really being trained to be competent in his field, to fully integrate the theoretical and practical parts of the program, when every new theory, technique or element of research is introduced in such a way that it resonates in each trainee's personal experience, in that which makes him different from other people, in his emotional and physical existence. If not, he will merely be accumulating vast quantities of unintegrated technical and theoretical knowledge. For him to be capable of integrating that knowledge, the trainers themselves should have had several years of comprehensive training. They should maintain contact with the irrational or spiritual part of their being. And they should stay constantly attuned to their bodies, their emotions, their defense mechanisms, their imagination, their creativity and their intellect while they teach.

These are the things a competent trainer should do in order to turn out creative nondirective helpers. And these are the things that participants in CNDA training courses are invited to do. The trainees learn to work with who they are because their trainers have integrated what they have to teach; they do not communicate a disembodied knowledge based on theories and their applications, but a knowledge that has been channeled through their very being and that is confirmed by their attitude. The ability to teach in this way is not acquired through generally accepted teaching methods, which concentrate exclusively on impersonal learning. It can only be acquired in an environment where the operation of both the mind and the brain are equally respected, by dealing with each individual's emotional and subjective experience. The sort of competence these trainers display relies, among other things, on letting go.

b) *Letting go*

Working with integrated knowledge means working with oneself, and being able to recognize one's own limits as regards one's role within the helping relationship. For example, if the helper feels powerless to help someone in a given situation, and uses his rational faculties to search for the ideal theory or technique to resolve his difficulty, he often finds that his assistance is ineffective. For, during the course of the therapeutic process, the therapist does indeed sometimes come up against his own personal limitations, and the limits of his theoretical and practical knowledge. At this point, he should simply let go, and trust in the irrational force that resides within him. The individual who has integrated his training will know how to ignore his conscious attempts at control, as well as the theoretical and technical know-how that makes him feel secure, and trust his instinct. When knowledge is truly integrated, it becomes part of who we are, and tuning out the one-dimensional reality of the intellect is usually all it takes to bring to mind the relevant idea, gesture or turn of phrase that will resolve a seemingly inextricable situation.

A helper needs to be really competent, according to the definition given above, in order to have sufficient self-confidence to let go. Letting go means realizing when our rational attempts to solve a problem are not working, when our attempts to help are ineffective, and giving up on those attempts. In certain instances the psychotherapist has to know that it is time to put his rational functions aside, and give free rein to the irrational ones, namely his intuition, his feelings or, for those who can identify with this term, that reflection of the divine that resides within. My training and psychotherapy work are a constant reminder of the importance of letting go in helping relationships, the importance, in certain situations, of opening myself up to what reason alone cannot perceive, and to trust in the unlimited resources of the unconscious to lead me in a direction that will be suitable for the helpee. When knowledge is integrated, the most appropriate response to a situation often comes into our conscious mind when we stop searching for it, and call upon our irrational faculties. Letting go will help us accomplish this, based as it is on inner work, integrated knowledge and an ability to recognize and accept the limits of reason alone when helping others. Paradoxically, as we learn to let go, we should also learn how to be self-disciplined.

c) *Discipline*

Self-actualization is not possible without self-discipline. As Scott Peck (1987) observes, "Discipline is the most important tool we have for solving life's problems." It is also a vital ingredient in the shift to creative action, the actualization of creative potential and any kind of personal evolution and growth. It also provides us with a sense of inner security, without which we are forced to walk hesitantly and on tiptoe in the obscurity generated by a "laissez-faire" attitude.

As I have mentioned earlier, a life without structure and discipline is usually a life filled with frustration, disappointment and, in many cases, outright failure. Discipline helps us take control of our lives; without it, we are guided by external events, and are blown this way and that like a weathervane. Unless we are disciplined, we get caught up in power games, trying to defend a freedom that is "free" in name only, for true freedom is based on self-discipline.

A great deal of inner work has to be accomplished before the CNDA-trained psychotherapist can be said to have acquired the necessary discipline. This inner work leads the student to the very core of his deepest insecurities and his most intense fears. Perhaps he is afraid of commitment, of responsibility, of being invaded, of losing his freedom, of losing someone else's love or of disappointing someone. These are the kinds of fears that prevent the helper from giving structure to his life. Here we come up against yet another paradox: by allowing structure and its consequences to enter his life, he is freed from his fears. However, before he can take this step, he must have developed the will and the ability to choose, to make decisions, to define his limits and to organize his time. The more self-disciplined the helper is, the greater control he has over his life and the more able he is to achieve and create. His achievements help to lessen his feelings of insecurity and inferiority, and increase the self-confidence that is such an essential ingredient to on-going growth. Self-discipline helps us take control of our lives and paves the way to success in our careers and in our relationships, to outstanding achievements and exciting creativity. Paradoxically, it also paves the way to pleasure.

d) *Pleasure*

The concept of pleasure is of paramount importance in the training programs for creative nondirective psychotherapists. By "pleasure," I mean the fundamental emotional state that constitutes one of the focal points of our affective experience, the other being pain. We might define pleasure as an agreeable sensation or emotion that we feel when a need or a desire is fulfilled in the course of vital, healthy activities.

Although, during the course of their inner work, therapist trainees may go through times of trouble, or experience isolated painful incidents, their training is basically pleasurable. After all, since the student is constantly working towards his own personal goals as he concentrates on his training, and since he is committed to his course of study on an ongoing and personally applicable basis, he is always interested and motivated by what he learns. The course content allows plenty of room for the students to play, move around and relax. They cannot help but evolve in a classroom atmosphere that accepts personal differences as a matter of course, and they take pleasure in learning about themselves as they learn the course material.

The training program for creative nondirective psychotherapists amounts to 1,200 hours spread out over 3 years. During the course of the program, intensive training periods take place once every three or four weeks, to allow the student to integrate what he has learned and apply it to his everyday life. Divided as it is into progressive stages, this structure is essential to any person-centered training program because it ensures an almost "reverential" respect for the trainee and the pace at which he can evolve, since the student has permanently invested his entire physical, emotional, intellectual, social and spiritual being in it.

2. Stages in the training

The training program for creative nondirective psychotherapists is divided into several stages. At the Montreal Counselling Centre, we provide an initial period of basic training that lasts 1,200 hours, spread out over three years, at a rate of one weekend of courses per month and three intensive, seven-day workshops. We also offer a specialized program at a more advanced level to our graduate students.

a) Stage 1

The first section of the program, entitled Self Awareness, lasts a year and is basically a time for the student to learn, individually or in groups, how to tune in to the messages coming from his body, and how to listen to his emotions. During this first year, the approach used by the trainers helps him to discover and integrate the way his psyche operates and what his needs, his fears, his defense mechanisms and his patterns might be. In an atmosphere of mutual respect, he learns to accept and love himself as he is. When he is ready, he will be able to utilize the protective mechanisms that will satisfy his needs and provide him with the necessary resources to develop his creative potential and learn about freedom. Since this learning process is not solely on the theoretical level, but also aims at integration, only the student who invests his time and energy in it will get the most out of it.

During the first year, in addition to their group activities, the students begin a one-on-one psychotherapeutic relationship, at no extra cost to them, with the final-year students. They can also, if they choose, pursue their inner work with an experienced creative nondirective psychotherapist. The goal of giving them this wide variety of options is to enable them, in every situation they encounter, to be aware of what is happening within them, to listen to what their body is telling them, to feel their emotions, to acknowledge their needs and to observe the behavior that deprives them of the ability to satisfy their basic needs. Finally, the goal is to enable them to face up to their fears, if they are ready to do so, and so to choose the protective mechanisms that will guarantee them more effective communication and healthier, happier relationships.

The road leading to that goal is not without obstacles. Nevertheless, it is rare indeed for a student not to continue until he has reached the end of the road. They press on because they are conscious of the remarkable changes taking hold in their lives, because they have a better understanding of what is happening within them and because the training provides them with a sense of security thanks to the attention and respect they receive there. However, perhaps the most important reason for their perseverance is that the CNDA teaches them that they are the sole architects of their own freedom, change and happiness. This realization gives them a sense of confidence in their abilities, and the feeling that they are in control of their lives.

b) *Stage 2*

The vast majority of people who go through the first year move on to the second and third year of the program. This involves two years of professional training entitled Counseling Theories and Techniques.

The fundamental principle of the program is that the helper is the most important element in the CNDA. Because of this, the thrust of the student's inner work changes at this point, to enable him to help others. The greater his ability to observe himself, to be attuned and open to himself, the more he will develop his ability to be open to others. Whenever the trainer introduces a new technique or a new theory, he starts by relating it first to the helper-in-training as a person. The new material is thus well and truly integrated, rather than being grafted on.

Workshops centered on practical application are followed by written assignments emphasizing reflection and analysis. Each assignment is carefully perused by an educational psychotherapist, who writes comments on the papers and meets with the students to ensure they are on the right path. Qualified supervisors sit in on "practice" counseling done by the students, and these sessions are also recorded on videotape, so that the student can gauge his own progress and change his approach if necessary. During this second stage, the students work on defining the goals of their personal and professional life. In addition to emphasizing the importance of ongoing inner work, this stage concentrates on integrated theoretical knowledge, practical learning, analysis and written assignments; it also introduces the student to the value of research.

At the end of this basic training period, the student receives a diploma that allows him to become a member of an association representing therapists and that allows him also to sign up for the graduate program at the Montreal Counseling Centre.

c) Stage 3

The basic training program, totaling 1,200 hours spread out over three years, is followed by a graduate program. Anyone who successfully completes it will receive a DESA (*diplôme d'études supérieures avancées* or diploma of advanced graduate studies) in counseling.

This program, which continues to focus on the helper as the most important element in the counseling process, places a greater amount of emphasis on specialization, on professional practice and on research. The program lasts 1,400 hours, spread out over four years. During this time, the student must take five specialized weekend courses per year, do 300 hours of supervised practicum, take part in research seminars and, with the help of competent research directors, write a thesis of significant length, which he will have to defend at the end of the program. When he graduates from this program, he will receive a DESA, or diploma of advanced graduate studies.

3. Course methodology

These two programs, which, for those interested in continuing their training, can be followed by additional courses of study, never deviate from the methodology that informs all teaching at the Montreal Counselling Centre. Every course begins with "centering" and interiorization exercises. The activities that follow these exercises are meant to build on the program's subject matter, but are also based on the students' input. They are designed to bring the participants into constant interaction with one another.

Since counterproductive psychic processes generally originate in relationships, this constant interaction provides the student with an opportunity to get in touch with himself. He learns to become attuned to the messages his body sends him (breathing, muscle tension, malaises), to feel his emotions, to recognize and express them, to pay attention to the images his mind conjures up, such as fantasies, daydreams and interior monologues. Each course allows him to get progressively more in touch with himself. By moving at his own pace through the stages in the CNDA's process of liberation and change, he will come to accept himself as he is, to assume his responsibilities and to observe how he behaves in everyday situations as well as in therapy sessions. Finally, he will be able to confront his Minotaur, armed with the sort of protective mechanisms that will help him achieve satisfaction of his fundamental needs.

Each activity included in the course syllabus is followed by a supervised period of intense reflection, the results of which are to be recorded in the student's logbook. Throughout his training, the student should constantly refer to this, his most invaluable tool. Individual reflection is followed by a time of sharing, in pairs or in small groups, so that everyone can have a chance to speak. A similar exercise then follows, but with a larger group. After this time of sharing are the theoretical foundations of the course brought up. These are never discussed for their own sake, but always in relation to the subject matter under discussion, the exercises being done, and the situations that arise from the exercises or the personal history that has been shared. The theory is always presented in such a way that it responds to the needs of the moment. Thus it is guided by the content of the course, the group, the situations and the times of sharing.

The learning process always follows the same pattern of centering, activities, reflection, sharing and theoretical deductions. After the course, the students are asked to assess, in writing, how the course content pertains to everyday life. After a few days they should review this assessment and then write down their conclusions. All the assessments are read and extensively annotated by an educational psychotherapist; his comments are confidential, and specifically geared to each participant.

4. Trainers

This whole process, as the reader can see, places a great deal of emphasis on the helper as a person, whether he be a psychotherapist, an educational psychotherapist or a trainer. The trainer has a particularly important role to play at every stage of the process, especially when the students gather in large groups to share their experiences.

Sharing in the large group is an important aspect of the training program. The students are not obliged to take part in this activity unless they feel ready to do so. However, this is a stage that can be helpful for all concerned: those who do not actively participate can at least hear the experiences of those who do speak out, and get in touch with the emotions that those experiences give rise to in them. Also, it gives all the students in the program the opportunity to see the trainer "in action," so to speak, as he conducts a brief, one-on-one therapy session with the person who is sharing. This practice inevitably opens new doors for the helpee because, thanks to his familiarity with the CNDA, the trainer can ensure that the person who speaks up in a group situation is never left with an unsatisfying, incomplete sharing experience.

In such a situation, the helpee feels satisfied and has evolved because the trainer has accompanied him through the gradual, gentle release of the emotion or trouble in question. He does this in such a way that the helpee, depending on his need, can find his own solution to his problem, his own way out of a dead end or his own hope in the midst of doubts. This is not a miraculous ability. The trainer is able to bring this about because he knows how to perceive, observe and elucidate what the participant is expressing both verbally and non-verbally, and is able to accompany other people through their emotional experiences without making them feel either inhibited, panicky or insecure. Since most people, even those who are attuned to the ebb and flow of their inner world, fear emotion more than anything else, it is important that the individual should not feel alone with his emotions, whether in an individual or a group situation. Thus the trainer or psychotherapist can be said to "accompany" the participant, in the sense that he helps him conquer his emotional world, by discovering it and, over time, entering it.

The process of learning these abilities begins with the basic program for creative nondirective psychotherapists, continues through the graduate program and culminates in "trainer training." The trainer who learns to stay in constant contact with his own emotions, his own feelings of unease, his own needs, even as the individual or group therapy session is unfolding, exerts a profound influence. This most important ability enables him to maintain his relationship with the trainees. Unless he manages simultaneously to be a trainer that observes, rephrases and elucidates and one that feels and is aware that he feels, and who does not deny that irrational part of himself that can sometimes guide him, then he cannot maintain that relationship.

Once accepted into the program following a personal interview, the trainer for the creative nondirective approach is not only trained to become a competent psychotherapist; his studies also prepare him to be a teacher, group leader, regulator or supervisor. The training he receives at the Montreal Counselling Centre teaches him to listen, observe, elucidate and intervene in a creative nondirective manner; it teaches him to accompany the participant in front of the group for anywhere from five to twenty minutes, in such a way that the participant feels satisfied, but that does not imply that the trainer assumes responsibility for the participant's feelings; nor does he attempt to find a solution to his troubles. By leaving him with this responsibility, the trainer is not abandoning him by the roadside, so to speak. Rather, he is letting the participant guide him toward the appropriate helping procedure. It is precisely this guiding, or induction, that makes his actions so satisfying for the helpee.

Induction is an important element in the creative nondirective approach. Knowing how to let oneself be led by an individual or a group means being sufficiently observant, sufficiently attuned to the person or the group in question (empathy) as well as to one's own feelings (congruence) to intervene in an appropriate manner and give pertinent explanations. He who neither acknowledges his own feelings nor those of others cannot possibly use induction in his approach. Certain teachers in training have to work on this for years. Once they have mastered it, good psychotherapists or trainers use the helpee himself as their starting point, so that they are not merely mechanically repeating the same helping procedures with each individual, or repeating the same exercises, steps and explanations with each group.

The approach of a CNDA trainer also takes into consideration the overall functioning of the human brain, as it is defined in this book, the functioning of the psyche, and the different ways of perceiving and learning represented by the members of his group. When he is with them in class, he ensures that time is set aside for some form of rhythmic movement, because he is aware that this is an important factor in integrating knowledge. In fact, the courses at the Montreal Counselling Centre make full use of the fundamental evocative and relaxing powers of music. It is used in many ways: as a means of leading into some exercises, or as a subtle background presence for others. Music draws us in, gets us involved, and has the ability to affect every aspect of our being. Lozanov recognized this, making it an important element in suggestopedic teaching. Its effect on rhythm and movement promotes learning because of the emotional echoes that are set off within the psyche, and that help to make it whole. This is the reason why the CNDA trainer has frequent recourse to it as well. In addition, he uses a multidimensional approach toward people that is based on the most profound respect for each participant's individual rate of progress.

Becoming a CNDA trainer, then, requires a great deal of experience working with the creative nondirective approach, combined with a commitment to lifelong learning and inner work. We must keep in mind that the primary tool of the trainer, or the psychotherapist, or, indeed, anyone who uses the CNDA is himself as a person. Primarily intended for all physical and mental health professionals (that is, psychologists, psychotherapists, sexologists, physiotherapists, doctors, social workers, nurses, teachers and various kinds of massage therapists) CNDA training also applies to anyone who has pursued his own inner work and who now wishes to improve his relationships with others. Whether he is a manager, supervisor or department head, he can learn to approach his job on a more personal level, and use better communication techniques. Finally, CNDA training is aimed at everyone who wishes to place human beings ahead of structures, ideologies and power games. Whatever their reason for being there, the participants are enriched by their experiences within the group. The differences in personal or professional background contribute greatly to the group as a whole, as does the unifying desire of all the participants to continue their inner work and increase their self-acceptance and self-love. Their ultimate goal is to give to others the best of who they can be.

CONCLUSION

Being a creative nondirective teacher, psychotherapist or trainer means learning to integrate the directivity/nondirectivity dialectic into one's life, to integrate responsibility, acceptance and self-love in such a way as to create oneself, and to participate in the self-creation of others. It also means using one's inner work and the learning assimilated during the training process as a means of acknowledging both the right and left side of the helpee's brain, both the rational and irrational side of his nature. Being a creative nondirective helper also means being able to respect, in the context of a helping relationship, the way the other's psyche functions, his way of perceiving the world and his individual rate of progress.

All of this, as we have seen, requires that one thoroughly integrate both theoretical and practical knowledge. The process of learning about the CNDA cannot be undertaken by everyone, since it involves a great deal more than just the intellect, and a person's technical and methodological abilities. The most important selection criteria, then, are not the applicant's book-learning, nor even his aptitude with this or that technique, but rather his life experience, and the manner in which he has integrated the theoretical and practical knowledge those experiences have brought him.

Moreover, the CNDA training programs have been set up in such a way that the only ones who complete them are those whose life experiences make them capable of applying what they learn in the courses to their own lives; who can deal with that factual content from within, rather than placing themselves above it, or else keeping it external to them, and hence non-integrated. Those who need to control everything rationally, for whom knowledge is a veritable lifeline, whose sense of security resides primarily if not exclusively in the number of facts they can accumulate, or the number of hours they spend practicing techniques and methods, such people will have great difficulty going through with the CNDA training program for the simple reason that it is not meant for them.

The vast majority of training programs have not paid much attention to the concept of integrated knowledge. Some stress intellectual knowledge, others emphasize the practical application of that knowledge, while still others underline the importance of personal growth or psychotherapy. The programs that do include all three of these elements tend to consider them as separate entities. The integrated learning program provided by the CNDA incorporates and combines all these elements throughout the duration of both the basic and the graduate training programs, using the trainee himself as the focal point.

The CNDA sees the helping relationship as being directly related to the helper's self-knowledge and self-love. The intimate connection I make between the helping relationship and self-love is based on my experiences of interpersonal relationships, which had a determining effect on many areas in my life. And, whether I like it or not, all my relationships have been affected by the first relationship I became involved in, and the one that we too often blame for all our psychological problems: my relationship with my parents.

I was the oldest of seven children. I cannot truthfully say that I retain many happy memories from my childhood. Because of my vulnerability, I experienced sometimes unbearable fear and psychological suffering. Certain events were, indeed, so painful that I repressed them completely for many years before I was finally able to free myself from them. However, I was fortunate enough to have been taught to view suffering as a means of inner work and of personal evolution rather than as something to be avoided at all costs. Today, I know that I have been liberated from the memory of those difficult experiences. Of my mother, I remember especially, her great generosity, her eternal youthfulness and her openness to new experiences; of my father, I retain mostly his wisdom, and his exceptional personal qualities. These memories are propulsive, urging me on toward total self-actualization. Because I used my suffering as a springboard to self-knowledge and self-acceptance, I gradually learned to love myself for who I really am and, consequently, was able to see the undeniably rich inheritance my parents had given me, although, before, I had been unable to perceive it. I learned to love my vulnerability, and to see it as a great asset to my interpersonal relationships. I learned to love my intense need to be loved and acknowledged. I learned to love my fears, and to learn how to face up to them.

Everything that I learned in the school of life taught me how to love and understand others and, because in the midst of my suffering I still felt loved, I emerged strengthened from these experiences. The love I am speaking of here is the love that is the foundation of the helping relationship, and is the *primum mobile* of all relationships between children and their parents, students and teachers, clients and psychotherapists. I will conclude by recounting one particular event in my relationship with my father that proved to me the importance of love in the helping relationship. My father was a farmer and had little formal schooling. However, he was a self-taught man and, as such, was respected both within our family and within the community where we lived. Everyone acknowledged that he had a real gift for interpersonal relationships, that he knew how to listen and that he had a great deal of love and respect for others.

I have always loved and admired that man, who taught me what it means to work with people. His congruent attitude, which conveyed both his abiding trust in human nature and his deep love for others and himself, influenced me in a way that no book, course or teacher was subsequently able to duplicate. He died on April 27, 1980 and, until that time, I had always believed that I had a very special place in his heart. That same day, and the two days that followed he taught me something that I hadn't been able to understand before. An incredible number of people came to pay their final respects. Relatives and friends came and, in addition, a great many people who had known him through the different organizations he had been a member of during his lifetime. As I watched them walking by the casket, many of them stopped to talk to me, and they all said more or less the same thing: "Your father and I were very close; I think that I had a special place in his heart." I know that they were telling me how much they had loved my father. But I also know that, throughout his life, this man's attitude and his attentiveness to each person in his entourage and circle of acquaintances had given all of them the feeling that they were special to him in a unique and wonderful way.

This experience taught me an important lesson that I was able to apply to all my personal and professional relationships. Today I am convinced that being a helper means having the self-love and love for others necessary to bring each helpee to the point where he feels important enough to acknowledge himself. By being with him, giving him our undivided attention, and showing the acceptance, trust, and love we have for him, we can help him develop self-love and, consequently, manifest his differences and his creativity.

I would say that this self-love is indeed the very cornerstone of the creative nondirective approach, whether it is used in education or in psychotherapy. The philosophy on which this approach is based has the ability to completely transform interpersonal relationships, making them more genuine and hence more satisfying and propulsive. This self-love is the soil in which our creative potential can blossom into vivid and beautiful reality and in which happiness, liberty and inner harmony can send forth their deepest roots.

BIBLIOGRAPHY

Chalvin, D. 1986. *Utiliser tout son cerveau. De nouvelles voies pour accroître son potentiel de réussite.* Paris: Éditions ESF. 193 pp.

Chevalier, J. 1984. "La pensée rationnelle n'a pas réussi à tuer la pensée symbolique." *3ᵉ millénaire. Les symboles dans notre vie quotidienne,* no. 12. Paris: Éditions du 3ᵉ millénaire, pp. 414.

Freud, S. 1969. *An Outline of Psycho-Analysis.* Trans., ed. James Strachey. New York: Norton. 75 pp.

Freud, S. 1982. *Le Moi et les mécanismes de défense.* 2d ed. Trans. A. Berman. Paris: PUF. 166 pp.

Geshurnd, N. 1979. "Les specialisations du cerveau humain." *Pour la science,* no. 25, p. 132.

Heimann, P., M. Little, L. Tower and A. Reich. 1987. *Countertransference.* Ed. H.S. Strean. Howarth Press. 131 pp.

Jung, C.-G. 1976. *Collected Works.* Trans. R.F. Hull, ed. G. Adler et al. Princeton: Princeton University Press.

Jung, C.-G. 1963. *Psychology of the Unconscious: A Study of the Transformations and Symbolisms of the Libido, a Contribution to the History of the Evolution of Thought.* Trans. ed. B.M. Hinkle. New York: Dodd, Mead. 566 pp.

KRISHNAMURTI, J. 1953. *Education and the Significance of Life.* San Francisco: Harper, 125 pp.

LANDRY, Y. 1983. *Créer, se créer. Vers une pratique méthodique de la créativité.* Montréal: Québec/Amérique. 450 pp.

LAVIGNE, F. 1987. "La personnalité socio-affective." *Psycho-Mag,* vol. 1, no. 4, Montréal: Les publications Domaines, p. 13.

LERÈDE, J. 1980. *Les troupeaux de l'aurore.* Boucherville: Éditions de Mortagne. 285 pp.

LERÈDE, J. 1980. *Suggérer pour apprendre.* Québec: Les Presses de l'Université du Québec. 320 pp.

LOBROT, M. 1974. *Les effets de l'éducation.* 2nd ed. Paris: Éditions ESF. 284 pp.

LOBROT, M. 1983. *Les forces profondes du Moi.* Paris: Economica. 322 pp.

LOZANOV, G. 1978. *Suggestology and Outlines of Suggestopedy.* Psychic Studies, vol. 2. New York: Gordon & Breach. 377 pp.

MISCH, F.C. et al., eds. 1983. *Webster's Ninth New Collegiate Dictionary.* Springfield, Mass.: Merriam-Webster. 1568 pp.

MOREAU, A. 1983. *La Gestalt-thérapie. Chemin de vie.* Paris: Maloine S.A. éditeur. 207 pp.

MUCCHIELLI, R. 1980. *Les complexes personnels.* Paris: Éditions ESF. 166 pp.

PECK, M.S. 1978. *The Road Less Traveled: A New Psychology of Love, Traditional Values, and Spiritual Growth.* New York: Simon & Schuster. 316 pp.

PERLS, F.S., R.F. HEFFERLINE and P. GOODMAN. 1951. *Gestalt Therapy: Excitement and Growth in the Human Personality.* New York and Toronto: Bantam. 551 pp.

PETIT, M. 1984. *La Gestalt. Thérapie de l'ici et maintenant.* Paris: Éditions ESF. 156 pp.

PORTELANCE, C. 1985. "La suggestopédagogie. Pour une pédagogie des communications inconscientes et de l'approche multidimensionnelle." Doctoral thesis. Université de Paris-VIII. 638 pp.

RACLE, G. 1983. *La pédagogie interactive. Au croisement de la psychologie moderne et de la pédagogie.* Paris: Retz. 202 pp.

ROGERS, C.R. 1st ed. 1942, 6th ed. 1985. *Counseling and Psychotherapy: Newer Concepts in Practice.* Boston: Houghton Mifflin. 450 pp.

ROGERS, C.R. 1961. *On Becoming a Person: A Therapist's View of Psychotherapy.* Boston: Houghton Mifflin. 420 pp.

ROGERS, C.R. 1969. *Freedom to Learn: A View of What Education Might Become.* Columbus, Ohio: Merrill. 358 pp.

ROGERS, C.R. 1980. *A Way of Being.* Boston: Houghton Mifflin. 395 pp.

ROSENTHAL, R.A. and L. JACOBSON. 1968. *Pygmalion in the Classroom: Teacher Expectation and Pupils' Intellectual Development.* New York: Holt, Rinehart and Winston. 240 pp.

SAFOUAN, M. 1988. *Le transfert et le désir de l'analyste.* Paris: Seuil. 251 pp.

SEARLES, H.F. 1979. *Countertransference and Related Subjects: Selected Papers*. New York: International Universities Press. 625 pp.

SILLAMY, N. 1983. *Dictionnaire usuel de psychologie*. Paris: Bordas. 767 pp.

SIRIC. 1982. *Communication ou manipulation. La vie quotidienne vue à la lumière du fonctionnement du cerveau*. Montréal: Empirika et Boréal Express. 339 pp.

WINNICOTT, D.W. 1965. *The Maturational Processes and the Facilitating Environment: Studies in the Theory of Emotional Development*. New York: International Universities Press. 296 pp.

COLETTE PORTELANCE

Authentic Communication

In Praise of Intimate Relationships

PSYCHOLOGY SERIES